Lecture Notes in Computer Science   11403

More information about this series at http://www.springer.com/series/7407

Lawrence Rauchwerger (Ed.)

Languages and Compilers for Parallel Computing

30th International Workshop, LCPC 2017
College Station, TX, USA, October 11–13, 2017
Revised Selected Papers

 Springer

Editor
Lawrence Rauchwerger
Texas A&M University
College Station, TX, USA

ISSN 0302-9743 ISSN 1611-3349 (electronic)
Lecture Notes in Computer Science
ISBN 978-3-030-35224-0 ISBN 978-3-030-35225-7 (eBook)
https://doi.org/10.1007/978-3-030-35225-7

LNCS Sublibrary: SL1 – Theoretical Computer Science and General Issues

This Springer imprint is published by the registered company Springer Nature Switzerland AG
The registered company address is: Gewerbestrasse 11, 6330 Cham, Switzerland

To our friend and colleague, Dr. Utpal Banerjee (1943 – 2017), who gave us fast and practical dependence analysis, its theoretical framework and uni-modular loop transformations. He also co-founded the LCPC workshop.
Photo provided by Utpal Banerjee's daughter, Sanchita Saxena.

David Kuck and James Browne having a conversation in the "Oval Office" of the George H.W. Bush Presidential Library.
The photo was taken by David Ramirez. Used with permission.

Participants of the LCPC Workshop 2017.
The photo was taken by David Ramirez, USA. Used with permission.

Preface

The 30th Workshop on Languages and Compilers for Parallel Computing (LCPC) was held October 11-13, 2017 in College Station, Texas. It was organized by the Parasol Lab and the Department of Computer Science and Engineering at Texas A&M University. The workshop gathered together more than 60 researchers from academia, corporate and government research institutions spanning three continents.

This year we celebrated the 30th anniversary of the workshop. In honor of the occasion we included in the program both new contributions as well invited retrospective presentations of 30 years of compiler and language research for parallel computing. The program included 17 regular papers, 11 invited presentations and 5 keynote lectures. We received 26 regular paper submissions which were double blind reviewed by three PC members each. The program committee met online and accepted 13 full length papers and 4 short papers. In addition, four papers where invited to be presented as posters.

The program also included a panel discussion appropriately named for the 30th anniversary of the workshop: "Compilers and Languages for Parallel Computing - What have we Achieved?" The panel was moderated by the Program Chair and the panelists were selected from the long time contributors to LCPC: James Browne (University of Texas), Henry G. Dietz (University of Kentucky), David Kuck (Intel), Monica Lam (Stanford University), Keshav Pingali (University of Texas), and Harry Wijshoff (Leiden University). The workshop took place in three different venues on the campus of Texas A&M University and enabled participants to interact during breaks in a relaxed environment. On the second day, the workshop was held on the grounds of the George H.W. Bush (41) Presidential Library. It allowed participants to visit the museum at leisure and "travel" through modern American history. The traditional banquet was held at Messina Hof, the local winery just outside of town, and included a presentation about wine making and tasting.

Finally, the 30th LCPC Workshop was also an occasion to give tribute to Dr. Utpal Banerjee's life and accomplishments. On the first day of workshop, in a special gathering, his friends and colleagues reminded everybody of his amazing life story and his great technical achievements. He gave us the theoretical basis of data dependence analysis and uni-modular loop transformations. He was also a founder of this workshop. He was remembered by his friends, colleagues and Ph.D. adviser. His daughter Sanchita was also present and received an award on behalf of her father.

November 2017   Lawrence Rauchwerger

Organization

General and Program Chair

Lawrence Rauchwerger   Texas A&M University, USA

Workshop Organizing Committee

Nancy M. Amato   Texas A&M University, USA
Jeff Huang   Texas A&M University, USA
Lawrence Rauchwerger   Texas A&M University, USA

Steering Committee

David Padua   University of Illinois, USA
Alexandru Nicolau   University of California, Irvine, USA
Rudolf Eigenmann   University of Delaware, USA
Lawrence Rauchwerger   Texas A&M University, USA

Program Committee

Nancy M. Amato   Texas A&M University, USA
John Criswell   University of Rochester, USA
Tim Davis   Texas A&M University, USA
Chen Ding   University of Rochester, USA
Matthew Fluet   Rochester Institute of Technology, USA
Mary Hall   University of Utah, USA
Jeff Huang   Texas A&M University, USA
Jaejin Lee   Seoul National University, South Korea
Sam Midkiff   Purdue University, USA
Jose Moreira   IBM, USA
Frank Mueller   North Carolina State University, USA
Peter Pirkelbauer   University of Alabama at Birmingham, USA
Xipeng Shen   North Carolina State University, USA
James Tuck   North Carolina State University, USA
Peng Wu   Huawei, USA

Sponsors

Parasol Lab	Texas A&M University, USA
Texas A&M Engineering Experiment Station	Texas A&M University, USA
Institute for Applied Mathematics and Computational Science	Texas A&M University, USA
Huawei	China
Intel	USA

Keynote Talks

Making Sparse Fast

Saman Amarasinghe

MIT, USA

Abstract. Achieving high performance is no easy task. When it comes to programs operating on sparse data, where there is very little hardware, programming language or compiler support, getting high performance is nearly impossible. As important modern problems such as deep learning in big data analytics and physical simulations in computer graphics and scientific computing operate on sparse data, lack of performance is becoming a critical issue. Achieving high performance was so important from the early days of computing, many researchers have spent their lifetime trying to extract more FLOPS out of critical codes. Hardcore performance engineers try to get to this performance nirvana single handedly without any help from languages, compilers or tools. In this talk, using two examples, I'll argue that domain specific languages and compiler technology can take most of the performance optimization burden even in a very difficult domain such as sparse computations. The first example I will describe is TACO, an optimizing code generator for linear and tensor algebra. TACO introduces a new techniques for compiling compound tensor algebra expressions into efficient loops. TACO-generated code has competitive performance to best-in-class hand-written codes for sparse, dense and mixed tensor and matrix expressions. Next, I will introduce Simit, a new language for physical simulation. Simit lets the programmer seamlessly work on a physical system both in its individual geometric elements as a graph as well as the behavior of the entire system as a set of global tensors. We demonstrate that Simit is easy to use: a Simit program is typically shorter than a Matlab program; that it is high performance: a Simit program running sequentially on a CPU performs comparably to hand-optimized simulations; and that it is portable: Simit programs can be compiled for GPUs with no change to the program, delivering 4 to 20? speedups over our optimized CPU code.

Software Challenges for Extreme Heterogeneity

Vivek Sarkar

Georgia Institute of Technology, USA

Abstract. It is widely recognized that a major disruption is under way in computer hardware as processors strive to extend, and go beyond, the end-game of Moore's Law. This disruption will include new forms of heterogenous processor and memory hierarchies, near-memory computation structures, and, in some cases, Non-von Neumann computing elements. In this talk, we summarize the software challenges for these levels of "extreme heterogeneity", with a focus on the role of programming systems, which encompass programming models, compilers, and runtime systems. These challenges anticipate a new vision for programming systems that goes beyond their traditional role of mapping a specific subcomputation to a specific hardware platform, to an expanded world view in which programming systems control the global selection of computation and data mappings of subcomputations on heterogeneous subsystems. We will discuss recent trends in programming models, compilers, and runtime systems that point the way towards addressing the challenges of extreme heterogeneity.

A New Framework for Expressing, Parallelizing and Optimizing Parallel Applications

Harry Wijshoff

University of Leiden, The Netherlands

Abstract. The Forelem framework was initially introduced as a means to optimize database queries using optimization techniques developed for compilers. Since its introduction, Forelem has proven to be more versatile and to be applicable beyond database applications. In this talk we show that the original Forelem framework can be adapted to express general applications and demonstrate how this framework can be used to express and optimize applications. More specifically, we will demonstrate the effectiveness of this framework by applying it to k-Means clustering and PageRank, resulting in automatically generated implementations of these applications. These implementations are more efficient than standard, hand coded, and state of the art MPI C/C++ implementations of k-Means and PageRank, as well as significantly outperform state-of-the-art Hadoop implementations.

Languages and Compilers for Exascale Science

Katherine Yelick

UC Berkeley, Lawrence Berkeley National Laboratory, USA

Abstract. In the next few years, exascale computing systems will become available to the scientific community. They will require new levels of parallelization, new models of memory and storage, and a variety of node architectures for processors and accelerators. They will enable simulations with unprecedented scale and complexity across many fields from fundamental science to the environment, infrastructure design, and human health. These systems will also offer exascale data analysis capabilities, allowing genomes, images, and sensor data to be processed, analyzed, and modeled using machine learning and other analytics techniques. But several programming challenges remain as architectures are diverging and data movement continues to dominate computation. In this talk, I will describe some of the latest communication-avoiding algorithms and open questions on automating the communication optimizations. Using example from genomics, MRI image analysis, and machine learning, I will argue that we can take advantage of the characteristics of particular science domains to produce compilers, libraries and runtime systems that are powerful and convenient, while still providing scalable, high performance code.

Thingtalk: A Distributed and Synthesizable Programming Language for Virtual Assistants

Monica Lam

Stanford University, USA

Abstract. Virtual assistants, such as Alexa, Siri, and Google Home, are emerging as the super app that intermediates between users and their IoT devices and online services. As an intermediary, the virtual assistant sees all our personal data and has control over the services and vendors we use. A monopolistic virtual assistant would pose a great threat to personal privacy as well as open competition and innovation. This talk presents Almond, an open-source project to create an open virtual assistant platform that protects user privacy. At the core of the project is ThingTalk, a domain-specific language which lets end users use natural language to describe sophisticated tasks involving an open world of skills. It also protects privacy by letting users share data and devices while keeping their credentials and data on their personal devices.

Invited Speakers

Programming in a Spatial World

James Brodman

Intel

Abstract. Moore's Law provided ever increasing performance gains for decades. However, power has become a limiting factor for architectural improvements. The increasing success of accelerators like GPUs and FPGAs shows willingness to trade off general purpose flexibility for greater efficiency and performance. This talk will examine generating high-performing programs for FPGAs. While existing data parallel programming models are capable of generating good results, a few simple extensions to these models can exploit the unique nature of these devices. Several architecture-specific optimizations will be discussed as well as difficulties that arise due to optimization tradeoffs that differ from those for CPUs or GPUs.

Is Parallelization Technology Ready For Prime Time?

Rudolf Eigenmann

University of Delaware, USA

Abstract. Our language and compilers community has created a large body of work in parallelization techniques over the past three decades. Nevertheless, current practical compilers make little use of these contributions. Automatic parallelization tools have a mixed reputation at best. This situation contrasts with the expectation of the now over two-years-old National Strategic Computing Initiative (NSCI). The NSCI, in addition to pushing high-end compute capabilities, wants to make high-performance computing available to the large majority of non-experts in parallel computing. In this talk, after a brief review of the past, I will plot a path forward that aims to ensure that the technology our community has put so much energy in, will be harnessed and benefit a large number of HPC users. Elements of this path include highly interactive translators, options that can set the degree of automation versus user involvement, and tight involvement with the applications community, giving us constant feedback on how to improve the tools.

Compilers for Program Execution Models Inspired By Dataflow - A Personal Reflection of 30 Years (1987–2017)

Guang Gao

University of Delaware, USA

Abstract. Recently we have witnessed a rapid growing Interests and activities on dataflow program execution models and systems – from academia and industry. In this talk, I will present a personal reflection on compiler technology evolution for dataflow-inspired parallel architectures in the past 30 years. Remarks will be made on aspects that may be particularly useful in exploring future innovative system design assisted by modern hardware/software technologies especially when facing the challenges from applications in advanced data analytics and machine learning.

Autotuning Stencil Computations
with Structural Ordinal Regression Learning

Ben Juurlink

Berlin University of Technology, Germany

Abstract. Stencil computations expose a large and complex space of equivalent implementations. These computations often rely on autotuning techniques, based on iterative compilation or machine learning (ML), to achieve high performance. Iterative compilation autotuning is a challenging and time-consuming task that may be unaffordable in many scenarios. Meanwhile, traditional ML autotuning approaches exploiting classification algorithms (such as neural networks and support vector machines) face difficulties in capturing all features of large search spaces. This presentation proposes a new way of automatically tuning stencil computations based on structural learning. By organizing the training data in a set of partially-sorted samples (i.e., rankings), the problem is formulated as a ranking prediction model, which translates to an ordinal regression problem. This approach can be coupled with an iterative compilation method or used as a standalone autotuner. Its potential is demonstrated by comparing it with state-of-the-art iterative compilation methods on a set of nine stencil codes and by analyzing the quality of the obtained ranking in terms of Kendall rank correlation coefficients.

Multigrain Parallelization and Compiler/Architecture Co-design for 30 Years

Hironori Kasahara

Waseda University, Japan

Abstract. Multicores have been attracting much attention to improve performance and reduce power consumption of computing systems facing the end of Moore's Law. To obtain high performance and low power on multicores, co-design of hardware and software especially parallelizing and power reducing compiler is very important. OSCAR (Optimally Scheduled Advanced Multiprocessor) compiler and OSCAR multiprocessor/multicore architecture have been researched since 1985. This talk includes OSCAR multigrain parallelization compiler that hierarchically exploits coarse grain task parallelism, loop parallelism, and statement level parallelism, global data locality optimization over coarse grain tasks for cache and local memory automatic power reduction controlling frequency and voltage control, clock and power gating, heterogeneous task scheduling with overlapping data transfers using DMA controllers software coherence controls by OSCAR compiler local memory automatic management with software-defined block and its replacement, performance and power consumption of real applications including automobile engine control, cancer treatment, scientific applications and so on various multicore systems, such as Intel, ARM, IBM, Fujitsu, Renesas, Tilera and so on.

When Small Things Cause Big Problems

Paul Petersen

Intel, USA

Abstract. Effective performance optimization requires knowledge of the target application's dynamic behavior. Measuring this behavior without excessive effort or substantially perturbing the applications execution has been a common request from developers. For many applications, we have today effective tools which can give you a good understanding of the dynamic behavior of an application at rather low cost. But this is only when certain assumptions are met. The typical assumption being that the application execution is sufficiently long relative to the sampling period, and that the behavior of the functions are relatively uniform without unexpected actions occurring on the system. But problems arise when you violate these assumptions. What if you care about small execution paths (< < 100K instructions), but your sampling period is >100K instructions. What if you care about minimizing the cost of outliers more than reducing the average behavior of these short sequences? What if these outliers are not necessarily caused by the program itself, but by the interaction of the program with other things being managed by the OS? These problems can be solved with the help of hardware support for collecting fine-grain execution traces. In this talk we will walk through some simple examples illustrating these problems, and show what is possible with the instruction tracing features available on today's systems.

Thirty Years of the Polyhedral Model: Let's Return to the Origins

Sanjay Rajopadhye

Colorado State University, USA

Abstract. Even after thirty years, the polyhedral model is far from being an unequivocal success, even on the restricted domain where it is applicable. Despite impressive recent progress, we do not (yet) have compilers for general-purpose processors that can generate code approaching either the machine peak, or the algorithmic peak of the source program, or even hand tuned libraries developed by "heroes" of high performance computing. I will try to explain why this is so by arguing that although the theory is elegant and beautiful, we have been solving the wrong problems. We are also targeting the wrong platforms. I will suggest a plan of how we can improve this state of affairs by targeting accelerators, building analytical models, and using discrete nonlinear optimization.

On Using Data Movement Lower Bounds To Guide Code Optimization

P. (Saday) Sadayappan

Ohio State University, USA

Abstract. The four-index integral transform is a computationally demanding calculation used in many quantum chemistry software suites like NWChem. It requires a sequence of four tensor contractions that each contract a four-dimensional tensor with a two-dimensional transformation matrix. Loop fusion and tiling can be used to reduce the total space requirement, as well as data movement within and across nodes of a parallel supercomputer. However, the large number of possible choices for loop fusion and tiling, and data/computation distribution across a parallel system, make it challenging to develop an optimized parallel implementation. Lower bounds on data movement as a function of available aggregate physical memory in a parallel computer system are used to identify and prune ineffective fusion configurations. This enables a characterization of optimality criteria and the development of an improved parallel implementation of the four-index transform - with higher performance and the ability to model larger electronic systems than feasible with previously available implementations in NWChem.

Experiences on Generalizing Redundancy Removal

Xipeng Shen

North Carolina State University, USA

Abstract. Born soon after the advent of the first computer, as one of the oldest branches in Computer Science, Compiler Technology is often regarded as a mature field. However, recent observations led Dr. Shen and his group to believe that some dramatic, hidden power of compilers has remained untapped, especially for modern computing. When the power gets exerted, computing efficiency may improve by up to hundreds of times, and even automatic algorithm derivations become possible. In this talk, Dr. Shen will discuss the findings by drawing on their recent experiences in generalizing redundancy removal into a large scope and a high level. (The talk is based on his publications at PLDI'2017, OOPSLA'2017, ICDE'2017, VLDB'2015, ICML'2015.)

The Route To Automation

Armando Solar-Lezama

MIT, USA

Abstract. Traditionally, there has been a trade-off between the level of abstraction afforded by a language and the performance one can expect from the resulting code. In this talk, I will describe how a new class of techniques based on program synthesis could help introduce more automation into high-performance programming tasks. The goal is to help to reduce programmer effort without sacrificing performance.

Hiding the High Overheads of Persistent Memory

Yan Solihin

NSF/North Carolina State University, USA

Abstract. Byte-addressable non-volatile memory technology is emerging as an alternative for DRAM for main memory. This new Non-Volatile Main Memory (NVMM) allows programmers to store important data in data structures in memory instead of serializing it to the file system, thereby providing a substantial performance boost. However, computer systems reorder memory operations and utilize volatile caches for better performance, making it difficult to ensure a consistent state in NVMM. Intel recently announced a new set of persistence instructions, clflushopt, clwb, and pcommit. These new instructions make it possible to implement fail-safe code on NVMM, but few workloads have been written or characterized using these new instructions. In this talk, I will discuss a new logging approach for durable transactions that achieves the favorable characteristics of both prior software and hardware approaches. Like software, it has no hardware constraint limiting the number of transactions or logs available to it, and like hardware, it has very low overhead. Our approach introduces two new instructions: one that indicates whether a load instruction should create a log entry, and a log flush instruction to make a copy of a cache line in the log. We add hardware support, primarily within the core, to manage the execution of these instructions and critical ordering requirements between logging operations and updates to data. We also propose a novel optimization at the memory controller that is enabled by a battery backed write pending queue in the memory controller. Our experiments show that our technique improves performance by 1.48?, on average, compared to a system without hardware logging and 10.5% faster than ATOM. A significant advantage of our approach is dropping writes to the log when they are not needed.

Contents

Parallel Programming and Abstractions

GPU Applications

Posters

Compilers for Parallel Computing

Using Hardware Counters to Predict Vectorization

Neftali Watkinson[1($\boxtimes$)], Aniket Shivam[1], Zhi Chen[1],
Alexander Veidenbaum[1], Alexandru Nicolau[1],
and Zhangxiaowen Gong[2]

[1] Department of Computer Science, University of California, Irvine, Irvine, USA
{watkinso, aniketsh, zhic2, alexv, anicolau}@uci.edu
[2] Department of Computer Science, University of Illinois, Urbana-Champaign,
Champaign, USA
gongl5@illinois.edu

Abstract. Vectorization is the process of transforming the scalar implementation of an algorithm into vector form. This transformation aims to benefit from parallelism through the generation of microprocessor vector instructions. Using abstract models and source level information, compilers can identify opportunities for auto-vectorization. However, compilers do not always predict the runtime effects accurately or completely fail to identify vectorization opportunities. This ultimately results in no performance improvement.

This paper takes on a new perspective by leveraging the use of runtime hardware counters to predict the potential for loop vectorization. Using supervised machine learning models, we can detect instances where vectorization can be applied (but the compilers fail to) with 80% validation accuracy. We also predict profitability and performance in different architectures.

We evaluate a wide range of hardware counters across different machine learning models. We show that dynamic features, extracted from performance data, implicitly include useful information about the host machine and runtime program behavior.

Keywords: Machine learning · Compilers · Auto-vectorization · Profitability

1 Introduction

During the last decades, numerous techniques have been proposed for automatically transform code to improve performance and optimize the use of resources. When a compiler is performing optimizations, most of the transformations are applied early in the compilation process relying on an abstract model of the host machine configuration. Because of this, it is expected that only a few optimizations will take full advantage of the host's architecture and hardware configuration.

Among these transformations, there are some designed to take advantage of different levels of parallelism found in modern architectures. These may range from parallel functional units in a CPU core, to using special instruction sets and parallel thread execution. Such is the case for Single Instruction Multiple Data (SIMD)

© Springer Nature Switzerland AG 2019
L. Rauchwerger (Ed.): LCPC 2017, LNCS 11403, pp. 3–16, 2019.
https://doi.org/10.1007/978-3-030-35225-7_1

instructions. They apply an operation on "vectors" of data simultaneously. Hence the transformation of code to take advantage of these instructions is called "vectorization".

However, obstacles like data dependency, function calls, or complex memory access patterns could prevent vectorization. Most compilers rely on static information (gathered at the source level and/or at the intermediate representation) to decide when to vectorize.

The compiler's analysis faces challenges as well. The two most common ones are: lack of running-time information (e.g. the behavior depends on the input data) and inaccurate profitability prediction due to an incomplete model of the host architecture. In [6] we can see that three of the widely used (and arguably best) C compilers (IBM XL, Intel's compiler, GCC) failed to vectorize over 30% of loops inside a benchmark. Manual analysis showed that many of these loops were clearly vectorizable.

With the increasingly complex modern architectures with highly constrained vector instructions (i.e. with a specific purpose for the architecture), multiple levels of parallelism exploitation (e.g. vector instructions, instruction-level parallelism (ILP), multi-core processing), and complex memory hierarchies, it is also increasingly hard for compilers to create an accurate model.

Recent approaches have tried to design a model that is self-adaptable (i.e. can be applied to different machine configurations) and capable of predicting vectorization and its profitability. Fursin et al. [10] create models from dynamic and static data that can be used to identify parallelism and profitable scheduling policies for loops inside a code. Kennedy et al. [5] use dependence information extracted at the source and intermediate level to optimize a compiler. However, these are not specific to vectorization and use only static information. Cammarota et al. [3] use hardware counters and unsupervised learning to find similarity among different applications that translate into performance improvement through the application of similar optimizations among clusters. This shows that dynamic information extracted at run time contains a different representation than the one provided by static models.

We focus on evaluating dynamic data (hardware counters) in supervised machine learning models for the prediction of vectorization. We predict whether a loop-nest can be vectorized, manually or by a compiler, and if vectorization will be profitable. The prediction is done for two major compilers, the Intel C Compiler (ICC) and the GNU Compiler Collection (GCC), using their respective auto-vectorization options.

To fully evaluate the performance of dynamic data, we make use of six machine learning algorithms: Support Vector Machines, Naïve Bayes, K-Nearest Neighbors, Random Forest Trees and Logistic Regression. In our experiments, we could predict when vectorization is successful with up to 94% accuracy on cross-validation, and profitability with up to 92% accuracy. In the last experiment, we extend our dataset to include loops that can be manually vectorized but the compiler fails to do so. We created a validation set using these loops and we achieved 80% accuracy in predicting whether the loops could be manually vectorized.

The rest of this paper is organized as follows: The section Approach explains the tools and the methodology that we used, the key concepts needed to understand the problem and the solution. In Experiments, we present the tests we performed and the results obtained with six different sets of classification models and discuss the applicability of hardware event features. The section Related work gives a brief overview of other projects and a comparison of their approaches with ours, including a similar approach that used only static information. Finally, in Conclusion we analyze the implication of our results and explain why this approach to the problem has potential to grow further and be used in other areas of compiler optimization as well.

2   Approach

In most of supervised Machine Learning workflows, there is a dataset from which one can extract features, then build a classifying model using these features and one of the available algorithms, and finally validate that model. Our dataset is built from loops that were compiled, executed and profiled to collect runtime data from the hardware event counters. That data is then used to build the feature vector. We select the features that are more relevant for the classifier. Finally, the features are evaluated using several machine learning algorithms. Figure 1 illustrates the workflow.

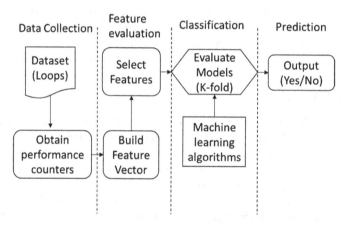

Fig. 1. Flow diagram for our machine learning approach.

2.1   Data Collection

For our training dataset, we used the TSVC (Test Suite for Vectorizing Compilers) benchmark [6]. It contains 151 loops written in C. It was designed to evaluate auto-vectorization capabilities in different compilers. Each loop is also nested inside a control loop that repeats the run to record execution time accurately.

We reevaluated the work in [6] to update the number of loops that newer versions of the GCC (5.6) and ICC (15) compilers can vectorize. By using – O3, there are 105 loops that are vectorized by ICC and 57 by GCC (114 in the union set of both compilers). However, by disabling the cost estimation model and force the compiler to vectorize (using the -vec-threshold0 flag on ICC and -fvect-cost-model = unlimited on GCC), the report yielded 116 from Intel and 78 from GCC (with 123 total). For our first experiment, we disregard the profitability of vectorization and focus only on whether the loop can or can't be vectorized.

Adding the information about manual vectorization and IBM compiler in [6] we end up with 137 loops that are vectorizable (compared to the 124 originally reported in [6]). Note that for our approach we consider a loop vectorizable if either of the compilers report some level of vector transformations applied to the loop or there was a way to vectorize it manually.

To create a separate validation data for our last experiment, we used the extracted loops from LORE [15]. We isolated the loops that are not vectorized by ICC and then performed manual vectorization to identify the ones that could be vectorized. There was a total of 490 loops that could not be vectorized by the compilers. Out of those, 123 could be vectorized manually. We profiled these loops using the same method described for TSVC.

2.2 Hardware Performance Counters

We built the features using performance data gathered with Linux Perf [13] and Intel Vtune Amplifier XE 2016 [8]. Since we want to predict vectorization only, the data comes from non-vectorized code (with O3 enabled but vectorization turned off). Some of the hardware events include branching, micro operations, cycles, memory flow, and time-based events, among others. These are also called dynamic features, because they depend on the performance of the program and change with each architecture.

2.3 Feature Evaluation

When working with a new set of features, it is important to evaluate and discard those that - related to the model's output - are irrelevant or introduce noise to the dataset. This list of features may be different for each ML model and algorithm depending on the problem being solved. Since we use every hardware counter available to build our feature vector, we use filter based feature selection [7].

We selected features using Information Gain (IG), a ratio useful for identifying those features that reduce bias in decision trees. It builds a decision tree for each feature and measures the difference in entropy before and after splitting the instances. The higher the IG value the better the feature is in dividing the dataset. In Sect. 3 we discuss the features selected in each experiment, as well as in general terms the ones that we found to be most useful across the experiments.

2.4 Classification

There are several machine learning techniques and algorithms for classification. We focused on applying the most common ones. We used Orange 3.2 [4] to build and evaluate the models.

Support Vector Machine (SVM)

This algorithm creates a virtual space with multiple dimensions (hyperspace) and then represents each instance as a point in that space using features as coordinates. It then divides the space by using a hyperplane via support vectors that define the limits for each class. When a new data point is evaluated, depending on which side of the decision hyperplane it falls, the model will define the predicted class. Along with feature filtering, it is a very powerful classifier for discriminative classification, and it is also very versatile since the user can define the number of dimensions the kernel that the SVM will use.

K-nearest Neighbors (KNN)
Similar, to SVM, this algorithm also deals with a vector space in the sense that it represents the instances as points in it using features as coordinates. However, instead of dividing the data into two spaces, it calculates the distance between the data point to be predicted and the ones nearest to it. The predicted value will be equal to the majority of the k neighbors nearest to it. The distance can be measured with different metrics, we use Manhattan distance (distance following a strictly horizontal and vertical axis [7]).

Naïve Bayes
This is a generative model that makes a statistical assumption: the features are conditionally independent to the predicted value. Once trained, the probability of each class is computed given the new example's feature. It then classifies the example as having the most likely class label [7].

Random Decision Forest
This algorithm builds a set of classification trees using the training data and outputs the mode for all the trees built. This is done to countermeasure the tendency of classification trees to overfit. Each tree is built using a subset of the features chosen stochastically [12]. The predicted value comes from the average of the trees selected in training.

Logistic Regression
This algorithm assigns weights to each of the features and fits a sigmoid function where the instances are assigned a probability of being part of a class or not [7].

2.5   Validation

We validate most of our models using leave-one-out cross validation, which is a variance of K-fold Cross validation [14]. We use all the instances but one for training, and validate on the remaining one, iterating until all the instances have been used once for validation. No classifier is ever tested on examples used in training it, which maintains the statistical integrity of the procedure. For the last experiment, we have previous knowledge of the features that are good predictors and we include more loops in the dataset so we can create a separate validation set by randomly splitting the data 70/30 (70% for training and 30% for validation). We do leave-one-out cross validation on the training set to select the features that perform the best and then use the validation set for accuracy.

3   Experiments

The first four experiments are designed to identify a relationship between hardware counters (dynamic features) and auto-vectorizability (whether a compiler can or cannot vectorize the given loop). The first and second experiment consider Harpertown and

Haswell architecture respectively but each with a different set of hardware counters. The third experiment analyzes the use of hardware counters with a different compiler. The fourth experiment uses the data from [6] to predict vectorization in general (vectorization with any of the compilers and manual vectorization). The fifth experiment analyzes profitability, and compares our results to the Intel Compiler model. The sixth and final experiment tests the models using an extended dataset consisting of non-vectorized loops.

3.1   Hardware Setup

Since our approach is designed to be independent of the architecture, or more accurately, adaptable to it, we performed our experiments on three different Intel processors. Table 1 shows the hardware configuration for our experiments, we used Harpertown for the first and sixth experiment, and Sandy Bridge and Haswell systems for the rest.

For every architecture, we compiled and ran the TSVC dataset using ICC 15.0.4 and GCC 5.3.0 with O3 optimization minus vectorization (-fno-tree-vectorize option for GCC and –no-vec for ICC) to obtain the hardware counters without vector transformations. Next, we compiled and ran the dataset again but enabling vectorization and using the default cost model for each compiler (the default flags are "-fvect-cost-model = dynamic" for GCC and "-vec-threshold100" for ICC), which will vectorize only when the compiler estimates that there is going to be favorable speedup (over 1.0). Finally, we performed the same experiment but now ignoring the cost model ("-fvect-cost-model = unlimited" for GCC and "-vec-threshold0") to obtain runtimes for the loops that the compiler's cost models predict to have no speedup. We consider that a compiler is capable of vectorizing a loop, if for any of the two cost models the compiler report one or more vector transformations.

Table 1. Hardware configuration of the three systems

Microarchitecture	Harpertown	Sandy Bridge	Haswell
Hardware setup			
Operating system	CentOS Linux 6.6 (x64)	Linux Ubuntu 14.04 (x64)	Linux Ubuntu 14.04 (x64)
Processor	Xeon E5450	Intel Core i7-2600	Intel Core i7-4770
Vector instruction set extensions	SSE 4.1	SSE 4.1/4.2, AVX	SSE 4.1/4.2, AVX 2.0
Processor Frequency	3.00 Ghz (4 cores)	3.40 Ghz (4 cores)	3.40 Ghz (4 cores)
RAM	32 GB	8 GB	8 GB
Compiler version			
Intel C compiler	ICC 15.0.4		
GNU compiler collection	GCC 5.3.0		

3.2   EXP1: Predicting Vectorization on Harpertown

Our Harpertown architecture has vector instructions up to SSE 4.1, so we expected the evaluation to find the loops that are vectorized by ICC to be different than the other two systems. Due to compatibility issues with Intel Vtune Amplifier, for the Harpertown System we used Linux Perf to obtain the hardware counters. For this experiment, our machine learning models are predicting whether ICC can vectorize the loops with any of the profitability models. In this case the significant features used were: L1 Cache loads misses, LLC store misses, LLC stores, D-TLB load misses, cache-references and branch-misses. Table 2 shows the results for the top classification models. Of all the models, Random Forest had the best result for accuracy on leave-one-out cross validation.

The class distribution for this experiment is 77% are vectorizable by ICC (yes class), and 33% are not (no class).

Table 2. Accuracy for Xeon processor (EXP I)

Harpertown	
Algorithm	Overall accuracy
Class distribution	0.77 (YES)
Random forest	0.83

3.3   EXP2: Prediction on a Different Architecture

For this experiment, we evaluate the models for predicting vectorization by ICC in the Haswell system. To take full advantage of the hardware counters available, we used Intel Vtune Amplifier's analysis to obtain our data for the feature vector. Due to the availability of AVX instructions, ICC yields different results when vectorizing the code.

The features selected by the filter were instructions retired, Micro-operations issued, Retired load micro-operations, Stalls pending (cycle activity), micro-operations executed, micro-operations dispatched by port, and load misses in D-TLB levels.

Table 3 shows that the two best classification models for this dataset are SVM and KNN. Results are consistent with our previous experiment in the increase of accuracy over the baseline. It is important to note that all the classification models are using the same set of features and the same cross validation. We don't fine tune the experiment separately for each model. This is in order to focus on the performance of hardware counters as features and not on evaluating a specific instance of a classifier. In a separate experiment, Haswell's results were almost identical to Sandy Bridge's, so for the sake of space we will not discuss them.

Table 3. Accuracy for ICC auto-vectorization (EXP 2)

Haswell	
Algorithm	Overall accuracy
SVM	0.80
KNN	0.81

3.4   EXP3: Prediction Using GCC

For this experiment, we turn our focus to the GCC compiler and used its vectorization report to feed the model. For the feature vector, we profiled a GCC's non-vectorized version of the benchmark.

In Table 4, the class distribution for this experiment is 50% (equally distributed between GCC vectorized, and not vectorized) for both Harpertown and Haswell. SVM and Naïve Bayes are the best models with up to 75% accuracy. For Haswell, the filter chose Instructions retired, Micro-operations issued, Micro-operations dispatched by port (8 ports total), and Micro-operations retired. For Harpertown, the features selected were CPU Cycles, Cache References, L1 D-Cache Load Misses, L1 D-Cache pre-fetches, L1 I-Cache loads and bus cycles. The models had very similar results, with up to 25 percentage point improvement over the baseline.

Since GCC uses a vectorization model that doesn't change much with the host architecture (vectorization results are the same regardless of the architecture, while ICC produces different results based on the cost estimation), we believe that the loops vectorized by it will have some degree of similarity between them, forming clusters that are easily detectable by the classifier. The difference in features from the previous experiment is due to that clustering difference. While we considered testing with LLVM compiler, the results in the vectorization report (number of loops vectorized) for TSVC were not better than GCC's.

Table 4. Accuracy for GCC's auto-vectorization (EXP 3)

Algorithm	Overall accuracy
Vectorizable with GCC in Harpertown	
Class distribution	0.5
SVM	0.75
Naïve Bayes	0.67
Vectorizable with GCC in Haswell	
SVM	0.73
Naïve Bayes	0.76

3.5   EXP4: Predicting Vectorization Across Compilers

As mentioned in Sect. 2, TSVC was used in [6] to test vectorization capabilities of different compilers. For this experiment, we used their data to build a separate set of models to predict vectorizability by either GCC, ICC, IBM XL or manual vectorization. The output class is whether a loop can or can't be vectorized by any of the mentioned compilers, and/or manually. We used the feature data from the ICC non-vectorized version ran on the Haswell system. Table 5 shows the result from this experiment.

Table 5. Accuracy for all auto-vectorization (EXP 4)

Vectorizability	
Algorithm	Overall accuracy
SVM	0.94
Logistic regression	0.91

Class distribution for this experiment is 92% yes, 8% no. SVM obtained the highest overall accuracy with 94%. The results seem to be consistent with the other experiments since the features selected were: Memory Micro-operations retired, Cycle stalls, Micro-operations dispatched by port, and L1 D-Cache replacements.

3.6   EXP5: Predicting Profitability

Since on Haswell and Sandy Bridge systems, ICC uses a profitability model to decide when to vectorize a loop, we designed this experiment to analyze the performance of hardware counters to predict the profitability of vectorization. The main challenge for this model is that profitability will change per the architecture.

We collected data by running a vectorized version and comparing the runtime for each loop. We removed the loops that cannot be vectorized by ICC, and then defined every loop with at least 1x speedup as profitable, which is the same threshold the compiler uses.

In these models, the significant features selected for Haswell were Instructions Retired, Micro-operations retired, Micro-operations dispatched by port, and Memory Micro-operations retired. For the Sandy Bridge model, the features selected where Instructions Retired, Micro-operations issued, Micro-operations retired, Memory Load Micro-operations, L2 Cache hits, and IDQ Micro-operations not delivered.

Table 6 shows the results for the experiment. Interestingly, Sandy Bridge's models have highest accuracy when predicting profitability than Haswell's models do.

Table 6. Accuracy for profitability classification (EXP 5)

Profitability	
Algorithm	Overall Accuracy
Haswell	
Majority	0.84
Naïve Bayes	0.88
KNN	0.85
Logistic regression	0.85
Intel compiler	0.86
Sandy Bridge	
Majority	0.90
SVM	0.93
Naïve Bayes	0.92
KNN	0.91
Logistic regression	0.91
Intel compiler	0.91

While in previous models, comparing to the compiler was somewhat impossible (the compiler vectorizes what it can without making any prediction), we can compare to the compiler's Cost Estimation Model. We don't know how this model is computed, but we can get the output value by using the -vec-report = 9 flag which lets us calculate an accuracy for their model. Note that the compiler uses information obtained very early in the compilation process. Through informal experiments we identified that it will predict different values depending on the architecture, which leads us to think that the model includes some abstract representation of the host system.

The compiler correctly predicts profitability in 86% of the loops ran on Haswell and 91% on Sandy Bridge. Note that we only consider profitability, however the value obtained from ICC's cost model is not always close to the actual speedup. It is worth noticing that with the newer architecture (Haswell), a lower number of loops have profitable vectorization and the compiler has lower accuracy in predicting it. This could be because the cost model is not keeping up with the changes of architecture, or the newer architectures have other optimizations that make vectorization less critical, depending on the loop.

Our best models are 2% more accurate than Intel's Model and are completely agnostic to the information the compiler uses to estimate speedup. These results may be used in future work to fine tune the compiler's model.

EXP6: Finding opportunities for Vectorization with a Validation Set
TSVC is biased towards already vectorizable loops (most the loops are vectorized by ICC). Therefore, for this experiment we combined the dataset with the loops from LORE that ICC couldn't vectorize. Out of those, we identified the loops that are manually vectorizable. We partitioned the data so that 70% of this extended dataset would be used for training, and the rest of the loops could be used as a validation set. We first performed cross validation on the training set to select the best features using an Information Gain filter. In this case the features chosen were LLC loads, LLC stores, D-TLB load misses, Branch loads, L1 Cache prefetches and Instructions per cycle. We then tested our model using the validation dataset.

Table 7. Accuracy for validation set (EXP 6)

Algorithm	Overall Accuracy
Cross Validation for 70%	
Majority	0.62
SVM	0.72
Naïve Bayes	0.70
KNN	0.71
Random forest	0.78
Validating on 30%	
Majority	0.61
SVM	0.75
Naïve Bayes	0.70
KNN	0.71
Random forest	0.80

Table 7 shows that the improvement over the majority classifier is much greater. This gives us a better sense of the potential that hardware counters have in detecting vectorization. When testing on the validation set, Random Forest performs best with 80% accuracy in detecting loops with opportunities for vectorization - recall that these loops were not originally vectorized by the compiler. This prediction could be used to detect loops that require a deeper analysis for improvement.

3.7   Result Analysis

The results on vectorizability from the first four experiments give us an insight on the effect vectorization has on the loop nests. Table 8 shows the different groups of features and how they were used in each of the 6 experiments. While Vtune and Perf don't have the same hardware events, we can group them and correlate them by the type of hardware counter.

Table 8. Features used by experiment

Features used by experiment

Feature class	Exp1	Exp2	Exp3	Exp4	Exp5	Exp6
Instructions related counters	✓	✓	✓	✓	✓	✓
Last Level Cache (LLC) counters	✓		✓			✓
L1 Data Cache counters	✓	✓	✓			✓
Others	✓	✓	✓	✓	✓	✓

The experiments show evidence that there is information about the opportunities for vectorization hidden in the runtime data. In this experiment, all the features were extracted from non-vectorized implementations of the code. While some experiments are designed to show that it is possible to predict vectorization using dynamic features, the output of those models is easily obtained by running the compiler. However, for our last experiment the output is not so trivial. By using the validation set, we are finding loops that the compiler is not able to vectorize but with manual analysis could be vectorized. This can be applied to detect optimization opportunities where today's tools fail.

Going back to the dynamic features, there were some that may seem counterintuitive but they still yielded good results in the classification models. Possible explanations behind some features being prominent across the different models are:

- **IPC (Instruction per Cycle):** The loops with higher IPC values seem to be well-suited for vectorization. The higher IPC correlates to higher parallelism at instruction level, to computation-bound loops and low cache miss rates, and predictable branches. The high scalar IPC also indicates that multiple operations available in same or near cycles, which indicates a potential to vectorize.
- **Branch Instructions:** Number of branch instructions had significant impact on predicting vectorization. Branching leads to inefficiency in generating vector

instructions since even after several compiler optimizations (Flattening-IFs, Index Set Splitting, etc.) it may be not possible to eliminate branches. Also, branch misprediction introduce stalls and reduce IPC.

- **L1 Data Cache**: Misses in L1 D-Cache may indicate that access to data inside the loop is not consecutive across iterations and hence vector instructions may not profitable. The fetching or storing of each data element needs to be performed as a scalar access and moved to/from an SIMD register separately. While the computation is now a vector instruction, but scalar moves are costly.
- **LLC Loads and Stores:** The LLC accesses are costly and LLC misses even more so. Both can significantly lower the IPC, ultimately making the program memory bound. SIMD instructions may not give speedup when the memory hierarchy dominates performance.
- **TLB:** A TLB miss also introduces significant delays and has the same effect on IPC as cache misses.

The results from our last experiment demonstrate that the accuracy of the models is not random. Being able to predict vectorization in a "blind" validation test, implies that the correlation between runtime data and vectorization potential is strong. The static information that compilers use to vectorize the code is insufficient.

4 Related Work

The use of static models and dependence analysis for vectorization has been studied for at least three decades ([2] and [5]). However, the use of machine learning for compiler optimization is new and growing. In [3] a feature-agnostic model is used to predict performance, it deals mainly with finding parallelism and it doesn't need any previous knowledge of the program because it uses unsupervised learning. [1] uses a set of hand written rules guided by a combined set of static and dynamic features to generate suggestions for the programmer on where to apply transformations that will help to vectorize code using SIMD instructions. Their decision system is designed to work at the source level and it only deals with possible vectorization opportunities that need to be validated by the user.

The work presented in [9] applies an SVM model to detect basic block vectorization specific to unroll factors (they populate a dataset using TSVC with different unroll factors from 0 to 20, ending with a dataset of 151×20 loops) and get a final classification accuracy of about 70% in binary (yes/no) classification to determine whether unrolling would be profitable or not. They use static features only.

In [11] they make a good case about using profiling information by showing that it improves the classification model considerably. In their specific case, it is applied towards identifying auto-parallelization, which represents a different challenge than auto-vectorization, the latter being a more constrained problem. They use an SVM predictor to identify if a parallel execution would be profitable and identify which scheduling policy to choose and rely on the user to approve the cases where static correctness cannot be proved.

Our approach stands out from the others mentioned because it evaluates a wide array of dynamic features and machine learning models, and compares it with the state of the art which is what the compiler uses today. The cost estimation models used by compilers are applied very early in the compilation process so they disregard the effects of other optimization transformations and the differences in architectures, therefore the use of only static features will likely have the same outcome. However, static features are not to be discarded, in future work we are going to explore dependence analysis information to our models.

5 Conclusion

We evaluated the use of hardware counters in machine learning to predict if vectorization can be applied and how profitable it will be. We predicted loops that contain opportunities for manual vectorization that the compilers miss with 80% accuracy. As of now, this model can already be applied to find potential candidates for vectorization, without having to manually analyze each loop that the compiler can't vectorize.

In other experiments, we built different models that predict the vectorizability of a loop-nest when using GCC (with 76% accuracy), ICC (80% accuracy), and manual vectorization (94% accuracy), as well as vectorization profitability (93% accuracy). This shows viability towards the use of runtime data to identify optimization opportunities. This gives new insight into code optimization. We can identify optimization opportunities that a commercial compiler misses.

Dynamic information can be used to further optimize the compilers. Since our approach is not constrained to a specific compiler or architecture, it can be further implemented to predict how the combination of the two will produce different gains in performance.

Acknowledgements. This material is based upon work supported by the National Science Foundation under Award 1533912.

References

1. Aumage, O., Barthou, D., Haine, C., Meunier, T.: Detecting SIMDization opportunities through static/dynamic dependence analysis. In: an Mey, D., et al. (eds.) Euro-Par 2013. LNCS, vol. 8374, pp. 637–646. Springer, Heidelberg (2014). https://doi.org/10.1007/978-3-642-54420-0_62
2. Banerjee, U.: An introduction to a formal theory of dependence analysis. J. Supercomput. **2** (2), 133–149 (1988)
3. Cammarota, R., Beni, L.A., Nicolau, A., Veidenbaum, A.V.: Optimizing program performance via similarity, using a feature-agnostic approach. In: Wu, C., Cohen, A. (eds.) APPT 2013. LNCS, vol. 8299, pp. 199–213. Springer, Heidelberg (2013). https://doi.org/10.1007/978-3-642-45293-2_15
4. Demšar, J., et al.: Orange: data mining toolbox in python. J. Mach. Learn. Res. **14**(1), 2349–2353 (2013)

5. Kennedy, K., Allen, J.R.: Optimizing Compilers for Modern Architectures: A Dependence-Based Approach (2001)
6. Maleki, S., Gao, Y., Garzarán, M.J., Wong, T., Padua, D.A.: An evaluation of vectorizing compilers. In: Parallel Architectures and Compilation Techniques - Conference Proceedings, PACT, pp. 372–382 (2011)
7. Manning, C.D., Raghavan, P., Schütze, H.: Introduction to information retrieval. In: Americas, vol. 32, pp. 2473–10013. Delhi Cambridge University Press (2008)
8. Reinders, J.: VTuneTM Performance Analyzer Essentials Measurement and Tuning Techniques for Software Developers (First.). Intel Press (2005)
9. Trouvé, A., et al.: Using machine learning in order to improve automatic SIMD instruction generation. Procedia Comput. Sci. **18**, 1292–1301 (2013)
10. Fursin, G., et al.: Milepost GCC: machine learning enabled self-tuning compiler. Int. J. Parallel Prog. **39**(3), 296–327 (2011)
11. Tournavitis, G., Wang, Z., Franke, B., O'Boyle, M.F.M.: Towards a holistic approach to auto-parallelization: integrating profile-driven parallelism detection and machine-learning based mapping. In: ACM SIGPLAN Notices, pp. 177–187 (2009)
12. Breiman, L.: Random forests. Mach. Learn. **45**(1), 5–32 (2001)
13. Weaver, V.M.: Linux perf_event features and overhead. In: The 2nd International Workshop on Performance Analysis of Workload Optimized Systems, FastPath, p. 80, April 2013
14. Kohavi, R.: A study of cross-validation and bootstrap for accuracy estimation and model selection. In: IJCAI, vol. 14, no. 2, pp. 1137–1145, August 1995
15. Chen, Z., et al.: LORE: a loop repository for the evaluation of compilers. In: 2017 IEEE International Symposium on Workload Characterization (in press)

Software Cache Coherent Control
by Parallelizing Compiler

Boma A. Adhi$^{(\boxtimes)}$, Masayoshi Mase, Yuhei Hosokawa, Yohei Kishimoto,
Taisuke Onishi, Hiroki Mikami, Keiji Kimura, and Hironori Kasahara

Department of Computer Science and Engineering,
Waseda University, Tokyo, Japan
{boma, onishi, hiroki, kimura, kasahara}@kasahara.cs.waseda.ac.jp

Abstract. Recently multicore technology has enabled development of
hundreds or thousands core processor on a single chip. However, on such
multicore processor, cache coherence hardware will become very complex, hot and expensive. This paper proposes a parallelizing compiler
directed software coherence scheme for shared memory multicore systems without hardware cache coherence control. The general idea of the
proposed method is that an automatic parallelizing compiler parallelize
coarse grain task, analyzes stale data and line sharing in the program,
then solves those problems by simple program restructuring and data
synchronization. The proposed method is a simple and efficient software
cache coherent control scheme built on OSCAR automatic parallelizing
compiler and evaluated on Renesas RP2 with 8 SH-4A cores processor.
The cache coherence hardware on the RP2 processor is only available
for up to 4 cores. The cache coherence hardware can also be turned off
for non-coherence cache mode. Performance evaluation was performed
using 10 benchmark programs from SPEC2000, SPEC2006, NAS Parallel
Benchmark (NPB) and MediaBench II. The proposed method performed
as good as or better than hardware cache coherence scheme while still
provided correct result as the hardware coherent mechanism. For example, the proposed software cache coherent control (NCC) gave us 2.63
times speedup for SPEC 2000 equake with 4 cores against sequential
execution while got only 2.52 times speedup for 4 cores MESI hardware
coherent control. Also, the software coherence control gave us 4.37 speed
up for 8 cores with no hardware coherent mechanism available.

1 Introduction

For many years, cache coherent SMPs have been widely used as the core component of all classes of machines, from smartphones, IoTs, PCs, and embedded
systems all the way to HPC systems. Typically, a hardware cache coherence
mechanism, either snoopy or directory based, is employed to ensure every change
made into a shared line in one processor's private cache is always reflected in the
content of all private cahces so that coherency is maintained. Hardware cache
coherence mechanism scales well for current generation multicore processor [1],

© Springer Nature Switzerland AG 2019
L. Rauchwerger (Ed.): LCPC 2017, LNCS 11403, pp. 17–25, 2019.
https://doi.org/10.1007/978-3-030-35225-7_2

e.g. Intel Xeon Phi [2], Tilera Tile64 [3]. However, despite its common usage among current generation multicore processor, this kind of hardware will too complex, hot and expensive for the upcoming hundreds to thousands core massively parallel multicore system to avoid the complexity of the hardware based cache coherency.

Research on software controlled started in the late 80's. One of the prominent contributions is [4] which proposed fast selective invalidation scheme and version control scheme for compiler directed cache coherence. More recent research [5] proposes a compiler support for software based cache coherency. A practical and ready to use solution for software based coherence is yet to be proposed.

This paper proposes a new software coherent control scheme to guarantee coherency by avoiding stale data and false sharing. This method is novel, simple, powerful and give us delivers the same performance as the hardware implementation of cache coherency. Next, we present an overview of OSCAR's parallelization strategy followed by a discussion of the techniques to handle sate data and false sharing.

2   Software Cache Coherent Control by Parallelizing Compiler

The proposed method is built into the OSCAR parallelizing compiler, which analyzes and decomposes programs into tasks using control flow and data dependence. Based on the data access range of each task, the compiler addresses stale data and false sharing. Our proposed method may be applied to almost any kind of interprocessor networking as our method uses the main shared memory for synchronization and does not rely on communication between CPU cores. Next, we present an overview of OSCAR's parallelization strategy followed by a discussion of the techniques to handle sate data and false sharing.

2.1   Coarse-Grain Task Parallelization

The OSCAR compiler is a multi-grain parallelizing compiler. The compiler generates C or Fortran program extended with invocations to OSCAR API [6] routines in this way, OSCAR compiler generated parallel multicore code that can be compiled for any shared memory multicore available in the market using a conventional compiler. The OSCAR compiler starts the compilation process by dividing the source program into three types of coarse-grain tasks, or Macro Tasks (MTs): Basic Blocks (BBs), Repetition Blocks (RBs), and Subroutine Blocks (SBs). RBs and SBs are hierarchically decomposed into smaller MTs if coarse-grain task parallelism still exists within the task. Then, as all MTs for the input program are generated, they are analyzed to produce a Macro Flow Graph (MFG). An MFG is a control flow graph among the MTs having the data dependence edges. A Macro Task Graph (MTG) is generated by analyzing the earliest executable condition of every MT and tracing the control dependencies and data dependencies among MTs on the MFG. Based on this information, the compiler generates appropriate cache coherence control code [7].

2.2   Handling the Stale Data Problem

A hardware based cache coherence ensures information on changes made to
the data in one of the CPU cores cache line is propagated to other cores so
that each copy of this data in other cores can be invalidated. The process of
notifying the other processors in a snoopy based cache coherence may impact
the performance of the processor. With directory based mechanism, simultaneous
access to directory may become a performance bottleneck. Meanwhile, without
any hardware cache coherence, these bottlenecks do not exist, but access to stale
data should be manually managed by the compiler.

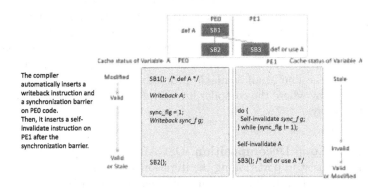

Fig. 1. Cache control code inserted by the compiler to prevent reference to stale data.

Based on the coarse grain scheduling result, to manage stale data problem,
the compiler generates explicit cache manipulation instructions to the processor,
i.e. writeback, self-invalidate, and purge. Writeback command tells the processor
to write the modified cache line to the main memory. The self-invalidate is a
command for invalidating the line of the cache memory. The purge command
executes the self-invalidate after the writing back (writeback) of the data stored
in the line of the cache memory.

Figure 1 is an example of the compiler generated code to prevent stale data
reference. Core 0 defines a new value for a shared variable, A. The compiler automatically inserts a writeback instruction and an assignment to a synchronization
flag on core 0's code. The compiler also inserts a self-invalidate instruction on
core 1 right after testing the synchronization flag. The compiler then schedules
the task in a way that minimize the delay caused by the synchronization. In
addition, if multiple cores retain the same data at the same time, the compiler
schedules all cores in way to prevent the data to be simultaneously updated.
These cache manipulation instructions are inserted only for Read-after-Write
data dependence. Meanwhile for Write-after-Read and Write-after-Write, only
synchronization instruction is inserted. By using this approach, stale data can be
avoided. Moreover, the overhead caused by the transmission of invalidate packets
associated with hardware based mechanism can be eliminated.

2.3   Handling the False Sharing Problem

False sharing is a condition in which two or more data items share a single cache line. Whenever one of those data is updated, inconsistency may occur. This is due to the granularity of the cache writeback mechanism usually works with line instead of byte or word sized. To address this problem, OSCAR compiler uses one of the following four mechanisms:

Variable Alignment and Array Expansion. To prevent unrelated variables from sharing a single cache line, the compiler aligns each variable to the beginning of a cache line. Not only for scalar variables, but this approach is also applicable for small sized one-dimension array. The array can be expanded so that each element is stored in a single cache line. While not very efficient due to potentially wasting cache space, this approach effectively prevents false sharing. Data alignment works best for one-dimension array whose size is smaller than the number of cache line in all available processor cores. It also works well for indirect access array where the compiler has no information regarding the access pattern of the array.

Cache Aligned Loop Decomposition. OSCAR compiler applies loop decomposition which consist in partitioning the iteration space of a loop to create several tasks. Instead of assigning the same number of iterations to each partial task, the compiler decomposes loops taking into account the cache line size as seen in Fig. 2(A).

Array Padding. It is not always possible to partition a two-dimension array cleanly along cache line boundaries. This happens when the lowest dimension of the array is not an integer multiply of the cache line size. In this case, OSCAR compiler inserts padding to the end of the array to match the cache line size. This approach is depicted in Fig. 2(B). It should be noted that this approach may also waste cache space.

Data Transfer Using Non-cacheable Buffer. When cache aligned loop causes a significant load imbalance or array padding consumes too much cache space or none of the former approaches cannot be applied, OSCAR compiler uses a non-cacheable buffer. The compiler designates a an area in the main memory that should not be copied to the cache and places the shared data in that area. Figure 3 depicts the usage of non-cacheable buffer.

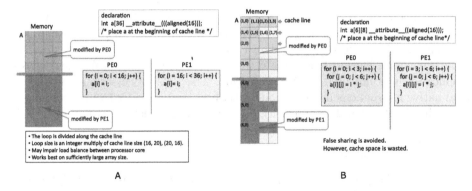

Fig. 2. (A)Cache alligned loop decomposition is applied to a one-dimension matrix to avoid false sharing. (B)Array padding is applied to a two-dimention matrix to avoid false sharing.

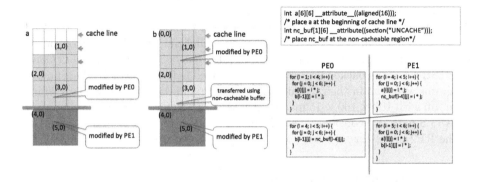

Fig. 3. Non-cacheable buffer is used to avoid false sharing.

3 Performance of the Software Coherent Control on Embedded Multicore

This section shows the performance of the proposed method on an embedded multicore the Renesas RP2 for benchmark programs from SPEC, NAS Parallel and MediaBench.

3.1 The RP2 Processor

The Renesas RP2 is an 8-core embedded processor configured as two 4-core SH-4A SMP clusters, with each cluster having MESI protocol, jointly developed by Renesas Electronics, Hitachi Ltd. and Waseda University under support from the METI/NEDO Multicore Processors for Real-time Consumer Electronics Project in 2007 [8]. Each processor core has its own private cache. However, there is no hardware coherence controller between the cluster for hard real-time applications like automobile engine control; hence, to use more than 4 cores across the cluster, a software based cache coherency must be used. The MESI hardware coherence mechanism can be disabled completely. The RP2 board as configured for this experiment has 16 kB of data cache with 32-byte line size and 128MB shared memory. The local memory, which was provided for hard real-time control application was not used in this evaluation. The RP2 processor supports several native instructions in NCC mode: writeback operation (OCBWB instruction), cache invalidate (OCBBI instruction), cache flush (OCBP instruction).

3.2   Benchmark Applications

To evaluate the performance of the proposed method, we used 10 benchmark applications from SPEC2000, SPEC2006, NAS Parallel Benchmark (NPB) and Mediabench II. While the selection of the benchmark program is somewhat limited due to the main memory size of the current board, the selected benchmark represents several different types of scientific and multimedia application. These benchmarks were written in C and converted to Parallelizable C [9] which is similar to MISRA-C used in embedded field. Then these programs were compiled by the OSCAR source-to-source automatic parallelizing compiler. The output C program by the OSCAR compiler was compiled by the Renesas SuperH C Compiler (SH C) as the backend compiler as mentioned before. The SPEC benchmark programs were run in their default configuration and datasets except lbm which were run with $100 \times 100 \times 15$ matrix. All NPB benchmarks were configured with CLASS S data size considering small shared memory or main memory (128 MB) of the RP2 processor.

3.3   Experimental Results and Analysis

Figure 4 is a graph showing the speedups by multiple cores of the proposed method on RP2 Processor. The lighter bars show the baseline performance on a Symmetric Multiprocessor (SMP) cluster with MESI hardware coherence control. The darker bars show the performance of the proposed software coherence control method on NCC architecture. The single core performance on SMP machine was selected as the baseline.

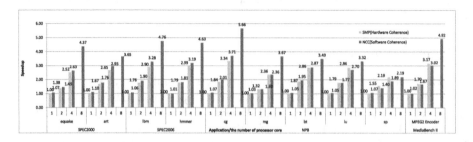

Fig. 4. The performance of the proposed method on RP2 Processor.

Figure 5 depicts the performance impact of each proposed methods. Five different plots are presented for four of the benchmark programs executing in 1, 2 and 4 cores: **SMP** is a normal shared memory architecture with native hardware based coherence. This is selected as the baseline of the measurement.

Stale data handling: stale data handling method with hardware based coherence control still turned on. We can see here that the performance is negatively impacted. This is to be expected since stale data handling method wastes CPU cycles since the hardware already handles this problem. But we can see here the effect of the stale data handling negatively impacted the performance of lbm.

False sharing avoidance: false sharing handling which comprises data alignment, cache line aligned data decomposition, and other layout transformation with hardware coherence control still turned on. We can see here that there is almost no significant performance impact. The cache line wasting effect is insignificant. In certain benchmarks, most notably lbm, this approach improves the performance. This is to be expected since false sharing is also bad even for hardware based cache coherence control. Removing false sharing problem will improves the performance of a hardware based coherence control. **NCC (hardware coherence):** this graph measures the overhead of both proposed method for handling stale data and false sharing with hardware coherence still active. **NCC (software coherence):** this graph shows the performance of the proposed method with hardware coherence control completely turned off.

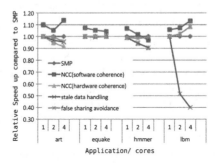

Fig. 5. The performance impact of software cache coherence.

The performance of the proposed software cache coherence method give us roughly 4%–14% better performance compared to hardware based coherence. With hardware based coherence, an overhead is imposed due to frequent transmission of invalidation packet between processor cores via the interconnection bus. On the other hand, the software does not require the transmission of such packet as the compiler will insert self-invalidate instruction to the required processor core. For art, quake and lbm benchmark, is positively affected by this performance benefit of software based coherence. The data structure of "lbm" is also unique that it has a lot of false sharing. We can see here that our proposed false sharing avoidance method improves the performance significantly.

While not offering huge performance benefit, compared to hardware based approach, the proposed method has enabled the usage of 8 cores in RP2 processor which does not have cache coherence mechanism. Before, using our proposed method, it was impossible to run an application with 8 cores without very complicated hand-tuned optimization.

4 Conclusions

This paper proposes a method to manage cache coherency by an automatic parallelizing compiler for non-coherent cache architecture. The proposed method incorporates control dependence, data dependence analysis and automatic parallelization by the compiler. Based on the analyzed stale data, any possible false sharing is identified and resolved. Then, software cache control code is automatically inserted. The proposed method was evaluated using 10 benchmark applications from SPEC2000, SPEC2006, NAS Parallel Benchmark and MediaBench II on Renesas RP2 8 core multicore processor. The performance of the NCC architecture with the proposed method was similar or better than the hardware based c herenc mple, the hardware coherent mechanism using MESI protocol gave us 2.52 speedup on 4 core against one core SPEC2006 "equake", 2.9 times speedup on 4 cores for SPEC2006 "lbm", 3.34 times speedup on 4 cores for NPB "cg", 3.17 times speedup on 4 cores for MediaBench II "MPEG2 Encoder". On the otherhand, the proposed software cache coherence control method implemented on OSCAR Multigrain Parallelizing Compiler gave us 2.63 times on 4 cores, 4.37 times on 8 cores speedup for "equake", 3.28 times on 4 cores and 4.76 times on "lbm", 3.71 times on 4 cores and 5.66 times on 8 cores for "cg", 3.02 times on 4 cores and 4.92 times on 8 cores for "MPEG2 Encoder". Those result shows the proposed software coherent control method allow us to obtain comparable performance with the MESI hardware coherence control mechanism for the same number of processor cores. Furthermore, it gives us good speedup automatically and quickly for many processor cores without the hardware coherent control mechanism although up until now application programmers had to spend huge development time to use the non-coherent cache architecture.

Acknowledgement. Masayoshi Mase and Yohei Kishimoto are currently working for Hitachi, Ltd. and Yahoo Japan Corp respectively. Their works contained in this paper were part of their study at Waseda University. Boma Anantasatya Adhi is part of Universitas Indonesia and currently a PhD student at Waseda University supported by Hitachi Scholarship.

References

1. Martin, M.M.K., Hill, M.D., Sorin, D.J.: Why on-chip cache coherence is here to stay. Commun. ACM **55**(7), 78–89 (2012)

2. Chrysos, G.: Intel & ®Xeon Phi Coprocessor-the Architecture. Intel Whitepaper (2014)
3. Bell, S., et al.: TILE64 - processor: a 64-Core SoC with mesh interconnect. In: 2008 IEEE International Solid-State Circuits Conference - Digest of Technical Papers, pp. 588–598, February 2008
4. Cheong, H., Veidenbaum, A.V.: Compiler-directed cache management in multiprocessors. Computer **23**(6), 39–47 (1990)
5. Tavarageri, S., Kim, W., Torrellas, J., Sadayappan, P.: Compiler support for software cache coherence. In: 2016 IEEE 23rd International Conference on High Performance Computing (HiPC), pp. 341–350, December 2016
6. Kimura, K., Hayashi, A., Mikami, H., Shimaoka, M., Shirako, J., Kasahara, H.: OSCAR API v2. 1 : extensions for an advanced accelerator control scheme to a low-power multicore API. In: 17th Workshop on Compilers for Parallel Computing (2013)
7. Kasahara, H., Kimura, K., Adhi, B.A., Hosokawa, Y., Kishimoto, Y., Mase, M.: Multicore cache coherence control by a parallelizing compiler. In: 2017 IEEE 41st Annual Computer Software and Applications Conference (COMPSAC), vol. 01, pp. 492–497, July 2017
8. Ito, M.: An 8640 mips soc with independent power-off control of 8 cpus and 8 rams by an automatic parallelizing compiler. In: 2008 IEEE International Solid-State Circuits Conference - Digest of Technical Papers, pp. 90–598, February 2008
9. Mase, M., Onozaki, Y., Kimura, K., Kasahara, H.: Parallelizable c and its performance on low power high performance multicore processors (2010)

Polyhedral Compilation Support for C++ Features: A Case Study with CPPTRAJ

Amit Roy[1], Daniel Roe[2], Mary Hall[1(✉)], and Thomas Cheatham[2]

[1] School of Computing, University of Utah, Salt Lake City, UT 84112, USA
mhall@cs.utah.edu
[2] Department of Medicinal Chemistry, University of Utah,
Salt Lake City, UT 84112, USA

Abstract. This paper reveals challenges in migrating C++ codes to GPUs using polyhedral compiler technology. We point to instances where reasoning about C++ constructs in a polyhedral model is feasible. We describe a case study using CPPTRAJ, an analysis code for molecular dynamics trajectory data. An initial experiment applied the CUDA-CHiLL compiler to key computations in CPPTRAJ to migrate them to the GPUs of NCSA's Blue Waters supercomputer. We found three aspects of this code made program analysis difficult: (1) STL C++ vectors; (2) structures of vectors; and, (3) iterators over these structures. We show how we can rewrite the computation to affine form suitable for CUDA-CHiLL, and also describe how to support the original C++ code in a polyhedral framework. The result of this effort yielded speedups over serial ranging from 3× to 278× on the six optimized kernels, and up to 100× over serial and 10× speedup over OpenMP.

1 Introduction

CPPTRAJ is a biomolecular analysis code that examines results of simulations that are represented as time series of three-dimensional atomic positions (i.e., coordinate trajectories) [1]. CPPTRAJ is an MPI and OpenMP code distributed as part of the AmberTools suite, a widely-used set of tools for complete molecular dynamics simulations, with either explicit water or implicit solvent models [2], and is also available on GitHub [3]. Historically, the analysis function is less compute-intensive than the simulation, and less attention has been paid to its parallelization. As Amber simulations scale to larger supercomputing systems, it is desirable to perform analysis functions in situ during simulation to reduce data movement and storage. Thus, analysis has become a more significant component of simulation time, and worthy of renewed attention paid to its parallelization, especially in light of new architectures.

Parallelization within the `Action` class computations offered an unexploited opportunity for thread-level parallelism on GPUs. We adapted one of the more time-consuming analyses in CPPTRAJ, the `Action_Closest`, which determines the N closest solvent molecules to M solute atoms where N and M are both user-specified. This calculation can require millions of distance calculations for each

© Springer Nature Switzerland AG 2019
L. Rauchwerger (Ed.): LCPC 2017, LNCS 11403, pp. 26–35, 2019.
https://doi.org/10.1007/978-3-030-35225-7_3

trajectory frame, to use GPUs. To ease the programming challenges of migrating CPPTRAJ to use GPUs, we employed CUDA-CHiLL, which generates CUDA code from a sequential implementation [4,5]. CUDA-CHiLL is a lightweight GPU-specific layer for CHiLL, a source-to-source code translator that takes as input sequential loop nest computations written in C, performs transformations, and generates optimized sequential or parallel C. A separate input called a *transformation recipe* describes high-level code transformations to be applied to the code; this recipe can either be automatically generated [5] or specified by the programmer. The underlying compiler technology relies on a *polyhedral* abstraction of loop nest computations, where loop iteration spaces are represented as polyhedra.

CUDA-CHiLL has a C++ frontend, but has primarily been applied to C codes. We discovered that some of the C++ features are difficult to represent in a polyhedral framework: (1) structures of arrays; (2) C++ iterators; and, (3) a vector library. We initially modified the code so that CUDA-CHiLL could analyze it and generate GPU code. The resulting code achieves high performance, meeting the goals of the optimization exercise and providing a template to the CPPTRAJ team for further parallelization. We then considered how to extend CUDA-CHiLL to support these features. The contributions of this paper are: (1) a description of a successful parallelization of CPPTRAJ for GPUs; (2) analysis of barriers to automatic parallelization in CUDA-CHiLL; and, (3) extensions to polyhedral compiler technology to support the C++ features of this code.

2 Background and Related Work

We describe the foundations of polyhedral transformation and code generation technology, and tease out key concepts in extending its support.

2.1 Polyhedral Compiler Frameworks

Polyhedral frameworks describe the iteration space for each statement in a loop nest as a set of lattice points of a polyhedron. Loop transformations can then be viewed as mapping functions that convert the original iteration space to a transformed iteration space, providing the compiler a powerful abstraction to transform a loop nest without being restricted to the original loop structure [6]. To verify correctness of iteration space remappings, the compiler employs *dependence analysis*, which detects possible accesses to the same memory location, where one of the accesses is a write. Reordering a statement's execution order is valid as long as it preserves all data dependences [7]. Once transformations are proven safe through dependence analysis, the code corresponding to the transformed iteration space may then be generated by polyhedra scanning [8–12].

Let us consider for example, the loop permutation transformation applied to the loop nest in Fig. 1(a), with the iteration space I represented as an integer tuple set. The original statement is replaced by a statement macro as shown in Fig. 1(b). The loop permutation transformation T in Fig. 1(c), which permutes

a. Original loop nest

```
for (i=0;i<N;i++) {
    for (j=1;j<M;j++) {
SO:   a[i][j] = b[j] − a[i][j-1];


I = {[i,j] | 0<=i<N ∧ 1<=j<=M}
```

b. Statement macro

```
#define SO(i,j) a[(i)][(j)] = b[(j)] − a[(i)][(j-1)]
```

c. Transformed loop nest

```
T = {[i,j] →[j,i]}

for (j=1;j<M;j++) {
    for (i=0;i<N;i++) {
SO:   a[i][j] = b[j] − a[i][j-1];
```

d. Dependence relation for SO

```
{[i,j] →[i',j'] | 0<=i,i'<N ∧ 1<=j,j'<M ∧
             (i=i' ∧ j=j'-1)}
```

Fig. 1. An example of a loop permutation transformation.

the order of the loops, takes I as input and returns an output integer tuple. The code generator then employs polyhedra scanning of the resulting iteration space to generate the output code shown. To determine safety of the transformation, dependence relations are extracted from examining the iteration space and array accesses, as in Fig. 1(d). In this case, while there is a dependence between reads and writes of a, permutation is safe because it does not reverse the dependence on a. The statement is not specified in the set representation, and therefore the loop body contains statement macros. The transformed loop need only pass to the statement macro the original iterators for the statement as functions of the new loop iterators.

2.2 Support for C++ Code

Many polyhedral frameworks are embedded into C and C++ compilers and leverage parsing of C++ code into an abstract syntax tree (e.g., PolyOpt, PSSC [13], Polly [14]). Some polyhedral compilers generate CUDA code as in this work [15,16]. Such compilers typically look for analyzable regions of code amenable to polyhedral optimization, called Static Control Parts (SCoPs) such that all loop bounds and conditionals are affine functions of enclosing loops. Certain C++ code constructs may appear to be non-affine to a polyhedral compiler, and therefore these portions of the code would be ignored and not optimized, even though they could be rewritten into an affine form. Notably, analysis and transformation merely needs to extract dependence relations and statement macros as functions of loop indices. *We consider in this paper such examples whereby we reason about C++ code and represent the code in statement macros, extract iteration spaces to facilitate transformation and code generation, and extract dependence relations to determine safety of transformations.*

3   Code Modifications and Extensions for CPPTRAJ

This section highlights the C++ features that we modified to pass the CPPTRAJ code through CUDA-CHiLL, and discusses possible extensions.

```
 1  void  Action_Closest :: Action_NoImage_Center (Frame&,  double  maxD)
 2  {
 3    double  Dist ;
 4    int  smol ;
 5    std :: vector<int >:: const_iterator  satom ;
 6
 7    Vec3  maskCenter = frmIn .VGeometricCenter ( distanceMask_ ) ;
 8    for  (smol=0;  smol < Nsmols_;  smol++) {
 9      SolventMols_ [smol ].D = maxD;
10      for  (satom = SolventMols_ [smol ]. solventAtoms . begin () ;
11           satom != SolventMols_ [smol ]. solventAtoms . end () ;
12           ++satom )
13    {
14
15      double *a1 = maskCenter . Dptr () ; //center of solute  molecule
16      double *a2 = frmIn .XYZ(* satom ) ;
17
18      double x = a1 [0]  − a2 [0];
19      double y = a1 [1]  − a2 [1];
20      double z = a1 [2]  − a2 [2];
21
22      Dist = (x*x + y*y + z*z ) ;
23
24      if  (Dist < SolventMols_ [smol ].D)
25        SolventMols_ [smol ].D = Dist ;
26    }
27  }
28  }
29  \vspace*{ −.1in}
```

Listing 1.1. Original code for `Action_Closest`.

3.1   Changes Irrelevant to a Polyhedral Framework

The original C++ code is shown in Listing 1.1. A few constructs not supported by CUDA-CHiLL are not fundamental, and extensions to the implementation are straightforward. The required changes, which will not be discussed further, include (1) use of member functions of a class, and reference to member fields, which should be replaced with C functions and parameters; (2) control flow simplifications that would benefit from more sophisticated data-flow analysis; and, (3) the *min* calculation over `Dist`, which should be recognized as a reduction.

3.2   Other Ways of Expressing Loops over Arrays in C++

Additional required changes show C++ constructs that are comparable to standard loop nests over dense arrays, but are expressed differently from C. The reference in line 15 to `maskCenter` returns a variable of type `Vec3`, which is a simple datatype for representing 3D coordinates. The reference in line 16 to `frmIn.XYZ` returns a pointer to the position inside the Frame datatype's internal 3D coordinate array corresponding to atom **n**. Since these are read-only variables, it is sufficient to ignore the references since they cannot carry a dependence. However, in the more general case where they may also be written, it is useful to recognize that these types actually represent an array of three doubles.

The second kind of vector represented by `SolventMols_` adds more complexity to the analysis. It is declared as `std::vector⟨MolDist⟩`. That is, it uses the vector data type from the C++ standard template library. The code loops over the elements of this vector using a C++ iterator, `satom`.

A key observation is that these are implemented similarly to unit-stride access to arrays, but the compiler must be extended to recognize this. For our experiments, we have made these changes explicit. Referring back to Sect. 2.1, it is realistic to support these because we only need to extract three things from the code: (1) the iteration space of the loop nest; (2) the statement macro; and, (3) the dependence relations.

First, the loop nest needs to be rewritten in the code representation leading to an affine iteration space. The following rewrite is safe if you know that these vectors are stored contiguously in memory and the meaning of the `begin()`, `end()` and `size()` functions [17].

```
ub = SolventMols_[smol].solventAtoms.size();
I = {[smol,satom] | 0<=smol<Nsmols_ && 0<=satom<ub}
```

For the statement macros, we can leave line 15 as written in this case. But for line 16, we would like to rewrite so that if we are to modify the iteration space for the `satom` loop, we will be able to update the access in the context of the loop indices. The same is true for the reduction statement at lines 24 and 25. Therefore, the statement macros are as follows:

```
#define S16(smol,satom)
    double *a2 = SolventMols_[(smol)].solventAtoms[(satom)]
#define S24(smol,satom)
    SolventMols_[(smol)].D = min(Dist,SolventMols_[(smol)].D)
```

Finally, we consider the dependence relations arising from the statements that reference these vectors. As the statements at lines 15 and 16 are read-only accesses to the `maskCenter` and the data associated with the solvent atom, there are no dependence relations. For the access at lines 24 and 25, after the reduction transformation is performed as described above, the following dependence relation arises between read and write of `SolventMols_[smol].D`.

```
{[smol,satom]->[smol',satom'] | 0<=smol,smol'<NSmols_ &&
                                0<satom,satom'<ub && smol=smol'}
```

This discussion assumes that the compiler can perform dependence analysis on fields in structures. This is a straightforward extension, where indexed fields are treated as arrays, and distinct fields are considered independent.

3.3   CUDA Code Generation and Application Integration

CUDA-CHiLL was applied to manually modified code to arrive at the output kernel code in Listing 1.2 and scaffolding code (not shown). The problem size is fixed to the sample input used for the experiments in Sect. 5. The generated code was derived using the CUDA-CHiLL script below.

```
--global-- void Action_No_image_GPU(double *D_,double *maskCenter,
    double (*SolventMols_)[965][3])
{
  int satom;
  int bx;
  int tx;

  double maxD;
  double Dist;
  double newVariable0;

  bx = blockIdx.x;
  tx = threadIdx.x;
  newVariable0 = D_[tx + 32 * bx];
  newVariable0 = maxD;

  for (satom = 0; satom <= 15021; satom += 1) {
    Dist = (pow(maskCenter[0] - SolventMols_[smol][satom][0],2) +
            pow(maskCenter[1] - SolventMols_[smol][satom][1],2) +
            pow(maskCenter[2] - SolventMols_[smol][satom][2],2));
    newVariable0 = (min(Dist,newVariable0));
  }
  D_[tx + 32 * bx] = newVariable0;
}
\vspace*{-.1in}
```

Listing 1.2. Kernel output of CUDA-CHiLL.

```
init("simple_action_noImage.c", "Action_NoImage_Center",0)
NA=15022
NM=965
TI=32
TJ=3*NM/TI
tile_by_index(0,{"smol"}, {TI}, {l1_control="ii"}, {"ii","smol"})
cudaize(0,"Action_No_image_GPU",
          {D_=NM*3, SolventMols_=NA*3,maskCenter=3},
          {block={"ii"}, thread={"smol"}},{})
copy_to_registers(0, "satom", "D_")
```

It is only safe to parallelize the outermost loop as the inner loop carries a dependence on D_[smol]. Therefore, this simple script creates two levels of parallelism for the outermost loop using the tile_by_index command. Each thread then computes one element of D_. To avoid unnecessary memory accesses, the copy_to_registers command is used to locally store D_[smol] in newVariable0 during the majority of a thread's execution. The cudaize command marks the outermost two loops to serve as block and thread indices, whose sizes are controlled by TI and TJ derived from tuning. Note that different transformation recipes will lead to very different generated codes.

Five more member functions were also replaced with CUDA kernels. These all had similar structure and C++ features as compared to the code in Listing 1.1, but some had more computation at each point. We used the generated CUDA code as a template for the other kernels, and replaced the computation at the innermost loop. The CUDA code was then integrated back into the application with some additional functions calls from the Action_Closest class. We also inserted timing functions within a combined CUDA harness code for the kernels. Therefore, the impact in terms of coding changes on the application was not significant, but the performance gains were substantial, as shown in Sect. 5.

4   Incorporating Knowledge of Library or Class Properties

The previous section shows it is certainly feasible to represent the C++ constructs in this code as affine. However, the question arises as to how to embed knowledge into the compiler of the C++ STL or even a user class. For something as widely used as the STL, we could treat it as part of the C++ language and integrate these transformations into the CHiLL compiler directly. However, this approach would not apply to any user-defined class.

We propose to take advantage of CHiLL's existing *transformation recipe* interface to extend the compiler to convey this additional information. This concept of programmability of transformation recipes has been used before in adding CUDA support through a programming language interface [4], but in that case it was composing and reinterpeting existing CHiLL commands and modifying the output only. Here, we need a way of reinterpreting the input. We propose a new command in a transformation recipe called *scopInfo*:

```
scopInfo(loop, IS={affine_relation}, SM={statement_macros},D={deps})
```

This is one way to convey information to the compiler, before it attempts to analyze the code, that this analysis should permit extensions to whatever is already supported by CHiLL. This approach is similar to rewrite rules that are supported in domain-specific compiler frameworks such as DeLite [18], but specifically provides the inputs of a polyhedral framework to facilitate dependence analysis, iteration space reordering and code generation.

While such an extension could make it possible for a programmer to add *scopInfo* commands to their recipes, it may be too low-level for the average programmer. However, a custom preprocessing phase could be added to the framework to derive specialized information such as this in a domain-specific or library-specific way, particularly if the recipes are automatically generated as in [5]. We foresee such an extension would make it possible to convey other information to the compiler useful to loop nest optimization for HPC applications, such as for example, how to interpret user-defined domain decompositions.

5   Experimental Results

The GPU-enabled version of CPPTRAJ was then executed on the NCSA Bluewaters supercomputer, and compared against an MPI-only implementation and an MPI+OpenMP implementation. Bluewaters has two types of nodes, namely *XE* or *XK*. *XE* nodes have 2 AMD 6276 Interlagos processors while *XK* nodes have a single Interlagos processor and a GPU accelerator, an NVIDIA GK110 (K20X) Kepler GPU with 2688 CUDA cores. Both *XE* and *XK* nodes have 64 GBytes of memory. We used a molecular system for our experiment as a good proxy for typical real world usage, consisting of 4143 solute atoms and 15022 solvent molecules, resulting in up to 62M distance calculations for each frame.

As described in Sect. 3, the CPPTRAJ code was extended to replace six `Action` member functions with calls to CUDA kernels. The six kernels are divided into two groups: one group calculates distance with respect to the solvent molecule's center as represented by the code in Listing 1.2; the other calculates distance with respect to each atom contained within the solvent molecule. Figure 2(left) compares speedup over serial for each GPU kernel. Speedups range from 3× to 278×, with the *Non-center* kernels exhibiting a higher speedup. Each of the 3 kernels in each group is furthermore separated by the type of imaging method they use during the distance calculation. The labels *Ortho* and *Non-Ortho* refer to orthorhombic and nonorthorhombic, respectively, indicating the unit cell shape. Non-orthorhombic distance calculations are more compute-intensive as they check the "self" unit cell plus 26 images.

We now compare performance of the *Non-Center, Non-Ortho* kernel to the original OpenMP code within the full CPPTRAJ MPI code in Fig. 2(right). On a single node, the GPU version is rougly 10× faster than the OpenMP version. The substantial parallelism exhibits strong scaling as we deploy the application across multiple nodes, ranging from 1 to 32.

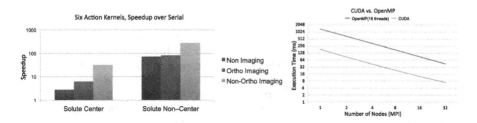

Fig. 2. Performance measurements on Blue Waters, showing speedup over serial of all Action kernels (left); OpenMP comparison and strong scaling within MPI code (right).

6 Conclusion

This paper has explored using polyhedral compiler technology to parallelize for GPUs key computations in CPPTRAJ, a real-world analysis code used for molecular dynamics trajectory data written in C++. The primary goal of this work was to derive high-performance GPU code for CPPTRAJ. At the same time, we explored the gaps in the CUDA-CHiLL framework for supporting C++ code and proposed how to extend polyhedral compiler technology to support C++ features, including the vectors in the standard template library.

We believe interactions such as this between HPC tool researchers and application developers on real applications lead to tools that better meet user needs while aiding applications in their migration to the variety of current and future architectures that require significant application changes.

Acknowledgment. This research is part of the Blue Waters sustained-petascale computing project, which is supported by the National Science Foundation (awards OCI-0725070 and ACI-1238993) and the state of Illinois. Blue Waters is a joint effort of the University of Illinois at Urbana-Champaign and its National Center for Supercomputing Applications.

References

1. Roe, D.R., Cheatham, T.E.: Ptraj and cpptraj: software for processing and analysis of molecular dynamics trajectory data. J. Chem. Theory Comput. **9**(7), 3084–3095 (2013). https://doi.org/10.1021/ct400341p. pMID: 2658398
2. http://ambermd.org
3. https://github.com/Amber-MD/cpptraj
4. Rudy, G., Khan, M.M., Hall, M., Chen, C., Chame, J.: A programming language interface to describe transformations and code generation. In: Cooper, K., Mellor-Crummey, J., Sarkar, V. (eds.) LCPC 2010. LNCS, vol. 6548, pp. 136–150. Springer, Heidelberg (2011). https://doi.org/10.1007/978-3-642-19595-2_10
5. Khan, M., Basu, P., Rudy, G., Hall, M., Chen, C., Chame, J.: A script-based autotuning compiler system to generate high-performance cuda code. ACM Trans. Archit. Code Optim. **9**(4), 31:1–31:25 (2013). https://doi.org/10.1145/2400682.2400690
6. Feautrier, P.: Automatic parallelization in the polytope model. In: Perrin, G.-R., Darte, A. (eds.) The Data Parallel Programming Model. LNCS, vol. 1132, pp. 79–103. Springer, Heidelberg (1996). https://doi.org/10.1007/3-540-61736-1_44
7. Allen, R., Kennedy, K.: Optimizing Compilers for Modern Architectures: A Dependence-Based Approach. Morgan Kaufmann Publishers, Burlington (2002)
8. Ancourt, C., Irigoin, F.: Scanning polyhedra with DO loops. In: Symposium on Principles and Practice of Parallel Programming, April 1991
9. Kelly, W.A.: Optimization within a unified transformation framework. Ph.D. dissertation, University of Maryland, December 1996
10. Quilleré, F., Rajopadhye, S.: Generation of efficient nested loops from polyhedra. Int. J. Parallel Program. **28**(5), 469–498 (2000)
11. Vasilache, N., Bastoul, C., Cohen, A.: Polyhedral code generation in the real world. In: Mycroft, A., Zeller, A. (eds.) CC 2006. LNCS, vol. 3923, pp. 185–201. Springer, Heidelberg (2006). https://doi.org/10.1007/11688839_16
12. Chen, C.: Polyhedra scanning revisited. In: Proceedings of the 33rd ACM SIGPLAN Conference on Programming Language Design and Implementation, ser. PLDI 2012, pp. 499–508, June 2012
13. Adamski, D., Jablonski, G., Perek, P., Napieralski, A.: Polyhedral source-to-source compiler. In: 2016 MIXDES - 23rd International Conference Mixed Design of Integrated Circuits and Systems, pp. 458–463, June 2016

14. Grosser, T., Armin, G., Lengauer, C.: Pollyâperforming polyhedral optimizations on a low-level intermediate representation. Parallel Process. Lett. **22**(04), 1250010 (2012)
15. Baskaran, M.M., Ramanujam, J., Sadayappan, P.: Automatic C-to-CUDA code generation for affine programs. In: Proceedings of the International Conference on Compiler Construction, March 2010
16. Leung, A.: A mapping path for multi-GPGPU accelerated computers from a portable high level programming abstraction. In: Workshop on General-Purpose Processing using GPUs, September 2010
17. http://en.cppreference.com/w/cpp/container/vector
18. Sujeeth, A.K., et al.: Delite: a compiler architecture for performance-oriented embedded domain-specific languages. ACM Trans. Embed. Comput. Syst. **13**(4s), 134:1–134:25 (2014). https://doi.org/10.1145/2584665

Language-Agnostic Optimization and Parallelization for Interpreted Languages

Michelle Mills Strout[✉], Saumya Debray, Kate Isaacs, Barbara Kreaseck,
Julio Cárdenas-Rodríguez, Bonnie Hurwitz, Kat Volk, Sam Badger,
Jesse Bartels, Ian Bertolacci, Sabin Devkota, Anthony Encinas, Ben Gaska,
Brandon Neth, Theo Sackos, Jon Stephens, Sarah Willer, and Babak Yadegari

Department of Computer Science, University of Arizona, Tucson, AZ, USA
mstrout@cs.arizona.edu

Abstract. Scientists are increasingly turning to interpreted languages, such as Python, Java, R, Matlab, and Perl, to implement their data analysis algorithms. While such languages permit rapid software development, their implementations often run into performance issues that slow down the scientific process. Source-level approaches for parallelization are problematic for two reasons: first, many of the language features common to these languages can be challenging for the kinds of analyses needed for parallelization; and second, even where such analysis is possible, a language-specific approach implies that each language would need its own parallelizing compiler and/or constructs, resulting in significant duplication of effort.

The Science Up To Par project is investigating a radically different approach to this problem: automatic parallelization at the machine code level using trace information. The key to accomplishing this will be the static and dynamic analysis of executables and the reconstitution of such executables into parallel executables. The key insight is that with trace information it should be possible optimize out the interpreter and other dynamic features in a language-agnostic manner and create parallelized executables for multicore architectures. If successful, this can enable scientists to continue to develop in programming environments that most conveniently support their scientific exploration without paying the performance overheads currently associated with many such environments.

1 Introduction

Scientific communities, such as medical imaging, the life sciences, and planetary sciences, rely extensively on computer software to process and analyze the wealth of data they and others are generating. In recent years, interpreted languages such as Python, Perl, and R have come to dominate data analysis software development in many areas of science: for example, most of the bioinformatics software developed in the last five years was implemented in Python,

© Springer Nature Switzerland AG 2019
L. Rauchwerger (Ed.): LCPC 2017, LNCS 11403, pp. 36–46, 2019.
https://doi.org/10.1007/978-3-030-35225-7_4

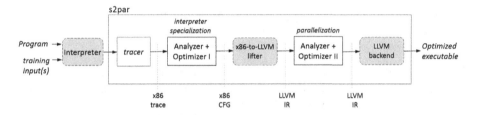

Fig. 1. s2par tool. Solid boxes are modules being developed as part of this project; dashed shaded boxes represent third-party software.

JavaScript, or Perl [7]. Such languages have been referred to as productivity languages [2]. The high-level abstractions supported by such languages enable rapid prototyping that, together with the re-use of contributed code from the scientific community, has led to productivity gains in the development of data analysis and simulation programs.

Unfortunately, some of the features that make these languages productive, e.g., dynamic typing, dynamic error checking, not requiring programmers to specify the parallelization strategy, and being interpreted, incur significant run-time overheads and lead to execution times that are orders of magnitude more than programming languages such as Fortran, C/C++, and parallel programming languages. Scientists can therefore either work within the constraints of inefficient software, which can limit the problem sizes they can address; or rewrite their software in a different programming language, where they would also have to port their colleagues' algorithms to reuse sub-routines and/or compare results. Neither alternative is very appealing because of the iterative nature of data analysis algorithm development that involves evolving the algorithms based on feedback from evaluating such algorithms on large datasets. The Science Up To Par project, presented in this paper, aims to provide the advantages of current alternatives while mitigating their disadvantages.

Our goal is to bring multicore parallelism to scientists while still allowing them to use programming environments that most conveniently support their scientific exploration. *We are developing a language-agnostic, trace-guided optimization tool that operates directly on the productivity-language software written by scientists. This tool will combine dynamic instrumentation and analysis with aggressive optimization and parallelization to create specialized and parallelized executables for use with large datasets based on example runs with small representative datasets.* Figure 1 illustrates the Science Up To Par optimization tool (s2par) and the dynamic analysis toolchain that s2par is built on.

Scientists will extend their development cycle with a step where they let the Science Up To Par optimization tool trace the processing of small example datasets. The optimization tool will provide a specialized, optimized, and parallelized executable based on the traces. Scientists will then be able to analyze their larger datasets with the provided executable. Our usage goal is for the tool to "just work" as illustrated in the following example:

```
s2par --profile <profile_name>  python myprog.py <parameters>
s2par --optimize <profile_name> -o newexec
./newexec <parameters for larger datasets>
```

Thus, scientists will be able to continue using the programming languages that they are most productive in while still being able to leverage multicore resources to analyze large datasets with scientifically useful turnaround times.

To achieve these goals, we need to solve the following technical problems:

– Given an execution trace (a sequence of machine instructions), how can we separate out the control-flow and data-flow logic of the interpreted program (the *interpretee*) from those of the interpreter?
– How representative are traces of small inputs in scientific codes?
– How can we detect parallel and/or reduction loops in the recovered control flow graphs?
– How can we implement the parallel loops without assuming an underlying memory model, (i.e., without assuming arrays are being used)?
– How can we efficiently catch control-flow that did not occur in the traced input execution but does for larger datasets?

The remainder of this paper overviews the progress we have made in solving these problems.

2   Control-Flow and Data-Flow Separation

The machine-level instruction sequence observed in an execution trace reflects control flows and data flows resulting from a combination of the program logic of the interpreter and the interpreted program. This intermingling of the logic of these two programs can hamper parallelization. For example, branch instructions in the interpreter's dispatch code can result in spurious control dependencies, while data movement to and from the interpreter's expression evaluation stack can result in spurious data dependencies. To permit effective parallelization, therefore, we have to separate out the program logic of the interpreted program from that of the interpreter. This involves a number of nontrivial challenges, for example:

– Translating from the input program to the interpreter's internal representation (IR) of that code involves the interpreter's front-end (possibly including the compiler that generates the IR), whose logic can be complex and difficult to untangle.
– Different interpreters may use different IRs, e.g., a linear array of byte code instructions, as in Python and Java, or a tree representation, as in Perl and some implementations of Ruby.
– The dispatch mechanism may be different, e.g., byte code as in Python and Java, direct-threading as in Ruby.
– Some of the interpreter code may be created dynamically at interpreter startup time, as in the Hotspot template-based interpreter for Java [6].

– Depending on the optimizations performed by the interpreter front end, the dispatch code may be replicated, resulting in multiple different dispatch instructions in the executed code (e.g., as in optimized CPython).
– An interpreter that supports multi-threading (or simulates it, as with the `thread` library in CPython) may have multiple virtual instruction pointers (vips), making it necessary to untangle the code corresponding to the different vips.

Many of these issues arise from the diversity of design choices available for implementing interpreters, and they mean that a language-agnostic system such as that proposed here cannot make *a priori* assumptions about any particular design choice. For example, we cannot assume that the IR is a byte-code, or that it occupies a contiguous region of memory. Coming up with effective ways to identify and reason about interpreters and interpreted programs under weak assumptions is a major research thrust of this research.

2.1 Control-Flow Separation

Control-flow separation refers to the process of untangling and separating the control flow logic of the interpreted program from that of the interpreter. Furthermore, in an interpreted execution of a program, control dependencies in the input program are mapped to data dependencies through the interpreter's virtual instruction pointer (vip) [14]. For example, a conditional branch in the input program is implemented by updating the value of the vip appropriately, thereby inducing a data dependence through that variable. These data dependencies have to be identified, and the corresponding control dependencies reconstructed, when separating out the control flow logic of the interpreter from that of the input program (see Fig. 2).

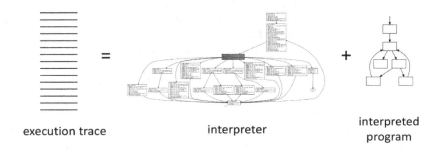

execution trace   interpreter   interpreted program

Fig. 2. Illustrating the process of deriving the interpreters control flow graph from a trace and then specializing then deriving the control flow graph of the program being interpreted.

We are decomposing the interpreter specialization problem into a collection of smaller and simpler problems.

1. Given the file from which the input program is read (specified, for example, as a command-line argument), identify the memory regions corresponding to the IR of the program being interpreted. An example of such an IR is the byte code for the input program.
2. Given the set of locations comprising the input program's IR, identify the control transfers corresponding to the dispatch instruction(s) of the interpreter.
3. Given the set of dispatch instructions, identify the machine instructions corresponding to the handler for each byte code instruction and thereby reconstruct the control flow graph of the input program.
4. Given the control flow graph of the input program, identify and optimize out inefficiencies due to interpretation.

We propose to use *dynamic taint analysis* [10] (augmented to deal with implicit flows through control dependencies) to follow the flow of values through the computation: e.g., from the input program through the front end to the IR; and from the IR to the dispatch code. To obtain accurate results, it will be essential to minimize imprecision arising from over-tainting; we propose to apply ideas from our earlier work on bit-precise architecture-aware taint analysis [12,13] to address this issue.

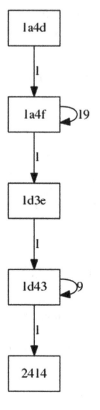

Fig. 3. Example recovered CFG

To explore the viability of these ideas, we have experimented with a simple prototype tool for analyzing interpreter traces for a variety of different languages, including Java, Perl, Python, and Ruby. These experiments have helped identify, and clarify our understanding of, many of the research challenges identified above. This prototype does not address the issues that arise from the interactions between the interpreter's code and data structures (e.g., the interpreter's expression stack) as well as interactions with other components of the runtime system (e.g., the garbage collector). Nevertheless, we have been able to make progress on the third research subproblem mentioned above: namely, given a set of dispatch instructions, reconstruct the control flow graph of the input program.

We recover the control flow graph using a method broadly analogous to that of Sharif *et al.* [11], though significantly different in details. Like Sharif et al, we employ a multi-label taint analysis to identify the dispatch of an interpreter; unlike that work, however, we do not make any assumptions about the interpreter or the interpreted IR (e.g., Sharif *et al.* assume a bytecode interpreter where the executed bytecode is laid out as a contiguous array of memory locations—assumptions that do not hold for AST interpreters as for Perl and direct-threaded interpreters as for Ruby). The generality of our approach, while important for applicability to a wide variety of interpreters, can sometimes result in an over-approximation of the bytecode executed. Additionally, we extend past Sharif's work by using the identified bytecode to construct a CFG of the input source file, allowing us to determine not only what x86 instructions are related to a particular bytecode instruction, but also what x86 instructions execute a particular instance of a bytecode instruction. With this information, we believe the interpreter can be optimized for a particular input program using techniques similar to those employed by trace based JIT compilers [1].

Experiments using the above approach on a few small programs have been encouraging. Figure 3 shows the control flow graph of a histogram loop written in Python, recovered from the dynamic trace using our method. Each node represents a basic block of byte codes, each bytecode is composed of multiple x86 instructions, and the label on the node represents the address of the first x86 instruction in the basic block. The edge labels represent dynamic trip count. Our method correctly retrieves two loops, one to generate the histogram and another to write it out and reconstitutes them into a working executable.

2.2   Data-Flow Separation

Data-flow separation refers to the process of separating the data-flow logic of the interpreted program from that of the interpreter and the runtime system. The issue arises because computations of data values in the interpreter involve data movement into and out of a set of locations used for expression evaluation (e.g., an expression stack, as in the Java Virtual Machine and CPython interpreter; or virtual registers, as in the Dalvik virtual machine and the SPIM interpreter for MIPS assembly code). The reads and writes involving these locations can then induce spurious dependencies between instructions. Such dependencies can also arise from data movements in the runtime system, e.g., due to garbage collection or just-in-time compilation.

We plan to apply compiler optimization techniques to effect data-flow separation. For example, using an SSA representation may allow us to identify and separate out distinct uses of expression evaluation locations in the interpreter, such as the expression stack, without having to presuppose any particular mechanism for expression evaluation. There may also be complexities arising from architectural features, e.g., the stack of floating point registers on x86 and x86-64 processors.

3   Small Datasets Appear Representative

A potential drawback of optimization based on dynamic analysis is that of code coverage: the only code paths observed in dynamic analyses are those executed with the profiling inputs. This can be problematic if the "real" datasets exercise code paths that deviate from those observed on profiling runs. Avoiding correctness problems resulting from such deviations requires adding additional runtime checks into the code, which then incur some runtime overhead.

As an initial check that the dynamic analyses performed on small input data are representative enough to be applied to larger-scale target inputs without loss of correctness, we examined coverage between the training and reference inputs of twelve SPECfp-2006 benchmarks.[1] We used our binary-level dynamic analysis toolset to determine, for each benchmark program tested, the fraction of the machine code executed on the reference inputs that was also executed on the training inputs.

Our experiments indicate that, on average, 96.5% of the code executed on the reference inputs is also executed on the training inputs, with ten of the programs having >99% coverage. Only one, `calculix`, had a significant difference (69%) in coverage of the scientific features. This suggests that while smaller training inputs may not always provide complete coverage of the code executed on the reference inputs, in most cases the difference will likely be small. To guide scientists in choosing a set of small representative inputs, we plan to automatically pre-check inputs and provide feedback when coverage tools exists for their language. Examples of such tools include Figleaf for Python, simplecov for Ruby, and Devel::Cover for Perl.

When coverage is incomplete, we must insert appropriate and efficient runtime checks to ensure correctness should a given input attempt to access a non-traced feature of the software. Interpreter specialization will impose strong assumptions regarding facets of the program such as control flow and data types. We will identify the locations of these assumptions, encode those assumptions as checks, and insert the checks into the control flow where they dominate the assumption. For example, the Python interpreter includes many conditional checks involving type information. We can assume types do not change while data analysis is being performed, assume the largest version of the datatype (e.g., double vs. float) used during training runs on representative inputs should be used throughout, and therefore remove extraneous conditional checks.

We also plan an in-depth analysis of these scripts to determine the characteristics of the aliasing used in their data structures, with a focus on multiply-referenced values in the same data structure, amount of indirection, and the differences between small and large inputs with respect to these measures. Multiply referenced values could affect the correctness of our parallelization. This analysis will guide our strategy in handling these cases.

4 Parallelism Exists

Data analysis scripts contain significant parallelism. In current and previous work [3,4], we have been collaborating with scientists who write data analysis codes in Python, Perl, Matlab, and Julia. These data analysis codes typically have a single bottleneck loop. The bottleneck is often a reduction of some kind:

---

[1] We had problems building and running the remaining five benchmarks in the SPECfp-2006 suite. Some of these problems may have been due to non-standard-conformant code in the benchmarks.

adding items to a list, set, or matrix or performing some calculation and maintaining summary information.

As part of an in depth analysis of scientific data analysis codes, done in conjunction with a graduate level course, we ported Matlab and Perl scientific data analysis codes to new parallel programming models, leading to significant speedups (60x for a medical imaging analysis) [3,5]. Although some of this speedup was due to porting a snap-shot of the program to a compiled programming language, through this process we also discovered significant parallelism in the computations causing performance bottlenecks (in [5] over 6× speedup on 8 cores for an orbital analysis code in Python and in [3] over 7× speedup for a medical imaging analysis code in Matlab).

Finding the parallelism in a trace that includes the interpreter code as its interpreting is more challenging than finding parallelism of a compiled program. Oh et al. [8,9] showed that if an interpreter is specialized for a specific input program, it is possible to find pipeline and speculative loop-level parallelism at the LLVM IR level. They found that performing profiling at the LLVM level significantly reduced the speculation overhead thus leading to decent parallel scaling with some Lua and Perl programs.

5   Implementing the Parallelism

We plan to implement loop-level parallelism by breaking the LLVM IR instructions from time-consuming loops into two sets: the instructions that perform the (parallelizable) work and the instructions that determine the next iteration, including the loop completion. A master thread will execute the iterator code and then spawn off tasks to a task pool implementation.

The proposed work includes plans to raise the interprocedural control flow graph of x86 instructions into annotated LLVM and then analyze for parallelism. In our initial experiments, we determined how to find parallelism in the full x86 traces using a back tainting analysis (e.g., equivalent to backward slicing. The example code was a C++ loop traversing an input linked list, performing some busy work computation in the form of a loop of sin() calls, and writing the sum of those sin() call results into a node of the output linked list.

Figure 4(a) illustrates the split of x86 instructions for one loop iteration into a master thread that deals with the linked list traversal that needs to be serialized and the task instructions (minus the sin() loop due to space considerations) for tasks that can be computationally overlapped. We have also started experimenting with finding the parallelism in the traces. The algorithm for finding the split involves identifying loop-exit branches and upwards-exposed reads per iteration and placing the instructions that influence those into the master thread. The leftover instructions can be encapsulated into a worker task function.

To implement the found parallelism, we use POSIX threads (pthreads). Using a hand-implemented version of the example loop at the C level, we see promising results. The goal of these tests were to determine the size of work tasks required to see a performance increase over serial execution. To see execution speeds on

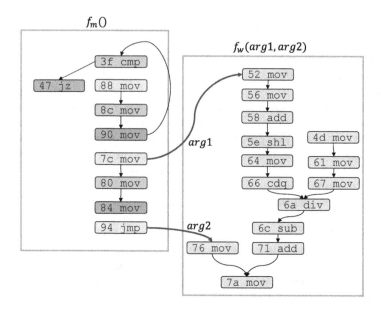

(a) The x86 instructions of one loop iteration are split into those to be serialized by the master thread (pink) and those that can be parallelized into tasks (green). Parameters needed by the tasks are also determined (red lines).

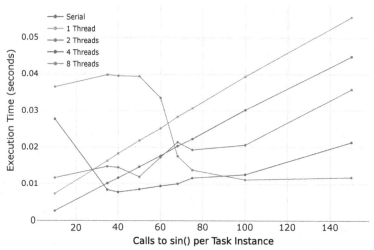

(b) Execution time scaling with number of threads and amount of discovered parallel work. As the work per iteration crosses the equivalent of 35 calls to sin(), our method run on four threads executes faster than the original C serial code.

Fig. 4. Proof of concept identification of serial master thread and parallel worker instructions from an x86 trace of a C program and performance of an initial pthreads implementation. (Color figure online)

par with the serial execution, the work function must execute 8,000 instructions with two worker threads, 5,000 with four, and 11,000 with eight. This corresponds to 50, 40, and 70 calls to sin(), respectively. Figure 4(b) summarizes these results.

Another major issue that will need to be addressed is the detection of reduction dependences in the loop and implementing their parallelism. Their detection and implementation will be somewhat intertwined, because it will be more complex than a read, add, and update operation on a register. Some of the values experiencing a reduction might be values in a dictionary. Therefore the reduction operation will have to be detected within a trace through memory loads and stores as well as operations on registers. We plan to leverage the existing research on source-level detection of reductions and other commutative operations and extend that to the LLVM IR.

One possible approach for handling reductions is that once the loads and stores involved have been detected, the implementation will be built by putting off the loads and stores to the shared memory accesses. Each thread could be given its own map that maps memory addresses to value and address pairs at runtime. At end of executing all tasks in a loop, all thread maps would be reduced into shared memory.

With reduction and loop parallelism detected, the next step will be experimenting with implementation approaches that leverage that parallelism while amortizing overhead. The most problematic overhead will probably be the serial bottleneck of the master thread. Providing each thread its own address space and then mapping results back into shared spaces once large-grained tasks are complete might help break this bottleneck, but will introduce memory copying overhead. Experimentation and modeling of the various tradeoffs will be needed.

6   Conclusion

This research aims to develop software analysis, optimization, and parallelization techniques to obtain significant performance improvements in research software developed by scientists (including several collaborators from a diversity of scientific disciplines). Our goal is to do this in a way that (a) is language-agnostic and transparent to the scientists, so that they can continue to work in the programming language of their choice and (b) leverages state-of-the-art compiler technology to effectively utilize multicore parallelism. The impact of this research will be two-fold: first and foremost, it will benefit a wide variety of scientists—most immediately medical imaging analysis and life sciences at the University of Arizona but also elsewhere—by boosting the speed of their research software with little to no additional effort on their part; second, it will benefit computer science research by developing new techniques for software performance optimization and thereby giving rise to additional new and exciting research problems.

References

1. Bolz, C.F., Cuni, A., Fijalkowski, M., Rigo, A.: Tracing the meta-level: Pypy's tracing JIT compiler. In: Proceedings of the 4th Workshop on the Implementation, Compilation, Optimization of Object-Oriented Languages and Programming Systems, pp. 18–25. ACM (2009)
2. Catanzaro, B., et al.: SEJITS: getting productivity and performance with selective embedded JIT specialization. Technical report UCB/EECS-2010-23, EECS Department, University of California, Berkeley, March 2010
3. Danford, F., Welch, E., Cárdenas-Ródriguez, J., Strout, M.M.: Analyzing parallel programming models for magnetic resonance imaging. In: Ding, C., Criswell, J., Wu, P. (eds.) LCPC 2016. LNCS, vol. 10136, pp. 188–202. Springer, Cham (2017). https://doi.org/10.1007/978-3-319-52709-3_15
4. Gaska, B.J.: Parforpy: loop parallelism in python. Master's thesis, University of Arizona (2017)
5. Gaska, B.J., Jothi, N., Mohammadi, M.S., Volk, K., Strout, M.M.: Handling nested parallelism, load imbalance, and early termination in an orbital analysis code. Technical report arXiv:1707.09668, University of Arizona (2017)
6. Kotzmann, T., Wimmer, C., Mössenböck, H., Rodriguez, T., Russell, K., Cox, D.: Design of the Java hotspot™ client compiler for Java 6. ACM Trans. Archit. Code Optim. 5(1), 7:1–7:32 (2008)
7. Lindenbaum, P.: Programming language use distribution from recent programs/articles, April 2017. https://www.biostars.org/p/251002/
8. Oh, T., Beard, S.R., Johnson, N.P., Popovych, S., August, D.I.: A generalized framework for automatic scripting language parallelization. In: Proceedings of the 26th International Conference on Parallel Architectures and Compilation Techniques (PACT) (2017, to appear)
9. Oh, T., Kim, H., Johnson, N.P., Lee, J.W., August, D.I.: Practical automatic loop specialization. In: Proceedings of the Eighteenth International Conference on Architectural Support for Programming Languages and Operating Systems, ASPLOS 2013, pp. 419–430. ACM, New York (2013)
10. Schwartz, E.J., Avgerinos, T., Brumley, D.: All you ever wanted to know about dynamic taint analysis and forward symbolic execution (but might have been afraid to ask). In: Proceedings of IEEE Symposium on Security and Privacy, pp. 317–331 (2010)
11. Sharif, M., Lanzi, A., Giffin, J., Lee, W.: Automatic reverse engineering of malware emulators. In: 2009 30th IEEE Symposium on Security and Privacy, pp. 94–109. IEEE (2009)
12. Yadegari, B., Debray, S.: Bit-level taint analysis. In: IEEE International Working Conference on Source Code Analysis and Manipulation (SCAM) (2014)
13. Yadegari, B., Debray, S.: Symbolic execution of obfuscated code. In: Proceedings of 22nd ACM Conference on Computer and Communications Security (CCS), October 2015
14. Yadegari, B., Debray, S.: Control dependencies in interpretive systems. In: Lahiri, S., Reger, G. (eds.) RV 2017. LNCS, vol. 10548, pp. 312–329. Springer, Cham (2017). https://doi.org/10.1007/978-3-319-67531-2_19

Performance Modeling and Instrumentation

Memory Distance Measurement for Concurrent Programs

Hao Li, Jialiang Chang, Zijiang Yang$^{(\boxtimes)}$, and Steve Carr

Western Michigan University, Kalamazoo, MI, USA
{hao.81.li,jialiang.chang,zijiang.yang,steve.carr}@wmich.edu

Abstract. Memory distance analysis, the number of unique memory references made between two accesses to the same memory location, is an effective method to measure data locality and predict memory behavior. Many existing methods on memory distance measurement and analysis consider sequential programs only. With the trend towards concurrent programming, it is necessary to study the impact of memory distance on the performance of concurrent programs. Unfortunately, accurate measurement of concurrent program memory distance is non-trivial. In fact, due to non-determinism, the reuse distance of memory references may differ with the same input set across multiple runs. Since memory distance measurement is fundamental to analysis, we propose a measuring approach that is based on randomized executions. Our approach provides a probabilistic guarantee of observing all possible interleavings without repeated executions. In order to evaluate our approach, we propose a second symbolic execution based approach that is more rigorous but much less scalable than the first approach. We have compared the two approaches on small programs and evaluated the first one on Parsec benchmark suite and a large industrial-size benchmark MySQL. Our experiments confirm that the randomized execution based approach is effective and practical.

1 Introduction

Nowadays, widespread multicore hardware has put us at a fundamental turning point in software development. Although we have seen incrementally more programmers writing multithreaded programs in the past decade, the vast majority of applications today are still single-threaded and cannot benefit from the hardware improvement without significant redesign. Applications will need to be well-written concurrent software programs in order to benefit from the advances in multicore processors.

The main reason to develop concurrent programs, which are much more sophisticated than sequential programs, is to enhance the performance of an application. To achieve the performance, developers usually make extra effort to hand tune the programs. One aspect of performance enhancement is data locality because of its significant effect on cache. In order to manage locality, developers need to measure the memory distance of their programs.

© Springer Nature Switzerland AG 2019
L. Rauchwerger (Ed.): LCPC 2017, LNCS 11403, pp. 49–64, 2019.
https://doi.org/10.1007/978-3-030-35225-7_5

The *memory distance* of a reference is a dynamic quantifiable distance in terms of the number of different memory references between two accesses to the same memory location [1]. It is a widely accepted concept in analyzing program cache performance. The speed gap between the processor and memory has resulted in what is known as the memory wall. To overcome this wall and speed up program performance, data locality is an important factor that developers must consider. Memory distance analysis [1–4] is an effective method to measure data locality and predict memory behavior.

Much existing work on memory distance measurement and analysis considers sequential programs only. With the trend towards concurrency, we need to do such measurement on concurrent programs. Unfortunately, adapting existing approaches that were designed for sequential programs is not feasible. Due to the inherent non-deterministic behavior under fixed inputs for concurrent programs, measuring concurrent memory distance is fundamentally different from that of sequential programs.

Table 1. Memory reference of a program execution

Index	1	2	3	4	5	6	7	8	9	10	11	12	13	14	15	16
Reference accessed	A	B	C	A	C	C	B	A	C	B	A	C	B	B	A	C
Memory distance	∞	∞	∞	2	1	0	2	2	2	2	2	2	2	0	2	2

Consider the example shown in Table 1. The first row lists the indices of the events in a program execution under input vector v. The second row gives the symbolic memory address being accessed and the third row computes the memory distance. In the following, we use an index as the superscript to differentiate the instances of the same memory addresses in the execution trace. The memory distance of A^1, denoted as $\Delta_v(A^1)$, is ∞ because it is the first appearance of A. For the same reason we have $\Delta_v(B^2) = \Delta_v(C^3) = \infty$. $\Delta_v(A^4) = 2$ because there are two accesses to other memory locations between the current access and the previous access to A. Note that $\Delta_v(B^7) = 2$, because although there are four accesses between B^2 and B^7, three out of the four access visit the same memory location. It can be easily observed that the minimal and maximal memory distances under v are 0 and 2 (not considering ∞), respectively. All the existing memory analysis approaches are in general based on such computation, with minor variants [1].

However, the minimal and maximal memory distances under v may not be 0 and 2 if the program under analysis is concurrent. For example, the trace in Table 1 may be from a concurrent program with two threads as shown in Table 2. That is, the first eight memory accesses are from Thread 1 and the remaining eight are from Thread 2. The execution trace in Table 1 corresponds to the case

---

[1] For example, some approaches may report $\Delta_v(B^7) = 4$ because there are four accesses between B^2 and B^7 regardless same memory locations are accessed.

Table 2. Motivating example

Index	1	2	3	4	5	6	7	8
Memory references in thread 1	A	B	C	A	C	C	B	A
Memory references in thread 2	C	B	A	C	B	B	A	C

where Thread 2 starts its execution after Thread 1 completes. However, this is not the only possibility. Many other interleavings are possible, as illustrated in Table 3.

Table 3. Memory distance results in different interleavings

idx	Reference accessed	Memory distance
1	$\{C_2,B_2,A_2,C_2,B_2,B_2,A_2,C_2,A_1,B_1,C_1,A_1,C_1,C_1,B_1,A_1\}$	$\{\infty,\infty,\infty,2,2,0,2,2,1,2,2,2,1,0,2,2\}$
2	$\{C_2,B_2,A_2,C_2,A_1,B_1,C_1,A_1,C_1,C_1,B_1,A_1,C_2,B_2,B_2,A_2\}$	$\{\infty,\infty,\infty,2,1,2,2,2,1,0,2,2,2,2,0,2\}$
3	$\{A_1,B_1,C_1,C_2,B_2,A_2,C_2,A_1,C_1,C_1,B_1,A_1,C_2,B_2,B_2,A_2\}$	$\{\infty,\infty,\infty,0,1,2,2,1,1,0,2,2,2,2,0,2\}$
4	$\{A_1,C_2,B_2,B_1,C_1,A_2,C_2,A_1,C_1,C_2,B_2,C_1,B_1,A_1,B_2,A_2\}$	$\{\infty,\infty,\infty,0,1,2,1,1,1,0,2,1,1,2,1,1\}$
5	$\{A_1,C_2,B_1,B_2,C_1,A_2,C_2,A_1,C_1,C_2,C_1,B_2,B_1,B_2,A_1,A_2\}$	$\{\infty,\infty,\infty,0,1,2,1,1,1,0,0,2,0,0,2,0\}$
6	$\{C_2,B_2,A_1,B_1,A_2,C_2,C_1,A_1,B_2,B_2,C_1,C_1,A_2,C_2,B_1,A_1\}$	$\{\infty,\infty,\infty,1,1,2,0,1,2,0,2,0,2,1,2,2\}$
7	$\{C_2,A_1,B_2,B_1,A_2,C_1,A_1,C_2,B_2,B_2,C_1,A_2,C_1,C_2,B_1,A_1\}$	$\{\infty,\infty,\infty,0,1,2,1,1,2,0,1,2,1,0,2,2\}$

This simple example illustrates the challenge in measuring memory distance for concurrent programs. Multiple executions of a concurrent program with the same input might exercise different sequences of synchronization events possibly producing different results each time. To obtain accurate memory distances for a given input, *all execution traces* permissible under that input must be examined. However, in current execution environments a developer has no control over the scheduling of threads. Furthermore, when executing a concurrent program by running it repeatedly on a lightly-loaded machine, the same thread interleaving, with minor variations, tend to be exercised since thread schedulers generally switch among threads at the same program locations. The net effect of these impediments is that only a few interleavings end up being examined. This leads to an incomplete picture of memory distances.

In this paper, we present an approach to measure memory distance of concurrent programs. Given the fact that we cannot possibly explore all the thread interleavings of a concurrent program, our approach introduces randomness in repeated executions. By adapting a method called PCT [5], our approach provides a mathematical guarantee to detect memory distances of given triggering depths. That is, if there exists a memory distance d between memory accesses to m with triggering depth δ_m^d (definition to be given in Sect. 4), our approach guarantees its detection with probability of $1/(n \times k^{\delta_m^d - 1})$, where n and k are the approximated number of threads and the approximated number of events, respectively, of the given program. We have implemented our method in a tool called DisConPro (Memory <u>Dis</u>tance measurement of <u>Con</u>current <u>Pro</u>grams with <u>Pro</u>babilistic Guarantee).

In order to validate the effectiveness of DisConPro, we propose a more rigorous but much less scalable approach to measure memory distance based on symbolic execution. The second approach utilizes the symbolic execution engine that we developed to exhaustively explore all intra-thread paths and inter-thread interleavings. We name this tool DisConSym (Memory <u>Dis</u>tance measurement of <u>Con</u>current Programs based on <u>Sym</u>bolic Execution Guarantee). DisConSym can only handle small programs due to its inherent path explosion. By comparing DisConPro against DisConSym on small programs, we are able to determine if DisConPro covers a similar memory distance spectrum as DisConSym.

The contributions of this paper include the following:

1. To the best of our knowledge, we are the first to propose a feasible approach to measure the memory distance of concurrent programs. Our approach is based on randomized executions and provides probabilistic guarantees.
2. We propose a second approach that is more rigorous but less scalable than the first approach. Although such a symbolic execution based approach can only handle small benchmarks, it allows us to evaluate the effectiveness of the first approach.
3. We have implemented two prototypes DisConPro and DisConSym and conducted experiments on medium-sized Parsec [6] benchmarks and a large industrial size benchmark MySQL with DisConPro.

The rest of the paper is organized as follows. The background knowledge of concurrent program execution is described in Sect. 2, followed by the explanation of our two approaches in Sects. 3 and 4, respectively. The experimental results are given in Sect. 5. Section 6 discusses the related work. Finally Sect. 7 concludes the paper.

2   Background: Execution of Concurrent Programs

Figure 1 gives a code snippet of a concurrent program with two threads. Depending on the values of a and b, different branches in the two threads can be observed across executions. Depending on the synchronization and operating system scheduling policies, different interleavings can also be observed. In order to present intra-thread paths and inter-thread interleavings, we use the *generalized interleaving graph*(GIG) [7,8] to illustrate all possible executions of a concurrent program.

Figure 1 depicts the GIG of the code snippet on its left, where black and blue edges represent an execution step of Threads $T1$ and $T2$, respectively. The dashed lines with the same source (defined as b-PP node) denote a branch within a thread and the solid lines with the same source (defined as i-PP node) denote a context switch between two threads. Note that a node can be both b-PP and i-PP. In order to measure memory distance accurately, all the paths in a GIG must be considered. This is what our symbolic execution based approach, described in Sect. 7, attempts to accomplish. However, enumerating all possible executions is obviously impractical. Thus, we present a practical approach in Sect. 4.

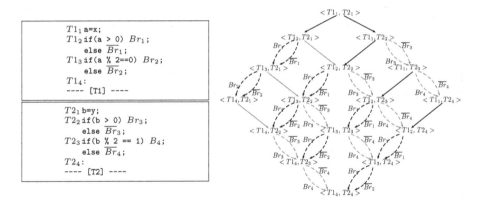

Fig. 1. Code snippet of a concurrent program and its generalized interleaving graph(GIG).

3   Memory Distance Measurement Based on Symbolic Execution

In this section, we present a symbolic execution based approach that is able to systematically explore all the intra-thread branches and inter-thread interleavings. The pseudo-code is shown in Algorithm 1, which is based on the symbolic execution algorithm proposed in [8], and follows the Concolic [9] framework. The algorithm uses a recursive procedure TRACKSTATE to explore paths. The first path is randomly chosen. When a new b-PP node with condition c is encountered, TRACKSTATE checks whether the current path condition appended with c if satisfiable. If so, it continues the execution along the branch while pushing the other branch $\neg c$ on the stack S. The satisfiability is checked by an SMT solver such as Z3 [10]. If the SMT solver fails to find a solution, it indicates that no inputs or interleavings can continue the execution along the branch. In this case, the current execution backtracks by popping its stack S. If an i-PP node is first encountered, TRACKSTATE randomly choose one interleaving while pushing the other one on the stack. For a more detailed explanation, please refer to [8].

The measurement of memory distance occurs during backtrack. That is, when the current execution reaches an end state $normal\_end\_state$ or reaches an infeasible branch. In GETMEMDIST, a path is treated as a sequence of member accesses $\langle acc_1, \ldots, acc_n \rangle$. Each acc_i is a pair $(addr, d)$ of memory address and distance. All the global memory accesses are analyzed to calculate the memory distance. Initially the memory distance of any memory access is set to -1. The algorithm continuously checks the next access acc_j. If acc_j accesses a memory address different from $acc_i.addr$, $acc_j.addr$ is added to the set $memorySet$. Otherwise, the size of $memorySet$ is the memory distance between acc_i and acc_j.

Algorithm 1. SymbolicExecution(P)

let Stack $S \leftarrow \emptyset$ be the path constraints of a path;
1: TRACKSTATE(s)
2:     S.push(s);
3:     **if** (s is an i-PP node or b-PP node)
4:         **while** ($\exists t \in (s.enabled \setminus s.done \setminus s.branch)$)
5:             $s' \leftarrow$ NEXT(s, t);
6:             TRACKSTATE(s');
7:             $s.done \leftarrow s.done \cup \{t\}$;
8:     **else if** (s is an local thread node)
9:         $t \leftarrow s.next$;
10:         $s' \leftarrow$ NEXT(s, t);
11:         TRACKSTATE(s');
12:     $path \leftarrow S$.pop();
13: NEXT(s, t)
14:     let s be $\langle pcon, \mathcal{M} \rangle$;
15:     **if** (t instanceof **halt**)
16:         $s' \leftarrow$ normal_end_state;
17:         GetMemDist($path$);
18:     **else if** (t instanceof **branch(c)**)
19:         **if** ($s.pcon$ is unsatisfiable under $\mathcal{M}$)
20:             $s' \leftarrow$ infeasible_state;
21:             GetMemDist($path$);
22:         **else**
23:             $s' \leftarrow \langle pcon \wedge c, \mathcal{M} \rangle$;
24:     **else if** (t instanceof $X = Y$ op Z)
25:         $s' \leftarrow \langle pcon, \mathcal{M}[X] \rangle$;
26:     **return** s';
27: GETMEMDIST($path$)
28:     let $path$ be $\langle acc_1, \ldots, acc_n \rangle$;
29:     **for** (int $i \leftarrow 0, i < n - 1, i++$)
30:         $memorySet \leftarrow \emptyset$;
31:         **for** (int $j \leftarrow 1, j < n, j++$)
32:             **if** ($acc_i.addr = acc_i.addr$
33:                 $acc_i.d \leftarrow memorySet$.size();
34:                 break;
35:             **else**
36:                 $memorySet$.insert($acc_j.addr$);

4 Memory Distance Measurement with Random Scheduling

In this section, we present our main approach that computes memory distances with random scheduling. We begin with the concept of memory distance minimal depth δ_m^d. Given a memory location m, δ_m^d is defined as the minimal number of constraints for any pair of accesses to m that have a memory distance of d. Consider the example given in Table 4. There are four threads with eight events

$e_1, \ldots, e_8$ that access four memory locations A, B, C and D. Among the total 2520 interleavings, the memory distances between a pair of accesses to A range from 0 to 3. The memory distance of 3 occurs only if $e_1 \prec e_2 \wedge e_1 \prec e_3 \wedge e_1 \prec e_4$, where $\prec$ denotes the happens-before relation. That is, $\delta_A^3 = 3$ because there are three constraints.

Table 4. Four threads with eight memory accesses.

Thread1	Thread2	Thread3	Thread4
$< e1, A >$	$< e2, B >$	$< e3, C >$	$< e4, D >$
$< e5, A >$	$< e6, A >$	$< e7, A >$	$< e8, A >$

4.1 PCT Algorithm

We adapt the PCT [5] algorithm that was proposed to detect concurrent bugs with a probabilistic guarantee. The basic idea is to add a random scheduling control mechanism to randomize scheduling to avoid redundant executions.

In [5], a concurrent bug depth is defined as the minimum number of order constraints that are sufficient to guarantee to find the bug. The algorithm attempts to find the concurrent bug with depth of d by controlling the thread scheduling as the following.

- The scheduling is controlled by giving each thread a priority. A thread executes only if it has the highest priority or the threads with higher priorities are waiting.
- It assigns n initial priorities $d, d+1, d+2 \ldots d+n-1$ to the n threads.
- It randomly picks $d-1$ change points from k instructions, where k is the estimated number of instructions. The program is then executed with the following rules.
  - Each time only the enabled instruction from the thread with the highest priority can be executed. During execution all the instructions are counted.
  - If the instruction to be executed is counted as the number k-th and k is equal to any of k_i, change the priority value of the current thread to i. This causes a context switch.

4.2 Measure Memory Distance with Random Scheduling

We propose an approach called DisConPro, which adapts the PCT [5] algorithm to measure the memory distance in concurrent programs. As demonstrated above, memory distances may be different with different interleavings.

The basic idea of DisConPro is to measure the memory distance in multiple executions with the PCT scheduling control menchanism. At the begining, DisConPro generates a random schedule following PCT [5]. Then it executes the program following the schedule. The memory distance is measured during the execution. Each memory access is recorded in a memory access trace and memory distances are calculated based on the memory access traces.

In practice, the statically computed scheduling is not always feasible. However, the infeasible cases only deviate from the planned interleavings but do not lead to execution error. For example, DisConPro may attempt to execute an instruction that is disabled by the operating system. In this case, the execution will choose the next thread with highest priority until an enabled instruction is found.

Algorithm 2. DisConPro(P,n,k,d,m)

Input: P is a program
Input: n is the number of threads
Input: k is the number of events
Input: d is memory distance minimum depth
Input: m is a memory address on which memory distance is measured
1: **Var: Trace** is a list that records every memory access events
2: **Var: Distance** is an array of memory distances
   Distance[i] is the memory distance between **i-th** and **(i+1)-th** access to **m**
3: **Trace** = Empty List
4: Generate a random schedule **S** based on PCT algorithm
5: Schedule **n** threads based on **S** and execute those **k** events
6: **for each memory access event e do**
7:     Trace.add(e)
8: **end for**
9: Calculate **Distance** based on **Trace**

4.3   Probabilistic Guarantee Inheritance

The PCT algorithm provides a probabilistic guarantee to find a concurrent bug. By adapting it, our approach can provide a probabilistic guarantee to find a particular memory distance d with a depth of δ_m^d. The probability is at least $1/(n \times k^{\delta_m^d - 1})$. Now we now give the proof by adapting the proof for finding a concurrent bug found in [5].

Definition 1. *DisConPro(m, n, k, P) is defined as a set of memory distances of a memory object m. DisConPro finds memory distances during one execution of program P, containing n threads and k instructions.*

Theorem 1 (Probabilistic Guarantee Theorem). *If there exists a memory distance d with a minimum depth memory distance of δ_m^d, the probability of DisConPro finding it in one execution is*

$$Pr(d \in DisConPro(m, n, k, P)) > 1/(n \times k^{\delta_m^d - 1}) \tag{1}$$

Proof. We define an assert statement $assert(m, d)$ as that d is not the memory distance of memory object m in the execution. We define a bug B that can be flagged if the assertion fails. If bug B is detected, d is found as the memory distance of memory m. We define event E_1 as $DisConPro$ finds bug B and event E_2 as DisConPro finds d as the memory distance of m. Base on the definition of E_1 and E_2, we can argue that $E_1 \equiv E_2$. Let $Cons$ be a minimum set of constraints that are sufficient for E_1 to happen. We argue that $Cons$ is one of the minimum set of constraints that are sufficient for E_2 to happen. This bug B is not different from other concurrent bugs hidden in rare schedules. The depth of B equals δ_m^d, which is the size of $Cons$. We define E_3 as PCT algorithm find B in one execution. Since DisConPro adapts PCT algorithm, we can argue that $Pr(E_2) = Pr(E_3)$. By the definition, we have

$$Pr(E_1 : d \in DisConPro(m, n, k, P)) = Pr(E_2 : DisConPro \ finds \ B) \quad (2)$$

$$Pr(E_2 : DisConPro \ finds \ B) = Pr(E3 : PCT \ finds \ B) \quad (3)$$

It has been proved that (see [5])

$$Pr(E_3 : PCT \ finds \ B) > 1/(n \times k^{\delta_m^d - 1}) \quad (4)$$

Then,

$$Pr(E_1 : d \in DisConPro(m, n, k, P)) > 1/(n \times k^{\delta_m^d - 1}) \quad (5)$$

5   Experiments

5.1   Implementation

We implement DisConPro using PIN [11], a dynamic binary instrumentation(DBI) framework that allows users to insert analysis routines to the original program in binary form. DisConSym is based on Cloud9 [12], a symbolic execution engine built upon LLVM [13,14] and KLEE [15]. DisConSym has an extension for analyzing concurrent programs since Cloud9 only partially supports concurrency. The extension of Cloud9 follows the algorithm and implemention given in [16]. With the extension, DisConSym can analyze the interleavings not only due to synchronization primitives, which is also supported by Cloud9, but also due to global variables. The latter is essential and a prerequisite to analyze the memory distance of a concurrent program.

5.2   Comparison Between DisConPro and DisConSym on Small Programs

We compare DisConPro with DisConSym to answer the following questions.

– Can DisConPro discover the same memory reuse range as DisConSym does?
– Can DisConPro cover all valid tracks as DisConSym does?
– Is DisConPro more scalable than DisConSym?

Table 5. Impact of the number of global variables comparing with DisConSym and DisConPro

	Thread number = 3	2 mem_global	3 mem_global	4 mem_global	5 mem_global
DisConSym	mem_global 1	−1, 0, 1	−1, 0, 1, 2	−1, 0, 1, 2, 3	−1, 0, 1, 2, 3, 4
	mem_global 2	−1, 0, 1	−1, 0, 1, 2	−1, 0, 1, 2, 3	−1, 0, 1, 2, 3, 4
	mem_global 3	N/A	−1, 0, 1, 2	−1, 0, 1, 2, 3	−1, 0, 1, 2, 3, 4
	mem_global 4	N/A	N/A	−1, 0, 1, 2, 3	−1, 0, 1, 2, 3, 4
	mem_global 5	N/A	N/A	N/A	−1, 0, 1, 2, 3, 4
DisConPro	mem_global 1	−1, 0, 1	−1, 0, 1, 2	−1, 0, 1, 2, 3	−1, 0, 1, 2, 3, 4
	mem_global 2	−1, 0, 1	−1, 0, 1, 2	−1, 0, 1, 2, 3	−1, 0, 1, 2, 3, 4
	mem_global 3	N/A	−1, 0, 1, 2	−1, 0, 1, 2, 3	−1, 0, 1, 2, 3, 4
	mem_global 4	N/A	N/A	−1, 0, 1, 2, 3	−1, 0, 1, 2, 3, 4
	mem_global 5	N/A	N/A	N/A	−1, 0, 1, 2, 3, 4

Since DisConSym is not scalable, we compare the two tools on several small concurrent programs with an adjustable number of threads and global variables. All the programs have less than 100 lines of code. Table 5 gives the experimental results. In the experiments we set the number of threads to 3, as indicated by the heading of Column 2, and the number of global variables to be 2–5. DisConSym is not able to handle a program with more threads and global variables. Columns 3–6 indicate the number of global variables created in each group of experiments. Each row in the table gives the memory distance observed for each individual global variable. When a variable does not exist in an experiment, e.g. mem_global3 in an experiment with only two global variables in Column 3, N/A is given. In the table, the top half of the rows give the results under DisConSym and the bottom half show the results under DisConPro. For all the experiments done by DisConPro, we set depth to be 5 and run each program 100 times. The table indicates that memory distances can be affected by the number of global variables. It can also be observed that for the small programs DisConPro can find as many memory distances as DisConSym.

Although for small programs DisConSym and DisConPro generate the same results in measuring memory distance, the cost is significantly different. Table 6 gives the number of paths and time usage of the seven groups of experiments with various numbers of threads and global variables. It can be observed that even for such small programs DisConPro is more than 1000 times faster. As concurrent programs become larger, the gap will be wider. Although we cannot guarantee DisConPro can detect as many memory distances as DisConSym does for non-trivial programs, we believe DisConPro achieves a nice trade-off between accuracy and efficiency.

5.3 DisConPro on Public Benchmarks

We evaluate DisConPro with 9 applications in the Parsec benchmark suite [6], as well as the real-world application MySQL with more than 11 million lines of code.

Table 6. Tracked paths and time cost result for DisConSym and DisConPro

Threads and *mem_global* setting	Approach	# Paths	Time (seconds)
3 threads, 2 *mem_global*	DisConSym	90	2
	DisConPro	100	25
3 threads, 3 *mem_global*	DisConSym	1680	27
	DisConPro	100	25
3 threads, 4 *mem_global*	DisConSym	34650	930
	DisConPro	100	25
3 threads, 5 *mem_global*	DisConSym	>200000	>6794
	DisConPro	100	25
2 threads, 3 *mem_global*	DisConSym	20	1
	DisConPro	100	25
4 threads, 3 *mem_global*	DisConSym	>200000	>9609
	DisConPro	100	25
5 threads, 3 *mem_global*	DisConSym	>200000	>11473
	DisConPro	100	25

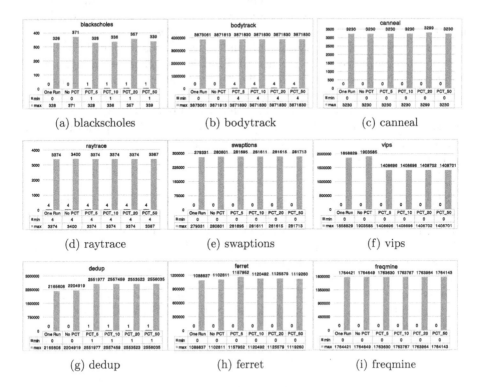

(a) blackscholes   (b) bodytrack   (c) canneal

(d) raytrace   (e) swaptions   (f) vips

(g) dedup   (h) ferret   (i) freqmine

Fig. 2. Parsec results

For each application, we conduct 6 groups of experiments. Group one measures the memory distance by only running the test cases once without scheduling control. Groups 2 to 6 measure the memory distances by running each test case 30 times. Group 2 uses random scheduling. Groups 3–6 set the predefined depth to 5, 10, 20 and 50, respectively. For each application, we perform memory distance analysis on global variables only. For a large application with too many global variables, we randomly choose several global variables to measure their memory distances.

Parsec Benchmark. Figure 2 gives the results of the experiments on Parsec [6]. The data in the sub-tables and sub-figures present the range of memory distances. Each column gives the minimum and maximum distances of all the global variables we evaluate. The figures show that in most cases the ranges that DisConPro finds are larger than those detected by Random_Schedule, which in turn are larger than the ranges discovered by Single_Run. However, the range gaps achieved by PCT are not comparable to those obtained by random algorithm or even single runs. This is because the ranges reported in the figure are for all the global variables that we have evaluated. Assume that there exists a global variable that is accessed at the beginning of an execution and is re-accessed before the program terminates, its memory distance span is large and does not change much under all the possible interleavings. In this case, this variable hides the differences of the ranges exhibited in other variables.

For the application *vips*, single and random executions without PCT detect a larger memory distance span. Since PCT randomly generates change points to enforce context switches, it may disturb program executions significantly. For this reason, PCT may observe memory distances that are less diverse than those without PCT. This phenomenon is further amplified by the facts that we aggregate all variables in the same figure. To understand the performance of PCT algorithms further, we choose to illustrate the data per variable in MySQL experiments.

MySQL. Figure 3 gives the experimental results on MySQL. We randomly choose 6 memory objects whose addresses are listed in the table. The figure depicts the ranges of the minimum and maximum memory distances that we have observed from each group of experiments. It can be observed that the memory ranges in Groups 2 to 6 are larger than that in Group 1. By comparing the results of Group 2 to Groups 3–5, we can conclude that DisConPro is more effective than the random scheduling algorithm. The best performance algorithms for the six memory objects are PCT_5, PCT_50, PCT_5 or PCT_10 or PCT_50, PCT_10, PCT_5 or PCT_10, PCT_50, respectively. For measuring the memory distances of individual variables, DisConPro can find a range that is 30% larger than Random_Schedule.

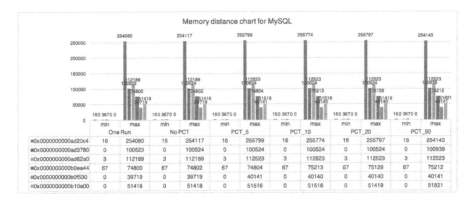

Fig. 3. MySQL result

6 Related Work

Cache performance heavily depends on program locality. In the past there were studies that indirectly measure program locality by simulating its execution on a set of probable cache configurations. Such simulations are not only time consuming but also inaccurate. In [17], Ding and Zhong proposed to measure program locality directly by the distance between the reuses of its data because data reuse is an inherent program property and does not depend on any cache parameters. They designed two algorithms with one targeting efficiency and the other one targeting accuracy. Their work inspired further improvements that exploits sampling [16] and statistical methods [1]. These methods work well for sequential programs. However, they do not consider that non-deterministic thread scheduling and thus not applicable to concurrent programs.

In recent years there has been research on multicore reuse distance analysis [18–21]. Schuff et al. [18] propose a sampled, parallelized method of measuring reuse distance profiles for multithreaded programs. Whereas previous full reuse distance analysis tracks every reference, sampling analysis randomly selects individual references from the dynamic reference stream and yields a sample for each by tracking unique addresses accessed until the reuse of that address. The sampling analyzer can account for multicore characteristics in much the same way as the full analyzer. The method allows the use of a fast-execution mode when no samples are currently active and allows parallelization to reduce overhead in analysis mode. These techniques result in a system with high accuracy that has comparable performance to the best single-thread reuse distance analysis tools. While our work also conducts reuse distance analysis of multithreaded programs, there exists fundamental difference between their approach and ours. Schuff et al. focus on the hardware while we focus on software. Their goal is to efficiently measure the distance on a more sophisticated multicore. Thus efficiency is a major concern of their research. With the help of the their findings a system designer may design a better cache. We aim to provide a feasible approach that measures the reuse distance of a particular multithreaded program. Therefore non-deterministic thread scheduling is the major concern of our work. With our approach we hope to let programmers understand the behavior of their multi-threaded programs regardless of the cache configurations. The two methods are orthogonal and can potentially be integrated. While we strive to diversify the executions of a multithreaded program, the approach proposed in [18] can be used to monitor each execution.

The goal of the approaches in [19–21] are similar to that of [18]. They apply reuse distance analysis to study the scalability of multicore cache hierarchies, with the goal to help architects design better cache systems. In particular, Jiang et al. [19] introduce the concept of concurrent reuse distance (CRD), a direct extension of the traditional concept of reuse distance with data references by all co-running threads (or jobs) considered. They reveal the special challenges facing the collection and application of CRD on multicore platforms, and present the solutions based on a probabilistic model that connects CRD with the data locality of each individual thread. Wu et al. [20] present a framework based on concurrent reuse distance and private reuse distance (PRD) profiles for reasoning about the locality impact of core count. They find that interference-based locality degradation is more significant than sharing-based locality degradation. Wu and Yeung [21] extend [20] by using reuse distance analysis to efficiently analyze multicore cache performance for loop-based parallel programs. They provide an in-depth analysis on how CRD and PRD profiles change with core count scaling, and develop techniques to predict CRD and PRD profile scaling. As we mentioned, our focus is to examine program behavior rather than the cache performance. Thus we measure memory distance from a completely different perspective from [19–21].

There exists work that studies reuse distance from other perspectives. Keramidas et al. [22] propose a direct way to predict reuse distance and apply their method to cache optimization. Zhong et al. [23] focus on the effect of input on reuse distance. They propose a statistical, pattern-matching method to predict reuse distance of a program based on executions under limited number of inputs. Shen et al. [24] introduce the time-efficiency model to analyze reuse distance with time distance. Retaining the high accuracy of memory distance, their approach significantly reduces the reuse-distance measurement cost. Niu et al. [25] present the first parallel framework to analyze reuse distance efficiently. They apply a cached size upper bound to restrict a maximum reuse distance to get a faster analysis. Although these approaches are not optimized for multithreaded programs, many of their ideas can potentially be adopted to extend our work.

Our repeated executions of a multithreaded program relies on PCT [5, 26], a randomized algorithm originally designed for concurrent program testing. The advantage of PCT over total randomized algorithms is that PCT provides a probabilistic guarantee to detect bugs in a concurrent program. There has been recent work that adopts PCT for various purposes. For example, Liu et al. [27] introduce a pthread library replacement that applies PCT to support analyzing data races and deadlocks in concurrent programs deterministically. Cai and Yang [28] propose to add a radius to the PCT algorithm so the revised algorithm can efficiently detect deadlocks. However, to the best of our knowledge, we are the first to apply PCT in applications that are not intended to detect concurrency bugs.

7 Conclusion

In this paper, we have presented an approach to measure the memory distance of concurrent programs. Given the fact that we cannot possibly explore all the thread interleavings of a concurrent program, our approach introduces randomness in repeated executions. By adapting the scheduling method PCT, our approach provides a mathematical guarantee to detect memory distances of given triggering depths.

Acknowledgements. This work was supported in part by the National Science Foundation (NSF) under grant CSR-1421643.

References

1. Fang, C., Carr, S., Onder, S., Wang, Z.: Instruction based memory distance analysis and its application to optimization. In: 14th International Conference on Parallel Architectures and Compilation Techniques (PACT 2005), pp. 27–37. IEEE (2005)
2. Ding, C., Zhong, Y.: Predicting whole-program locality through reuse distance analysis. In: Proceedings of the ACM SIGPLAN 2003 Conference on Programming Language Design and Implementation, PLDI 2003, pp. 245–257 (2003)
3. Fang, C., Carr, S., Önder, S., Wang, Z.: Reuse-distance-based miss-rate prediction on a per instruction basis. In: Proceedings of the 2004 Workshop on Memory System Performance, MSP 2004, pp. 60–68 (2004)
4. Marin, G., Mellor-Crummey, J.: Cross-architecture performance predictions for scientific applications using parameterized models. In: Proceedings of the Joint International Conference on Measurement and Modeling of Computer Systems, SIGMETRICS 2004/Performance 2004, pp. 2–13 (2004)
5. Burckhardt, S., Kothari, P., Musuvathi, M., Nagarakatte, S.: A randomized scheduler with probabilistic guarantees of finding bugs. In: Fifteenth Edition of ASPLOS on Architectural Support for Programming Languages and Operating Systems, pp. 167–178 (2010)
6. Bienia, C., Kumar, S., Singh, J.P., Li, K.: The PARSEC benchmark suite: characterization and architectural implications. In: International Conference on Parallel Architecture and Compilation Techniques, pp. 72–81 (2008)
7. Wang, C., Mahmoud, S., Gupta, A., Kahlon, V., Sinha, N.: Dynamic test generation for concurrent programs, 12 July 2012. US Patent App. 13/348,286
8. Guo, S., Kusano, M., Wang, C., Yang, Z., Gupta, A.: Assertion guided symbolic execution of multithreaded programs. In: Proceedings of the 2015 10th Joint Meeting on Foundations of Software Engineering, pp. 854–865. ACM (2015)
9. Sen, K.: Scalable automated methods for dynamic program analysis. Technical report (2006)
10. de Moura, L., Bjørner, N.: Z3: an efficient SMT solver. In: Ramakrishnan, C.R., Rehof, J. (eds.) TACAS 2008. LNCS, vol. 4963, pp. 337–340. Springer, Heidelberg (2008). https://doi.org/10.1007/978-3-540-78800-3_24

11. Luk, C.-K., et al.: Pin: building customized program analysis tools with dynamic instrumentation. In: ACM Sigplan Notice, vol. 40, pp. 190–200. ACM (2005)

12. Ciortea, L., Zamfir, C., Bucur, S., Chipounov, V., Candea, G.: Cloud9: a software testing service. Oper. Syst. Rev. **43**(4), 5–10 (2009)

13. Lattner, C., Adve, V.: LLVM: a compilation framework for lifelong program analysis & transformation. In: Proceedings of the International Symposium on Code Generation and Optimization: Feedback-Directed and Runtime Optimization, p. 75. IEEE Computer Society (2004)

14. Lattner, C.: LLVM and Clang: next generation compiler technology. In: The BSD Conference, pp. 1–2 (2008)

15. Cadar, C., Dunbar, D., Engler, D.R.: KLEE: unassisted and automatic generation of high-coverage tests for complex systems programs, pp. 209–224 (2008)

16. Shen, X., Zhong, Y., Ding, C.: Locality phase prediction. ACM SIGPLAN Not. **39**(11), 165–176 (2004)

17. Ding, C., Zhong, Y.: Reuse Distance Analysis. University of Rochester, Rochester (2001)

18. Schuff, D.L., Kulkarni, M., Pai, V.S.: Accelerating multicore reuse distance analysis with sampling and parallelization. In: Proceedings of the 19th International Conference on Parallel Architectures and Compilation Techniques, pp. 53–64. ACM (2010)

19. Jiang, Y., Zhang, E.Z., Tian, K., Shen, X.: Is reuse distance applicable to data locality analysis on chip multiprocessors? In: Gupta, R. (ed.) CC 2010. LNCS, vol. 6011, pp. 264–282. Springer, Heidelberg (2010). https://doi.org/10.1007/978-3-642-11970-5_15

20. Wu, M.-J., Zhao, M., Yeung, D.: Studying multicore processor scaling via reuse distance analysis. In: ACM SIGARCH Computer Architecture News, vol. 41, pp. 499–510. ACM (2013)

21. Meng-Ju, W., Yeung, D.: Efficient reuse distance analysis of multicore scaling for loop-based parallel programs. ACM Trans. Comput. Syst. (TOCS) **31**(1), 1 (2013)

22. Keramidas, G., Petoumenos, P., Kaxiras, S.: Cache replacement based on reuse-distance prediction. In: 25th International Conference on Computer Design, ICCD 2007, pp. 245–250. IEEE (2007)

23. Zhong, Y., Shen, X., Ding, C.: Program locality analysis using reuse distance. ACM Trans. Program. Lang. Syst. (TOPLAS) **31**(6), 20 (2009)

24. Shen, X., Shaw, J., Meeker, B., Ding, C.: Locality approximation using time. In: ACM SIGPLAN Notices, vol. 42, pp. 55–61. ACM (2007)

25. Niu, Q., Dinan, J., Lu, Q., Sadayappan, P.: PARDA: a fast parallel reuse distance analysis algorithm. In: 2012 IEEE 26th International Parallel & Distributed Processing Symposium (IPDPS), pp. 1284–1294. IEEE (2012)

26. Burckhardt, S., Kothari, P., Musuvathi, M., SNagarakatte, M.: A randomized scheduler with probabilistic guarantees of finding bugs. In: ACM Sigplan Notices, vol. 45, pp. 167–178. ACM (2010)

27. Liu, T., Curtsinger, C., Berger, E.D.: Dthreads: efficient deterministic multithreading. In: Proceedings of the Twenty-Third ACM Symposium on Operating Systems Principles, pp. 327–336. ACM (2011)

28. Cai, Y., Yang, Z.: Radius aware probabilistic testing of deadlocks with guarantees. In: Proceedings of the 31st IEEE/ACM International Conference on Automated Software Engineering, ASE 2016, 3–7 September 2016, Singapore, pp. 356–367 (2016)

Efficient Cache Simulation
for Affine Computations

Wenlei Bao[1][✉], Prashant Singh Rawat[1], Martin Kong[2],
Sriram Krishnamoorthy[3], Louis-Noel Pouchet[4], and P. Sadayappan[1]

[1] The Ohio State University, Columbus, USA
{bao.79,rawat.15,sadayappan.1}@osu.edu
[2] Brookhaven National Laboratory, Upton, USA
mkong@bnl.gov
[3] Pacific Northwest National Laboratory, Richland, USA
sriram@pnnl.gov
[4] Colorado State University, Fort Collins, USA
pouchet@colostate.edu

Abstract. Trace based cache simulation are common techniques in
design space exploration. In this paper, we develop an efficient strategy to
simulate cache behavior for affine computations. Our framework exploits
the regularity of polyhedral programs to implement a cache set partition transformation to parallelize both trace generation and simulation.
We demonstrate that our framework accurately models the cache behavior of polyhedral programs while achieving significant improvements in
simulation time. Extensive evaluations show that our proposed framework systematically outperforms the time-partition based parallel cache
simulation.

1 Introduction

Modern computer architectures leverage memory hierarchies to bridge the speed
gap between fast processors and slow memories. At the top of this hierarchy sits
the fastest, smaller, and most expensive memory, i.e. registers; at the bottom
of the hierarchy, one can find much slower, larger, and cheaper memories (e.g.
DRAM, or other permanent media storage such as disks). The intermediate levels of this hierarchy provide temporary storage between two or more levels. This
avoids making time-expensive trips to lower memory levels. These intermediate
levels are often known as caches, and their main characteristic is to store frequently used data under some pre-determined storage and replacement policy
(e.g. LRU, FIFO, etc.).

The behavior of a cache is defined by a number of properties and policies,
the most obvious being its memory capacity, the possible locations where a
unit of data can be stored, as well as mechanisms for identifying and searching data. Other intricacies of caches include determining when data should be
evicted or when it should be committed to a more permanent memory, so as to

© Springer Nature Switzerland AG 2019
L. Rauchwerger (Ed.): LCPC 2017, LNCS 11403, pp. 65–85, 2019.
https://doi.org/10.1007/978-3-030-35225-7_6

keep all levels synchronized [17, 27]. In system design, different cache architectures and configurations are thoroughly evaluated to gauge the effectiveness of their use. It is easy to see that the aforementioned cache characteristics increase the complexity of this task. Furthermore, this evaluation is generally performed by trace-driven simulation, which is more flexible and accurate compared to execution-driven cache simulation [25] and modeling approaches [30]. The relevance of cache simulation is also observed in the design of new compiler analyses and transformations. In order for a simulation to be preferred, it must produce the same output as the real program execution while simultaneously being faster or more cost effective. Therefore, fast, reliable and accurate cache simulators are an important tool for engineers and researchers.

Techniques to reduce the complexity of cache simulation have been widely studied in the past. The stack processing algorithm [25] was introduced to reduce the complexity of sequential cache simulation. It was later extended to simulate several cache configurations in a single pass [39], and reduce space complexity by compressing program traces [30].

Trace-driven cache simulation is one of the preferred methods primarily due to the accuracy of its results. However, with the increase in complexity of the cache architectures, trace-driven methods incurs longer simulation times and requires storing large program traces (which store the referenced addresses) to generate accurate results. Therefore, it is imperative to study and develop techniques to overcome these shortcomings. One such technique is the parallel simulation approach [15, 26] that exploits the parallelism of current processors to reduce the simulation time.

Previous research efforts in the context of parallel simulation approaches can be divided into two major classes – time-partitioning simulation [15], and set-partitioning simulation [6]. Time-partitioning methods separate the program trace into a number of sequential subtraces of equal length. All the subtraces are used to concurrently simulate cache behavior with identical configuration, and generate partial simulation results. In set-partitioning simulation, a program reference is mapped to a single cache set for a given cache configuration. Each cache set can be simulated independently by a different processor. The parallelism of the set-partitioning approach is therefore limited by the number of sets within the cache configurations.

Time-partitioning parallel simulation can be more efficient than the set-partitioning simulation under certain conditions [6]. However, the accuracy of results for time-partitioning is often lower than set-partitioning because it ignores the initial cache state of each program trace. Subtle algorithmic tweaks are employed to correct/improve the accuracy of the simulation result by performing re-simulation. The added overhead and cost of re-simulation can potentially overcome the benefits from parallelism. Moreover, the time-partitioning scheme involves a preprocessing step that divides the entire program trace into subtraces in order to enable the concurrent simulation. Clearly, the entire trace of the program has to be stored in memory, which may be problematic when the trace size exceeds the system storage.

In this work, we propose a novel parallel cache simulation framework based on set-partitioning for affine programs (where cache set partition based on compile-time analysis in the paper is possible), which achieves up to $100+\times$ speedup against sequential simulation on 64 nodes cluster among 60 evaluations of 10 benchmarks with 6 different cache configurations.

Unlike previous parallel simulation approaches that generate the trace in sequential fashion, our approach also parallelizes the trace production. Moreover, compared to previous set-partitioning approaches [6] that compute the cache set number while performing the trace analysis, our approach organizes the trace by cache set at the very beginning of its generation. It thus avoids costly operations such as insertion and synchronization by maintaining the traces in lexicographic order. To the best of our knowledge, our work is the first to adopt this approach. Experimental evaluations validate the correctness and also demonstrates the performance of our framework.

In summary, we make the following contributions:

- We introduce a novel compiler technique that classifies the program references by their targeted cache set. This allows to parallelize the trace generation, and accelerates the overall cache simulation.
- We propose a program transformation that exploits the inherent parallelism exposed by classifying the program references by cache sets, and leverage two standard parallel runtimes, OpenMP and MPI, to increase the cache simulation speed.
- We provide a fully automated tool that, given a C source file containing a polyhedral program region as input, performs the cache set partition transformation and generates code that could conduct the program cache simulation in parallel.
- We perform an extensive evaluation to demonstrate the accuracy of the simulation in terms of cache miss and efficiency in terms of simulation time for our proposed approach.

The rest of the paper is organized as follows: Sect. 2 describes the motivation, Sects. 3 and 4 introduce the background and present the algorithm to perform the cache set partition. Section 5 summarizes our parallel cache simulation framework. Section 6 shows the evaluation results. We conclude the paper with Sect. 7.

2   Motivation

The problem of cache simulation has been extensively studied in the past decades [1,8,16,19,21,25,32,34,38]. Accurate and fast simulation techniques are necessary in order to do extensive architectural space exploration as well as devising new compiler optimization strategies. This problem will become even more important in the current and next generation of computer systems, where

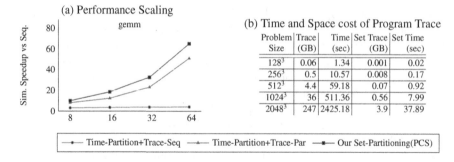

Fig. 1. Motivation example of Gemm

massively parallel processors will effectively have hundreds and thousands of cores. Therefore, good parallel hierarchical cache simulator will play a critical role.

Previous research efforts have demonstrated the benefits of exposing and exploiting parallelism in cache simulations [6,15,31,37]. In particular, parallelization approaches for trace-driven techniques have taken two directions – time-partitioning and set-partitioning. Time-partition approach suffers from inaccuracy and resimulation overhead as previously described. Set-partition approach simulates each cache set independently, does not suffer from the re-simulation problem, and obtains better accuracy. Nevertheless, the achievable speedup is limited to the number of available cache sets. Additionally, most of the previously proposed set-partitioning techniques suffer from the following limitations:

1. Inefficient sequential trace generation phase could dominate the simulation time.
2. Long program runs produce large trace files (potentially in the order of hundreds of GB), which could exceed the storage capacity of a single node.

We now demonstrate the problems in detail with the example of matrix multiplication, *Gemm*, on a real-world cache configuration: a 3-Level cache memory hierarchy with 32 KB 4-way L1, 256 KB 4-way L2 and 8 MB 16-way L3 cache.

Space Complexity of Trace Generation. Table 1b in Fig. 1 lists the space needed to store the trace file for different matrix sizes for *Gemm*. It is easy to observe that even for a problem size of 2048^3, the storage required for the trace file is as huge as 247 GB. Therefore, cache simulation on full-size problems will demand significant storage space, which is impractical.

Time Complexity of Trace Generation. The plot in Fig. 1 illustrates the speedup obtained over the sequential simulation across different number of nodes for problem size of 256^3. *Time-partition + Trace-seq* represents the speedup with time-partition simulation and sequential trace generation, while *Time-partition + Trace-par* shows the speedup of time-partition but with parallel trace

```
1    for (t = 0; t <T; t++)
2      for (i = 1; i <N; i++)
3        for (j = 1; j <N; j++)
4        /* reference c */   /* reference a */      /* reference b */
5    S1:     A[i][j]       =      A[i-1][j]      +      A[i][j-1];
```

Fig. 2. Simplified Seidel-2d benchmark (actual benchmark has 5 read references).

generation. The difference clearly demonstrates that the trace generation phase can dominate the whole simulation time, making the parallel simulation inefficient. Columns *set trace* and *set time* indicate the storage space and time needed if the trace generation phase get parallelized by set-partitioning with 64 nodes. We can observe significant improvements in both space and time consumption. Moreover, the parallelization of trace generation allows the subsequent simulation process to be more efficient compared to previous approaches [6].

   Therefore, we propose an efficient parallel cache simulation framework for a class of computationally intensive programs known as affine programs, which automatically transforms the program, and parallelizes the cache simulation along with the trace generation process based on set-partitioning.

3   Program Representation

The compute-intensive kernels of many linear algebra methods, image processing applications [41,43–45], and physics simulations [9,14,40,42] can be expressed as an affine/polyhedral program [2,4,11,14]. Extracting a high performance for such kernels often requires an effective utilization of cache hierarchies.

   A property of polyhedral program is that the loop bounds, conditionals, and array indices in the program must be affine functions. The mathematical structures used in this work to represent polyhedral program are: iteration domain, data access relations, and schedule of iterations. The operations on these structures, such as composition and inverse, are the same as [3,5], and not listed here because of the space limitations.

Iteration Domains. Iteration domains capture the set of runtime executions of a statement, using integer sets where the loop bounds are used to constrain the number of points in the set. Each statement S is associated with an iteration vector i_S with one component per surrounding loop, and the values i_S are captured by defining its iteration space $\mathcal{D}_S$. For example the iteration domain of S1 in Fig. 2 is:

$$\mathcal{D}_{S1} = [T, N] \rightarrow \{S1[t, i, j] : 0 \leq t < T \wedge 1 \leq i < N \wedge 1 \leq j < N\}$$

Data Access Functions. An essential part of our cache simulation framework is the cache analysis based on representing the data accessed by each program iteration. For polyhedral programs, the function that maps a statement instance to the array element being accessed is by definition an affine relation, including surrounding loop iterators and parameters. The access relation maps an iteration domain to the multidimensional array index being accessed. For example, the function that relates the iterations of $S1$ with the location read in array A for the reference $A[i-1][j]$ in Fig. 2 is:

$$\mathbf{Read}_{S_1}^A = \{S_1[t,i,j] \mapsto A[i_2,j_2] : (i_2 = i-1) \wedge (j_2 = j)\}$$

We note **Write** for the write references. Furthermore, one can build the relation that is restricted to the set of iterations of $S1$ by computing $\mathbf{S} = \mathbf{Read}_{S1}^A \cap \mathcal{D}_{S1}$, that is embed the constraints on the possible values for $S_1[t,i,j]$ directly in the relation.

Finally, we note **ProgRefs** the union of all access relations for the program, **ReadRefs** the union of all read-only access relations for the program, and **WriteRefs** the union of all write-access relations in the program. We have **ProgRefs** = **ReadRefs** $\cup$ **WriteRefs**.

Program Execution Order. Schedule is used to specify the execution order of statements in program by mapping statement instances in iteration domain to timestamps of iteration space combed with values to indicate orders. As such, statement instances in the iteration domain are executed following the lexicographic ordering $\prec$ of their associated timestamp. $\prec$ is defined as $(a_1,\ldots,a_n) \prec (b_1,\ldots,b_m)$ iff there exists an integer $1 \leq i \leq min(n,m)$ s.t. $(a_1,\ldots,a_{i-1}) = (b_1,\ldots,b_{i-1})$ and $a_i < b_i$.

The program schedule can be denoted by $2d+1$ timestamps, where d is the maximum depth of loop in program [14]. A schedule can be constrained by the iteration domain of its statement, e.g., via $Sched_{S1} \cap \mathcal{D}_{S1}$, and the set of all distinct statement iterations in the program can be built by the union of all schedules constrained by the respective statement iteration domain as **Sched**.

4 Cache Set Partition Analysis

4.1 Cache Access Modeling

The core polyhedral abstractions are obtained from the C code via the PET [36]. In order to model the events corresponding to accessing different cache lines, we must first translate the underlying virtual memory address of each individual array reference into the unique cache line, and the associated set in the cache. For the moment, we will assume that the referenced variable has already been translated to a virtual memory address. Definition 1 defines the steps of the conversion from a given virtual memory address to the associated and accessed cache set.

Definition 1 (Set-associative cache). *A set-associative cache C with associativity K, cache line (i.e., block) size of B bytes, and size n bytes contains S sets, with $S = n/B/K$. A virtual memory address addr maps to a unique line index $L_{id} = floor(addr/B)$, and a line maps to a unique set $S_{L_{id}} = L_{id}\%S$.*

The previous definition essentially assumes that the cache size in bytes (n), the number in bytes of a cache line (B), and associativity degree (K) are given.

We now explain how the translation from a particular array reference to its virtual memory address is performed. The first step is to linearize the access relation. Therefore, for each distinct variable (array or scalar) a vector of fixed dimension sizes is provided at compile-time. The reason for requiring fixed sizes is that the exact virtual memory address must be determined before computing the associated cache set. To complete the linearization, we also require an offset address for each program variable, which in this case, can be either a program parameter or a fixed numerical integer value. If a fixed value is preferred, we can simply estimate the address offsets by taking the declaration order, and computing each array size with the dimension sizes and the floating point precision used. For example, the linearization transformation from a 2D access relation $\mathbf{R}^A$ for array A, with sz the size of A and start_A its starting address can be written as:

$$\mathbf{Linearize} = \{[i,j] \mapsto [m] : m = \mathrm{start}_A + i * sz_1 + j\}$$

Then the unique cache line index is given by applying the relation:

$$\mathbf{MemToLineId} = \{[m] \mapsto [lid] : lid = \mathrm{floor}(m/B)\}$$

Computing the set to which a cache line maps to is given by the relation:

$$\mathbf{LineIdToCacheSet} = \{[lid] \mapsto [cset] : cset = lid \% S\}$$

Definition 2 (Array to Cache set index). *Given an access function* $\mathbf{R}^A$ *of an array reference A with sizes sz and starting address start_A, for a cache as defined in Definition 1. The associated cache line in cache C is identified by* **AccessToLine** *as:*

$$\mathbf{AccessToLine} = \mathbf{R}^A \circ \mathbf{Linearize}(sz, \mathrm{start}_A) \circ \mathbf{MemToLineId}$$

The composition of the obtained relation with the **LineIdToCacheSet** *relation provides the corresponding cache set in C that is referenced by the array and identified by* **AccessToSet** *as:*

$$\mathbf{AccessToSet} = \mathbf{AccessToLine} \circ \mathbf{LineIdToCacheSet}$$

Thus, for every array access within the program, we can determine in a static fashion which cache set it maps to given cache configuration based on above relations.

4.2   Cache Set Partition

In order to distribute and parallelize the trace generation and program simulation, we first need to construct a map from the time space (space of timestamps assigned to each lexical statement) to the accessed cache set. This relation is easily built by composing the inverse of the program schedule with the composition of the union of access relations with the union of maps that translate the access relation to a specific cache set instance:

$$\textbf{TimeToCacheSet} = \textbf{Sched}^{-1} \circ (\textbf{ProgRefs} \circ \textbf{AccessToSet})$$

where the composition of **ProgRefs** and **AccessToSet** provides the relation from program statements to the cache set index they are mapped to. In a nutshell, the complete equation essentially determines all the timestamps that affect a particular cachet set. The composition is done via the statement instances being accessed. The benefits of having in a closed form all the timestamps mapped to a cache set, is that we can easily determine the subset of statement instances that are associated to the timestamps, and that impact a specific cache set. Obviously, this also allows us to use the schedule map (**Sched**) to generate the necessary array references in the order required by the original program. This step is vital to maintain the program semantics, thereby keeping the original locality and avoiding to insert fake access patterns or remove real ones. Thus, the expression **TimeToCacheSet** calculates the mapping between all assigned timestamps to all different cache sets for affine programs, under the constraints previously discussed.

Hierarchical Cache. To handle multi-level cache hierarchies, we remark that it is easy to build the formulation with the expression above. It can be achieved by editing the cache parameters in **MemToLineId** and **LineIdToCacheSet**, e.g., block size B in **MemToLineId** and number of sets S in **LineIdToCacheSet**. Besides the changes of the formulation for set-partition, the trace analysis algorithm also needs to support multi-level cache simulation, which is shown in the later section. Therefore, an iterative algorithm for program reference behaviors, specializing **TimeToCacheSet** for each cache set value $S_i \in [0, S]$ is built. It can be easily parallelized using either OpenMP or MPI since there are no interactions needed between different threads but a simple accumulation, which compulsory to form the union of cache behaviors such as cache misses for all cache sets.

4.3   Code Generation

The code generation in our framework leverages the result from the previous steps that (a) partition the program statement instances into distinct and individual cache sets; and (b) generate the code that can be execute to conduct the cache simulation in parallel.

There are two phases to achieve the goal of code generation. During the first phase, the union of all statements within an iteration space is scanned using the provided global lexicographic ordering specified by the program schedule, and loop nests in the target program are generated that execute the statement instances in the new lexicographic order. During the second phase, the primary tasks of post-AST processing are (1) Adding parallel/distributed primitives such as OpenMP or MPI for parallel execution; (2) Instrument code to construct and analyze the trace for cache simulation; (3) Place the reduction code to accumulate the simulation result of each cache set.

Algorithms 1 and 2 detail the code generation steps. Algorithm 1 takes the relation **TimeToCacheSet** together with iteration domains $\mathcal{D}$, and access relations and the original program schedule as input. The overall idea here is that the generated code must contain the original access sequence of the input code; each lexical program statement is decomposed into as many array references as it has; and the original loop nests must be surrounded by an outer parallel loop. This outer loop effectively iterates over all cache sets. In terms of standard loop transformations, this is akin to strip-mining all the original dimensions by the cache set index being accessed.

Line 7 in Algorithm 1 deserves further explanation. The role of **ComputeNewProgramSchedule** is to build the new program schedule from the **TimeToCacheSet** union map. It achieves this by creating a new union map, where the domain is the **TimeToCacheSet** map, wrapped into a set, while the range is a second wrapped map. The second wrapped map has in its domain the same dimensions as the domain of **TimeToCacheSet** with an additional fixed dimension which represents the array reference ID of a specific statement, the **i** argument of the function. The range of the second wrapped map is almost identical to its domain, but where the leading dimension (at position zero) is inserted, and set to the cache set index (which is also the unique dimension in the image of **TimeToCacheSet**). Furthermore, the domains of the second wrapped union map are also properly renamed to prevent fusion among the same points of different statements. Finally, after this map of wrapped union maps to wrapped union maps is computed, we apply a *range* operation to it and return this result.

Algorithm 2 details the post processing steps. It takes the previous generated program as input, and traverse it to enable the instrumentation and proper calls to the parallel runtime of choice. In summary, at this stage we: (1) enable the parallel execution, (2) perform trace generation and analysis and (3) collect the final simulation results by a reduction. Line 1 inserts the parallel primitives for the outer most loop in the transformed program, where the outer most loop is the one to iterate all different cache sets and thus can be easily parallelized. e.g. using #pragma omp for. When using MPI, the described transformations equate to adding a filter to handle the case where many cache sets are assigned to a single process, i.e., we add a filter such as **if (cache_set % comm_size == my_rank)**. Lines 2 to 7 traverse the program to instrument the code for trace production and analysis. Line 8 places the reduction code the collect the final simulation results from parallel processes or distributed nodes. The *AnalyzeTrace* function is responsible of performing the trace analysis and counting the number of cache misses and hits, etc.

Example. Figure 3 presents an example generated by our parallel simulation framework using *Seidel* as the sequential source program. Line 1 to 3 declare the number of sets in the cache configuration and number of nodes available. Line 4 is the loop that decides which cache sets to execute, and depends on the set id and node id match. Line 7 to 10 perform the simulation by construct-

---

Algorithm 1. Cache Set Partition Code Generation

Input: Program statement iteration domains: $\mathcal{D}^S, s \in S$
   Program access relations: $\mathcal{A}^S, s \in S$
   TimeToCacheSet relations
   Program schedule with cache set dimension: $\theta^S, s \in S$
Output: Cache set partitioned program: $\mathcal{P}$
 1: **for all** statements S **do**
 2:    Sort array references of S by lexicographic order and make the write reference the last one
 3:    **for all** array references A_i^S in the current lexical statement S **do**
 4:       // Create iteration domains, access relations and schedules for each reference

 5:       $\mathcal{D}^{S,A,i} \leftarrow$ copy $\mathcal{D}^S$, rename set to S_A_i, append fixed dimension and fix to i
 6:       $\mathcal{A}^{S,A,i} \leftarrow$ copy $\mathcal{A}_i^S$, rename the map's domain to S_A_i, append fixed dimension to domain of map and fix it to i
 7:       $\theta^{S,A,i} \leftarrow$ ComputeNewProgramSchedule (*TimeToCacheSet,i*)
 8:       // Establish the order among array references of a single statement
 9:       Append to the image of $\theta^{S,A,i}$ a fixed dimension with value i
10:       // Add computed abstractions to their respective unions
11:       $domain \leftarrow domain \cup \mathcal{D}^{S,A,i}$
12:       $access \leftarrow access \cup \mathcal{A}^{S,A,i}$
13:       $schedule \leftarrow schedule \cup \theta^{S,A,i}$
14:    **end for**
15: **end for**
16: $\mathcal{P} \leftarrow$ codegen($domain,access,schedule$)
17: **return** Generated program $\mathcal{P}$;

---

ing and analyzing the traces on different threads (if using OpenMP) or process ranks (if MPI is preferred). Finally, line 11 is the reduction function to collect the simulation results from all nodes.

Algorithm 2. Post AST processing

Input: Cache set partitioned program: $\mathcal{P}$
Output: Parallel cache simulation program: $\mathcal{P}_S$
 1: $\mathcal{P}_S \leftarrow$ Add parallel primitives for outer most loop
 2: **for all** Statements S_i **do**
 3:    **for all** Array reference R **do**
 4:       $T_R \leftarrow$ Construct trace based on reference R
 5:       $\mathcal{P}_S \leftarrow$ Instrument trace analysis code *AnalyzeTrace(T_R)*
 6:    **end for**
 7: **end for**
 8: $\mathcal{P}_S \leftarrow$ Add parallel reduction code *ParReduction* to collect results
 9: **return** Parallel cache simulation program: $\mathcal{P}_S$;

```
1  #define SET num_of_cache_sets
2  #define NODE num_of_nodes
3  #define DIM SET/NODE
4  for (c0 = Id*DIM; c0 < (Id+1)*DIM; c0++)//Execute when setId match NodeId
5    for (c1 = lb1; c1 < ub1; c1++)
6      for (c2 = lb2; c2 < ub2; c2++)
7        for (c3 = lb3; c3 < ub3; c3++) {
8          AnalyzeTrace(ConstTrace(A[c2-1][c3],c0,c1,c2,c3)); //reference a
9          AnalyzeTrace(ConstTrace(A[c2][c3-1],c0,c1,c2,c3)); //reference b
10         AnalyzeTrace(ConstTrace(A[c2][c3] , c0,c1,c2,c3));}//reference c
11 Reduction() {...}; // Reduction code not shown
```

Fig. 3. Example of generated code for Seidel by our framework

5   Parallel Cache Simulation Framework

The overall flow diagram of our set-partition based parallel cache simulation framework is shown in Fig. 4. Our automatic simulation framework works as follows. The input source program is scanned and parsed, the affine computation kernels are extracted and analyzed to construct the relations such as **ProgRefs**, **Sched**, which is performed using ISL. Then the cache set partition analysis and transformation, which is the critical part within the framework, is performed as described in the previous sections. The partition is achieved by the relation **TimeToCacheSet**, which is built upon the cache accessing model and cache set partition formulation, together with the polyhedral analysis. We view this step as *cache set partition transformation*, which reorganizes the programs statements and execution order so that the references accessing the same cache set are grouped together. Next, the code generation algorithm generates the code skeleton of the transformed program, where memory references are grouped based on the calculated cache set number. After that, the post-AST processing algorithm adds the necessary parallel primitives and trace analysis code to generate code for simulation. This is denoted as the *code generation* part in the flow diagram. Finally, during *parallel cache simulation* step, the generated code is compiled and executed in parallel to conduct the trace-driven cache simulation. Thus, the program traces are generated and analyzed in parallel with respect to cache set to produce cache simulation results.

The parallelism of our cache simulation framework comes from set-partition. However, it is better than previous set-partitioning simulation techniques in mainly two aspects. One is the parallelization of trace generation, which exploits

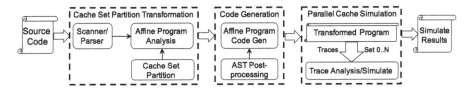

Fig. 4. Parallel trace-driven cache simulation framework

more parallelism within the simulation process and improves the overall performance. The other is the trace analysis process. Previous approaches need to calculate the set number for each trace that involves expensive operations such as trace insertion and synchronization, making the simulation inefficient. In contrast, our approach avoids these operations via the proposed cache set partition transformation, separating the trace based on cache set at source level, which makes the trace analysis much more efficient.

6   Experimental Evaluation

6.1   Experiment Setup

Implementation Details. Our framework takes a sequential C program, cache parameters, array sizes and starting addresses as input. Polyhedral Extraction Tool [36] detects affine regions and extracts the polyhedral model from C source code. ISL [35] is used to perform the cache partition transformation described in previous sections. CLooG [7], a state-of-the-art polyhedral code generator, is used to generate the code based on the algorithm described previously.

Benchmarks. We validate the accuracy and efficiency of our parallel cache simulation framework via the PolyBench/C benchmark suite [29], which is a collection of benchmarks with static control parts that meets our requirements. For the experiments, We select 10 representative benchmarks that are listed in Table 1.

Tools and Setup. To conduct the comparison experiments to validate the performance and correctness with our proposed parallel cache simulation framework, we use DineroIV, a trace-based cache simulator that can handle hierarchical set associative caches, to perform the sequential cache simulation. All experiments are performed on a cluster with a maximum of 64 nodes, each with an Intel Xeon E5640 processor at frequency 2.67 GHz. The programs are all compiled using MPI with MVAPICH2 version 2.1 with -O3 optimization and using one process for each node [18,22–24]. All reported results are the average of 5 runs with single precision used for the benchmarks.

6.2   Experiments Results

We use single- and multi- level set associative caches to validate our framework in both accuracy and efficiency. Note our experiments only show the simulations of most commonly used LRU replacement policy and write allocate write back policy in the evaluation process. However, other replacement policies (FIFO, random, etc.) and write policies (non write-allocate, write through, etc.) are seamlessly handled: their processing is independent from proposed parallel trace generation and simulation.

Single Level Set Associative Cache. We first perform the validation on single level cache with 4 different cache sizes ranging including 4 KB, 8 KB, 16 KB and 32 KB, with block size 64 bytes and 8-way associativity.

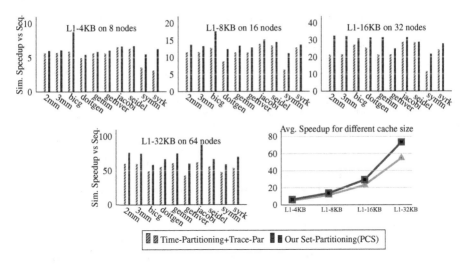

Fig. 5. Summary of simulation speedup for single level cache

Accuracy. The number of cache misses is one of the most important metrics that users want to obtain from the cache simulation to better understand a program's behavior. Table 1 compares the cache miss results for all sizes of single level caches between the sequential simulation with DineroIV and our parallel simulation framework (PCS).

We observe an exact match of the cache misses of the two simulations, which results in an error rate of 0% for all benchmarks across different cache sizes. We can also observe from the table that the cache miss count decreases along with the increasing of cache size until all data can be hold by the cache.

Table 1. Cache misses for single level cache

Sim.	Bench.	Cache configurations				Sim.
		L1-4KB	L1-8KB	L1-16KB	L1-32KB	
Dinero	2 mm	33,846,272	33,709,056	33,709,056	33,708,032	PCS
serial	3 mm	50,769,408	50,563,584	50,563,584	50,562,048	
	bicg	3,146,240	3,146,240	3,146,240	3,146,240	
	doitgen	270,893,056	270,893,056	270,860,288	270,796,800	
	gemm	16,923,136	16,854,528	16,854,528	16,854,016	
	gemver	5,767,936	5,523,312	5,261,165	4,732,719	
	jacobi	12,558,336	12,558,336	8,408,992	8,376,320	
	seidel	6,279,168	6,279,168	2,097,152	2,097,152	
	symm	200,525,957	200,524,323	200,523,289	200,430,141	
	syrk	134,348,800	71,753,728	67,305,472	67,305,472	
Sum.	Error rate	0%	0%	0%	0%	

Efficiency. To further evaluate the performance of our simulation framework, we also compare PCS with *a nearly ideal time-partitioning* based parallel simulation besides the sequential simulation. The time-partition cache simulation divides the whole program trace into multiple, roughly equal sized subtraces, and simulates them in parallel. In our time-partitioning implementation we assume that only one partition requires re-simulation. So the real performance gap between it and PCS could effectively be larger.

Table 2. Summary of cache misses for hierarchical cache

Sim.	Benchmark	Cache configurations							Sim.
		L1	L2	L3-Conf1	L3-Conf2	L3-Conf3	L3-Conf4	L3-Conf5	
Dinero serial	2 mm	33,708,032	707,844	20,480	20,480	20,480	28,399	285,897	PCS
	3 mm	50,562,048	1,061,766	28,672	28,672	28,672	32,784	49,104	
	bicg	3,146,240	1,049,600	1,049,600	1,049,600	1,049,600	1,049,600	1,049,600	
	doitgen	8,387,648	8,384,064	8,371,360	262,144	1,046,424	262,144	285,144	
	gemm	4,332,830	4,329,184	24,800	12,288	12,288	12,288	16,128	
	gemvel	4,732,719	4,722,357	4,721,994	4,722,186	4,722,282	4,323,120	4,722,351	
	jacobi	935,584	934,808	6,873	12,288	12,288	16,128	8,029,984	
	seidel	2,016,000	2,016,000	63,000	63,000	2,016,000	2,016,000	2,016,000	
	symm	200,429,973	192,265,358	49,090	49,090	3,175,278	70,699,265	164,684,202	
	syrk	67,305,472	67,305,472	261,960	1,043,743	67,305,472	67,305,472	67,305,472	
Sum.	Error rate	0%	0%	0%	0%	0%	0%	0%	

Furthermore, normally in time-partitioning based simulation, the whole program trace would need to be first generated and then split into subtraces. This incurs in an inefficient sequential trace generation phase as we already demonstrated in the previous section. It is for this reason that we also combine the time-partitioning scheme with our parallel trace generation. This effectively removes the big performance gap between both schemes. Moreover, here we assume a perfect accuracy of time-partition simulation results even it suffers accuracy problem in reality because of the unknown cache initialization state at the beginning of each subtrace.

Figure 5 illustrates the efficiency of simulation by comparing the speedup of sequential simulation vs. parallel simulation on varying number of nodes. The 4 bar charts in Figure present the simulation speedup between time-partitioning and our framework on different degree of parallelism for all benchmarks across different cache sizes.

We observe that for all the cases, our set-partitioning simulation achieved better speedup compared to time-partitioning. In fact, our set-partitioning simulation constantly outperforms time-partitioning across all the benchmarks. There are several reasons: First of all, the re-simulation phase of time-partitioning approach takes extra cost. In practice, the time cost of the re-simulation phase to correct the simulation results will often make the simulation time much longer than the optimal case we considered here in the experiments. Besides, our set-partitioning approach has better memory efficiency. The memory trace accessed by the program has smaller footprint compared to time-partitioning. This effect is more obvious in hierarchical cache shown later in this section. Line chart in Fig. 5 shows average speedup of all benchmarks for different cache sizes. This is because more parallelism can be achieved for large cache compared to small ones.

Hierarchical Set Associative Cache. We perform similar experiments for multi-level caches for further validation. We consider 5 real world scenario configurations: a 3-Level cache hierarchy with 32 KB 4-way set-associative L1 and

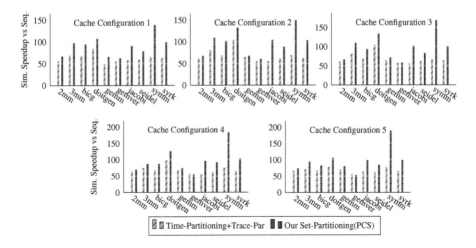

Fig. 6. Summary of simulation speedup for hierarchical cache

256 KB 4-way set-associative L2, and L3 cache with size and associativity reduce by 2 for each configuration start from 8 MB 16-way for Conf1. The block size is 64 Bytes across all levels.

Accuracy. Table 2 compares cache miss count between DineroIV and our parallel simulation framework (PCS) for all evaluated configurations.

Again we observation that *for all cache configurations, our framework produces exactly the same results as DineroIV.* For all benchmarks the cache miss count decreases when moving from the L1 to the L3 cache as expected.

Efficiency. Figure 6 shows the results of performance speedup comparison between time-partitioning and our approach against sequential simulation when using 64 nodes and 1 process for each node (make sure each process has enough computation resources such as cache and memory). We observe that our framework outperforms the time-partitioning approach for all the benchmarks, and across different cache hierarchies.

To illustrate the benefits of our parallel cache simulation framework, we analyze the results of benchmark *symm* in detail. As shown in the chart, *symm* achieves the highest speedup compared to time-partitioning approach among all benchmarks. The underlying reason is that, *symm* uses three matrices of size 512×512, and among the array references, 5 out of 6 of them incur on high-strides. Thus, the non-efficient memory access pattern leads to large cache memory footprints when simulating the full cache. This phenomenon happens again in time-partitioning simulation, as the order of the memory references and cache footprint in trace file remains unaltered. Moreover, the cache set partition transformation changes the memory access order (in simulation) and also the simulation cache footprint. Because every memory reference within each trace is mapping to the same cache set, which has a much smaller cache footprint when

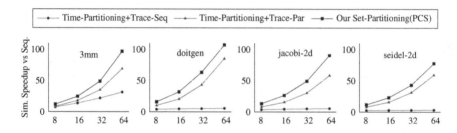

Fig. 7. Summary of performance scaling on cache Conf1

simulating the full cache. Furthermore, the benefits also come from the fact that trace analysis algorithm does not need to spent time on calculating and searching cache set and other related operations in our framework. Therefore, our framework uses a smaller cache footprint during the full cache simulation, and performs much better than the time-partitioning counterpart for benchmark *symm*. Opposing *symm* we have the *gemm* benchmark, which also uses three matrices, but wherein 3 out of 4 matrix references within the innermost loop have stride-1 access. This clearly leads to having rather smaller cache memory footprint compared to *symm*. Thus, the benefits over the time-partitioning on *gemm* are not as large as with *symm*.

Performance Scaling. Figure 7 illustrates the performance scaling of our framework, which is the simulation speedup across different number of nodes (8, 16, 32, 64) with cache configuration *Conf1*. There are three different curves in each subfigure. *Time-partitioning+Trace-Seq* represents time partition parallel simulation with sequential trace generation; *Time-partitioning+Trace-Par* represents time partition parallel simulation with parallel trace generation; *Set-partitioning(PCS)* represents our parallel cache simulation framework. Note we only show 4 benchmarks here because of the space.

It is more than obvious that the simulation with sequential trace generation has limited performance scaling. This demonstrates again the necessity of trace generation parallelization. We also observe that both approaches show strong scaling when increasing the number of nodes. However, our simulation framework outperforms the time-partitioning approach for all the benchmarks by showing a stronger scaling of performance. At this point we also recall that our implementation of the *Time-partitioning+Trace-Par* variant is a nearly ideal and inaccurate simulation, unlike PCS which is as accurate as the serial simulation.

Readers may also observe the super-linear scaling in some benchmarks (e.g. *doitgen*). The reason behind is the cache effect resulting from the different memory hierarchies. With more nodes involved in the computation, the accumulated cache memory (for simulation purposes) also becomes larger, and with larger accumulated cache sizes, more or even all of the working sets can fit into caches and the memory access time reduces dramatically, which causes the extra speedup in addition to that from the actual computation.

7   Related Work

Cache simulation is used to evaluate different cache architectures during new system design. The seminal paper of [25] proposed to use simulation in virtual memory. Their technique computed, in a single pass of the trace file, the miss ratios for all memory capacities, and also introduced notions such as set-refinement and inclusion. However, it was limited to a number of constraints, among of which was a fixed page size. Their work had many applications, in particular, simulation of hierarchical caches.

Due to the constant increase in complexity of cache architectures, a broad range of techniques have been proposed along the years [12,15,28,30,33]. The main difference among the techniques is their cost-efficiency ratio, that is, how much accuracy one is willing to sacrifice in exchange for faster simulation speeds. On one end of the spectrum, parametric analytical models that estimate the number of cache misses are faster and more general available [1,12,13]. On the other end, non-parameterized and less general models combined with trace-driven techniques can be used to produce more accurate simulations, at expense of longer simulation times [8,21,34]. These two classes of work are complementary, and can be used at different stages of the design process.

Compare to cache modeling analysis, simulation still provides a wider coverage of cache architectures and better accuracy. Among all simulation approaches, trace-driven simulation [34], has better accuracy and flexibility. In this context, two directions have been preferred: single pass optimization and trace parallelization strategies. The former one attempts to optimize the simulation in a single sequential pass. This is usually achieved by reducing the trace file size, either by sampling or judicious address selection, and leveraging data structures such as linked lists and trees [8,32] to represent the cache state. Within this research branch, Dinero [10], which is a uniprocessor cache simulator that can handle hierarchical set-associative caches as well as numerous replacement and write policies, thereby characterizing program cache behavior with varying degrees of fidelity.

The second direction aims at partitioning the simulation so that partitions of traces can be executed in parallel [15,19,21,37]. There are two major approaches to exploit the parallelism in cache simulation: time-partitioning and set-partitioning. The idea behind time partitioning is to divide the input program trace into chunks, which can then be simulated in parallel. However, an extra step is necessary to assign the correct cache state between every pair of chunks. Furthermore, depending on the cache configuration and the input program, a number of re-simulation might be necessary and could potentially overcome all parallel benefits, thereby making it even slower than the sequential version. The approach of set partitioning does not require this re-simulation step, since it divides the trace file by the sets addresses by each variable reference. However, the degree of parallelism is limited by the number of sets of cache configuration. Barriga et al. [6] presented a straightforward implementation of cache simulation that exploited set-partitioning. However, their approach included expensive operations such as insertion and synchronization during the trace generation.

Works such as [37], use GPU to exploit the set-partitioning parallelism and simulate multiple cache configurations at one time. Despite utilizing GPUs, their approach still suffers from the inefficiency of processing program traces, specifically, during the address sorting stage.

To the best of our knowledge, in context of trace-driven simulation, all previous works have assumed that the trace generation stage to be inherently sequential. This makes trace-driven cache simulation less efficient as the time spent on generating traces could dominate the simulation time and overcome the benefits achieved via parallelization. Thus, our approach also parallelizes this phase to achieve better efficiency.

Finally, in the general field of simulation, approximate techniques have also been devised. The idea behind this is that results accuracy can be sacrificed in exchange for faster execution times [20]. These techniques have also been adapted for time-parallel cache simulation [19].

8   Conclusion

Exploiting parallelism to accelerate trace-driven cache simulation is a well-studied problem. Previous works have typically focused on two major aspects: (a) the time-partitioning based parallel simulation; and (b) the set-partitioning based approach. These approaches are inefficient when generating and processing large program traces.

In this paper, we propose a novel *parallel* cache simulation framework for *polyhedral programs* to perform accurate, and efficient cache simulation. Compared to previous state-of-the-art works, our approach exploits not only the parallelism in the trace analysis, but also improves the trace generation phase based on cache set partition transformation. Our approach avoids inefficient operations such as trace insertion and synchronization, which are necessary in other set-partitioning methods. We demonstrate that for affine programs, we can achieve better simulation speedup and better memory efficiency compared to time-partition approach. Experimental evaluations validate the accuracy of the proposed framework, showing significant simulation speedup on representative benchmarks against the time-partition parallel simulation.

Acknowledgments. We thank the anonymous referees for the feedback and many suggestions that helped in improving the presentation. This work was supported in part by the U.S. Department of Energy, Office of Science, Office of Advanced Scientific Computing Research under Awards 66905 and DE-SC0014135, program manager Lucy Nowell, by the U.S. National Science Foundation through awards 1513120 and 1731612, and by computational resources from the Ohio Supercomputer Center. Pacific Northwest National Laboratory is operated by Battelle for DOE under Contract DE-AC05-76RL01830.

References

1. Agarwal, A., Hennessy, J., Horowitz, M.: An analytical cache model. ACM Trans. Comput. Syst. (TOCS) **7**(2), 184–215 (1989)

2. Bao, W., Tavarageri, S., Ozguner, F., Sadayappan, P.: PWCET: power-aware worst case execution time analysis. In: 2014 43rd International Conference on Parallel Processing Workshops, pp. 439–447, September 2014
3. Bao, W.: Power aware WCET analysis (2014)
4. Bao, W., et al.: Static and dynamic frequency scaling on multicore CPUs. ACM Trans. Arch. Code Optim. (TACO) **13**(4), 51:1–51:26 (2016). https://doi.org/10. 1145/3011017
5. Bao, W., Krishnamoorthy, S., Pouchet, L.N., Rastello, F., Sadayappan, P.: Poly-Check: dynamic verification of iteration space transformations on affine programs. SIGPLAN Not. **51**(1), 539–554 (2016). https://doi.org/10.1145/2914770.2837656
6. Barriga, L., Ayani, R.: Parallel cache simulation on multiprocessor workstattions. In: 1993 International Conference on Parallel Processing, ICPP 1993, vol. 1, pp. 171–174. IEEE (1993)
7. Bastoul, C.: Generating loops for scanning polyhedra: CLooG users guide. Polyhedron **2**, 10 (2004)
8. Conte, T.M., Hirsch, M.A., Hwu, W.M.: Combining trace sampling with single pass methods for efficient cache simulation. IEEE Trans. Comput. **47**(6), 714–720 (1998)
9. Dundar, M., Kou, Q., Zhang, B., He, Y., Rajwa, B.: Simplicity of kmeans versus deepness of deep learning: a case of unsupervised feature learning with limited data. In: 2015 IEEE 14th International Conference on Machine Learning and Applications (ICMLA), pp. 883–888. IEEE (2015)
10. Edler, J., Hill, M.D.: Dinero IV trace-driven uniprocessor cache simulator (1999). http://www.cs.wisc.edu/markhill
11. Feautrier, P.: Some efficient solutions to the affine scheduling problem, part II: multidimensional time. Int. J. Parallel Prog. **21**(6), 389–420 (1992)
12. Ghosh, S., Martonosi, M., Malik, S.: Precise miss analysis for program transformations with caches of arbitrary associativity. In: Proceedings of the Eighth International Conference on Architectural Support for Programming Languages and Operating Systems, ASPLOS VIII, pp. 228–239. ACM, New York (1998). https:// doi.org/10.1145/291069.291051
13. Ghosh, S., Martonosi, M., Malik, S.: Cache miss equations: a compiler framework for analyzing and tuning memory behavior. ACM Trans. Program. Lang. Syst. (TOPLAS) **21**(4), 703–746 (1999)
14. Girbal, S., et al.: Semi-automatic composition of loop transformations. Int. J. Parallel Prog. **34**(3), 261–317 (2006)
15. Heidelberger, P., Stone, H.S.: Parallel trace-driven cache simulation by time partitioning. In: 1990 Proceedings of the Simulation Conference, Winter, pp. 734–737. IEEE (1990)
16. Hill, M.D., Smith, A.J.: Evaluating associativity in CPU caches. IEEE Trans. Comput. **38**(12), 1612–1630 (1989)
17. Hong, C., et al.: Effective padding of multidimensional arrays to avoid cache conflict misses. SIGPLAN Not. **51**(6), 129–144 (2016). https://doi.org/10.1145/2980983. 2908123
18. Zhang, J., Lu, X., Panda, D.: High performance MPI library for container-based HPC cloud on InfiniBand clusters, August 2016
19. Kiesling, T.: Approximate time-parallel cache simulation. In: Proceedings of the 36th Conference on Winter Simulation, pp. 345–354. Winter Simulation Conference (2004)

20. Kiesling, T., Pohl, S.: Time-parallel simulation with approximative state matching. In: Proceedings of the Eighteenth Workshop on Parallel and Distributed Simulation, pp. 195–202. ACM (2004)

21. Lauterbach, G.: Accelerating architectural simulation by parallel execution of trace samples. In: 1994 Proceedings of the Twenty-Seventh Hawaii International Conference on System Sciences, vol. 1, pp. 205–210. IEEE (1994)

22. Li, M., Lu, X., Hamidouche, K., Zhang, J., Panda, D.K.: Mizan-RMA: accelerating Mizan graph processing framework with MPI RMA. In: 2016 IEEE 23rd International Conference on High Performance Computing (HiPC), pp. 42–51, December 2016

23. Li, M., Potluri, S., Hamidouche, K., Jose, J., Panda, D.K.: Efficient and truly passive MPI-3 RMA using InfiniBand atomics. In: Proceedings of the 20th European MPI Users' Group Meeting, EuroMPI 2013, pp. 91–96. ACM, New York (2013). https://doi.org/10.1145/2488551.2488573

24. Li, M., Hamidouche, K., Lu, X., Subramoni, H., Zhang, J., Panda, D.K.: Designing MPI library with on-demand paging (ODP) of InfiniBand: challenges and benefits. In: Proceedings of the International Conference for High Performance Computing, Networking, Storage and Analysis, SC 2016, pp. 37:1–37:11. IEEE Press, Piscataway (2016). http://dl.acm.org/citation.cfm?id=3014904.3014954

25. Mattson, R.L., Gecsei, J., Slutz, D.R., Traiger, I.L.: Evaluation techniques for storage hierarchies. IBM Syst. J. $9(2)$, 78–117 (1970)

26. Nicol, D.M., Greenberg, A.G., Lubachevsky, B.D.: Massively parallel algorithms for trace-driven cache simulations. IEEE Trans. Parallel Distrib. Syst. $5(8)$, 849–859 (1994)

27. Patterson, D.A.: Computer Architecture: A Quantitative Approach. Elsevier, Amsterdam (2011)

28. Pieper, J.J., Mellan, A., Paul, J.M., Thomas, D.E., Karim, F.: High level cache simulation for heterogeneous multiprocessors. In: Proceedings of the 41st Annual Design Automation Conference, pp. 287–292. ACM (2004)

29. Pouchet, L.N.: Polybench: the polyhedral benchmark suite (2012). http://www.cs.ucla.edu/pouchet/software/polybench

30. Puzak, T.R.: Analysis of cache replacement-algorithms (1985)

31. Schuff, D.L., Kulkarni, M., Pai, V.S.: Accelerating multicore reuse distance analysis with sampling and parallelization. In: Proceedings of the 19th International Conference on Parallel Architectures and Compilation Techniques, PACT 2010, pp. 53–64. ACM, New York (2010). https://doi.org/10.1145/1854273.1854286

32. Sugumar, R.A., Abraham, S.G.: Set-associative cache simulation using generalized binomial trees. ACM Trans. Comput. Syst. (TOCS) $13(1)$, 32–56 (1995)

33. Sugumar, R.A.: Multi-configuration simulation algorithms for the evaluation of computer architecture designs (1993)

34. Uhlig, R.A., Mudge, T.N.: Trace-driven memory simulation: a survey. ACM Comput. Surv. (CSUR) $29(2)$, 128–170 (1997)

35. Verdoolaege, S.: isl: an integer set library for the polyhedral model. In: Fukuda, K., Hoeven, J., Joswig, M., Takayama, N. (eds.) ICMS 2010. LNCS, vol. 6327, pp. 299–302. Springer, Heidelberg (2010). https://doi.org/10.1007/978-3-642-15582-6_49

36. Verdoolaege, S., Grosser, T.: Polyhedral extraction tool. In: Second International Workshop on Polyhedral Compilation Techniques (IMPACT 2012), Paris, France (2012)

37. Wan, H., Gao, X., Long, X., Wang, Z.: GCSim: a GPU-based trace-driven simulator for multi-level cache. In: Dou, Y., Gruber, R., Joller, J.M. (eds.) APPT 2009. LNCS, vol. 5737, pp. 177–190. Springer, Heidelberg (2009). https://doi.org/10. 1007/978-3-642-03644-6_14
38. Wu, M.J., Yeung, D.: Efficient reuse distance analysis of multicore scaling for loop-based parallel programs. ACM Trans. Comput. Syst. 31(1), 1:1–1:37 (2013). https://doi.org/10.1145/2427631.2427632
39. Wu, Y., Muntz, R.: Stack evaluation of arbitrary set-associative multiprocessor caches. IEEE Trans. Parallel Distrib. Syst. 6(9), 930–942 (1995)
40. Zhang, B., et al.: Trust from the past: Bayesian personalized ranking based link prediction in knowledge graphs. In: SDM Workshop on Mining Networks and Graphs (MNG 2016) (2016)
41. Zhang, B., Dundar, M., Hasan, M.A.: Bayesian non-exhaustive classification a case study: online name disambiguation using temporal record streams. In: CIKM 2016 Proceedings of the 25th ACM International Conference on Information and Knowledge Management, pp. 1341–1350. ACM (2016)
42. Zhang, B., Dundar, M., Hasan, M.A.: Bayesian non-exhaustive classification for active online name disambiguation. arXiv preprint arXiv:1708.04531 (2017)
43. Zhang, B., Hasan, M.A.: Name disambiguation in anonymized graphs using network embedding. In: The 26th ACM International Conference on Information and Knowledge Management (CIKM 2017) (2017)
44. Zhang, B., Mohammed, N., Dave, V., Hasan, M.A.: Feature selection for classification under anonymity constraint. Trans. Data Priv. 10, 1–25 (2017)
45. Zhang, B., Saha, T.K., Al Hasan, M.: Name disambiguation from link data in a collaboration graph. In: 2014 IEEE/ACM International Conference on Advances in Social Networks Analysis and Mining (ASONAM), pp. 81–84. IEEE (2014)

ADLER: Adaptive Sampling for Precise Monitoring

Arnamoy Bhattacharyya[✉] and Cristiana Amza

Department of Electrical and Computer Engineering, University of Toronto,
Toronto, Canada
{arnamoyb,amza}@ece.utoronto.ca

Abstract. In this paper, we present ADLER, a tool for profiling applications using a sampling frequency that is tuned at program runtime. ADLER can not only determine the adaptive sampling rate for any application, but also can instrument the code for profiling so that different parts of the application can be sampled at different frequencies. The frequencies are selected to provide enough information without collecting redundant data. ADLER uses performance models of program *kernels* and prepare the kernels for sampling according to their complexity classes. We also show an example use case of real-time anomaly detection, where using ADLER's execution models, the anomalies can be detected 23% quicker than static sampling.

1 Introduction

Application sampling is widely used for a number of scenarios: (1) application phase detection [15], (2) anomaly detection [5] (3) improving energy efficiency [13]. Choosing an appropriate sampling frequency to correctly capture the behaviour of an application is quite important. Choosing a high frequency may give rise to redundant data thus incurring unnecessary storage and analysis overhead, while sampling at a low frequency may fail to capture enough information. Moreover, different applications have parts of code that show different execution behaviour. Therefore, setting a static sampling frequency is not the right choice for correctly capturing the behaviour of an entire application.

Correctly capturing data though application profiling at an optimal sampling frequency is also necessary for other use cases, for example, anomaly detection in the cloud [5]. In large-scale cloud systems like Cassandra, HBase, stateful components are expected to be many, and failures are expected to be the rule rather than the exception; for example, one hardware failure per data center, per day is commonly reported. Moreover, the necessary maintenance activities for monitoring, diagnosis, inspection or repair can no longer be handled through frequent human intervention. New approaches that predict the resource consumption of cloud applications [1] and provide automatic solutions for anomaly detection are more applicable today. For fast and effective anomaly identification in real time, an adaptive strategy for monitoring application execution and resource usage

© Springer Nature Switzerland AG 2019
L. Rauchwerger (Ed.): LCPC 2017, LNCS 11403, pp. 86–100, 2019.
https://doi.org/10.1007/978-3-030-35225-7_7

is very important. Adaptive sampling provides a balance between the storage overhead of the profiled data and the processing time of the profiled data to detect anomalies.

In this paper we propose a compiler based tool called ADLER (ADaptive sampLER) that instruments the application for adaptive sampling. ADLER takes application bytecode and different input configurations. It then builds performance models for program kernels and cluster them according to their performance complexity classes. The output from ADLER is application code that is instrumented to set the sampling frequency on the fly as the application runs with a particular input. We show the effectiveness of ADLER in reducing the storage overhead from a high static sampling frequency sampling while still keeping enough information to correctly identify anomalies. We present results for a wide range of database server applications written in multiple programming languages. We show that ADLER is able to efficiently switch the sampling frequency at minimum performance penalty. We also show the effectiveness of adaptive sampling an example use case of real-time performance anomaly identification in database servers running in the cloud.

2 Motivational Experiment

In this section, we provide a motivational experiment to show that a proper sampling frequency is necessary for correctly capturing a program's runtime behaviour. For this experiment, we set up an Hbase server. We monitor the CPU utilization of the HBase process running the Yahoo! Cloud Serving Benchmark (YCSB) [5] workload over time.

Figure 1 shows the CPU utilization of a HBase server when the YCSB workload is run on it. The sampling frequency for the CPU utilization is set at 300 HZ. There is a *busy* phase when the workload is run in the server. Also before the beginning and at the end of the service, there are *setup* and *cleanup* phases that the application uses to set up and clean up tables for running the workload.

In Figs. 1(c) and (d) we introduce a disk anomaly during the setup phase (at around time 51 in Fig. 1(c)). This anomaly can be detected using a real-time anomaly detection technique using sampled data about resources [5].

Figures 1(b) and (d) show the same scenario but with a lower frequency of sampling (50 Hz). Here the CPU utilization patterns with and without the presence of an anomaly are not clearly distinguishable due to the sparse collection, therefore, the anomaly is not detected.

The motivational experiment clearly shows the necessity of a good choice of sampling frequency for understanding the behaviour of servers running in the cloud. The sampled data can not only be used for resource anomaly detection, but also for debugging the code, phase analysis, application optimization, VM migration decisions [9].

The sampling frequency should not be very high as well, because that may give rise to a lot of redundant data that incurs both storage and analysis complexity overhead. Therefore, a technique of adaptive sampling, where the frequency

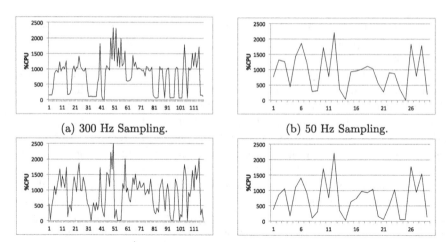

(a) 300 Hz Sampling.   (b) 50 Hz Sampling.

(c) 300 Hz Sampling with anomaly intro- (d) 50 Hz Sampling with anomaly introduced.   duced.

Fig. 1. Motivational Experiment with different sampling frequencies for a HBase server serving a YCSB workload. A higher sampling frequency captures more information, helping in Anomaly detection (at around time 51), but a lower sampling frequency, though can save space, fails to detect the same anomaly.

changes depending on the overall application structure is necessary. In the next section, we provide our methodology for adaptive sampling that can correctly capture the behavior of applications without incurring too much storage and analysis overhead.

3   A New Method for Adaptive Sampling

In this section, we provide a detailed description of our adaptive sampling technique. Our methodology consists of two main steps:

- Estimate a sampling frequency based on the execution time models of program *kernels*.
- Modify the sampling frequency on the fly according to the complexities of the *kernels* during the program execution for a given input.

3.1   Execution Time Modeling

The first step of the adaptive sampling methodology is to build precise performance models of *kernels*. An execution time model of a program *kernel* is a function that can estimate the execution time of a kernel based on the program inputs. We provide the definition of kernels and describe how we generate execution time models of those kernels below.

Program Kernels. We identify *loops* and *functions* in the program as program *kernels*. We represent the performance M of a program through the execution time models m of n *kernels*:

$$M = \{m_1, m_2, \ldots, m_n\} \tag{1}$$

We define the execution time model m of each kernel as a linear regression function of a set of *predictors* $p = \{p_1, p_2, \ldots, p_p\}$.

$$m = \sum_{i=1}^{|p|} \alpha_i \cdot p_i + \beta \text{ where } p_i \in p \tag{2}$$

A predictor p_i is a function of one or more program input parameters ι. If there are r input parameters that influence the performance of a *kernel*, the predictor set is formed by applying a set of transformations $\tau_1, \tau_2, \ldots \tau_v$ on those input parameters.

$$p = \{\bigcup_v \bigcup_r \tau_v(\iota_r)\} \tag{3}$$

Values of Model Parameters. The first task is to assemble a list of all input parameters that significantly influence the runtime of the application. We call such parameters *critical (input) parameters*.

Critical parameters should be scalar values such as sizes of dimensions, number of iterations or the percentage of reads and writes during a workload. If the execution time of the program is determined by an input file or a vector, then it should be condensed into the smallest number of scalar critical parameters (e.g., if the input file is a sparse matrix, the critical parameter could be the number of non-zero elements in the matrix). A domain expert has to determine the complete set of parameters and supply them. We identify the set of parameters as $P = (p_1, p_2, \ldots, p_n)$.

Model Fitting. We use an empirical method to determine the execution time model of the kernel in terms of its input parameters. In constructing models to predict performance and put locations into clusters, we make use of "least-squares linear regression and power law regression". Regression selects model parameters that minimize some measure of error. We use the LASSO statistical method proposed by Bhattacharyya et al. [6] to determine the execution time model of the kernel. Following this approach, the *predictors* are formed by applying powers and logarithm transformations on program inputs. The search space of *predictors* is constructed from program input parameters using the following normal form:

$$p = \{\iota_i^k \log^l \iota_i^k, \ k, l \in \mathbb{R}, \ \iota_i \in I\} \tag{4}$$

Here I represents the set of program input parameters. By assigning different values to k and l, the predictor set is constructed from the input parameters.

An example model from EPMNF for program input parameters ι_1 and ι_2 would be $c_1 \cdot \iota_1^2 + c_2 \cdot \iota_2 \log \iota_2$, where c_1 and c_2 are constants.

We generate execution time models for each *calling context* of a kernel. We define a calling context of a kernel following the Loop Call Graph (LCG) [4] of the program as following:

Definition 3.1 *A context C of a kernel is defined as the set of nodes of the LCG that are visited during a particular instance of execution.*

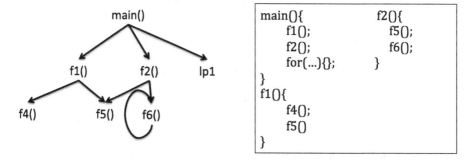

Fig. 2. Sample code with corresponding LCG.

Figure 2 shows a sample code and its corresponding LCG. According to our definition of context, the LCG will have the following contexts.

1. main → f1
2. main → f1 → f4
3. main → f1 → f5
4. main → f2
5. main → f2 → f5
6. main → f2 → f6
7. main → lp1

While profiling the kernels for the construction of execution time models, we model each calling context separately. Therefore, at the end of the execution time modeling step, we have one execution time model per kernel per calling context. It is possible for a kernel to have multiple execution time models due to execution from different calling contexts.

Measure of Fit. As our method for constructing execution time model is based on empirical method, the constructed model sometimes does not reflect the theoretical exact execution time model. Therefore, we need to measure the goodness of fit of the constructed model so that it can be effective utilized to tune the sampling rate in the following step. For measuring the goodness of fit of the constructed model, we use the adjusted R^2 (cite pemogen) statistic, a measure of the model's goodness-of-fit that quantifies the fraction of the variance in execution time accounted for by a least-squares linear regression on the inputs:

The adjusted R-square (ARS) of the predictions by the model is calculated on the test data:

$$R^2 \equiv 1 - \frac{\sum_{i=1}^{x} (y_i - f_i)^2}{\sum_{i=1}^{x} (y_i - \bar{y})^2} \tag{5}$$

$$ARS = R^2 - (1 - R^2)\frac{m}{x - m - 1} \tag{6}$$

Where x and m are the test data batch size and number of parameters respectively.

3.2 Adaptive Sampling

After we generate the execution time models for all the kernels in the program, we have to set execution points in the loop call graph of the program where we want to switch the sampling frequency. If we switch the sampling frequency for the execution of each kernel in each context, the overhead from sampling will be too high, resulting in a high drop in application throughput. Therefore, in this section we provide a novel approach for adaptive sampling based on complexity classes of the kernels at various calling contexts.

Complexity Classes. We cluster the execution time models of kernels as the following four main classes. This clustering of kernels helps to modify the sampling frequency switching to keep the sampling frequency switching at a minimum. Since the sampling frequency switching requires communication between the program and the sampler, a frequency switch at the beginning of execution of each kernel will produce too much runtime overhead.

1. Logarithmic Class: The kernels belonging to the logarithmic class have the following normal form of the execution time model.

$$p = \{\sum \log^l \iota_i, \ l \in \mathbb{R}, \ \iota_i \in I\} \tag{7}$$

2. Linear Class: The kernels belonging to the linear class has the following normal form of the execution time model.

$$p = \{\sum \iota_i^k, \ k \in \{1\} \ \iota_i \in I\} \tag{8}$$

3. Polynomial Class: The kernels in the polynomial class has the following normal form:

$$p = \{\iota_i^k \log^l \iota_i^k, \ k \in \{2, 3\}, l \in \mathbb{R}, \ \iota_i \in I\} \tag{9}$$

It is important to note that we consider two kernels with execution time models $O(n^2)$ and $O(n^2 * \log n)$ to be in the same complexity class because their asymptotic behaviour is roughly the same.

4. Unknown Class: All kernels whose execution time models do not achieve a good fit for the training data, belong to a Unknown complexity class. We consider a value of 0.95 for the ARS a good fit.

Grouping of Kernels. Once we have identified all the different complexity classes of the kernels, we instrument the code to prepare it for adaptive sampling. The instrumentation prepares the code to communicate with the sampling tool to modify the sampling frequency on the fly during application deployment. Our goal in this grouping step is to minimize the communication between the application and the sampling tool, while still collecting enough information through sampling to capture the complete behaviour of the application.

To group the kernels, we use two information:

- The complexity class of the kernel.
- The calling context of the kernel in the LCG.

Our grouping algorithm starts from the leaves of the LCG. For each leaf of the LCG, we also check the calling context of the kernel to determine its *level*. The instrumentation adds codes for either setting the sampling for the respective kernels. The result of the instrumentation is to produce a code that after adaptive sampling, will generate the same number of data points for each kernel at each calling context level. This means that a kernel with a higher execution time will need a lower sampling frequency while a kernel with a smaller execution time will be in need of a higher sampling frequency. The setting of sampling frequency uses both the static structure and the runtime information about the kernels.

During static check, all the kernels belonging to the same complexity class is sampled against the same frequency. Therefore, code for switching is added only once for these kernels of the same group. But if two kernels belong to different complexity classes (where the input parameters in the execution time model are different), we take a look at the execution time trends of the kernels obtained during the execution time model generation. If the trend shows that the kernels do not differ from each other by more that 5% in their execution time for the different input parameter values, we do not switch the sampling frequency during the kernels switch. The number 5%, according to our experiments, provides the sweet spot between the number of sampling switches and the quality of the collected data.

The static analysis begins with kernels at the deepest calling context level (the highest number of nodes in the calling context). It processes the leaf kernels at the same level of the LCG. Once the leaves at the lowest level have been processed, the analysis moves one level up and applies the same clustering strategy. Once the processing of all the leaves at all calling context levels is done, our instrumentation for the code necessary for frequency switching per context is complete.

Setting the Sampling Frequency. Once the instrumentation of the switching of sampling frequency is done, the setting of actual sampling frequency is done during the program execution as this is input specific.

At runtime, the switching code first calculates the predicted execution time of a kernel at a particular calling context based on the values of input parameters during that particular run. After calculating the execution time, based on the given number of data points necessary for capturing the program behaviour, the frequency is set. The required number of samples per kernel per calling context can be set by the analyst and that is a compromise between the resource one has vs. the amount of information one wants to collect about the program behaviour. For the kernels with *Unknown* execution time models, the execution time is conservatively predicted to be the minimum of all the execution times of that kernel during training and the sampling frequency is set according to that.

Example. In this section we give a complete example of sampling frequency switching using our kernel grouping heuristics. Listing 1.1 shows a sample code and Fig. 3 shows the corresponding LCG for the code. Figure 3 is also annotated with the execution time models of the relevant of the LCG.

Listing 1.1. Example code for Adaptive Sampling.

```
main(){
        f1();
        //non-kernel code
        for(...){
          f6();
        } //lp2
        //non-kernel code
        for(...){} //lp3
}
f1(){
        f4();
        //non-kernel code
        for(...){} //lp1
        //non-kernel code
        f5();
}
```

We first start our instrumentation for all the leaves in the LCG of the program. In the given LCG, there are five leaves: (1) f4() (2) loop1 (lp1) (3) f5() (4) f6() and (5) loop3 (lp3). As a first step, we have to identify all the leaves that belong to the same calling context. We can see from the graph that the three leaves (f4(), lp1 and f5()) belong to the same calling context which is main() → f1(). Therefore, first we process them. Here let us assume that during the execution time model generation with different input parameter values, the execution time trends of f4() and lp1 do not vary by more than 5%. Therefore, according to our heuristics, even though they have different input parameter values in their respective execution time models, they belong to the same linear

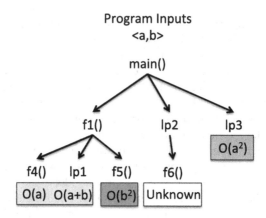

Fig. 3. Loop Call Graph and their respective sampling groups for the code in Listing 1.

complexity class. As a result, we do not have to switch sampling frequency during the kernel switch. But f5() belongs to a different (quadratic) complexity class. When the code switches from the execution of kernel lp1 to f5() we perform a sampling frequency switch.

Next we process the next leaf node of the graph that is f6(). This node alone belongs to the calling context main() → lp2. Therefore, this kernel is instrumented with its own sampling frequency code. As the kernel belongs to a Unknown complexity class, the sampling frequency will be set according to the smallest execution time of this kernel during the execution time model generation phase.

Once we finish processing of all the leaf kernels at the deepest level, we move one level up and process the leaf kernel lp3. lp3 has the calling context main() and it is the only kernel belonging to this context. Therefore, it will be instrumented with the sampling frequency according to the predicted execution time for the given input at runtime. Listing 1.2 shows the instrumented code with our adaptive sampling method.

Listing 1.2. Instrumented for Adaptive Sampling.

```
main(){
        f1();
        //non-kernel code
        for(...){
          predict_and_setfreq(f6);
          f6();
         } //lp2
        //non-kernel code
        predict_and_setfreq(lp3);
        for(...){} //lp3
}
f1(){
        predict_and_setfreq(f4);
```

```
    f4();
    //non-kernel code
    for(...){} //lp1
    //non-kernel code
    predict_and_setfreq(f5);
    f5();
}
```

4 Implementation

In this section we provide details about the implementation of our tool ADLER. As seen in Fig. 4, the tool is composed of three components.

1. **Execution time model Generator:** The execution time model generation engine of ADLER has all the capabilities built for generating the execution time models of the kernels in the program.
2. **Adaptive Sampler:** The adaptive sampler engine of ADLER takes the execution time models generated by the execution time model generator engine and then instruments the original code for adaptive sampling.
3. **Compiler Analysis:** The compiler component of ADLER has two compilers that support intermediate languages: (1) LLVM for C/C++ and (2) Soot [16] for Java. The execution time model generator and the adaptive sampler components both are connected to this component.

ADLER takes as input source code files and produces an instrumented version of the source code ready for adaptive sampling. If the source code is not available, ADLER can work with intermediate representations of the code as well. For the intermediate representation of C and C++ programs, we use the LLVM's intermediate language. The LLVM compiler is widely used by programming language research these days the intermediate representation of the code gives the flexibility to work across microarchitectures.

Similar to C/C++ applications, for Java ADLER supports both source code files and class/ jar files that are essentially intermediate representation of source code in the Java language.

The analyst supplies the source code files, the language of analysis and the values and names of the input parameters for the given code. ADLER first performs static analysis of the source code and instruments the source code for execution time model construction. This produces an instrumented version of the source code, which, when run by the user with different input parameter values, produces profile files with timing information per run.

Next, the profile files are fed back into the execution time model generator component of ADLER to learn the execution time models of the kernels inside the code. The execution time models of the kernels are written to files by the model generator engine.

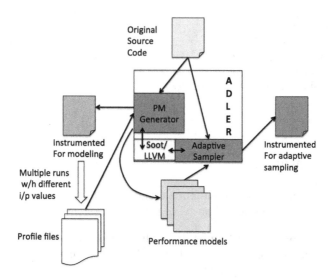

Fig. 4. Different components of ADLER and the complete workflow.

In the next step, the adaptive sampler engine of ADLER uses the execution time models learned at the previous step to perform instrumentation for preparing the code for adaptive sampling. The instrumentation in this step does not go on top of the previous instrumentation because our tool buffers the original code.

5 Experimental Evaluation

In this section, we present the effectiveness of adaptive sampling using ADLER for a number of popular cloud database servers written in both C/C+ and Java. Though our method for adaptive sampling is versatile and can be used in any use case where sampling needs to be performed, we focus our use case on real time resource anomaly detection on the cloud. We choose the YCSB [1] workloads for running on the cloud servers. The various parameters of the YCSB workloads give us different input values to train the execution time models of kernels. We first present the study on the kernel characteristics of the servers and how adaptive sampling is effective in grouping the kernels based on their complexity classes. Then we present a detailed study on an anomaly detection use case.

5.1 Execution Time Modeling

In this section, we present the results from the execution time modeling engine of ADLER. We report the total number of kernels in each of the databases we use for experiments and their complexity classes. We also report how many sampling frequency switching points are created by ADLER to show the effectiveness of

Table 1. The total number of kernels and their complexity classes for the codebases of our experiments.

Codebase	Language	# kernels	Log	Linear	Polynomial	Unknown	# Switching
Hbase-1.1.0	Java	488953	45	488529	279	100	2536
Cassandra-3.0	Java	133331	44	133141	89	57	4789
Elasticsearch-2.3.3	Java	134581	10	134416	90	65	2987
MongoDB-3.0.14	C/C++	298822	12	298735	45	30	546
ArangoDB-4.3.61	C++	1539	30	1473	20	16	656
Memcached-1.4.37	C	120	3	108	6	3	54

the grouping strategy. We run each database with 100 different input parameter combinations, each for 10 times.

As seen from Table 1, most of the kernels can be correctly classified into complexity classes, with a few unknowns. Also most kernels belong to a linear complexity class for the databases. We see in the last column of Table 1, that the number of switching points introduced by ADLER is relatively low, which shows the effective clustering of the kernels in these applications. Grouping a large number of kernels in a smaller number of clusters also indicate the existence of recurrent phases in applications that have a significant number of kernels with similar complexity classes.

5.2 Case Study: Anomaly Detection

In this section we show an example use case of ADLER in case of anomaly detection. We use the execution time models to detect the anomaly during program runtime. Our anomaly detection technique closely relates to the method proposed by Bhattacharyya et a. [5] in the sense that we annotate raw resource usage data with semantic information (with the kernels). But unlike them, we use the predicted execution time from the execution time models and compare against the actual execution time during a program run of kernels for detecting anomalies.

For building the execution time models, we use 10 different configurations of YCSB workload for a total of 1000 runs. Then for testing the accuracy of anomaly detection, we use the *systemtap* tool to simulate a faulty disk anomaly. During the execution of a YCSB workload on Cassandra, we inject a delay of 50 s each in 50% of the reads and 50% of the writes to disk coming from the database. We keep injecting the delay for a period of 10 s.

Table 2 shows the methods from Cassandra that represent the workload processing phase. The actual and predicted execution times for a *normal* run and the actual execution time of an *anomalous* run are also shown. It is clearly seen that by comparing the predicted execution time with the actual execution time at runtime, the anomaly can be detected.

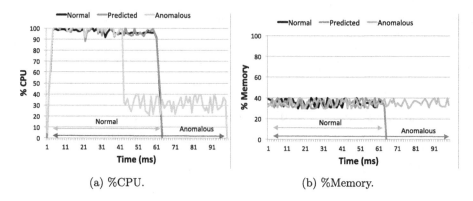

(a) %CPU.   (b) %Memory.

Fig. 5. The CPU and Memory consumption by the kernel org.apache.cassandra.io.util. ByteBufferOutputStream.write() for normal and anomalous runs for Cassandra.

Table 2. Predicted and actual execution times for Cassandra kernels for anomalous runs. Pred is Predicted execution time and Anom is Anomalous run.

Kernel	Normal	Pred	Anom
org.apache.cassandra.io.util.ByteBufferOutputStream.write()	150 ms	160 ms	300 ms
org.apache.cassandra.utils.PureJavaCrc32.update()	52 ms	60 ms	150 ms
org.apache.cassandra.io.util.ChecksummedOutputStream.write()	100 ms	95 ms	234 ms

Root-Cause Analysis. With our adaptive sampling methodology, we are able to perform a root cause analysis of the anomaly by correlating the monitored usage of different resources. Figure 5 shows the CPU and memory utilization of one of the Cassandra kernels (`org.apache.cassandra.io.util. ByteBufferOutputStream.write()`) during the normal and anomalous runs.

To learn the characteristics of normal runs, we use the method described by Bhattacharyya et al. [5]. By looking at the figure, it can be seen that there is not much change in the memory utilization for the disk fault anomaly but in CPU utilization, there is a noticeable difference. By correlating the resource utilization data with the execution time difference, we can identify this anomaly type. For a different anomaly e.g. memory leak, the difference in the memory usage pattern between a normal and anomalous run will become more significant.

Adaptive sampling can help in root cause analysis by reducing the analysis complexity of the amount of collected data. In an online setting, this is crucial. Using ADLER, we are able to perform the root cause analysis for the anomaly 23% faster after the end of the busy phase. Also, at a lower sampling frequency (e.g. the default sampling frequency of *gprof*), due to the lack of enough data points, the anomaly root cause analysis cannot be performed.

6 Related Work

Symantec i3 for J2EE [8] is a commercial tool that features the ability to adaptively instrument Java applications based on the application response time. Rish et al. [14] describe a technique, called active probing. Kumar et al. [10] apply transformations to the instrumentation code to reduce the number of instrumentation points executed as well the cost of instrumentation probes and payload. A technique to switch between instrumented and non-instrumented code is described by Arnold and Ryder [2]. Munawar and Ward [12] argue that a monitoring system should continuously assess current conditions by observing the most relevant data, it must promptly detect anomalies and it should help to identify the root-causes of problems. The magpie [3] and the Pinpoint [7] are also two well-known projects of the field. Magalhaes et al. [11] provides an approach for adaptive profiling and probably the closest to our work. But in contrary to them, our approach is not application and workload specific and it is not turned on only when anomaly is detected.

7 Conclusion

In this paper we present a tool for adaptive sampling – ADLER. ADLER can prepare applications that can self-adapt sampling frequencies on the fly based on the application input. We show an use case of ADLER in anomaly detection for web servers running on the cloud. Compared to a static sampling at high frequency, ADLER can improve the delay in anomaly root-cause analysis by 23%, making it very effective in real-time anomaly detection. ADLER can be used for any use case where sampling is necessary.

References

1. Yahoo Cloud Service Benchmarks. https://research.yahoo.com/news/yahoo-cloud-serving-benchmark/
2. Arnold, M., Ryder, B.G.: A framework for reducing the cost of instrumented code. ACM SIGPLAN Not. **36**(5), 168–179 (2001)
3. Barham, P., Donnelly, A., Isaacs, R., Mortier, R.: Using magpie for request extraction and workload modelling. In: OSDI, vol. 4, p. 18 (2004)
4. Bhattacharyya, A., Hoefler, T.: Pemogen: automatic adaptive performance modeling during program runtime. In: 2014 23rd International Conference on Parallel Architecture and Compilation Techniques (PACT), pp. 393–404. IEEE (2014)
5. Bhattacharyya, A., Jandaghi, S.A.J., Sotiriadis, S., Amza, C.: Semantic aware online detection of resource anomalies on the cloud. In: 2016 IEEE International Conference on Cloud Computing Technology and Science (CloudCom), pp. 134–143. IEEE (2016)
6. Bhattacharyya, A., Kwasniewski, G., Hoefler, T.: Using compiler techniques to improve automatic performance modeling. In: 2015 International Conference on Parallel Architecture and Compilation (PACT), pp. 468–479. IEEE (2015)
7. Chen, M.Y., Kiciman, E., Fratkin, E., Fox, A., Brewer, E.: Pinpoint: problem determination in large, dynamic internet services. In: Null, p. 595. IEEE (2002)

8. Symantec Corporation: Symantec i3 for J2EE - performance management for the J2EE platform
9. Jandaghi, S.J., Bhattacharyya, A., Sotiriadis, S., Amza, C.: Consolidation of under-utilized virtual machines to reduce total power usage. In: Proceedings of the 26th Annual International Conference on Computer Science and Software Engineering, pp. 128–137. IBM Corp. (2016)
10. Kumar, N., Childers, B.R., Soffa, M.L.: Low overhead program monitoring and profiling. ACM SIGSOFT Softw. Eng. Notes **31**(1), 28–34 (2006)
11. Magalhaes, J.P., Silva, L.M.: Adaptive profiling for root-cause analysis of performance anomalies in web-based applications. In: 2011 10th IEEE International Symposium on Network Computing and Applications (NCA), pp. 171–178. IEEE (2011)
12. Munawar, M.A., Ward, P.: Adaptive monitoring in enterprise software systems. SysML, June 2006
13. Padmanabha, S., Lukefahr, A., Das, R., Mahlke, S.: Trace based phase prediction for tightly-coupled heterogeneous cores. In: Proceedings of the 46th Annual IEEE/ACM International Symposium on Microarchitecture, pp. 445–456. ACM (2013)
14. Rish, I., et al.: Adaptive diagnosis in distributed systems. IEEE Trans. Neural Netw. **16**(5), 1088–1109 (2005)
15. Sherwood, T., Perelman, E., Hamerly, G., Sair, S., Calder, B.: Discovering and exploiting program phases. IEEE Micro **23**(6), 84–93 (2003)
16. Vallée-Rai, R., Co, P., Gagnon, E., Hendren, L., Lam, P., Sundaresan, V.: Soot: a java bytecode optimization framework. In: CASCON First Decade High Impact Papers, pp. 214–224. IBM Corp. (2010)

How Low Can You Go?

Henry Dietz[✉]

University of Kentucky, Lexington, KY 40506, USA
hankd@engr.uky.edu,
http://aggregate.org/hankd

Abstract. It could be said that much of the evolution of computers has been the quest to make use of the exponentially-growing amount of on-chip circuitry that Moore predicted in 1965 – a trend that many now claim is coming to an end [1]. Whether that rate slows or not, it is no longer the driver; there is already more circuitry than can be continuously powered. The immediate future of parallel language and compiler technology should be less about finding and using parallelism and more about maximizing the return on investment of power.

Programming language constructs generally operate on data words, and so does most compiler analysis and transformation. However, individual word-level operations often harbor pointless, yet power hungry, lower-level operations. This paper suggests that parallel compilers should not only be identifying and manipulating massive parallelism, but that the analysis and transformations should go all the way down to the bit or gate level with the goal of maximizing parallel throughput per unit of power consumed. Several different ways in which compiler analysis can go lower than word-level are discussed.

Keywords: Precision · Accuracy · Bit-slice · Logic optimization

1   A Word About Words

Throughout the history of computers, programming systems have taken a multitude of different approaches: procedural, declarative, functional, ... However, in nearly all cases, typed data objects are treated as indivisible entities. A REAL in Fortran is a thing; it may be operated upon, but whatever happens to it happens to it as a whole unit. In lower-level languages like C, machine words can be dressed as abstract data types, but they retain all the properties of machine words. This paper suggests it is time for compiler technology to start looking inside basic word-level data and operations.

There are two different ways that sub-word analysis can be approached. The following section discusses methods by which words may be segmented into smaller words or fields to avoid processing meaningless bits. The section following that describes full bit-level analysis and optimization to remove unnecessary power use at the gate level.

© Springer Nature Switzerland AG 2019
L. Rauchwerger (Ed.): LCPC 2017, LNCS 11403, pp. 101–108, 2019.
https://doi.org/10.1007/978-3-030-35225-7_8

2   Not All the Bits, Not All the Time

In languages and compilers for parallel computing, the focus has largely been on utilizing as much parallelism as the hardware provides, with the expectation that the maximum speedup will be obtained. At Thinking Machines in the 1980s, the mantra was "all the wires all the time" – and this notion of keeping all the hardware busy all the time certainly predates the 1980s and has persisted. However, it is now practical to have far more circuitry on a chip than can be continuously powered. The implication is that languages and compilers must become more careful about not wasting power on unnecessary computation.

Whenever a programmer writes code manipulating numeric data, they will likely consider if the values are known to always be integers, and most often will declare the variable as `int` if so, and `double` otherwise. Even the `unsigned int` type is rarely used, which is strange given that array index values are normally non-negative. Accepting these sloppy type declarations implies extra work – and extra power consumption – for processing what are essentially useless bits.

2.1   Integer Range Analysis

In most modern programming languages, an integer is implemented by hardware operating on a word with at least 32 bits. In code you have written, does each integer really have values spanning the complete range of 32-bit integer values, from –2,147,483,648 to 2,147,483,647? Of course not.

For example, if an integer `int i;` is used to index an array declared as `double a[1000];`, it is fairly clear that i should be in the range 0..999. That range spans fewer than 1024 values, which means it fits within 10 bits. So, what happens to the other 22 bits of the 32-bit integer? The answer is everything – even though the result is to store the same 22-bit zero value that was already there into i's top bits. If the 10-bit value was treated as a 16-bit value, instead of 32-bit, less than half as much ALU and datapath circuitry would *need* to be active.

Originally, the C programming language did not specify how many bits were used to represent an `int` – it merely stated that an `int` was "an integer, typically reflecting the natural size of integers on the host machine" and listed as examples 16 bits for a DEC PDP-11, 36 bits for Honeywell 6000, and 32 bits for IBM 370 and Interdata 8/32 [2]. However, this made many programs non-portable between machines. To improve portability, programmers used macros to define portable names for declaring types of various common sizes, which eventually led to standards like `int32_t` meaning a 32-bit integer in C++. Ironically, the original C language includes a fully general syntax for specifying the exact number of bits in an integer, but the syntax was only allowed for fields of a `struct`. For example, `struct { int:5 a; unsigned:1 b; } ab;` specifies that `ab.a` is a 5-bit signed integer and `ab.b` is 1-bit unsigned integer.

Certainly, it makes sense for programming languages to allow specification of the number of bits in each value. However, there is even ambiguity in such a specification: does `int:5` mean "5-bit integer" or "integer of at least 5 bits"? As bitfield specifications, C treated the specification as the exact number of bits rather than a minimum, but arguably it would often be useful, for example, to store a 5-bit integer in an 8-bit byte to meet memory access alignment constraints.

From a compilation point of view, the key is not just tracking the size of data objects, but using analysis to determine the set of active bits. Thus, the loop index variable declared as `int i;` could be automatically transformed by compiler analysis into something like `unsigned i:10;`. The necessary compiler value range analysis has long been known and used to perform loop unrolling/unraveling, improve efficiency of array bounds checking, and support dependence analysis... and it was used to infer types of variables as early as the mid-1960s [3]! The suggestion of the current work is simply that this type of analysis of value range be used both to adjust the declared size and type (e.g., signed vs. unsigned), and also to restrict operations to cover the active bits within that value's storage representation. Reusing the loop index example, even if `i` is stored as `int i:32;`, it is perfectly valid to operate only on the bottom 16 (or 10) bits in code where the top bits are known to be unaffected.

2.2 Floating-Point Accuracy, Not Precision

While tracking the size of integers is straightforward, the logically equivalent analysis for floating-point values is significantly more complex.

Operations on floating-point representations are inherently imprecise. The whole concept of floating-point is based on using an approximate representation of values to allow greater dynamic range with fewer bits. New hardware supports several floating-point precisions with huge performance benefits in use of lower precisions while remaining in the same power budget. Peak performance of the AMD RADEON INSTINCT MI25 GPU [4] is 768 GFLOPS 64-bit, 12.3 TFLOPS 32-bit, and 24.6 TFLOPS 16-bit – a factor of 32X faster using the lowest precision instead of 64-bit `double`.

According to IEEE 754 [5], the larger exponent field of 64-bit `double` gives it greater dynamic range than a 32-bit `float`, but lack of dynamic range is rarely why `double` is specified. The 24-bit mantissa of a `float` is accurate enough to express nearly any physical measurement for input or output. However, it is difficult to analyze the accuracy resulting from errors compounded while performing an arbitrary computation; the 53-bit mantissa of a `double` is treated as having so many *guard bits* that the programmer is comfortable accepting the results as accurate. This is a false security; not only is efficiency sacrificed, but when `float` is insufficient, `double` often also fails to deliver accurate results [6].

Rather than requiring the programmer to specify the precision, perhaps needed accuracy should be specified, and the compiler tasked with picking the appropriate precision. Unfortunately, compile-time analysis of accuracy bounds is inherently conservative, disturbingly often revealing that even `double` arithmetic is insufficient to guarantee an acceptably accurate result for worst-case input data, although lower precisions might suffice for every dataset actually used. Most programming languages also lack syntax for specifying accuracy. Both these problems can be resolved by adding a language construct (or pragma) that allows a user-specified accuracy acceptance test [6], which can be used to speculatively perform each computation at the minimum feasible precision, automatically repeating the computation at higher precision if necessary.

There is yet another advantage to specifying accuracy rather than precision for floating-point values: the values do not need to be represented using floating-point at all! For example, it may be advantageous to use LNS (logarithmic number system) [7] or to map the computation into scaled integer arithmetic. IEEE floating-point formats are primarily portable data exchange representations.

2.3   Smaller Data Fits

A consequence of the transformations discussed above for both integer and floating-point data is that lower precision values can fit in a smaller memory footprint. That principle holds true whether the memory is DRAM used for main memory or SRAM registers in a processing element. Reducing memory footprint reduces power by implying transmission of fewer bits, and can result in far greater power savings if the smaller data can more often reside in a higher level of the memory hierarchy.

Originally, the concept of SWAR (SIMD within a register) [8] was primarily to obtain modest speedups by packing a vector of smaller data objects into each register and performing SIMD-parallel operations on the packed data. Nearly all processors provide support for such packing, most in the form of SWAR instructions as seen in Intel AVX [9] or ARM NEON [10], but also in the form of "Advanced Vector Extensions" in RISC-V [11]. Operations on packed data significantly reduce power consumption while facilitating parallel execution.

For non-SIMD non-vector code, this packing requires compiler tracking of the occupancy of portions of registers, not just complete registers. A 64-bit register might hold four 16-bit values, and the lifetimes of those values may be different; thus, it is possible that a fraction of the register might be free for reuse while other parts are occupied by live values. Early work attempting to create SWAR register packings was called common subexpression induction [12], and the tracking of partial liveness was mentioned, but the analysis was never fully developed. Perhaps it is now time? There is no need to restrict layout analysis to registers; similar benefits can be obtained packing cache lines.

3   From Bits to Words, and Back Again

In 1958, the vacuum-tube-based EDSAC 2 computer [13] used the innovative trick of bit-slicing: implementing word-level instructions by executing microcoded sequences of operations on a smaller number of bits at a time. This approach was very widely adopted throughout the 1970s; for example, the AMD Am2900-series bipolar logic chips [14] provided 4-bit slice components that were used in a wide variety of computers including various DEC PDP-11 models and the UCSD Pascal P-machine processor. Use of bit-slicing greatly simplified the hardware, lowering cost at the expense of serial execution speed. By the 1980s, circuitry was cheap enough for most computers to operate on full words at a time, with word size slowly increasing from 8, to 16, to 32, and finally to 64 bits.

Massively-parallel computers have largely followed the same pattern. Fewer gates per processing element meant more parallelism, hence greater speedup, so many parallel supercomputers reduced circuitry per processing element by slicing. The ICL Distributed Array Processor (DAP) [15], STARAN [16], Goodyear Massively Parallel Processor (MPP) [17], Thinking Machines CM and CM2 [18], and NCR GAPP [19] sliced at the single-bit level; the somewhat-later MasPar MP-1 [20] was built using 4-bit slices. As 32-bit microprocessors became cost effective, and especially with the birth of Linux PC cluster supercomputing in 1994, massively-parallel computers began to migrate to processing elements that operate on a word at a time. Now, even GPUs with thousands of processing elements on a single chip operate on at least 32-bit words.

The point is that word-parallel hardware was about speeding up serial operations on word data at the cost of higher circuit complexity per unit performance. For example, a 32-bit adder needs additional logic (e.g., implementing carry lookahead) to perform one 32-bit add as fast as 32 one-bit adders can each perform 1/32 of a 32-bit add. This difference has become critical in the power-limited world. As a result, I believe we are now in the early days of a rebirth in bit-level massively-parallel processing. This brings at least two new challenges for optimizing, parallelizing, compiler technology.

3.1 True Bit-Level Optimization

Mapping of word-level algorithms into optimized bit-level implementations must be addressed. Earlier bit-sliced systems generally did not do this; they would use a generic microcode subroutine to handle each word-level operator rather than optimizing at the bit level. An early example of true bit-level optimization is the BitC language and compiler [21]. For example, BitC generates 3,040 gate operations for an 8-bit multiply, but just 64 for 8-bit squaring.

The new bit-level targets are not just conventional gates, but include FPGAs and reconfigurable logic, adiabatic circuits, quantum logic, etc. For example, TrueNorth [22] is fundamentally a massively parallel bit-serial machine with a somewhat unusual gate structure; although there is some compiler infrastructure for mapping neural networks to it, there is no fundamental reason why parallel algorithms in general could not be transformed to target it (in fact, watching the TrueNorth videos, I have flashbacks of Danny Hillis talking about the interconnections between processors in the connection machine [18]).

3.2 Whole Program Scale Gate Optimization

Thus far, very little optimizing compiler work has attacked the problem of optimizing programs at what might be called the circuit model level. There are lots of gate-level circuit optimization tools, especially for SOP (sum of products) form using AND, OR, and NOT gates with arbitrary many inputs (e.g., Espresso [23]), but these tools are ill-suited to processing logic representing complete programs.

Optimizing more realistic hardware designs also using XOR gates, or using only a single, fixed number of inputs, universal gate such as NAND, NOR, or MUX (1-of-2 multiplexor), is also an unsolved problem. Genetic algorithms and other machine learning techniques can help.

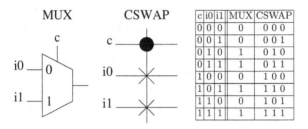

c	i0	i1	MUX	CSWAP
0	0	0	0	0 0 0
0	0	1	0	0 0 1
0	1	0	1	0 1 0
0	1	1	1	0 1 1
1	0	0	0	1 0 0
1	0	1	1	1 1 0
1	1	0	0	1 0 1
1	1	1	1	1 1 1

Fig. 1. MUX and CSWAP (Fredkin) gates and logic functions

In addition, a variety of new types of gates have been created for adiabatic and quantum computation. One of the more promising is the Fredkin, or CSWAP (conditional swap), gate. As Fig. 1 shows, CSWAP is essentially a MUX with an extra output, so it is obviously universal, but has the interesting property that the number of 1 bits entering and leaving is preserved, making it particularly suitable for adiabatic (thermodynamically reversible, very low power) implementation. A quantum CSWAP implementation was reported last year [24]. Thus, converting programs into CSWAP logic could be a path to very low power consumption and high performance. A key complication is that CSWAP gates do not allow fanout; minimizing the number of *ancilla* "garbage" wires added to copy signals while conserving the number of 1s is a non-trivial design problem.

4   Conclusion

Parallel languages and compilers had mostly been about the large. This paper suggests it is time to be looking at very large numbers of very small, low-level, details – many intricately intertwining compiler technology and architecture.

We have been slowly moving in the directions discussed in this paper for over two decades [6,12,21]. Earlier this year, we made a significant advance toward targeting various bit-level architectures, especially those involving adiabatic or quantum logic: a compiler that converts a program written in a subset of C directly into a full custom gate-level hardware design [25]. This compiler first performs conventional analysis and various optimizations, then inserts explicit manipulation of a state variable to implement control flow. Each word-level value is then decomposed into a vector of bit-level operation DAGs computing the individual bits, and the bit-level code for all basic blocks in the program is optimized as a single combinatorial logic circuit. The resulting circuit can be output in any of a variety of forms, including as a combinatorial Verilog module that implements the C code when fed a series of clock pulses. Of course, this compiler is just a crude proof of concept; there is still a long way to go.

References

1. Fletcher, S.: Computing after Moore's Law. Scientific American, 1 May 2015. https://www.scientificamerican.com/article/moores-law-computing-after-moores-law/
2. Kernighan, B.W., Ritchie, D.M.: The C Programming Language. Prentice Hall, Upper Saddle River (1978). ISBN 0-13-110163-3
3. Klerer, M., May, J.: Two-dimensional programming. In: Proceedings of the 30 November–1 December 1965, Fall Joint Computer Conference, Part I, pp. 63–75 (1965)
4. AMD: Radeon Instinct MI25. http://instinct.radeon.com/_downloads/radeon-instinct-mi25-datasheet-15.6.17.pdf. Accessed July 2017
5. IEEE: IEEE Standard for Binary Floating Point Arithmetic Std 754–1985 (1985)
6. Dietz, H., Dieter, B., Fisher, R., Chang, K.: Floating-point computation with just enough accuracy. In: Alexandrov, V.N., van Albada, G.D., Sloot, P.M.A., Dongarra, J. (eds.) ICCS 2006. LNCS, vol. 3991, pp. 226–233. Springer, Heidelberg (2006). https://doi.org/10.1007/11758501_34
7. Chugh, M., Parhami, B.: Logarithmic arithmetic as an alternative to floating-point: a review. In: 2013 Asilomar Conference on Signals, Systems and Computers, pp. 1139–1143 (2013)
8. Fisher, R.J., Dietz, H.G.: Compiling for SIMD within a register. In: Chatterjee, S., Prins, J.F., Carter, L., Ferrante, J., Li, Z., Sehr, D., Yew, P.-C. (eds.) LCPC 1998. LNCS, vol. 1656, pp. 290–305. Springer, Heidelberg (1999). https://doi.org/10.1007/3-540-48319-5_19. ISBN 978-3-540-48319-9
9. Lento, G.: Optimizing Performance with Intel Advanced Vector Extensions. Intel White Paper, September 2014
10. ARM: NEON. https://developer.arm.com/technologies/neon. Accessed July 2017
11. Waterman, A., Asanovic, K. (eds.): The RISC-V instruction set manual, volume 1: user-level ISA, Document Version 2.2. RISC-V Foundation, May 2017
12. Dietz, H.: Common subexpression induction. Technical report, TR-EE 92–5. School of Electrical Engineering, Purdue University, January 1992
13. Wilkes, M.V.: EDSAC 2. IEEE Ann. Hist. Comput. **14**(4), 49–56 (1992). ISSN 1058-6180
14. Advanced Micro Devices: The Am 2900 Family Data Book With Related Support Circuits. Advanced Micro Devices (1979)
15. Reddaway, S.F.: DAP - a distributed array processor. In: Proceedings of the 1st Annual Symposium on Computer Architecture, pp. 61–65, ACM Press (1973)
16. Batcher, K.E.: STARAN parallel processor system hardware. In: National Computer Conference, pp. 405–410 (1974)
17. Batcher, K.: Design of a massively parallel processor. IEEE Trans. Comput. **C–29**(9), 836–840 (1980)
18. Tucker, L.W., Robertson, G.G.: Architecture and applications of the connection machine. IEEE Comput. **21**(8), 26–38 (1988)
19. Morely, R.E., Sullivan, T.J.: A massively parallel systolic array processor system. In: Proceedings of the International Conference on Systolic Arrays, pp. 217–225 (1988)
20. Blank, T.: The MasPar MP-1 architecture. In: Thirty-Fifth IEEE Computer Society International Conference, Compcon, pp. 20–24 (1990)

21. Dietz, H.G., Arcot, S.D., Gorantla, S.: Much ado about almost nothing: compilation for nanocontrollers. In: Rauchwerger, L. (ed.) LCPC 2003. LNCS, vol. 2958, pp. 466–480. Springer, Heidelberg (2004). https://doi.org/10.1007/978-3-540-24644-2_30

22. Sawada, J., et al.: TrueNorth ecosystem for brain-inspired computing: scalable systems, software, and applications. In: IEEE/ACM SC16: International Conference for High Performance Computing, Networking, Storage and Analysis, pp. 130–141 (2016)

23. Brayton, R.K., Sangiovanni-Vincentelli, A.L., McMullen, C.T., Hachtel, G.D.: Logic Minimization Algorithms for VLSI Synthesis. Kluwer Academic Publishers, Dordrecht (1984). ISBN 0898381649

24. Patel, R.B., Ho, J., Ferreyrol, F., Ralph, T.C., Pryde, G.J.: A quantum Fredkin gate. Sci. Adv. **2**(3) (2016)

25. Dietz, H.G.: Spring 2017 EE599-006/EE699-007 optimizing compilers, "hardly software" class project. Electrical and Computer Engineering Department, University of Kentucky, 5 May 2017

Memory-Access-Pattern Analysis Techniques for OpenCL Kernels

Gangwon Jo[✉], Jaehoon Jung, Jiyoung Park, and Jaejin Lee

Center for Manycore Programming, Department of Computer Science
and Engineering, Seoul National University, Seoul 08826, Korea
{gangwon,jaehoon,jiyoung}@aces.snu.ac.kr, jaejin@snu.ac.kr,
http://aces.snu.ac.kr

Abstract. Previous pattern-by-pattern approaches for OpenCL/CUDA memory optimization require explicit user interventions to extract the kernel memory access patterns. This paper presents an automatic memory-access-pattern analysis framework called MAPA. It is based on a source-level analysis technique derived from traditional symbolic analyses and a run-time pattern selection technique. We propose formal notations of the memory access patterns, analysis algorithms based on the SSA form, and the integration method of MAPA with auto-tuners. The experimental results indicate that MAPA properly analyzes 116 real-world OpenCL kernels from Rodinia and Parboil benchmark suites. We also show an auto-tuner case study, Auto-Dymaxion, which exploits MAPA to automate a memory-access-pattern-based optimization approach.

1 Introduction

Despite of a great success of heterogeneous computing in the last decade [6,10, 11,17,20,26], efficiently exploiting accelerators remains a difficult, tedious, and error-prone task. A naïve OpenCL or CUDA program usually fails to achieve expected performance gain compared to the original sequential program even though the theoretical performance of an accelerator (*e.g.*, a GPU) is better than that of a CPU. One of the main reasons for not achieving the gain is the access overhead of off-chip memory that is shared by thousands of threads. To overcome this problem, the programmer has to apply well-known manual optimization techniques [1,18,23] by exploiting memory coalescing, vectorization, on-chip SRAM, and texture units of GPUs on a case-by-case basis.

This work was supported by the National Research Foundation of Korea (NRF) grant funded by the Ministry of Science and ICT (MSIT) (No. 2013R1A3A2003664), PF Class Heterogeneous High Performance Computer Development through the NRF funded by the MSIT (No. 2016M3C4A7952587), and BK21 Plus for Pioneers in Innovative Computing (Dept. of Computer Science and Engineering, SNU) through the NRF funded by the Ministry of Education (21A20151113068). ICT at Seoul National University provided research facilities for this study.

© Springer Nature Switzerland AG 2019
L. Rauchwerger (Ed.): LCPC 2017, LNCS 11403, pp. 109–126, 2019.
https://doi.org/10.1007/978-3-030-35225-7_9

1.1 Problems of Previous Approaches

There have been many proposals that use compiler and runtime techniques to overcome aforementioned problems. Particularly, some of them rely on memory access patterns of GPU kernels [4,8,25]. They decide which specific optimization technique (*e.g.*, code transformation and data movement) needs to be applied to a kernel by observing its memory access patterns on a case-by-case basis. Since most of memory accesses made in a typical GPU kernel have simple and regular patterns such as affine accesses and scatter/gather, such pattern-by-pattern approaches are adequate for GPU applications and may outperform a single, generic technique. Here are some examples:

- *Data reordering.* Dymaxion [8] reorganizes the layout of data stored in the off-chip memory to coalesce memory accesses. It classifies non-coalesced memory accesses into four patterns (row2col, diagonal, indirect, and arrstruct) and applies a different transformation to each of the patterns.
- *Data prefetching.* CudaDMA [3,4] reduces the memory access latency of a kernel by prefetching data from the off-chip memory to the on-chip SRAM. It supports three prefetching algorithms associated with sequential, strided, and indirect memory access patterns [3].
- *Workload and data distribution.* MAPS-Multi [25] automatically distributes the workload and data assigned to a single virtual GPU across multiple actual GPUs based on memory access patterns of kernels (eight patterns for input data and five patterns for output data).

However, all these techniques cannot automatically detect the memory access patterns. No prior studies address this issue seriously because no (open-source) automatic framework for OpenCL/CUDA applications has been proposed so far. Instead, developers are forced to explicitly annotate the memory access patterns in their code using language extensions and/or API functions. Consequently, many existing applications written in pure OpenCL or CUDA cannot benefit from the existing pattern-by-pattern approaches.

1.2 Proposed Techniques

The goal of this paper is to bridge the missing link between the previous pattern-by-pattern techniques and real-world OpenCL applications, and to encourage many future studies to adopt pattern-by-pattern-based methods.

We present a framework called *MAPA* that automatically determines and extracts memory access patterns of a kernel. MAPA is based on an observation that the architecture of widely used accelerators and programming model lead kernels to have characteristics that are beneficial to automating memory-access-pattern analyses. It relies on both a source-level compiler analysis technique derived from traditional symbolic analyses for parallelizing compilers [13,27] and run-time information (*e.g.*, kernel arguments). The current implementation of MAPA only supports OpenCL, but it can be easily extended to support CUDA and other heterogeneous programming models.

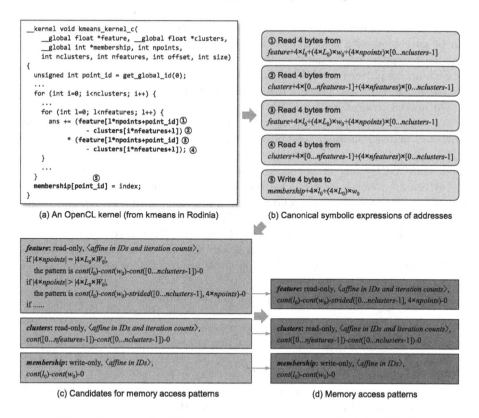

```
__kernel void kmeans_kernel_c(
    __global float *feature, __global float *clusters,
    __global int *membership, int npoints,
    int nclusters, int nfeatures, int offset, int size)
{
    unsigned int point_id = get_global_id(0);
    ...
    for (int i=0; i<nclusters; i++) {
        ...
        for (int l=0; l<nfeatures; l++) {
            ans += (feature[l*npoints+point_id] ①
                   - clusters[i*nfeatures+l]) ②
                   * (feature[l*npoints+point_id] ③
                   - clusters[i*nfeatures+l]); ④
        }
        ...
    }              ⑤
    membership[point_id] = index;
}
```

① Read 4 bytes from
$feature+4 \times l_0+(4 \times L_0) \times w_0+(4 \times npoints) \times [0...nclusters-1]$

② Read 4 bytes from
$clusters+4 \times [0...nfeatures-1]+(4 \times nfeatures) \times [0...nclusters-1]$

③ Read 4 bytes from
$feature+4 \times l_0+(4 \times L_0) \times w_0+(4 \times npoints) \times [0...nclusters-1]$

④ Read 4 bytes from
$clusters+4 \times [0...nfeatures-1]+(4 \times nfeatures) \times [0...nclusters-1]$

⑤ Write 4 bytes to
$membership+4 \times l_0+(4 \times L_0) \times w_0$

(a) An OpenCL kernel (from kmeans in Rodinia)　　　　(b) Canonical symbolic expressions of addresses

feature: read-only, ⟨*affine in IDs and iteration counts*⟩,
if $|4 \times npoints| = |4 \times L_0 \times W_0|$,
　　the pattern is $cont(l_0)\text{-}cont(w_0)\text{-}cont([0...nclusters-1])\text{-}0$
if $|4 \times npoints| > |4 \times L_0 \times W_0|$,
　　the pattern is $cont(l_0)\text{-}cont(w_0)\text{-}strided([0...nclusters-1], 4 \times npoints)\text{-}0$
if ......

feature: read-only, ⟨*affine in IDs and iteration counts*⟩,
$cont(l_0)\text{-}cont(w_0)\text{-}strided([0...nclusters-1], 4 \times npoints)\text{-}0$

clusters: read-only, ⟨*affine in IDs and iteration counts*⟩,
$cont([0...nfeatures-1])\text{-}cont([0...nclusters-1])\text{-}0$

clusters: read-only, ⟨*affine in IDs and iteration counts*⟩,
$cont([0...nfeatures-1])\text{-}cont([0...nclusters-1])\text{-}0$

membership: write-only, ⟨*affine in IDs*⟩,
$cont(l_0)\text{-}cont(w_0)\text{-}0$

membership: write-only, ⟨*affine in IDs*⟩,
$cont(l_0)\text{-}cont(w_0)\text{-}0$

(c) Candidates for memory access patterns　　　　(d) Memory access patterns

Fig. 1. An example of the memory access pattern analysis by MAPA.

Figure 1 shows a brief outline of how an OpenCL kernel is analyzed by MAPA and what its output is. Note that all notations in Fig. 1 will be explained in detail in Sect. 3. The kernel shown in Fig. 1(a) is from the kmeans in the Rodinia benchmark suite [7]. The kernel accesses three OpenCL buffers (*i.e.*, memory objects such as arrays), feature, clusters, and membership. The MAPA's source-level analyzer first identifies all memory accesses in the kernel. There are four reads and one write in Fig. 1(a). It converts the address of each access into a *canonical symbolic expression* as shown in Fig. 1(b). Then, it aggregates all addresses that belong to the same buffer together. For example, two reads ① and ③ belong to feature in Fig. 1(a), and their addresses in Fig. 1(b) are aggregated together in Fig. 1(c) under feature. Using this information, it determines the access pattern of each buffer. The memory access patterns extracted by the source-level analyzer is shown in Fig. 1(c).

When a read or write address is calculated from parameters of a kernel, the access pattern of the kernel *may* vary depending on the actual arguments given at run time. In this case, the MAPA's source-level analyzer generates all possible candidates for the access pattern (*e.g.*, feature in Fig. 1(c)). Then, the MAPA's pattern selector chooses one of the candidates immediately after the kernel arguments are set at run time, as shown in Fig. 1(d). This mechanism can be combined with a memory-access-pattern-based optimizer. For example, a kernel compiler may generate multiple optimized versions of the kernel, one for each access pattern candidate. Then, the runtime system can select a proper version at run time and execute it on the accelerator.

Optimizing compilers for CPU applications usually adopt the polyhedral model [5,12,19] to represent array references within a loop in a mathematical form (*i.e.*, access relations). The polyhedral model formulates data dependences in a loop, and its scope is restricted to *affine* array references. On the other hand, since GPUs rely on a relaxed memory consistency model, the pattern-by-pattern approaches for GPU applications do not concern about data dependences between threads inside a GPU kernel. Instead, they target a wider range of memory access patterns (*e.g.*, gather and scatter A[B[i]]).

Some prior studies [14,16,21] assume OpenCL/CUDA kernels contain only affine access patterns. This assumption is not true for many real-world benchmark applications, and MAPA may help these approaches to distinguish affine memory accesses from the others.

The major contributions of the paper are the following:

- We introduce an automatic memory-access-pattern analysis framework, called MAPA. It relies on two new ideas – a simple SSA-form-based analysis technique derived from traditional symbolic analyses and a run-time pattern selection technique.
- We propose formal internal representations of memory access patterns of OpenCL kernels. Previous approaches describe the target memory access patterns in an informal, verbose way.
- We evaluate the effectiveness of MAPA with a set of applications from Rodinia [7] and Parboil [24] benchmark suites. About 60% of the buffers are properly analyzed by MAPA. The result is wide enough to replace previous manual approaches because the 60% cover most of the memory access patterns used in the previous approaches. We also discuss how to improve MAPA to handle the remaining 40%.
- As a case study, we implement a MAPA-based auto-tuner called *Auto-Dymaxion*. It automates the data reordering techniques of Dymaxion [8].

2   Background and Observations

In this section, we briefly describe OpenCL and discuss some OpenCL kernel characteristics that are beneficial to automatic symbolic analyses.

2.1   OpenCL Platform and Execution Model

An OpenCL application consists of a *host program* and a set of *kernels*. A host program is written in a typical high-level programming language, such as C and C++. Kernels are written in OpenCL C derived from C99 with some extensions and restrictions. The host program runs on a CPU and issues a kernel execution command to an *OpenCL device* (*e.g.*, a GPU or an Intel Xeon Phi coprocessor). Then, many instances of the kernel execute on the device. An instance of the kernel execution is called a *work-item*.

The CPU and OpenCL device do not share an address space. Instead, an OpenCL device has its own *device memory*. The host program allocates a *buffer* in the device memory, and issues a memory command to the device to copy data between the main memory and a buffer. A buffer is a contiguous chunk of the device memory.

When the host program issues a kernel execution command, pointers to buffers and scalar values can be passed as arguments to the kernel. For example, the kernel in Fig. 1(a) receives three buffer pointers and five scalar values from the host program. All kernel instances have the same argument values. The address of a buffer in the device memory is managed by the OpenCL runtime and is not exposed to the host program. The host program obtains only a handle to the buffer object from the runtime.

The host program defines an N-dimensional index space ($1 \leq N \leq 3$) to specify how many work-items are created. Work-items are organized into *work-groups*. Each work-group in the index space is assigned to a *compute unit* (a streaming multiprocessor in CUDA), and work-items in the work-group are executed concurrently on *processing elements* (a scalar processor in CUDA) in the compute unit.

Each work-item has a unique *global ID* that is the index of the corresponding point in the index space and represented by an N-tuple with each dimension starting from 0. Similarly, each work-group has a unique *work-group ID*, and each work-item has a unique *local ID* within a work-group. Although all work-items execute the same kernel code, they can access different data and perform different tasks depending on their global ID, local ID, and work-group ID.

Let G_i be the size of the index space in dimension i ($0 \leq i < 3$). We treat all index spaces as if they were three-dimensional. When the space is one dimensional, the sizes in dimension 1 and 2 are ones. Similarly, when the space is two dimensional, the size in dimension 2 is one. The same thing applies to work-groups. Then, the total number of work-items in the index space is $\prod_{i=0}^{2} G_i$. Similarly, let L_i and W_i be the size of a work-group (*i.e.*, the number of work-items) and the number of work-groups in dimension i, respectively. Then,

$$G_i = L_i \times W_i \tag{1}$$

Let the global ID, the local ID, and the corresponding work-group ID of a work-item be (g_0, g_1, g_2), (l_0, l_1, l_2), and (w_0, w_1, w_2), respectively. Then,

$$g_i = L_i \times w_i + l_i \tag{2}$$

2.2   Observations

MAPA is based on the observation that the OpenCL platform model and the architecture of widely used accelerators (especially GPUs) lead OpenCL kernels to have some beneficial characteristics that make memory-access-pattern analyses much easier and more practical.

Specifically, an OpenCL device has a separated memory address space. The host program does not know the layout of the device memory. Thus, all values in a buffer stored by the host program can never be pointers to the device memory. The only pointers passed to a kernel are buffer pointers in the parameters. Buffer handles passed by the host to the kernel become buffer pointers at run time.

Moreover, programmers usually try to minimize the number of branches in an OpenCL kernel because branch divergence may significantly degrade the performance on GPUs. It is also very rare that a pointer points to different buffers depending on the control flow. Thus, it is not unnatural to assume that each pointer points to at most one buffer. Consequently, a conservative simple control-flow-insensitive analysis technique works well with OpenCL kernels rather than sophisticated but complicated analysis techniques [22].

MAPA's buffer-by-buffer analysis technique is facilitated by the fact that an OpenCL buffer typically contains a single data structure (*e.g.*, a matrix), and memory access patterns largely depend on data structures used. Finally, OpenCL does not allow using function pointers in kernels. Thus, MAPA can always determine the target of each function call.

3   Notations for Memory Access Patterns

In this section, we describe the categories of memory access patterns handled by MAPA and their notations.

3.1   Categories of Memory Access Patterns

We classify access patterns of an OpenCL buffer, say M_A, into ten categories that are listed below in the preferred order. That is, if more than one of the categories are matched, MAPA chooses the one that appears first in the list. We say a memory location is *affine in variables* if the location is determined by an affine function of the variables.

- ⟨*constant*⟩: All work-items in the index space access the same element(s) of M_A.
- ⟨*affine in IDs*⟩: Every work-item accesses exactly one element of M_A potentially more than once. The location is affine in local IDs and/or work-group IDs.
- ⟨*affine in IDs and iteration counts*⟩: Each loop iteration of a work-item accesses exactly one elements of M_A. The location is affine in local IDs, work-group IDs, and/or iteration counts.
- ⟨*set of offsets + affine in IDs*⟩: Each work-item accesses multiple elements of M_A. However, all of the elements have the same base address, and only constant offsets differ (*e.g.*, A[i], A[i+1], and A[i+2]). The base address is affine in local IDs and/or work-group IDs.
- ⟨*set of offsets + affine in IDs and iteration counts*⟩: Each loop iteration of a work-item accesses multiple elements of M_A. The elements have the same base address and different constant offsets. The base address is affine in local IDs, work-group IDs, and/or iteration counts.

- $\langle$*indirect , affine in IDs*$\rangle$: Each work-item accesses exactly one element of M_A using an element of another read-only buffer M_B as the index (*e.g.*, `A[B[...]]`). The location of the index is affine in local IDs and/or work-group IDs. This pattern corresponds to the access pattern of scatter or gather operations.
- $\langle$*indirect, affine in IDs and iteration counts*$\rangle$: Each loop iteration of a work-item accesses exactly one element of M_A using an element of another read-only buffer M_B as the index. The location of the index is affine in local IDs, work-group IDs, and/or iteration counts.
- $\langle$*contiguous in a work-item*$\rangle$: Every work-item accesses all elements in a contiguous region of M_A. However, the exact location of the region is not analyzable. This pattern is frequently used in important applications, such as graph traversals and sparse matrix operations.
- $\langle$*indirect, contiguous in a work-item*$\rangle$: Every work-item accesses elements of M_A using all elements in a contiguous region of another read-only buffer M_B as the indices. The exact locations of the indices are not analyzable.
- $\langle$*complex*$\rangle$: The access pattern of M_A does not match any of the above categories.

Table 1. Pattern categories of MAPA and previous manual approaches.

MAPA	Dymaxion [8]	CudaDMA [4]	MAPS-Multi [25]
$\langle$*constant*$\rangle$			reductive
$\langle$*affine in IDs*$\rangle$	row2col, diagonal		block, reductive, structured injective
$\langle$*affine in IDs and iter.*$\rangle$	row2col	sequential, strided	block
$\langle$*set of offsets + affine in IDs*$\rangle$	arrstruct, diagonal		window, structured injective
$\langle$*set of offsets + affine in IDs and iter.*$\rangle$	arrstruct	sequential, strided	window
$\langle$*indirect, affine in IDs*$\rangle$	indirect		
$\langle$*indirect, affine in IDs and iter.*$\rangle$	indirect	indirect	
$\langle$*contiguous in a work-item*$\rangle$			adjacency
$\langle$*indirect, contiguous in a work-item*$\rangle$			adjacency
$\langle$*complex*$\rangle$			traversal, permutation, unstructured injective, irregular

Table 1 compares the categories automatically analyzable by MAPA and those manually analyzed by previous approaches. Three access patterns of MAPS-Multi [25] (*i.e.*, traversal, permutation, and unstructured injective) are not analyzable by MAPA. However, these patterns are used in only a limited number of applications (*e.g.*, FFT).

3.2 Normal Form of Affine Functions

Six of the ten categories are related to affine functions. They contain a variety of sub-patterns depending on the value of coefficients in its associated affine function. To denote a memory access pattern more precisely, we make a category name followed by a notation for the associated affine function. This notation is called a *normal form* of the affine function. It emphasizes features of the affine function on which the memory-access-pattern-based techniques usually focus.

Consider an affine function $f(x_1, x_2, \cdots, x_k) = a_1 x_1 + a_2 x_2 + \cdots + a_k x_k + c$ that represents a memory access location within a buffer, where $a_i \neq 0$ and $0 \leq x_i < N_i$ for all $1 \leq i \leq k$. N_i indicates the constant upper bound of variable x_i. For example, if x_i indicates the local ID of work-items in dimension 0 (*i.e.*, l_0), N_i becomes L_0. L_0 denotes the size of a work-group in dimension 0, as described in Sect. 2.1. If x_i indicates the loop iteration count i in `for(i=0;i<100;i++)`, then N_i becomes 100. Without loss of generality, we assume $|a_i| \leq |a_{i+1}|$ for all $1 \leq i \leq k - 1$. We introduce two arbitrary values a_0 and N_0 in the following definitions. a_0 is 1, and N_0 is the width of the memory access (*e.g.*, 4 for int).

Definition 1. *An affine function is discrete if* $|a_{i-1} \times N_{i-1}| \leq |a_i|$ *for all* $1 \leq i \leq k$.

A discrete affine function is always *injective*. That is, a different point $(x_1, x_2, \cdots, x_k)$ corresponds to a different memory location. However, the inverse is not true.

Definition 2. *A variable* x_i *of a discrete affine function is contiguous if* $|a_{i-1} \times N_{i-1}| = |a_i|$. *Otherwise,* x_i *is strided by* a_i.

If x_i is contiguous, the difference between $f(\cdots, p_i, p_{i+1}, \cdots)$ and $f(\cdots, p_i+1, p_{i+1}, \cdots)$ is equal to the difference between $f(\cdots, N_{i-1}, p_{i+1}, \cdots)$ and $f(\cdots, 0, p_{i+1}, \cdots)$ (assume $a_i > 0$). Otherwise, the latter is larger than the former.

Definition 3. *The normal form of a discrete affine function* $f(x_1, x_2, \cdots, x_k)$ *is a sequence* $t_1 - t_2 - \cdots - t_k - c$, *where* t_i *is* $cont(x_i)$ *if* x_i *is contiguous, or* $strided(x_i, a_i)$ *if* x_i *is strided by* a_i. *The normal form of a non-discrete affine function* $f(x_1, x_2, \cdots, x_k)$ *is* f *itself.*

For example, consider a memory access `buf[`$l_0 + L_0 w_0 + (2L_0 W_0)w_1 + 1$`]`. Assume `buf` is an array of single-precision floating point numbers (*i.e.*, 4-byte elements). The memory location of the access is given by an affine function:

$$f(l_0, w_0, w_1) = 4 \cdot l_0 + (4L_0) \cdot w_0 + (8L_0 W_0) \cdot w_1 + 4 \tag{3}$$

This function takes three variables, l_0, w_0, and w_1. The constant upper bounds of the variables, N_1, N_2, and N_3, are L_0, W_0, and W_1, respectively. Moreover, $a_0 = 1$ and $N_0 = 4$ as mentioned above. The following is true:

$$|a_0 \times N_0| = |1 \times 4| = |a_1| \tag{4}$$

$$|a_1 \times N_1| = |4 \times L_0| = |a_2| \tag{5}$$

$$|a_2 \times N_2| = |4L_0 \times W_0| < |8L_0W_0| = |a_3| \tag{6}$$

Thus, this function is discrete, and l_0 and w_0 are contiguous (Eqs. (4) and (5)) while w_1 is strided by $8L_0W_0$ (Eq. (6)). Consequently, f can be represented by the following normal form:

$$cont(l_0) - cont(w_0) - strided(w_1, 8L_0W_0) - 4 \tag{7}$$

Table 2. Symbolic variables used in the analysis.

Variables	Description
l_0, l_1, l_2	The local ID of a work-item
w_0, w_1, w_2	The work-group ID of a work-item
L_0, L_1, L_2	The size of a work-group in each dimension
W_0, W_1, W_2	The number of work-groups in each dimension
buf_x	The kernel parameter x that stores a buffer pointer
$param_x$	The kernel parameter x that stores a scalar value
$ind(f, s)$	An induction variable that has the initial value 0, finishes with the value f, and increased by s

4   Memory Access Pattern Analysis

MAPA extracts the address of each buffer access (*e.g.*, Fig. 1(b)), and determines its memory access pattern (*e.g.*, Fig. 1(c)). If the access pattern varies according to the values passed by the host program at run time, MAPA generates all possible pattern candidates, each of which is annotated by a condition to choose the actual pattern at run time.

4.1   Internal Representation

MAPA uses the static single assignment (SSA) form [9] as its internal representation for kernels at the source level. Each scalar variable and structure field is replaced with an SSA variable unless its address is ever taken. In addition, each induction variable is replaced with a μ-function [2] (*i.e.*, a combination of an initial value, a loop bound, and an increment). All user-defined function calls in a kernel are inlined to make interprocedural analyses unnecessary.

4.2   Symbolic Analysis

MAPA performs a symbolic analysis to identify memory access patterns of each buffer. The symbolic analysis consists of two steps. First, it represents the value of each SSA variable in a symbolic expression. Then, it determines the address of each buffer access in a symbolic expression.

$$\llbracket expr \rrbracket \rightarrow \llbracket canonical\text{-}expr \rrbracket \mid \bot$$
$$\llbracket canonical\text{-}expr \rrbracket \rightarrow \llbracket buffer\text{-}address \rrbracket \mid \llbracket affine\text{-}expr \rrbracket$$
$$\llbracket buffer\text{-}address \rrbracket \rightarrow buf_x + \llbracket affine\text{-}expr \rrbracket \mid buf_x + \bot$$
$$\llbracket affine\text{-}expr \rrbracket \rightarrow \llbracket affine\text{-}term \rrbracket + \cdots + \llbracket affine\text{-}term \rrbracket$$
$$\llbracket affine\text{-}term \rrbracket \rightarrow \llbracket invariant \rrbracket \times \llbracket variant \rrbracket \mid \llbracket invariant \rrbracket$$
$$\llbracket invariant \rrbracket \rightarrow \texttt{constant} \mid param_x \mid L_i \mid W_i \mid \llbracket invariant \rrbracket \texttt{ op } \llbracket invariant \rrbracket$$
$$\llbracket variant \rrbracket \rightarrow l_i \mid w_i \mid ind(\llbracket canonical\text{-}expr \rrbracket, \llbracket invariant \rrbracket) \mid *(\llbracket buffer\text{-}address \rrbracket, \texttt{type})$$

Fig. 2. Definition of canonical symbolic expressions.

Input: V: a set of SSA variables, P: a set of kernel parameters.
Output: A: a set of buffer accesses.
1: $M \leftarrow \emptyset$
2: **for all** $x_i \in V$ **do**
3:     $M[x_i] \leftarrow \top$
4: **end for**
5: **for all** $p \in P$ **do**
6:     **if** p is a buffer pointer **then**
7:         $M[p_1] \leftarrow buf_p + 0$
8:     **else**
9:         $M[p_1] \leftarrow param_p$
10:     **end if**
11: **end for**
12: **for all** definitions $x_i = E$ for $x_i \in V$, in program order **do**
13:     $M[x_i] \leftarrow$ Canonicalize(Substitute(E, M))
14: **end for**
15:
16: $A \leftarrow \emptyset$
17: **for all** buffer accesses E that is one of $x[y]$, $*x$, or $x\text{->}f$ **do**
18:     $addr \leftarrow$ Canonicalize(Substitute($\&E$, M))
19:     $width \leftarrow$ sizeof(E)
20:     $rw \leftarrow$ one of $read$, $write$, or $read+write$
21:     $A \leftarrow A \cup \{(addr, width, rw)\}$
22: **end for**
23: **return** A

Fig. 3. The symbolic analysis algorithm.

A symbolic expression contains only variables listed in Table 2. Each symbolic variable represents a value that is determined at run time, either before or during the kernel execution. Since the work-item IDs, the size of a work-group, the number of work-groups, and the values of kernel arguments are not available at compile time, we treat them as symbolic variables. Note that the global ID of a work-item (g_i) and the size of the entire kernel index space (G_i) are not included in Table 2 because they can be represented with l_i, w_i, L_i, and W_i. In addition, an induction variable is also treated as a symbolic variable.

Since our goal is to discover regular buffer access patterns, we do not need to take all complicated symbolic expressions into account. Instead, we consider only *canonical symbolic expressions* defined in Fig. 2. If a value cannot be represented in the canonical form, it is just represented by $\bot$. $\bot$ means that the value is too complex to be analyzed by MAPA. In Fig. 2, $\llbracket invariant \rrbracket$ is an expression whose value is the same in all work-items in the index space. $\llbracket variant \rrbracket$ is an expression whose value can be different across work-items (*e.g.*, l_i and w_i) or across loop iterations within a single work-item (*e.g.*, $ind(\cdots)$). $ind(f, i)$ represents an induction variable whose final value is f and increment is i. The canonical form only contains induction variables whose final value is $[\![canonical\text{-}expr]\!]$ and increment is $[\![invariant]\!]$. All other induction variables are just ignored. $*(a, t)$ corresponds to a buffer element (*i.e.*, a value read from the device memory) whose address is a and data type is t.

The symbolic analysis algorithm implemented in MAPA is shown in Fig. 3. An associative array M maps each SSA variable x_i to its value $M[x_i]$. $\top$ indicates that the value of the variable is not yet analyzed.

The `Substitute`(E, M) function replaces all operands in E by their values represented in the canonical form. Every SSA variable x_i is substituted by $M[x_i]$, and every non-SSA variable (*e.g.*, a variable whose address is ever taken) is substituted by $\bot$. If some of the SSA variables have not been analyzed yet (*i.e.*, $M[x_i]$ is $\top$), they are also substituted by $\bot$.

The `Canonicalize`(E) function transforms E to a canonical symbolic expression or $\bot$. It traverses the abstract syntax tree of E from the leafs to the root. For each node, the corresponding canonical expression is constructed by merging the canonical expressions of the child nodes.

The result of applying the algorithm in Fig. 3 is a set of all buffer accesses in the kernel. Each buffer access is represented with its target address, data width (in bytes), and whether the access is a read (*e.g.*, $\cdots$ = `A[i]`), a write (*e.g.*, `A[i]` = $\cdots$), or both (*e.g.*, `A[i]` += $\cdots$). Our algorithm is control-flow insensitive.

4.3 Pattern Classification

Finally, MAPA identifies the memory access pattern (or multiple candidates for the pattern) of each buffer x using the result A of the symbolic analysis algorithm in Fig. 3. For example, in Fig. 1(b) and (c), the buffer `membership` is accessed by an affine function $f(l_0, w_0) = 4 \times l_0 + (4 \times L_0) \times w_0$. Since this function is definitely represented in a normal form $cont(l_0) - cont(w_0) - 0$, MAPA does not need to generate multiple candidates. On the other hand, the buffer `feature` is accessed by an affine function $f(l_0, w_0, i) = 4 \times l_0 + (4 \times L_0) \times w_0 + (4 \times npoints) \times i$, where $i = ind(nclusters - 1, 1)$. It can be represented in one of the following normal forms depending on the value of L_0, W_0, and $npoints$.

- $cont(l_0) - cont(w_0) - cont(i) - 0$ when $|npoints| = |L_0 \times W_0|$.
- $cont(l_0) - cont(w_0) - strided(i, 4 \times npoints) - 0$ when $|npoints| > |L_0 \times W_0|$.
- A non-discrete affine function when $0 < |npoints| < |L_0 \times W_0|$.
- $cont(l_0) - cont(w_0) - 0$ when $|npoints| = 0$.

Thus, MAPA generates four candidates for the pattern of `feature`, as shown in Fig. 1(c).

4.4 MAPA Framework

The MAPA framework consists of two parts: a *source-level analyzer* and a *pattern selector*. The source-level analyzer implements the compiler analysis described above, *i.e.*, it takes an OpenCL kernel source code as input and prints the memory access pattern (or multiple pattern candidates and their conditions) for each buffer. We have implemented the source-level analyzer by modifying a *clang*-based OpenCL C frontend developed by the Khronos Group [15]. The pattern selector chooses one of the pattern candidates according to the values of kernel parameters passed by the host program instance at run time, *i.e.*, it takes the kernel arguments as input and returns the selected pattern candidate.

5   Evaluation

In this section, we evaluate the effectiveness of MAPA using popular OpenCL benchmark applications.

Table 3. Benchmark applications used.

Application	LoC[a]	NoK[b]	NoBP[c]	Application	LoC	NoK	NoBP
Rodinia 3.1 [7]				Parboil 2.5 [24]			
backprop	90	2	8	bfs (base)	146	1	7
bfs	50	2	10	bfs (nvidia)	426	3	27
b+tree	220	2	15	cutcp (base)	203	1	4
cfd	284	5	19	cutcp (nvidia)	280	1	4
dwt2d	707	3	8	histo (base)	570	6	15
gaussian	49	2	5	histo (nvidia)	445	5	13
heartwall	2506	1	32	lbm (base)	422	1	2
hotspot	115	1	3	lbm (nvidia)	420	1	2
hotspot3D	50	1	3	mri-gridding (base)	601	9	25
hybridsort	341	7	23	mri-gridding (nvidia)	687	9	25
kmeans	61	2	6	mri-q (base)	288	2	9
lavaMD	393	1	4	mri-q (nvidia)	85	2	9
leukocyte	581	4	20	sad (base)	333	3	4
lud	162	3	3	sad (nvidia)	372	3	4
myocyte	1445	1	4	sgemm (base)	25	1	3
nn	21	1	2	sgemm (nvidia)	65	1	3
nw	202	2	6	spmv (base)	35	1	7
particlefilter	752	9	58	spmv (amd)	57	1	7
pathfinder	116	1	4	spmv (amd_vec)	75	1	7
srad	374	6	27	spmv (nvidia)	73	1	7
streamcluster	68	2	6	stencil (base)	40	1	2
				stencil (fermi)	52	1	2
				stencil (nvidia)	109	1	2
				tpacf (base)	206	1	3
				tpacf (nvidia)	228	1	3
Total						116	462

[a]LoC: Lines of code in OpenCL kernels.
[b] NoK: Number of kernels.
[c]NoBP: Number of buffer pointers.

We use all 116 kernels from applications in Rodinia 3.1 [7] and Parboil 2.5 [24] benchmark suites. Table 3 summarizes the applications. Some of them have multiple implementations optimized for different types of devices. For example, (nvidia) indicates a version optimized for NVIDIA GPUs. We use all applications except two versions of spmv in Parboil (tex and tex_nvidia) because they use OpenCL image objects. The last column labeled NoBP in Table 3 shows the total number of buffer pointers in the kernel parameters. In summary, we have 462 different buffer pointers to be analyzed by MAPA. Previous memory-access-pattern-based techniques are usually evaluated with a few simple applications.

Table 4 shows how the buffer pointers in Rodinia and Parboil are analyzed by MAPA. Since 13 buffer pointers are just passed to a kernel and never used, we focus on the remaining 449 buffer pointers. The result shows that 60% of the buffers are properly classified to 8 pattern categories. Other buffers are classified into ⟨complex⟩ because:

- The kernel has a buffer access whose base address is unknown. This happens only in one kernel from heartwall. Adopting a more precise pointer analysis [22] can resolve this problem.
- Some of the buffer addresses are not in the form of ⟦affine-expr⟧. Because of this reason, 25% of the buffers are classified into ⟨complex⟩. We can extend the definition of canonical symbolic expressions in Fig. 2 to overcome this problem.
- All buffer addresses are correctly analyzed by the symbolic analysis (Fig. 3), but there is no category that matches the addresses. Additional pattern categories may cover these kinds of access patterns.

The source-level analyzer generates multiple pattern candidates for a single buffer if there are more than one possible normal forms of the associated address function because of run-time parameters. Table 4 also shows how many buffers have multiple pattern candidates at compile time. Memory access patterns of 81 buffers are completely determined at run time by the pattern selector.

The result shows that MAPA can detect various memory access patterns used in the previous manual approaches (Table 1) in real-world OpenCL kernels automatically. Most of ⟨complex⟩ buffers identified by MAPA really have complicated access patterns and cannot be optimized by the previous manual techniques even though they can be detected manually. Note that the benchmark applications are highly optimized for GPUs. Thus, their memory access patterns are more complex than those of usual in-house OpenCL applications.

Table 4. Analysis result.

Pattern categories	# of buffers	Portion	#BwSP[a]	#BwMC[b]
⟨constant⟩	39	8.69%	39	–
⟨affine in IDs⟩	136	30.29%	96	40
⟨affine in IDs and iter.⟩	37	8.24%	12	25
⟨set of offsets + affine in IDs⟩	21	4.68%	14	7
⟨set of offsets + affine in IDs and iter.⟩	8	1.78%	1	7
⟨indirect, affine in IDs⟩	10	2.23%	8	2
⟨indirect, affine in IDs and iter.⟩	0	0.00%	0	0
⟨contiguous in a work-item⟩	5	1.11%	5	–
⟨indirect, contiguous in a work-item⟩	8	1.78%	8	–
Subtotal	**264**	**58.80%**	**183**	**81**
⟨complex⟩	185	41.20%		
- Stopped at Step 1 in Sect. 4.3	(34)	(7.57%)		
- Stopped at Step 2 in Sect. 4.3	(113)	(25.17%)		
- Not classified at Step 3 in Sect. 4.3	(38)	(8.46%)		
Total	**449**	**100.00%**		
(Not used in a kernel)	(13)			

[a]#BwSP: Number of buffers with a single pattern.
[b]#BwMC: Number of buffers with multiple candidates.

6   Case Study: Automatic Data Reordering

In this section, we show a case study, *Auto-Dymaxion*, which exploits MAPA to automate the memory-access-pattern analysis and perform auto-tuning with the analysis result.

As described in Sect. 1, Dymaxion [8] reorders buffer elements prior to kernel execution if the access pattern of the buffer is one of row2col, diagonal, indirect, and arrstruct. It eliminates non-coalesced memory accesses in the kernel. In addition, it overlaps data transfer between a CPU and a GPU with data reordering performed by the GPU to reduce the overhead caused by the data reordering.

Figure 4 shows how an OpenCL application is executed with Auto-Dymaxion. When a host-to-device copy command is issued, Auto-Dymaxion does not send data to the device memory immediately. Instead, it waits until a subsequent kernel execution command is arrived (①).

When a kernel execution command is issued, Auto-Dymaxion checks the buffer will be accessed by the kernel according to one of the Dymaxion's target access patterns (*i.e.*, row2col, · · · , arrstruct), using the analysis result from MAPA. For example, the MAPA pattern ⟨*indirect, affine in IDs*⟩ with a normal form of $cont(l_0) - cont(w_0) - c$ corresponds to the indirect pattern of Dymaxion. If a Dymaxion's pattern is detected, Auto-Dymaxion divides the data into multiple chunks, copies chunks to the device memory one by one (②), and executes the data reordering kernel for each chunk (③). Otherwise, Auto-Dymaxion simply copies the entire data to the device memory. Then, the kernel is executed on the

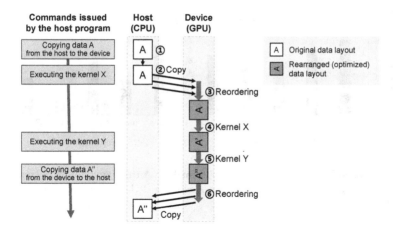

Fig. 4. Using Auto-Dymaxion.

device (④). The kernel compiler of Auto-Dymaxion replaces the index of every buffer reference in a kernel with a new (rearranged) index.

Once a buffer is stored in a rearranged form, whenever a new command is issued, Auto-Dymaxion checks whether the buffer layout should be restored or not. For example, in Fig. 4, if kernel Y has the same access pattern to the buffer A as that of kernel X, Auto-Dymaxion keeps the layout of A and executes kernel Y (⑤). On the other hand, if the subsequent kernel has a different access pattern or a device-to-host copy command is issued, Auto-Dymaxion restores the layout of the buffer immediately (⑥).

Table 5. The target system of Auto-Dymaxion.

GPU	NVIDIA GeForce GTX 480 (480 CUDA cores, 1.5 GB memory)
CPU	2× Intel Xeon X5660
Main memory	48 GB DDR3 PC3-10600
OS	CentOS 6.7
OpenCL	CUDA Toolkit 7.5
Compiler	gcc 4.4.7

At the time of Dymaxion's publication [8], it was evaluated on a NVIDIA GeForce GTX 480 GPU using four benchmark applications kmeans, nw, spmv, and nn [8]. We use the same target device and the same applications to compare the performance of Auto-Dymaxion and Dymaxion. Table 5 describes the specification of the target system.

Figure 5 shows the speedup of the four applications obtained by Auto-Dymaxion (*i.e.*, without any user intervention) over the execution time without data reordering. Auto-Dymaxion works correctly for all the applications,

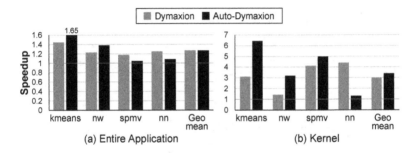

Fig. 5. (a) The speedup of applications obtained by Auto-Dymaxion and Dymaxion. (b) The speedup of the kernel functions (*i.e.* excluding PCI-E transfer and data reordering overhead).

and achieves 1.05x–1.65x. For comparison, Fig. 5 also shows the speedups from Dymaxion [8]. Auto-Dymaxion outperforms Dymaxion in kmeans and nw while it gets slower than Dymaxion in spmv and nn. The average speedup of Auto-Dymaxion is comparable to that of the manual approach (Dymaxion). Since the source code of Dymaxion is not available, we cannot analyze the reasons for speedup or slowdown.

7   Conclusions

This paper proposes MAPA, an automatic memory-access-pattern analysis framework for OpenCL applications. MAPA is based on an observation that accelerator architectures (especially GPUs) and programming models lead kernels to have characteristics that are beneficial to automating memory-access-pattern analyses. Memory access patterns in OpenCL kernels are classified into ten categories in MAPA. Some of them are further detailed by the normal form of the address functions associated to the patterns. The source-level analyzer in MAPA represents a kernel with an SSA form and determines the memory access pattern of each buffer accessed in the kernel using a symbolic analysis. If the pattern depends on a run-time parameter, the analyzer generates multiple candidates, and the pattern selector chooses the best suited one at run time. The evaluation results with 116 real-world OpenCL kernels and a case study of auto-tuners indicate that MAPA is effective enough to replace manual labor to identify the kernel memory access patterns. We plan to make the source code of MAPA publicly available.

References

1. AMD: AMD APP SDK OpenCL optimization guide (2015). http://amd-dev.wpengine.netdna-cdn.com/wordpress/media/2013/12/AMD_OpenCL_Programming_Optimization_Guide2.pdf

2. Ballance, R.A., Maccabe, A.B., Ottenstein, K.J.: The program dependence web: a representation supporting control-, data-, and demand-driven interpretation of imperative languages. In: Proceedings of the ACM SIGPLAN 1990 Conference on Programming Language Design and Implementation, pp. 257–271 (1990)
3. Bauer, M., Cook, H., Khailany, B.: CudaDMA. http://lightsighter.github.io/CudaDMA/
4. Bauer, M., Cook, H., Khailany, B.: CudaDMA: optimizing GPU memory bandwidth via warp specialization. In: Proceedings of 2011 International Conference for High Performance Computing, Networking, Storage and Analysis (2011)
5. Bondhugula, U., Hartono, A., Ramanujam, J., Sadayappan, P.: A practical automatic polyhedral parallelizer and locality optimizer. In: Proceedings of the 29th ACM SIGPLAN Conference on Programming Language Design and Implementation, pp. 101–113 (2008)
6. Brown, W.M., Wang, P., Plimpton, S.J., Tharrington, A.N.: Implementing molecular dynamics on hybrid high performance computers - short range forces. Comput. Phys. Commun. **182**(4), 898–911 (2011)
7. Che, S., et al.: Rodinia: a benchmark suite for heterogeneous computing. In: Proceedings of 2009 IEEE International Symposium on Workload Characterization, pp. 44–54 (2009)
8. Che, S., Sheaffer, J.W., Skadron, K.: Dymaxion: optimizing memory access patterns for heterogeneous systems. In: Proceedings of 2011 International Conference for High Performance Computing, Networking, Storage and Analysis (2011)
9. Cytron, R., Ferrante, J., Rosen, B.K., Wegman, M.N., Zadeck, F.K.: Efficiently computing static single assignment form and the control dependence graph. ACM Trans. Program. Lang. Syst. **13**(4), 451–490 (1991)
10. Eklund, A., Dufort, P., Forsberg, D., LaConte, S.M.: Medical image processing on the GPU - past, present and future. Med. Image Anal. **17**(8), 1073–1094 (2013)
11. Götz, A.W., Williamson, M.J., Xu, D., Poole, D., Le Grand, S., Walker, R.C.: Routine microsecond molecular dynamics simulations with AMBER on GPUs. 1. generalized born. J. Chem. Theory Comput. **8**(5), 1542–1555 (2012)
12. Grosser, T., Groesslinger, A., Lengauer, C.: Polly - performing polyhedral optimizations on a low-level intermediate representation. Parallel Process. Lett. **22**(4), 1250010 (2012)
13. Haghighat, M.R., Polychronopoulos, C.D.: Symbolic analysis for parallelizing compilers. ACM Trans. Program. Lang. Syst. **18**, 477–518 (1996)
14. Jang, B., Schaa, D., Mistry, P., Kaeli, D.: Exploiting memory access patterns to improve memory performance in data parallel architectures. IEEE Trans. Parallel Distrib. Syst. **22**(1), 105–118 (2011)
15. Khronos Group: SPIR generator/Clang. https://github.com/KhronosGroup/SPIR
16. Kim, J., Kim, H., Lee, J.H., Lee, J.: Achieving a single compute device image in OpenCL for multiple GPUs. In: Proceedings of the 16th ACM Symposium on Principles and Practice of Parallel Programming, pp. 277–288 (2011)
17. NVIDIA: cuDNN. https://developer.nvidia.com/cudnn
18. NVIDIA: CUDA C best practices guide (2015). http://docs.nvidia.com/cuda/cuda-c-best-practices-guide/
19. Pop, S., Cohen, A., Bastoul, C., Girbal, S., Silber, G.A., Vasilache, N.: GRAPHITE: polyhedral analyses and optimizations for GCC. In: Proceedings of the 2006 GCC Developers Summit (2006)
20. Schatz, M.C., Trapnell, C., Delcher, A.L., Varshney, A.: High-throughput sequence alignment using graphics processing units. BMC Bioinform. **8**(1), 1–10 (2007)

21. Seo, S., Lee, J., Jo, G., Lee, J.: Automatic OpenCL work-group size selection for multicore CPUs. In: Proceedings of the 22nd International Conference on Parallel Architectures and Compilation Techniques, pp. 387–397 (2013)
22. Steensgaard, B.: Points-to analysis in almost linear time. In: Proceedings of the 23rd ACM SIGPLAN-SIGACT Symposium on Principles of Programming Languages, pp. 32–41 (1996)
23. Stratton, J.A., et al.: Optimization and architecture effects on GPU computing workload performance. In: Proceedings of Innovative Parallel Computing (InPar) (2012)
24. Stratton, J.A., et al.: Parboil: a revised benchmark suite for scientific and commercial throughput computing. Technical report, IMPACT-12-01, IMPACT, University of Illinois at Urbana-Champaign (2012)
25. Tal, B.N., Levy, E., Barak, A., Rubin, E.: Memory access patterns: the missing piece of the multi-GPU puzzle. In: Proceedings of the International Conference for High Performance Computing, Networking, Storage and Analysis (2015)
26. Tomov, S., Dongarra, J., Baboulin, M.: Towards dense linear algebra for hybrid GPU accelerated manycore systems. Parallel Comput. **36**(5–6), 232–240 (2010)
27. Tu, P., Padua, D.: Gated SSA-based demand-driven symbolic analysis for parallelizing compilers. In: Proceedings of the 9th International Conference on Supercomputing, pp. 414–423 (1995)

Parallel Programming and Abstractions

Characterizing Performance of Imbalanced Collectives on Hybrid and Task Centric Runtimes for Two-Phase Reduction

Udayanga Wickramasinghe[1](✉) and Andrew Lumsdaine[2]

[1] Indiana University, Bloomington, IN, USA
uswickra@indiana.edu
[2] Pacific Northwest National Laboratory, Richland, USA
andrew.lumsdaine@pnnl.gov

Abstract. As clusters of multicore nodes become the standard platform for HPC, programmers are adopting approaches that combine multicore programming (e.g. OpenMP) for on-node parallelism with MPI for inter-node parallelism—the so-called "MPI+X". In important use cases, such as reductions, this hybrid approach can necessitate a scalability-limiting sequence of independent parallel operations, one for each paradigm. For example, MPI+OpenMP typically performs a global parallel reduction by first performing a local OpenMP reduction followed by an MPI reduction across the nodes. If the local reductions are not well balanced, which can happen in the case of irregular or dynamic adaptive applications, the scalability of the overall reduction operation becomes limited. In this paper, we study the impact of imbalanced reductions on two different execution models: MPI+X and Asynchronous Many Tasking (AMT), with MPI+OpenMP and HPX-5 as concrete instances of these respective models. We explore several approaches to maximizing asynchrony with the HPX-5 and MPI+OpenMP collective programming interfaces and characterize the imbalance using a specialized set of microbenchmarks. Despite maximizing MPI+OpenMP asynchrony, we find situations where scalability of the MPI+X programming model is significantly impaired for two-phase reductions. We report from 0.5X to 6.5X relative performance degradation of MPI+X in the AMT instance.

1 Introduction

The standard HPC platform today is a cluster of multicore nodes, perhaps also including some number of GPU resources. Historically, programmers have used shared-memory approaches for parallel programming of multicore machines and have used distributed-memory approaches (e.g. MPI) for programming clusters. Thus, the obvious approach for programming clusters of multicore machines is to marry the two approaches that have separately worked so well with shared and distributed memory. The general moniker for the resulting combination is "MPI+X" to reflect the fact that there is a multiplicity of shared-memory approaches but only one MPI.

© Springer Nature Switzerland AG 2019
L. Rauchwerger (Ed.): LCPC 2017, LNCS 11403, pp. 129–144, 2019.
https://doi.org/10.1007/978-3-030-35225-7_10

Of course the expectation, or at least the hope, is that the effect of MPI+X will provide the compounded benefits of each and enable scalability on today's largest machines as well as on future exascale machines. The problem with MPI+X, as has been famously noted, is in the "+".[1] That is, there are numerous problems in combining two separate parallel programming paradigms, as each carries its own interface, run-time system, and high-performance programming idioms. It is unlikely to expect independent approaches simply to compose a coherent system (programming or otherwise).

```
compute_kernel() {
  do {
    #pragma omp parallel private(val) reduction(+:sum)
    for (i = 0 ; i < C*nthreads ; i++) {
      val = work(i); //execute shared memory parallel region
      sum += val;
    }
    MPI_Allreduce(sum, global_sum, .., MPI_SUM, ... ); // allreduce SUM
  } while (time_step())
}
```

Listing 1: **General MPI+OpenMP pattern for a two-phase reduction**

In this paper we study one important use case in parallel programming, namely two-phase reduction, and we investigate the impact of the "+" in MPI+X—in our case we focus on MPI+OpenMP in particular. For example, in MPI+ OpenMP, a global parallel reduction can be performed by first performing a local OpenMP reduction, followed by an MPI reduction across the nodes (1). However, this approach imposes a serialization (albeit a coarse one) of the operations in the parallel reduction—i.e. it requires a reduction of the local variables followed by a further reduction over those intermediate values. Such a coarse serialization may not appear to be detrimental and, as the obvious approach presented by the two systems, would also seem to be the best possible approach. However, if the local reductions are not well balanced, which can happen in the case of irregular or dynamic adaptive applications, this serialization can cause problems and limit the scalability of the overall reduction operation. Any significant variation of thread arrival times at the OpenMP implicit synchronization barrier (that happens just before MPI_Allreduce in Listing 1) may cause cascading delays [1–3] across the overall operation. Additionally, such serialization constraints may reduce the amount of parallelism possible in a severely imbalanced local reduction.

One approach to ameliorating the effect of imbalance on collective operations is to make the collective operation non-blocking. This becomes problematic with a standard MPI+OpenMP approach because only the MPI collective operation is readily transformable into a non-blocking operation. That is, only the second half of the compound operation can be overlapped with other work – the local

---

[1] Quote attributed to Bill Gropp.

portion is not overlapped. However, when using more sophisticated approaches to asynchrony, an MPI+OpenMP programmer may work around this restriction.

Asynchronous Many Tasking (AMT) is an alternate approach to MPI+X for programming clusters of multicore systems. The basic paradigm of AMT is to expose and exploit maximum parallelism through large numbers of lightweight threads. In this paper we present a representative AMT system called "HPX-5" (based on the ParalleX execution model [4]) coupled with a fully asynchronous high-performance collective framework that is well suited for heavily imbalanced global reductions. We also compare and quantify the impact of imbalanced reductions on MPI+X vs AMT, with MPI+OpenMP and HPX-5 as concrete instances of these respective models.

This paper makes the following contributions:

- We analyze the problem of imbalance in two-phase reduction in detail for the MPI+X and AMT programming models. We also propose a generalized formal model that can be utilized to characterize imbalance for such configurations (Sect. 2).
- We implement a high-performance unified collective interface on a representative AMT called "HPX-5" and a portable framework to profile and instrument imbalance with various real-world load distributions into parallel regions of a distributed-memory application on MPI+OpenMP and AMT (Sect. 3).
- We empirically analyze effects of load variation (Sect. 4) on multiple runtime execution models, namely: MPI+OpenMP, MPI, and our AMT instance using a tunable collective microbenchmark.

2   Motivation

Collective communication is known to propagate and even amplify noise effects within an application life cycle. Numerous studies report the effects of external noise [1–3,5,6] on application scalability and the propagation of delays in the face of collective communication or global synchronization barriers. With MPI+X there is a necessary sequence of operations (local plus global) for realizing a single compound operation. The effect of computational irregularity becomes isomorphic to that of system noise but potentially orders of magnitude larger.

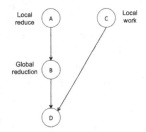

Fig. 1. General data-flow graph found in HPC

Figure 1 reports a simple but commonly found execution pattern of a two-phase reduction operation. One of the limitations of executing such a program in MPI+OpenMP is the strict ordering of the local reduction phase. The data flow graph depicts independent regions **A** and **C** (i.e. no directed edge) and regions **B** and **D** as dependent. Region **B** relies on the output of region **A** and then region **D** on both **B** and **C**. For irregular load conditions it would be especially beneficial to overlap the work of region **C** with **B**. However, the implicit synchronization barrier presents a limiting factor that makes it impossible to hide irregularities

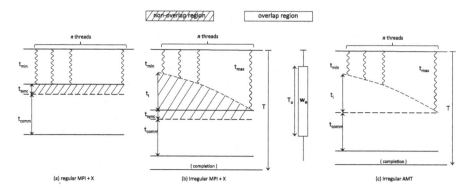

Fig. 2. Generic communication and computation models for two-phase reduction in MPI+X and AMT

in region **A**. Therefore a naive MPI+OpenMP model of programming can make it difficult to utilize available processing resources fully for applications with the aforementioned parallel data dependency characteristics.

Newer implementations of OpenMP (Version 3.0 and on) have attempted to mitigate some of these issues by embedding dynamic loop scheduling, work queues, and task parallelism techniques, e.g. by using new additions to its programming constructs like `pragma omp task`, `pragma omp sections`, and nested regions. An MPI-only approach for two-phase reduction may also use OpenMP as a thread substrate. In such cases special MPI per-threaded communicators[2] should be formed to accommodate local reductions on shared memory buffers. However, effectively controlling parallelism (task scheduling, granularity, etc.), and obscure details of performance tuning across different runtime boundaries (MPI and OpenMP) and compilers (Intel, gcc, etc.) may introduce many *performance* problems and significant discomfort for MPI+X application developers.

AMTs are the newest breed of distributed shared memory runtime systems that have had a significant influence on data-flow-driven parallel programming. We contend that AMTs provide a uniform approach to two-phase collectives even under severe imbalance. For example, due to the asynchronous nature of AMT runtimes, they can effectively overlap communication and computation of regions **A** and **B** (Fig. 1) and combine them with region **C**, thus avoiding wait time for any costly intermediate synchronization steps and thereby increasing throughput. Threads, in terms of early finishers, can compensate for late-comers by taking up any additional work while waiting for network completion.

2.1   Analysis of Two-Phase Reduction

We refer to Fig. 2 for a detailed analysis of the above problem. The leftmost diagram (in Fig. 2) shows a two-phase reduction by n threads conducted in MPI+X runtime under regular conditions (i.e. no outliers). The next two diagrams feature

---

[2] This can be superseded by MPI-4 Endpoints [16] if the proposal is accepted.

two-phase reduction when outliers are present in MPI+X and AMT, respectively. We state the following definitions and paramters for our evaluation.

Definition 1. *Overlap Region* – *An overlap region is a time window at which at least one idle processor is available to process any additional independent compute work (independent w.r.t. this reduction operation).*

Definition 2. *Non-overlap Region* – *A non-overlap region is a time window at which no idle processor is available (e.g. due to high contention or model-imposed constraint) to process any additional independent compute work effectively (independent w.r.t. this reduction operation).*

Definition 3. *Sequential Overlap* – *A sequential overlap is compute work executed on an overlap region that will run only on a single processor.*[3]

Definition 4. *Parallel Overlap* – *A parallel overlap is compute work executed on an overlap region that may run on any number of processors. A parallel overlap is assumed to be embarrassingly parallel.*

T An upper-bound on *total elapsed time* to complete a single two-phase reduction with an independent work of size W_o, across N number of nodes;

T_o *sequential latency* of a work of size W_o;

t_{min} *minimum latency* to complete a local reduction by one or more of total n worker threads;

t_{max} *maximum latency* to complete a local reduction by one or more of total n worker threads;

t_{sync} *synchronization overhead* incurred when switching from one runtime boundary to another;

t_{comm} average *communication latency* for a global reduction operation;

t_i *barrier latency* defined as time (remaining) to complete the local reduction barrier relative to the fastest thread. This implies that for regular reduction $\forall\, t_i \to 0$.

Our analysis of two-phase reduction is based on maximizing the overall parallelization (or minimizing latency) possible for MPI+X or AMT in the presence of extra computation work. However, as highlighted before, MPI+X and AMT differ in the execution of the overlap region. MPI+X has a smaller time window to leverage any overlap due to the coarse serialization of local and global reduction phases; it will only be able to overlap work during communication time (t_{comm} in Fig. 2(b)), whereas AMT's overlap region (Fig. 2(c)) is much larger. Therefore, quantification of such potential differentiation is necessary and useful for estimation of this behaviour. We have introduced a notation in-terms of t_{sync} which describe the synchronization overhead when control transfers

---

[3] We model sequential work as a compute segment with too many data dependencies such that any parallelization of respective code regions is either impossible or impractical.

between different executions, MPI and OpenMP in this particular case. A switch between heterogeneous execution environments may sometimes incur significant runtime overheads due to factors such as fork-join-like model-imposed barriers, implementation-specific constraints[4] as well as system-specific overheads related to coherency issues, instruction and data-level cache, TLB, and page misses. The probability of such occurrence in a homogeneous execution environment such as AMT is low, so we assume $t_{sync} \to 0$.

Table 1. Maximum overlap region sizes allowed in AMT two-phase reduction for optimal latency hiding on different load distributions

Distribution	Parallel overlap	Sequential overlap
Uniform (regular)	$(n-1) \cdot t_{comm}$	t_{comm}
Scaled	$(n-1) \cdot t_{comm} + n \cdot (t_{max} - t_{min})$	$t_{comm} + n \cdot (t_{max} - t_{min})$
Random uniform	$(n-1) \cdot t_{comm} + \frac{n \cdot (t_{max} - t_{min})}{2}$	$t_{comm} + \frac{n \cdot (t_{max} - t_{min})}{2}$
Gaussian	$(n-1) \cdot t_{comm} + (\frac{n}{\sqrt{2\pi\sigma^2}}) \cdot \int_0^{t_{max}} t \cdot e^{-\frac{(t-\mu)^2}{2 \cdot \sigma^2}} dt$	$t_{comm} + (\frac{n}{\sqrt{2\pi\sigma^2}}) \cdot \int_0^{t_{max}} t \cdot e^{-\frac{(t-\mu)^2}{2 \cdot \sigma^2}} dt$
Exponential	$(n-1) \cdot t_{comm} + n \cdot \int_0^{t_{max}} \frac{t \cdot e^{-\lambda} \lambda^t}{\Gamma(\lambda+1)} dt$	$t_{comm} + n \cdot \int_0^{t_{max}} \frac{t \cdot e^{-\lambda} \lambda^t}{\Gamma(\lambda+1)} dt$

2.2 Evaluating MPI+X

For MPI+X, minimum latency is achievable when additional parallel work W_o, is overlapped with the non-blocking MPI communication. However the overlap region starts only after t_{max}. Therefore the following relation holds true for total elapsed time when MPI+X reduction is executed with parallel overlap:

$$T_{par\_ov} = t_{max} + t_{sync} + \max (t_{comm}, \frac{T_o}{n-1}) \tag{1}$$

For sequential overlap, additional work cannot be executed in parallel (by definition). Therefore, work segment W_o must be delegated to a single thread.[5]

$$T_{seq\_ov} = t_{max} + t_{sync} + \max (t_{comm}, T_o) \tag{2}$$

Understandably, the potential for communication and computation overlap for MPI+X is higher in the case of parallel overlap, since the overlap region can be masked in the communication region of t_{comm}. However, time to complete the overall operation will depend on additional work when the amount of work (or noise) becomes sufficiently large $\frac{T_o}{n-1} > t_{comm}$ and $T_o > t_{comm}$ for parallel and sequential overlap, respectively. Furthermore, if significant synchronization overheads are incurred (t_{sync}), then potential for communication and computation overlap will decrease.

---

[4] For example MPI would need to execute in MPI_THREAD_MULTIPLE mode with OpenMP which may induce certain penalties compared to regular mode.

[5] Amdhal's Law can be applied for all other cases when both sequential and parallel code regions are present in W_o. However, this evaluation goes beyond the scope of this paper.

2.3   Evaluating AMT

For AMT, minimum latency is achievable when all or part of W_o overlaps with local reduction. Therefore the overlap region starts just after t_{min} (Fig. 2(c)). We formulate the following definition to continue our analysis.

Definition 5. T_l *Local Overlap* – *Local overlap is the maximum amount of work (in time units) that can be executed by all available idle processors during a local reduction phase (t_i). We model $t_i \in \{\mathbb{R} \mid t_i \geq 0\}$ as a continuous random variable, with a probability density function of $f(t)$. Let n be the total number of threads available, and $E(t)$ be average projected work (i.e. expected value) per thread, then T_l can be calculated by the following.*

$$T_l = n \cdot E(t_i)$$
$$= n \cdot \int_0^{t_i} t \cdot f(t)dt \tag{3}$$

Accordingly, for an imbalanced two-phase reduction in AMT, $T_l > 0$. Thus, for this case the Local Overlap facilitates the communication and computation overlap by reducing the amount of work that need to be parallelized during communication phase the (t_{comm}). By including T_l the following relation can be formulated for the total time of parallel overlap.

$$T_{par\_ov} = t_{max} + max \left(t_{comm}, \frac{T_o - T_l}{n - 1}\right) \tag{4}$$

Similarly, the following relation holds true for sequential overlap case.

$$T_{seq\_ov} = t_{max} + \max \left(t_{comm}, T_o - T_l\right) \tag{5}$$

Equations 4 and 5 highlight the significance of additional work size for the purpose of latency hiding. AMT two-phase reduction reaches optimal overlap[6] when the time required for additional work does not exceed global communication – that is $(n - 1) \cdot t_{comm} + T_l$ and $t_{comm} + T_l$ for parallel and sequential overlap, respectively. Thus, the best case for parallel overlap on AMT reduction allows overlap of an additional work region up to a size of $(n - 1) \cdot t_{comm} + T_l$, which is much larger than sequential case. Table 1 reports the maximum overlap allowed on AMT for many different probability distributions of load/noise. Barrier latencies (i.e. t_i) follow statistical properties of respective distributions as suggested by the formulae in Table 1, for example: $[t_{min}, t_{max}]$ for *uniform random* , (μ, σ) for *gaussian*, and λ for *exponential*.

2.4   MPI+X Vs AMT

Our model (cf. Eqs. 1 to 5) show that when $t_{comm} > T_o$ and the load configurations are the same AMT's imbalanced two-phase reduction enables execution of

---

[6] Optimal solution found when $T = t_{max} + t_{comm}$.

a larger overlap region than does MPI+X. This enables AMT to execute a global reduction very efficiently even under severe noise or load variation. Furthermore, even for the case in which heavy computation work ($T_o > t_{comm}$) is overlayed with the reduction, AMT performs better than MPI+X, as $\left(\frac{T_o - T_l}{n-1}\right) << \frac{T_o}{n-1}$. Therefore, according to our analysis AMT appears to be the best fit for use cases where distributed irregular reduction will be overlayed with useful parallel compute work. More importantly, such advantage of AMT has become increasingly evident as the amount of parallelism possible per node and the scale increases.

3   A Task-Centric Approach

```
struct elem[int id, long work, long overlap];

hpx_reduce_action(elem, allreduce){ /* two-phase reduction action */
    hpx_process_collective_allreduce_join( do_work(elem->id), allreduce);
}
run_kernel_action(elem_addr[], N, allreduce) {
    Future sync[N + 1] // create an array of futures to acquire results
    for ( i = 0 to N ) { /* call reduce action on each global element */
        sync[i] = hpx_call(elem_addr[i], hpx_reduce_action, &allreduce); }
    sync[N]=hpx_call(HPX_HERE, overlap, and, elem_addr); // parallel work
    hpx_wait_all(sync);
}
```

Listing 2: **HPX-5 pseudocode shows the parallel execution of two-phase reduction kernel and extra parallelizable work.**

In this paper we have selected the HPX-5 exascale runtime as our representative adaptive multithreaded runtime. Listing 2 reports a code listing for a global reduction of two-phase nature written in HPX-5 pseudo code. The reference implementation of HPX-5 [7] implements a conventional work-stealing scheduler [8] for local lightweight thread scheduling, a high performance Partitioned Global Address Space (PGAS) for active messaging and Remote Direct Memory Access (RDMA) operations, and uses a Photon RDMA library [9] for network transport. Importantly for this work, we introduce a novel non-blocking collective interface in HPX-5, which is assisted by its fully asynchronous lightweight thread runtime. As with MPI+OpenMP, threads interact via

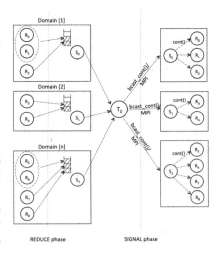

Fig. 3. Continuation driven collective design in HPX-5 for reduction operations

collectives through two phases: first joining the local domains and then communicating globally to arrive at the final value. However, unlike MPI+X, HPX-5 threads do not block during any stage of the collective reduction operation. Once the final reduced result is available, the HPX-5 scheduler will signal all suspended threads for completion.[7] This allows threads to overlap collective communication with computation and to tolerate both latency and irregularity. Our HPX-5 collective implementation has a *continuation-driven* [7] design, as shown in Fig. 3. Additionally, this implementation consists of optimizations such as shared memory, thread-local buffers, and virtual network topologies (binary, binomial trees, etc.) typical for any contemporary high-performance collective interface, implementation details [10] of which are beyond the scope of this paper. HPX-5 implements reduction operations using the HPX-5 collective interface `hpx_process_collective_allreduce_join` [7]. HPX-5 collective scheduling is naturally integrated into the HPX-5 runtime. This unified behavior eliminates model-imposed barriers that are fundamental to all MPI+X instantiations, and in Sect. 4 will be observed to be well-suited for tolerating noise and irregular behavior expected in exascale systems.

A Framework for Noise Injection. We developed a framework that injects various amounts of load into existing parallel programs to perform our analysis. Our framework uses the method of Fixed Work Quantum (FWQ) [1] to inject and measure load across application regions. FWQ assumes that minimum time t_u, or *unit work* (t_{min} in Fig. 2), represents the perfectly balanced execution of a program region. Our framework can inject $t_{max} - t_i$ delays into an application region. Thus, *unit work* is perturbed by injecting small delays, which we will refer to as "overhead" time or "t_o". Earlier work [2,5] used similar techniques in their noise-injection benchmarks that emulate minuscule amounts of system noise. We identified several important criteria to emulate imbalance. First, we enabled injection of load at varying amounts (amplitude) or conforming to a particular distribution. Second, we enabled injection of load at identified points – locality or light-weight processes/tasks of a distributed memory application. Finally, we implemented runtime-specific extensions for MPI, MPI+OpenMP, and HPX-5. Our model consists of a number of load distribution parameters for instrumentation: unit work (t_u), maximum overhead units (t_u/t_o %) to inject as a percentage of unit work, number of threads to inject in each locality (**tpn**), and a time or work resolution unit. Our emulation system varies load/noise amplitude by adjusting random distribution (Uniform Random, Gaussian, Poisson, etc.) parameters such as mean and standard deviation. A *scaled* version of distribution will scale just one load assignment with an overhead by a specified percentage relative to unit work. The *uniform* injection mode emulates the perfectly load-balanced base scenario.

---

[7] In fact, collectives in HPX-5 are data driven and not execution driven. The identity of the joining threads is inconsequential, and the completion of a collective operation triggers a set of registered continuations.

4   Results and Discussion

Our experiments have been conducted using a set of customized benchmarks that evaluate two-phase reduction in irregular conditions for three programming/execution models: MPI, MPI+OpenMP and HPX-5. We tested the maximum number of processing elements possible in each cluster in every experiment. We also tested realistic workload distributions with varying frequencies and amplitudes that may naturally occur within load-imbalanced applications. For statistical significance, each measure was repeated 100 times and special care was taken to limit any external interference on performance measures. We conducted all our experiments on two platforms: the small-scale HPC cluster "Cutter" (Intel Xeon E5 2.1 GHz processors, 16 cores per node, up to 256 cores with a **gcc/open-mpi** environment) at Indiana University and the large scale HPC cluster "Edison" (Cray X30 Intel 'Ivy Bridge' 2.4 GHz processors, 24 cores per node, up to 24576 cores with an **intel/cray-mpich** environment) on NERSC at Berkeley.

All microbenchmark experiments are based upon two categories of execution. First, we executed a two-phase allreduce operation[8] when outliers were present in parallel compute regions. Second, we executed the same experiment with an additional parallel work region (Fig. 1). We injected noise outliers for each thread (MPI+OpenMP), process (MPI-only), or task (HPX-5) using our emulation framework (cf. Sect. 3). For overlap we used model parameters, total overlapped region size (W_o), and overlapped work quantum ($\frac{T_o}{n-1} \sim$ work per thread). An overlapped region was emulated either with a sequential or a parallel region. The benchmarks currently implement different variants of these overlap regions for MPI, MPI+OpenMP, and HPX-5 via the `run_overlapped_work(uint64_t qw, uint64_t ow)` interface.

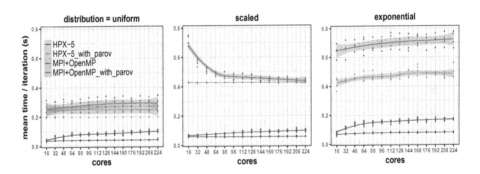

Fig. 4. Microbenchmark scaling with and without *parallel* overlap, for three distributions on Cutter (upto 224 cores)

---

[8] A collective (i.e. tree-based) algorithm was consistent across all experiments and runtime modes.

Each experiment pertaining to a particular random distribution was injected with a maximum overhead workload of t_{omax} value equating to 2x unit work t_u.[9] Next we adjusted statistical parameters accordingly to fit in the scaled range. For example the Gaussian mean was set at the mid range $2t_u$ and the sigma parameter was set at t_u. Similarly, random uniform distribution parameters $[a, b]$ were set between t_u and $3t_u$, etc. Using experimentation and empirical techniques as tools, we determined a minimum threshold where the cascading effects of noise irregularities became significant. For all microbenchmark experiments that followed, unit work t_u was determined at a constant value of 40 time units. Furthermore, all experiments report regression regions or error bars of a 90% confidence interval.

We first evaluated the performance of two-phase reduction with irregular noise on the Cutter cluster. Two experiments were conducted excluding and including parallel regions (the parallel overlap) on the reduction kernel. On each scatter plot in Fig. 4, we display the fitted lines (evaluated by non parametric LOESS regression) and confidence regions for MPI+OpenMP and HPX-5 for each case. The AMT instance completed the reduction faster than MPI+OpenMP on both these experiments. The uniform case (zero outliers) reported approximately same running times at a single node ($t_{comm} \rightarrow 0$), but, as the frequency of outliers and the scale increased, relative variance in running times became more significant. For exponential outliers HPX-5 reported a ~2.2X speedup when parallel regions were excluded, and when parallel regions were included HPX-5 reported a speedup of ~1.6X w.r.t. MPI+OpenMP.

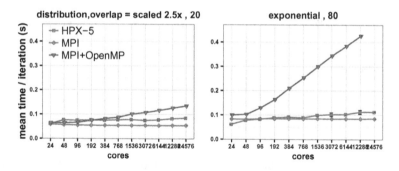

Fig. 5. Microbenchmark scaling results with *sequential* overlap on Edison (upto 24000+ cores)

Even though MPI+X and HPX-5 spent roughly the same time in global reduction (t_{comm}) on Cutter, MPI+X displayed higher synchronization costs ($\uparrow t_{sync}$), creating higher latencies than the AMT instance. For parallel overlap AMT showed a greater speedup than MPI+X on account of the higher potential for latency hiding when $T_o > t_{comm}$. We also noticed that the average latency

---

[9] Each parallel load injection t_i was scaled between t_u and $3.t_u$.

variation with exponential noise was more significant in MPI+OpenMP than in
HPX-5; the fitted model for MPI+OpenMP only explained 20% while HPX-5
explained 30% of the variability of data (Fig. 4 *exponential* plot). Interestingly,
the MPI+OpenMP allreduce benchmark with a parallel region and a single outlier (Fig. 4 *scaled* plot) displayed resilience by absorbing noise pressure as the
number of nodes increased. MPI+OpenMP was able to hide relatively smaller
delays (where $T_{comm} \simeq T_o$) by overlapping compute work in parallel regions.
Overall results suggested that HPX-5 was better at absorbing noise delays than
MPI+OpenMP for two-phase reduction on smaller node counts.

We show the performance of two-phase reduction on the Edison cluster with
scaling up to 24000+ cores in Fig. 5. More specifically, we tested a sequential
overlap region and started with a base case of scaled noise/load injection with
a lower overlap segment size setting (20 time units). In the base case running
times of two-phase reduction were about the same (within $+/-5\%$). As expected,
MPI+OpenMP two-phase reduction performed poorly with scale as compared
to MPI or AMT. For sequential overlapped segments on Edison, MPI+OpenMP
reported a maximum slowdown of $\sim$3X to $\sim$6.5X (on different distributions),
while MPI exhibited a marginal speedup of $\sim$0.25X w.r.t. HPX-5. Unlike the
case where overlap regions are parallelizable, the addition of a sequential region
imposed a sequential delay for MPI+OpenMP at the implicit barrier. At this
point, when $T_o \gg t_{comm}$ the overhead gap generated by MPI+X – (t_{sync} +
T_o), was much larger than in AMT ($T_o - T_l$). This resulted in amplification
of communication overheads with scale and thus a significant slowdown w.r.t.
HPX-5 and MPI allreduce.

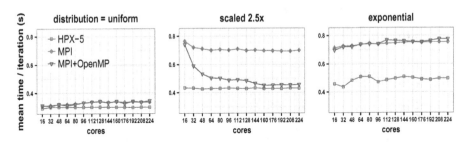

Fig. 6. Microbenchmark scaling with *parallel* overlap work ($t_u = 50$) for multiple
distributions on Cutter (upto 224 cores)

For parallel overlap cases, MPI+X performed much better than its sequential configuration (i.e. when uniform and scaled noise outliers were present), an
observation which matches the inferences derived by our model (cf. Eqs. 1 and
2). On Cutter (Fig. 6) both the MPI and MPI+OpenMP benchmarks reported
a relative slowdown of $\sim$10% to $\sim$50% compared to HPX-5 when outliers were
present. Here MPI+OpenMP absorbed noise pressure better when a single noise
outlier (scaled injection) was present. Interestingly, MPI proved slower in execution times, $\sim$10% to $\sim$50% w.r.t. MPI+OpenMP and HPX-5.

Our benchmark on Edison (up to 12000+ cores, Fig. 7), tested two additional modes of execution for MPI + OpenMP: OpenMP `sections` and `tasks`. The AMT instance performed better than the MPI and MPI+X runtime instances in a majority of these configurations. Importantly, we noted that it was able to absorb noise pressure at these large scales while maintaining a running time better than that of all MPI+OpenMP modes for two-phase reduction. More importantly, these observations are consistent with our model as well; AMT has better latency (T) than MPI+X, since $t_{max} + (\frac{T_o - T_l}{n-1}) << t_{max} + t_{sync} + \frac{T_o}{n-1}$. However, Fig. 7 shows that *exponential* and *random* distribution have relatively stable running times for the MPI+OpenMP two-phase reduction. This is because MPI+X does not depend on function $T_l(t_i)$ (Eq. 1), whereas AMT may be affected by cascading delays induced by variation of noise distributions $(T_l(t_i))$ across different nodes (cf. Table 1). Thus we observe that at larger scales the structure of noise between nodes is as important as the mode of execution for an global reduction. In contrast, this behaviour was not visible at smaller scales (Fig. 6), because for a small number of nodes significant amplification of delays is unlikely.

We observed a mean slowdown of ~2% to ~35% in MPI+OpenMP `task` execution while slowdown in MPI+OpenMP `sections` was ~2% to ~25% w.r.t. AMT. However, the MPI+OpenMP `sections` benchmark displayed its best performance in the presence of scaled noise outliers with ~6% speedup against our AMT instance. Both the MPI-only threaded mode and MPI+OpenMP regular version behaved similarly at scale with relative slowdowns ranging from ~2% to ~30% w.r.t. HPX-5. We also noticed some variance in performance characteristics in MPI+ OpenMP on the two cluster environments. Mainly, differences in runtime implementations of MPI+OpenMP (i.e. **open-mpi** vs **cray-mpich**) and programming environments (i.e. **gcc** vs **intel**) may have contributed towards this behavior. Synchronization costs when $\uparrow t_{sync}$, (costs on per-threaded communicators, progress engine, etc.) causes MPI execution higher penalties in certain cases (i.e. that of scaled outliers in Fig. 7) resulting in worse performance than MPI+OpenMP.

5   Related Work

Hoefler et al. have conducted a detailed analysis on the impact of external noise effects on communication synchronization. These effects include operating system [2] and network noise [5]. Other studies [6] shed further light on modeling noise to gain a more analytic perspective on the effect of noise on the scalability of collective operations. Ferreira et al. [2] use noise-injection techniques to assess the impact of noise on several large-scale applications using extremely lightweight kernels. Beckman [1] characterized sources of noise and analyzed performance on BlueGene/L systems, using a synthetic noise-injecting benchmark called "selfish detour".

Other research reports on MPI+OpenMP usage patterns [11–13] and how they can be applied to existing applications and possible challenges that may be encountered. Based on this evidence only a handful of hybrid execution patterns have been deemed successful in practice. The MPI+OpenMP programming

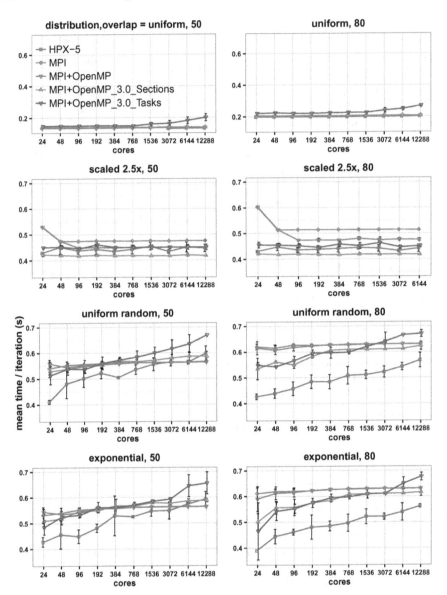

Fig. 7. Microbenchmark scaling with *parallel* overlap work segment size for 4 noise/load distributions on Edison (up to 12000+ cores).

model has been used for irregular application domains. Notably, Tafti et al. [14] have reported its early adoption for AMR. More recently, newer AMT runtimes, such as Legion [15] and OCR [17], too have grown in popularity for tackling large-scale irregular problems. However, the impact of irregularities and imbalance on the performance and scalability of applications has not been thoroughly studied on these systems. Our work differentiates from above efforts in that we focus our attention on the effects of imbalance for two-phase reduction in both the MPI+X and AMT execution models. Furthermore, we formalize imbalance in terms of a probabilistic model and characterize performance under a varying number of configurations.

6 Conclusion

Combining MPI and X for a two-phase reduction in a naive manner introduces a sequential barrier bottleneck between the X collective and the MPI collective. More involved combinations (e.g. by using OpenMP `tasks`) can eliminate that barrier but expose the disjoint nature of the MPI and X schedulers. As systems increase in size and real problems become more irregular, these effects will impact the scalability of applications using MPI+X. An AMT runtime with integrated collective support has unified scheduling, no sequential bottleneck, and is therefore not subjected to these same scalability limitations.

Our results indicate that given the above situations, MPI + OpenMP performance varied rapidly across different execution modes and environments. MPI+X asynchronous variants, such as OpenMP `tasks` and `sections`, performed better compared to the naive MPI+X implementation. The effectiveness of other alternatives, such as threaded MPI, largely depended on the size and structure of the irregularity. More importantly, on both small and large scales a reference AMT collective implementation was better able to withstand the pressure exerted by simulated noise than any implementation of MPI+X. However, both AMT and asynchronous MPI+X (i.e. OpenMP `tasks`) variants may not be entirely immune to noise at very large scales. We learned that, if the structure and the distribution of the noise changes significantly across nodes, then the tendency to cascade delays may influence the overall scalability of a two-phase reduction. Thus, we recognize that proper characterization of irregularity is essential to understanding the limits of existing parallel systems and address the issues of similar nature. We look forward to building on this framework to design accurate performance models, which will allow us to implement better parallel programming models and paradigms in the face of observed levels of irregularity in HPC systems.

References

1. Beckman, P., Iskra, K., Yoshii, K., Coghlan, S., Nataraj, A.: Benchmarking the effects of operating system interference on extreme-scale parallel machines. Cluster Comput. 11(1), 3–16 (2008). https://doi.org/10.1007/s10586-007-0047-2
2. Ferreira, K.B., Bridges, P., Brightwell, R.: Characterizing application sensitivity to OS interference using kernel-level noise injection. In: Proceedings of SC 2008, pp. 19:1–19:12. IEEE Press, Piscataway (2008). http://dl.acm.org/citation.cfm?id=1413370.1413390

3. Hoefler, T., Schneider, T., Lumsdaine, A.: The impact of network noise at large-scale communication performance. In: IPDPS 2009, pp. 1–8 (2009). https://doi.org/10.1109/IPDPS.2009.5161095

4. Kaiser, H., Brodowicz, M., Sterling, T.: Parallex an advanced parallel execution model for scaling-impaired applications. In: Proceedings of ICPPW 2009, pp. 394–401. IEEE Computer Society, Washington, DC (2009). https://doi.org/10.1109/ICPPW.2009.14

5. Hoefler, T., Schneider, T., Lumsdaine, A.: Characterizing the influence of system noise on large-scale applications by simulation. In: Proceedings of SC 2010, pp. 1–11. IEEE Computer Society, Washington, DC (2010). https://doi.org/10.1109/SC.2010.12

6. Agarwal, S., Garg, R., Vishnoi, N.K.: The impact of noise on the scaling of collectives: a theoretical approach. In: Bader, D.A., Parashar, M., Sridhar, V., Prasanna, V.K. (eds.) HiPC 2005. LNCS, vol. 3769, pp. 280–289. Springer, Heidelberg (2005). https://doi.org/10.1007/11602569_31

7. CREST: HPX-5. http://hpx.crest.iu.edu

8. Blumofe, R.D., Leiserson, C.E.: Scheduling multithreaded computations by work stealing. J. ACM **46**(5), 720–748 (1999)

9. Kissel, E., Swany, M.: Photon: remote memory access middleware for high-performance runtime systems. In: IPDPSW 2016, pp. 1736–1743 (2016). https://doi.org/10.1109/IPDPSW.2016.120

10. Wickramasinghe, U., DAlessandro, L., Lumsdaine, A., Kissel, E., Swany, M., Newton, R.: Evaluating collectives in networks of multicore/two-level reduction. Technical report, Indiana University, School of Informatics and Computing (2017)

11. Bova, S., et al.: Combining message-passing and directives in parallel applications. SIAM News **32**(9), 10–14 (1999)

12. Cappello, F., Etiemble, D.: MPI versus MPI+OpenMP on the IBM SP for the NAS benchmarks. In: Supercomputing, ACM/IEEE 2000 Conference, p. 12 (2000). https://doi.org/10.1109/SC.2000.10001

13. Corbalan, J., Duran, A., Labarta, J.: Dynamic load balancing of MPI+OpenMP applications. In: ICPP 2004, vol. 1, pp. 195–202 (2004). https://doi.org/10.1109/ICPP.2004.1327921

14. Huang, W., Tafti., D.: A parallel computing framework for dynamic power balancing in adaptive mesh refinement applications. In: Proceedings of Parallel Computational Fluid Dynamics, pp. 249–256 (1999)

15. Bauer, M., Treichler, S., Slaughter, E., Aiken, A.: Legion: expressing locality and independence with logical regions. In: Proceedings of the International Conference on High Performance Computing, Networking, Storage and Analysis, p. 66. IEEE Computer Society Press (2012)

16. Dinan, J., et al.: Enabling communication concurrency through flexible MPI endpoints. Int. J. High Perform. Comput. Appl. **28**(4), 390–405 (2014)

17. Dokulil, J., Sandrieser, M., Benkner, S.: OCR-Vx-an alternative implementation of the open community runtime. In: International Workshop on Runtime Systems for Extreme Scale Programming Models and Architectures, in Conjunction with SC15, Austin, Texas (2015)

Abstract Representation of Shared Data for Heterogeneous Computing

Tushar Kumar[1]([⊠]), Aravind Natarajan[1], Wenjia Ruan[1], Mario Badr[2],
Dario Suarez Gracia[3], and Calin Cascaval[4]

[1] Qualcomm Research, SantaClara, USA
{tushark,naravind,wenjiar}@qti.qualcomm.com
[2] University of Toronto, Toronto, Canada
mario.badr@mail.utoronto.ca
[3] Universidad de Zaragoza, Zaragoza, Spain
dario@unizar.es
[4] Barefoot Networks, Santa Clara, USA
cascaval@acm.org

Abstract. Data management across address spaces in heterogeneous platforms represents a significant performance bottleneck and energy cost for applications, particularly on mobile System-on-Chip (SoC). We propose a light-weight middleware layer to regulate concurrent access to shared data in a Heterogeneous SoC. Our approach uses acquire-release semantics to provide the following benefits: *(i)* enable high-level heterogeneous programming frameworks to easily maintain consistent non-device, non-platform-specific data abstractions for programmers, and *(ii)* provide an abstract memory interface with strong analyzable properties about the correctness and performance of the synchronization operations across memory-types. These benefits are achieved while retaining the ability to plug-in arbitrary types of heterogeneous memory frameworks and to enable platform-specific and inter-framework synchronization optimizations. We demonstrate that our approach avoids paying the "abstraction cost", achieving performance within 5% of manually optimized OpenCL while providing a simpler and understandable API.

Keywords: Heterogeneous system-on-chip · Memory synchronization · Memory concurrency · Data sharing

1 Introduction

Heterogeneous computing systems allow programmers to match parts of an application to the strengths of the different devices available [14]. The ultimate goal of heterogeneous computing is to obtain higher performance at lower power by judiciously balancing the computation. Prior work has focused on partitioning applications across heterogeneous devices. For example, the Fast Multipole

---

Qualcomm Research is a division of Qualcomm Technologies, Inc.

L. Rauchwerger (Ed.): LCPC 2017, LNCS 11403, pp. 145–162, 2019.
https://doi.org/10.1007/978-3-030-35225-7_11

Method has been shown to work better on a CPU-GPU architecture [10]. However, heterogeneous systems are not limited to CPUs and GPUs. As we scale to a more diverse set of accelerators, a major impediment to programmers becomes moving data across devices. Mobile Systems-on-Chip (SoCs) typically share data across devices using a contiguously-allocated block of memory (i.e., a buffer) that is modifiable by one device at a time. Without advanced hardware support [2] synchronization is *explicit*, placing a significant burden on programmers. We propose to simplify data movement across devices via intuitive abstractions.

Not all devices share a common view of system memory or even have access to it. For example, a device may not be cache coherent, and some devices may address 32-bit memory while others address 64-bit. Our approach leverages the familiar notion of a *buffer* augmented with acquire-release semantics to deal with this non-uniformity. We abstract the diverse mechanisms for data access into a uniform set of synchronization primitives that is implemented on top of hardware support. Put simply, in acquire-release semantics either the entire buffer is made available to a kernel or none of it is. This provides programmers with a familiar technique for sharing data in a heterogeneous system.

Currently, many frameworks exist to enable offloading data to a device. For example, OpenCL, CUDA, or OpenGL are used to offload computation to the GPU and to share data between the CPU and GPU [7,18,22]. Android ION is another industry standard that allocates memory accessible by any ION-compliant devices on an SoC. It is often used to share data between compute devices and custom-components of the SoC, such as image-processing accelerators [11]. However, to efficiently use ION from OpenCL kernels (i.e., to avoid unnecessary copying of data from ION into GPU-accessible memory regions), programmers must use specialized extensions of OpenCL API calls (typically vendor specific). This results in multiple versions of the application code to support the range of platforms. Prior work focused on establishing a cache-coherent shared memory model over multiple devices does not capture this level of intricacies [6].

The challenge of managing multiple frameworks for offloading data gets more complex as more devices are added to heterogeneous systems. For example, FPGAs and ML accelerators [1,17] will have their own mechanisms. Currently, a programmer looking to take advantage of all the compute devices available must:

1. Synchronize data across any combination of devices correctly and efficiently
2. Be aware of supported memory-optimizations for each target platform
3. Write application code to accommodate multiple device combinations

To alleviate the programmer's burden and enable heterogeneous applications, we propose an abstraction layer with a novel representation for a shared data buffer (Fig. 1). The synchronization state of a shared data buffer is maintained in a device- and platform-agnostic manner (*buffer state* – the middle of Fig. 1). An existing memory framework; e.g., OpenCL or ION, is plugged-in underneath the buffer-state via an abstract representation of memory called an *arena* (the bottom of Fig. 1). An arena provides generic operations to the buffer-state to

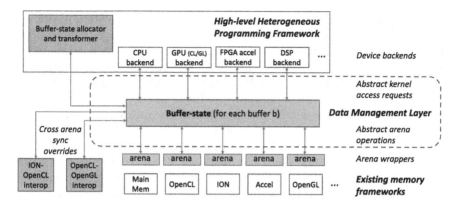

Fig. 1. The abstract representation of shared data decouples existing memory frameworks from their use by a high-level programming framework.

(1) allocate storage and (2) manage access to the storage, while hiding the particulars of the underlying memory framework. Each arena maintains an *arena state* capturing information sufficient for the buffer-state to correctly manage storage and synchronize data across arenas. The arena state includes the *map state*; i.e., which devices may currently access the storage (a generalization over OpenCL operations that burden the user to track state). Arenas serve as a wrapper around an existing memory framework, placing the onus on the platform developer rather than the application developer. For example, an OpenCL-arena would translate the arena operations into appropriate OpenCL API calls and correspondingly update the arena state. The arena and buffer-state transactions together ensure (1) correct storage allocation and synchronization of shared data across the memory frameworks, and (2) correct throttling of concurrent access by device kernels to the shared data based on the arena states. To ensure synchronization between any two arenas, the buffer-state requires the arenas to support a *default synchronization mechanism*, for example, require all arenas to allow the CPU to access their data, so the CPU may perform memory-copies between arenas. An ION-arena may simply provide a pointer to its ION-allocated storage, while an OpenCL-arena may use the OpenCL APIs to "read" or "map" data from the GPU memory into main memory (memory frameworks typically provide CPU-access mechanisms as current heterogeneous devices typically offload the CPU). The buffer-state synchronizes data across arenas using two interface functions: $can\_copy(src, dst)$ and $copy(src, dst)$. Under the default mechanism described above, $can\_copy(src, dst)$ would prevent synchronization between the *src* and *dst* arenas if granting access to the CPU would interfere with kernels already accessing the data in *src*, e.g., an OpenCL-arena in unmapped state may not be mapped for access by the CPU while GPU OpenCL kernels are accessing it. When permitted by $can\_copy(src, dst)$, $copy(src, dst)$ performs the data synchronization, including allocating storage inside *dst* if not already allocated.

The platform developer may override the default synchronization mechanism between two arenas with a *cross-arena synchronization mechanism* (bottom-left of Fig. 1) that is faster, requires less storage-allocation than the default, and/or provides alternative paths to synchronization. While the default *can_copy*() may disallow synchronization when the CPU cannot be granted access, the optimized *can_copy*() may evaluate use of platform-specific or memory-type-specific mechanisms to perform the synchronization without disrupting executing kernels. The corresponding *copy*() may also *bind-allocate* storage between arenas, e.g., the MainMem-arena and OpenCL-arena may directly use the storage allocated in the ION-arena instead of allocating their own. Crucially, the arena abstraction greatly alleviates the burden on the platform developer when implementing cross-arena optimizations – the developer may perform arbitrary transforms on the arena-state to carry out the synchronization, while easily verifying against the arena-state whether a transform impacts access to currently executing kernels.

Finally, the buffer-state itself provides an abstract representation that can be transformed by a high-level heterogeneous runtime in a fairly arbitrary manner to implement sophisticated program-specific and platform-specific optimizations, with an automatic guarantee of correctness (top-left of Fig. 1).

In this paper we make the following contributions:

1. We define an abstract representation of memory regions and synchronization primitives to maintain consistency across memory regions in the presence of multiple heterogeneous devices with different capabilities (Sect. 3).
2. We propose an overload mechanism, the cross-arena, that allows arbitrary memory synchronization optimizations to be plugged-in while retaining the ability to easily verify correctness of implementation (Sect. 3.2).
3. We implement these abstractions into a middleware, which we refer to as the *data management layer* (DML), that enables the creation of high-level programming frameworks with abstract representations of shared data, and provides portability across a range of platforms supporting any combinations of low-level memory-frameworks (Sect. 4).
4. We evaluate the proposed ideas by incorporating the DML into a C++ high-level programming framework, the Qualcomm® Symphony System Manager SDK [23,24] (*"the SDK"*). The SDK exploits its knowledge about program structure and data sharing patterns by performing transformations on the buffer-state abstraction, and plugs-in cross-arena optimizations to take advantage of platforms-specific synchronization mechanisms (Sect. 5).

In summary, our abstraction decouples the low level, platform-specific details of sharing and synchronizing memory regions from the high-level programming data abstraction and allows application programmers to write efficient, portable code. Next, we motivate our work with examples of the programmer burden.

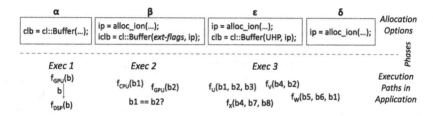

Fig. 2. Data management burden: the heterogeneous application developer is forced to track platform-specific functionality and the dynamic execution order of components.

2   Illustration of Programmer's Burden

Consider the application phases in Fig. 2. In the first phase, buffers are allocated for use with a CPU, GPU and DSP. On the given platform, ION is used to share data with the DSP, whereas an additional pool of memory is available to the GPU OpenCL driver for sharing data between the CPU and GPU. Option α allocates a buffer from GPU driver memory. Option β allocates from the ION pool and then uses the OpenCL-ION extensions available on some platforms to access ION memory efficiently from the GPU. Option ϵ allocates ION memory, but does not use the OpenCL-ION extensions, leading to the GPU OpenCL driver potentially copying data back and forth between the ION- and GPU-allocated storage. Option δ allocates ION storage for data that will only be shared between the CPU and DSP. For each buffer, the application programmer has to keep track of which buffer allocation option – α, β, ϵ or δ – was used. For data to be shared between the CPU, GPU and DSP, the programmer has to select at compile-time or run-time between options β and ϵ, to support platforms with and without support for the OpenCL-ION extensions.

Next, consider the data management challenges in the execution phase of the application. Exec 1 shows a producer-consumer relationship between a GPU and a DSP component using data buffer b. If b has format β, typically an OpenCL 'map' would be the correct synchronization operation. For format ϵ, however, an OpenCL 'read' may be more performant on some platforms, requiring the programmer to select synchronization operations based on platform. Exec 2 shows a CPU and a GPU component executing concurrently. When $b1$ and $b2$ are distinct data buffers, the two components may execute without any synchronization. However, when invoked on the same buffer, the programmer has to detect $b1 = b2$ during execution and serialize the components; e.g., by holding locks on the buffers. If f_{CPU} is serialized to execute before f_{GPU} and the buffer was allocated using option α or ϵ, the programmer must perform OpenCL 'unmap' or 'write' operations in between (whichever is more performant on the given platform), and 'map' or 'read' for the opposite execution order. With option β, 'unmap' or 'map' would correspondingly be used for the two serialization orders.

Of course, if the components only read the buffers, it would generally be feasible to execute them concurrently even when $b1 = b2$. Even so, option α

allocation may force a serialization if f_{GPU} executes first and the buffer has never been 'mapped' before—the f_{CPU} component is unable to access the data because the OpenCL buffer may not be 'mapped' while in use by the GPU.

Finally, Exec 3 shows a scenario of arbitrary concurrent components running on multiple heterogeneous devices (with more than one component possible on a device). Each component accesses multiple buffers. Depending on whether a given buffer, say $b4$, is read-only accessed by f_V and f_X or not, control serialization must be imposed between f_V and f_X. Similarly, every other buffer creates potential serialization between any of f_U, f_V, f_W and f_X. Correspondingly, there are a large combinations of data synchronization operations that must be judiciously selected between any serialized components to ensure correct and performant data management. This quickly becomes overwhelming for the programmer to manage, even at the level of relatively platform-abstract OpenCL and ION APIs.

3   Abstract Representation

Clearly a high-level programming runtime should alleviate the burden on the programmer by taking care of the data management, and consider a number of optimizations based on the memory access patterns: read-only accesses, concurrent access, allocation usage, etc. Toward this goal, our proposed data management layer (DML) introduces an abstract representation of the following concepts: *arena* to abstract operations over a device-specific memory, *buffer state* to abstract the distribution of a data buffer over multiple device-specific memories and to track the device kernels accessing the data, and *cross arena* to compartmentalize knowledge about platform-specific synchronization optimizations.

3.1   Arena

The arena representation captures the following *abstract state* information for a single type of memory or memory framework:

- **allocation state:** the storage of the underlying memory framework may be *unallocated, internally-allocated, externally-allocated,* or *bind-allocated.*
- **bind-arena:** identifies which other arena under the buffer state is this arena bind-allocated with (if at all).
- **native device:** a fixed attribute identifying which device accesses the memory wrapped by this arena to execute its kernels.
- **remote devices:** a fixed attribute identifying additional devices that are directly able to access the storage on this memory, not necessarily efficiently. By 'directly' we mean the remote device is able to access the data without involving another device (to perform a mem-copy, for example).
- **map handles:** for each remote device a handle that the device may use to access the data storage on this memory. For example, an OpenCL 'map' operation would provide the CPU with a 'map pointer' handle to access the

OpenCL-allocated memory in an OpenCL-arena. The map handle for a custom accelerator's memory arena may be a set of memory IDs that a remote CPU may use to program a DMA engine. Therefore, the map handle may have a platform- or memory-dependent format, but the handle is abstract in the sense that it is never interpreted by the buffer-state or arena abstractions.

- **map state:** either *unmapped*, *mapped* or *bimapped*. Unmapped implies that the data storage is currently accessible to the native device. Mapped implies that the data storage is available to an identified subset of remote devices using their corresponding map handles. Bimapped implies simultaneous access by the native device and an identified subset of remote devices.
- **ref-count:** tracks how many kernels executing on the native device have currently been granted access to the data storage on this memory.

The allocation state captures whether storage has been allocated for the data buffer on the memory wrapped by the arena. An internal-allocation implies that the arena itself has allocated the storage, which will be de-allocated when the buffer-state containing the arena is de-allocated. An external-allocation implies that the application program or some other entity in the high-level programming framework has already allocated storage on the wrapped memory, and wants the buffer-state to use the available storage and the data on it. Bind-allocated is crucial for optimizing the storage allocation and synchronization across different types of memory holding the shared data buffer. It implies that the storage has been allocated by another arena, and there is some specialized cross-arena mechanism available to synchronize data between this arena and the another arena. For example, an OpenCL-arena and a MainMem-arena may both bind-allocate to an ION-arena – this means that storage was initially allocated inside ION memory, and the OpenCL-arena and MainMem-arena are able to use the ION-allocated storage pointer instead of allocating from their own memory pool.

An *arena wrapper* over a memory framework consists of the following aspects:

1. **Abstract arena state:** as described above.
2. **Abstract arena operations API:** a device-, platform- and memory-agnostic API, used by the buffer state to manipulate the abstract arena state.
3. **Arena implementation:** concrete implementation that is highly specific to the memory-type. Ties the abstract state and the abstract operations to the specific memory-type or memory-framework wrapped by this arena; e.g., translate to OpenCL API calls in an OpenCL-arena.

For example, an OpenCL-arena would have native device as GPU, remote device as CPU, internal-allocation would allocate an OpenCL buffer, external-allocation would track a user-allocated OpenCL buffer, bind-allocate would create an OpenCL buffer using memory from a MainMem-arena or ION-allocated memory from an ION-arena, the map handle would be a CPU-accessible pointer, the map state would correspond to the map/unmap state of the contained OpenCL buffer, and ref-count would track how many GPU kernels currently access the contained OpenCL buffer. A MainMem-arena would have both the native and remote device as CPU, internal-allocation would malloc storage, external-allocation would save a user-pointer, bind-allocation would use the pointer from an ION-arena or the pointer provided by the OpenCL 'map' operation in an OpenCL-arena, the map-state would always be bimapped, and the ref-count would track how many CPU kernels currently access the MainMem-arena.

The abstract arena API provide the following operations to the buffer state:

- **allocate storage** – internal, external or bind-allocate.
- **request/revoke access** to one or more remote devices, or to the native device. Depending on the specific arena implementation, granting access may implicitly revoke access for another device, which the map state will reflect.
- **up-ref** tracks that one more kernel executing on the native device now has access to the arena's storage, while **down-ref** indicates a kernel completion.

The up-ref call increments the arena ref-count, while down-ref decrements it. A ref-count = 0 indicates no kernel on the native device is accessing the storage allocated in this arena, and hence any map-state changes are now permitted. A ref-count > 0 would disallow any map-state change that would disrupt access to executing kernels, possibly preventing data synchronization with another arena.

3.2   Cross-Arena

The cross-arena representation allows the following synchronization operations to be overridden by platform-specific implementations:

- bool **can_copy**(src-arena, dst-arena)
- **copy**(src-arena, dst-arena)

The buffer state provides a default implementation of these functions. In one possible default implementation, the CPU serves as a remote device for every arena, and the src and dst arenas can be mapped so the CPU may perform a mem-copy. In general, can_copy(src, dst) returns success if the data in the src arena can be used to update the storage in the dst arena. It may fail for the following reasons – *(i)* the src and dst do not share a common device in either their native or remote devices ("the sync device"), or *(ii)* using the sync device to access the data would require a change to src's map state, but ref-count > 0 in the src's arena state currently prevents that change. Note that when the buffer state invokes can_copy() or copy(), the dst arena does not contain valid data and has ref-count = 0, making any map-state change in dst feasible.

The cross arena interface in the DML provides a mechanism for plugging in platform-specific and memory-type specific overrides for any combination of src and dst arena types. The overridden copy() will also determine the best manner to allocate storage in the dst arena (whether to internal-allocate or bind-allocate), which frequently enables zero-copy optimizations. can_copy() can also return a cost to help buffer-state more precisely determine the cheapest copy mechanism.

The buffer-state abstract machine may evaluate multiple combinations of can_copy() calls to determine the cheapest or most optimal "sync sequence" currently available to synchronize data into a desired dst arena. On finding the best available sequence, the abstract machine will call one or more copy(src, dst) to enact data transfer on the chosen sequence. The copy() calls will allocate storage in their corresponding dst arenas if the storage was not already allocated. In this manner, more optimal bind-allocations that *minimize synchronization costs and the total amount of storage allocated* may be performed.

Overlapping remote and native devices across arenas create a path for the movement of data across corresponding memory types. Therefore, the buffer state essentially needs to find the 'shortest sync path' from any src arena currently holding *valid data* to the dst arena needing to get the shared data of the buffer. The path is over a graph whose nodes represent arenas, and an edge connects two arenas if they have a sync device in common. The edge cost is the cost returned by can_copy(). Overridden copy() and can_copy() may provide new mechanisms to synchronize data without changing the map-state of the src, and may also introduce alternative remote devices. *Therefore, platform-specific cross-arena overrides often enhance the degree of concurrency possible for executing kernels.*

As an example, consider that memory-type $m1$ (wrapped in arena $a1$) currently holds valid data. Suppose device $d2$, the native device of memory-type $m2$ (wrapped in arena $a2$) needs to execute a kernel that reads the data buffer. Suppose can_copy($a1, a2$) fails because $a1$'s map-state cannot be currently changed. The buffer-state's abstract machine can try can_copy($a1, a3$) and can_copy($a3, a2$) to accomplish can_copy($a1, a2$) if another arena $a3$ has sync devices in common with $a1$ and $a2$. This may also create bind-allocations between $a1$, $a2$ and $a3$.

Next, consider custom hardware accelerators *accel1* and *accel2* on an FPGA, with their corresponding private memory banks $m1$ and $m2$ wrapped by arenas $a1$ and $a2$, respectively. $a1$ has the CPU as remote device because $m1$ is connected to the system bus, but $a2$ only has *accel1* as remote device because *accel1* can also access $m2$. Such a situation may occur in custom FPGA designs, and our proposed abstractions will find a path to transmit data from the CPU to *accel2*.

3.3   Buffer-State

The buffer-state representation contains the following information:

- **arenas-set** – one arena for each type of memory.
- **valid-set** – which arenas currently have valid data.
- **requestor-set** – which kernels (over multiple devices) currently access the shared data buffer, what are their corresponding *access types* (read-only, write-invalidate, read-write), and which arena is accessed by each kernel.

The high-level programming runtime makes a *kernel-access request* to the buffer-state whenever a kernel k on device d needs to access data buffer b. Each data buffer maintains a distinct buffer-state. To grant a kernel-access request, the buffer-state's abstract machine must first ensure that the *access-type of the request does not conflict* with the accesses already granted; e.g., multiple read-only access requests may be granted, but only one write-invalidate or read-write request may exist in the requestor-set. Secondly, the buffer-state must ensure that an arena with native device d has been *(i)* storage allocated and *(ii)* the arena either already has valid data, or a sequence of can_copy() calls have been found that will make the latest data buffer contents available on the arena. If so, the buffer-state will issue the corresponding sequence of copy() calls, and return a "grant-success" to the high-level runtime. A "grant-failure" would prevent k from executing, whereby the DML would force a serialization in the runtime until one or more of the already executing kernels complete and are removed from the requestor-set. Completion of another kernel $k2$ may perhaps resolve an access-type conflict with k. Or, the arena $a2$ associated with $k2$ may now allow map state changes suitable for copying valid data out from $a2$ into the arena needed for executing k.

A kernel k may be represented in the requestor-set using any encoding scheme suitable for the high-level runtime. For example, a kernel could be represented simply by a pointer if the high-level runtime has a unique pointer to each kernel, or the kernel may be represented by a more complex data structure in the requestor-set. The only requirement is for the kernel representation to support an equality test, so the presence of a kernel k can be checked for in the requestor-set.

Our proposed data management layer relies on acquire-release semantics to provide kernels access to a shared buffer. Either the entire buffer is made available to a kernel or none of it is. For this reason, it is sufficient to maintain a valid-set, where each arena can be marked as holding valid data or as invalid. All arenas that are marked valid are considered to hold identical data contents.

3.4   Correctness Under Concurrent Kernel Access Requests

The following steps are taken by the buffer state on a kernel access request. Invariant properties at each step provide the requisite correctness guarantees under arbitrary concurrent requests from the high-level programming runtime.

Terms Given kernel k requesting access to shared buffer b:

1. $RS(b)$: Requestor-set of b, the kernels that currently access b.
2. Kernel's device d: the device k will execute on. Can be more specific than just the hardware component; e.g., d = cpu, gpucl, gpugl; when the GPU supports both OpenCL and OpenGL kernels.
3. Kernel's arena to access b: arena a under b's buffer-state that k will use to access the data buffer contents. The native device for a would be d.

Step 1: **Acquire**(k, b): the runtime makes a kernel access request to the DML

1. A lock is held on b to stall another concurrent request on b until the current request is granted or fails.

2. The access-type of k is checked against $RS(b)$ – request fails if a conflict is found with another kernel in $RS(b)$, e.g., if k requests read-write access to b.
3. If a does not have valid data, buffer-state determines a can_copy sequence to make a valid, or returns failure if no such sequence currently exists.
4. k and its access-type is added to $RS(b)$.
5. buffer-state executes the corresponding copy() sequence, to make a valid.
6. change a to unmapped state or bimapped state to allow access by k (unmapped vs bimapped depends on the arena-wrapper implementation).
7. a.upref()

Invariant: Either k fails to acquire b, or k's arena a is identified, has valid data, and has been put in a map-state suitable for access by k.

Step 2: Execute(k): runtime executes k after acquiring all its buffers.

1. No lock is held on b, allowing concurrent kernel access requests involving b to be made while k executes.
2. k executes and accesses the storage inside a. For example, an OpenCL k would be launched with the OpenCL buffer extracted from inside b's OpenCL-arena.

Invariant: The map-state of a will remain unmapped or perhaps become bimapped during the execution of k. No Acquire($k2$, b) or Release($k2$, b) for a concurrent kernel $k2$ may make a inaccessible to k. a will continue to hold the latest valid data of the shared buffer b until k completes execution.

Step 3: Release(k, b): runtime relinquishes access to b from k once k has completed execution.

1. A lock is held on b to update buffer-state of b safely.
2. k is removed from $RS(b)$.

A b-specific lock is held only for the duration of the Acquire and Release calls involving b. Kernel execution is allowed to happen without the lock held. The steps above have the annotated invariants that guarantee correctness. *High concurrency in kernel execution* is facilitated by *(i)* having individual locks for buffers, and *(ii)* only briefly holding those locks for associated Acquire and Release.

4   Use in a Heterogeneous Programming Runtime

We incorporate our proposed DML inside one high-level framework for C++ heterogeneous programming, the Qualcomm Symphony System Manager SDK [23,24] for mobile SoCs. Section 3 described how the DML ensures correct concurrent access to a single buffer. However, a kernel k often needs to access multiple buffers $b1$, $b2$, etc. during its execution. In accordance with our use of the acquire-release model, k must acquire all its buffers upfront before it can begin

```
void foo(float *a, float *b, int size, float& result_sum) {
  // Create buffers using storage and data from existing pointers
  auto buf_a = symphony::create_buffer<float>(a, size);
  auto buf_b = symphony::create_buffer<float>(b, size);

  // Pass 'hint' that buffer will be accessed by CPU, GPU and DSP devices. The hint enables optimal
  // allocation of storage by Symphony & DML on any platform, e.g., pre-allocate ION if available.
  auto buf_c = symphony::create_buffer<float>(size, {symphony::cpu, symphony::gpu, symphony::dsp});

  // Execute GPU task first
  auto t1 = symphony::launch(gpu_kernel, symphony::range<1>(size), buf_a, buf_b, buf_c);
  t1->wait_for();

  // Execute DSP and CPU tasks concurrently: both read buf_c, producing result_sum and buf_a.
  auto t2 = symphony::launch(dsp_kernel, buf_c, &result_sum);
  auto t3 = symphony::launch(cpu_kernel, buf_c, buf_a);

  t2->wait_for();
  t3->wait_for();
}                                                                                  1
```

Fig. 3. High-level compute APIs in the SDK enabled by the data management layer.

execution. If any buffer acquire fails, all previously acquired buffers must be released, and the whole operation to acquire buffers for k must resume from scratch.

Since the *Acquire* and *Release* operations hold a buffer's lock only for the duration of that operation, there is never a situation where a thread in the SDK would acquire a lock for $b2$ while holding a lock for $b1$. Thus, deadlock is avoided. Unfortunately, kernels $k1$ and $k2$ may acquire overlapping buffers in different orders, creating the possibility of livelock. The SDK avoids livelock by having each kernel acquire and release its buffers in a canonical order—the sorted order of the pointers to the DML's buffer-state objects representing the buffers.

The SDK supports a number of existing heterogeneous compute and memory frameworks. The SDK has *execution back-ends* that wrap the compute APIs of OpenCL, OpenGL and proprietary custom devices to launch kernels, while delegating the data allocation and synchronization aspects to the DML. Due to the DML, the SDK exposes very high-level programming APIs with an abstract representation for program data. As shown in the sample SDK program in Fig. 3, there are no explicit calls to allocate or synchronize data. In fact, the creation of buf_c does not imply any storage allocation for it. buf_a and buf_b illustrate the use of an externally-allocated MainMem-arena for each of them. However, buf_c only needs to allocate storage when accessed by a kernel. The execution of t1 requires OpenCL-arenas to be created under the buffer-states for buf_a, buf_b and buf_c, and OpenCL storage to be allocated inside them. Due to cross-arena optimizations, buf_a and buf_b bind-allocate their OpenCL arenas to the corresponding MainMem-arenas. The SDK accepted "program structure" hints for buf_c, indicating future access on the GPU and DSP. Therefore, the SDK relies on the program structure information to first create an ION-arena inside buf_c's buffer-state, so that the subsequent launch of t1 would cause the OpenCL-arena to bind-allocate to the ION-arena. Without the SDK's initial transformation of

Table 1. Comparison of operation counts and execution time.

Call	Vector-Add			Matrix-Multiply			BFS		
	hand	noopt	opt	hand	noopt	opt	hand	noopt	opt
CL map	1	3	1	0	3	0	0	20	0
CL unmap	0	2	0	0	2	0	0	18	0
CL read	0	0	0	1	0	1	13	0	13
CL write	2	0	2	2	0	2	18	0	18
CL kernel	1	1	1	1	1	1	24	24	24
alloc	-	6	3	-	6	3	-	14	7
bind	-	-	3	-	-	3	-	-	7
memcpy	-	3	0	-	3	0	-	31	0
Time (ms)	31.74	41.20	32.44	1011	1023	1015	149.57	156.31	154.54

buf_c's buffer-state to first allocate ION-storage, the DML would allocate arena storage in the order of use by kernels—allocating independent storage in the OpenCL-, ION-, and MainMem-arenas, and produce two unnecessary memory-copies at the launch of t2 and t3. The SDK also provides "programming pattern" constructs, such as heterogeneous pipelines and parallel-fors, which provide a much more precise order of device access than the hints, allowing the SDK to perform additional buffer-state transformations.

Table 2. Comparison of operation counts and execution time for SLAMBench.

Call	GPU			GPU-DSP		GPU-CPU	
	hand	noopt	opt	noopt	opt	noopt	opt
CL map	0	41480	12066	41480	12945	12314	5280
CL unmap	0	41479	12065	41479	12944	12308	5274
CL read	12066	0	0	0	0	0	1752
CL write	29414	0	28534	0	28534	0	4402
CL kernel	34252	34252	34252	33372	33372	10120	10120
alloc	-	58844	29429	57965	29429	10587	5297
bind	-	-	29415	-	28536	-	5290
memcpy	-	41480	0	41480	0	12314	0
Time (ms)	100447	109357	105356	119538	114187	112818	108484

5   Experimental Evaluation

We run experiments on a Qualcomm Snapdragon^{TM} mobile SoC [21] with multi-core CPUs and an integrated GPU and DSP. We port the following applications to the SDK, and benchmark against hand-optimized OpenCL versions.

1. **Vector-Add:** Adds two 1-million element vectors on the GPU.
2. **Matrix-Multiply:** Multiplies two 512×512-element matrices on the GPU.
3. **BFS** from the Rodinia benchmark suite [5]. Performs a breadth first search on a graph of 1 million nodes. Executes one kernel once on the GPU and a second kernel in a loop on the GPU.
4. **SLAMBench.** [15] solves the Simultaneous Localization and Mapping (SLAM) problem using the KinectFusion algorithm [16]. The algorithm consists of 9 kernels executed within multiple levels of loops. We use SLAM-Bench's reference data-set *living_room_traj2_loop.raw* consisting of 880 image frames.

Vector-Add and Matrix-Multiple execute a single kernel on the GPU once. The CPU creates the inputs and reads back the result to verify. BFS and SLAM-Bench are real-world applications that invoke multiple kernels repeatedly. There is repeated synchronization required between CPU steps and GPU kernels in each loop iteration. We also extend SLAMBench to execute the "mm2meters" kernel on the DSP. We count the number of OpenCL API calls in the SDK and hand-optimized versions—clEnqueue{Map, Unmap, ReadBuffer, WriteBuffer, NDRangeKernel}. We also compare execution times, averaged over 5 runs.

The hand-optimized implementations of the applications optimize performance and minimize use of the OpenCL calls based on the programmer's knowledge of the program structure and data access patterns. The SDK hides the low-level details from the programmer, while being conservative to ensure correct data synchronization at device kernel execution boundaries. We evaluate the SDK in two modes: (1) *non-optimized*, where all storage allocation and data synchronization decisions are defered to our proposed DML, which chooses the appropriate actions in the dynamic order of the kernel access requests received, and (2) *optimized* where the SDK plugs cross-arena optimizations into the DML and manipulates the buffer-state representation to force optimal storage allocation decisions based on advance knowledge of the program structure (Sect. 4).

Table 1 shows the count of CL operations and execution time for the hand-optimized OpenCL implementations (*hand*) against implementations using the SDK– both non-optimized (*noopt*) and optimized (*opt*). We also compare the number of storage allocations (*alloc*), the number of bind-allocations across arenas in a buffer-state (*bind*), and the number of memory-copies for data synchronization (*memcpy*). Vector-Add and Matrix-Multiply create two input buffers and one output buffer. Therefore, *hand* incurs two CL write operations to synchronize the inputs to the GPU, and one CL map or CL read to read back the GPU result. *noopt* allocates separate main-memory and GPU-memory storage for each buffer, resulting in an explicit mem-copy between the two allocated storages of the buffer, and a CL map or unmap. In contrast, in *opt* the SDK uses cross-arena optimizations to bind-allocate, creating a single storage per buffer and avoiding mem-copies. Therefore, *opt* matches both the CL operation count and the execution time of *hand*. The results for BFS show a similar trend.

Table 2 compares multiple implementations of the SLAMBench application: (1) hand-written OpenCL (*GPU-hand*), where all the kernels execute on the GPU, (2) SDK *GPU*, where all kernels execute on the GPU, (3) SDK *GPU-DSP*, where all kernels execute on the GPU except the "mm2meters" kernel which executes on the DSP, and (4) SDK *GPU-CPU*, which executes the "track" and "reduce" kernels on the CPU and the rest on the GPU. Each SDK implementation is evaluated in non-optimized (*noopt*) and optimized (*opt*) modes. Table 2 shows that *GPU-hand* executes the fastest, with *GPU-opt* within 5%. SDK *opt* versions show a substantially reduced number of OpenCL calls, storage allocations and mem-copies compared to *noopt*, resulting in execution time gains that range between 3.8 and 4.7%.

Overall, these results demonstrate that (1) the SDK does not substantially increase execution time over the hand-optimized implementations, successfully bounding the overheads of the DML, and (2) the DML abstractions allows the SDK to correctly and easily use platform-specific and program-structure knowledge to achieve significant performance improvements. Using the data management techniques presented in this paper and the SDK's high level abstractions we make it easy for programmers to get performance within 5–10% of hand optimized with much less effort.

6   Related Work

Distributed Shared Memory (DSM) is an abstraction that provides a shared address space over a multitude of, potentially heterogeneous, computing nodes. DSM enables the free sharing of pointers across the different nodes, ensuring a common logical memory space for accessing data. Several ideas have been proposed and implemented to improve the performance of DSM, such as reducing communication overhead by sending only the updates to a page as opposed to the entire page, and lazy release consistency—delaying the propagation of changes until the page is acquired by a node [12]. These systems address issues in which nodes are loosely connected and the latency of communication is high. InterWeave [6] assumes a distributed collection of servers and clients. Servers maintain persistent copies of shared data and coordinate sharing among clients by mapping cached copies of needed data into client local memory. The unit of sharing is a segment, with addresses represented as URLs. While such an approach works for large clusters of computers, it is too heavy for mobile SoCs.

Asymmetric DSM (ADSM) [9] is a programming model that implements a specialized DSM over a heterogeneous computing system, with CPUs and other accelerators. By allowing unidirectional CPU access to accelerator memory (the accelerator does not have access to the CPU memory), the overheads associated with ensuring coherency are significantly reduced.

Liu *et al.* describe a system that allows sharing of virtual memory between CPUs and accelerators [13]. Data transfer between the CPU and accelerator memories is achieved through an explicit communication buffer maintained by the runtime. The synchronization of data across the different memories is performed by the runtime, and programmers do not have finer control. Our system differs from this approach, in that we do not enforce a shared virtual address space.

A number of heterogeneous tasking models have proposed various mechanisms to address memory management: OmpSs [8] extends OpenMP [19] to enable concurrent execution of tasks on heterogeneous devices. Data transfers are inserted by the compiler, which performs array slice analysis to determine the necessary data movements. The programmer is responsible to define the read/write sets for the heterogeneous tasks. StarPu [4] is a task based heterogeneous runtime that allows the user to specify where the memory needs to be allocated via an API call. Fluidicl [20] is an OpenCL runtime that enables a kernel execution to be partitioned across the CPU and GPU. A data merge step on the GPU combines the partial results. OpenACC [3] supports heterogeneous systems where CPU and accelerator either share memory, or have separate memories. A "data" construct takes care of synchronizing data between the host and device memories.

Heterogeneous System Architecture (HSA) [2] provides a unified address space between CPUs and GPUs by performing memory management in hardware. In terms of synchronization, it offers cross-device atomic operations. This model is similar to shared memory programming in multi-core CPUs, with some additional restrictions on the size of coherence units and memory regions available for sharing, but it is too low level and requires expert knowledge of the underlying hardware.

7   Conclusions

We have proposed a data management layer based on a novel abstract representation over heterogeneous memory. The use of the data management layer hides the considerable complexity and platform-dependence that programmers of heterogeneous applications currently face. We advocate a software architecture where a high-level programming framework, whether general-purpose or domain-specific, may rely on our data management layer to easily avoid dealing with the complexities of multiple memory frameworks and platform variations. The high-level frameworks may focus on domain and application-specific optimizations and provide simpler high-level programming abstractions to the users, while relying on the data management layer to provide correct synchronization of data, optimized to the platform and program properties, and enhance the concurrent sharing of data over the available heterogeneous devices. We incorporated our data management layer into the Qualcomm Symphony System Manager SDK, and demonstrated using both micro-benchmarks and large multi-kernel workloads that the benefits of high-level user abstractions, platform-portability and strong correctness properties are achieved with less than 5% performance overhead compared to hand-optimized OpenCL applications.

Acknowledgement. Qualcomm and Snapdragon are trademarks of Qualcomm Incorporated, registered in the United States and other countries. Qualcomm Snapdragon and Qualcomm Symphony System Manager are products of Qualcomm Technologies, Inc.

References

1. IvyTown Xeon + FPGA: The HARP program. Intel Corp
2. HSA programmer's reference manual: HSAIL virtual ISA and programming model, compiler writer, and object format (BRIG). Technical report, HSA Foundation, July 2015
3. The OpenACC: Application Programming Interface. Technical report, OpenACC-Standard.org, October 2015
4. Augonnet, C., Thibault, S., Namyst, R., Wacrenier, P.-A.: StarPU: a unified platform for task scheduling on heterogeneous multicore architectures. Concurrency Comput.: Pract. Experience **23**(2), 187–198 (2011)
5. Che, S., et al.: Rodinia: a benchmark suite for heterogeneous computing. In: 2009 IEEE International Symposium on Workload Characterization, IISWC 2009, pp. 44–54, October 2009
6. Chen, D.Q., Dwarkadas, S., Parthasarathy, S., Pinheiro, E., Scott, M.L.: InterWeave: a middleware system for distributed shared state. In: Dwarkadas, S. (ed.) LCR 2000. LNCS, vol. 1915, pp. 207–220. Springer, Heidelberg (2000). https://doi.org/10.1007/3-540-40889-4_16
7. Compute unified device architecture (CUDA). http://www.nvidia.com/object/cuda_home_new.html
8. Duran, A., et al.: OmpSs: a proposal for programming heterogeneous multi-core architectures. Parallel Process. Lett. **21**(02), 173–193 (2011)
9. Gelado, I., Stone, J.E., Cabezas, J., Patel, S., Navarro, N., Hwu, W.W.: An asymmetric distributed shared memory model for heterogeneous parallel systems. In: Proceedings of the Fifteenth Edition of ASPLOS on Architectural Support for Programming Languages and Operating Systems, ASPLOS XV, pp. 347–358. ACM, New York (2010)
10. Hu, Q., Gumerov, N.A., Duraiswami, R.: Scalable fast multipole methods on distributed heterogeneous architectures. In: Proceedings of 2011 International Conference for High Performance Computing, Networking, Storage and Analysis, SC 2011, pp. 36:1–36:12. ACM, New York 2011
11. The Android ION memory allocator. https://lwn.net/Articles/480055/
12. Keleher, P., Cox, A.L., Dwarkadas, S., Zwaenepoel, W.: TreadMarks: distributed shared memory on standard workstations and operating systems. In: Proceedings of the USENIX Winter 1994 Technical Conference on USENIX Winter 1994 Technical Conference, WTEC 1994, p. 10. USENIX Association, Berkeley (1994)
13. Wei Liu, et al.: A balanced programming model for emerging heterogeneous multicore systems. In: Proceedings of the 2nd USENIX Conference on Hot Topics in Parallelism, HotPar 2010, p. 3. USENIX Association, Berkeley (1994)
14. Mittal, S., Vetter, J.S.: A survey of CPU-GPU Heterogeneous Computing Techniques. ACM Comput. Surv. **47**(4), 1–35 (2015)

15. Nardi, L., et al.: Introducing SLAMBench, a performance and accuracy benchmarking methodology for SLAM. In: 2015 IEEE International Conference on Robotics and Automation (ICRA), pp. 5783–5790, May 2015
16. Newcombe, R.A., et al.: KinectFusion: real-time dense surface mapping and tracking. In: 2011 10th IEEE International Symposium on Mixed and Augmented Reality (ISMAR), pp. 127–136, October 2011
17. Jouppi, N.P., et al.: In-datacenter performance analysis of a Tensor Processing Unit. In: Proceedings of the 44th Annual International Symposium on Computer Architecture, ISCA 2017, pp. 1–12. ACM, New York (2017)
18. OpenCL: The open standard for parallel programming of heterogeneous systems. http://www.khronos.org/opencl
19. The OpenMP API specification for parallel programming. http://www.openmp.org/
20. Pandit, P., Govindarajan, R.: Fluidic kernels: cooperative execution of OpenCL programs on multiple heterogeneous devices. In: Proceedings of Annual IEEE/ACM International Symposium on Code Generation and Optimization, p. 273. ACM (2014)
21. Qualcomm Snapdragon: Qualcomm Technologies Inc. https://www.qualcomm.com/products/snapdragon
22. Shreiner, D., The Khronos OpenGL ARB Working Group: OpenGL Programming Guide: The Official Guide to Learning OpenGL, Versions 3.0 and 3.1, 7th edn. Addison-Wesley Professional (2009)
23. Heterogeneous computing made simpler with the Symphony SDK. https://developer.qualcomm.com/blog/heterogeneous-computing-made-simpler-symphony-sdk
24. Qualcomm Symphony System Manager SDK. https://developer.qualcomm.com/software/symphony-system-manager-sdk

Parallel Roles for Practical Deterministic Parallel Programming

Michael Faes[(⊠)] and Thomas R. Gross[(⊠)]

Department of Computer Science, ETH Zurich, Zürich, Switzerland
{mfaes,trg}@inf.ethz.ch

Abstract. Deterministic parallel programming languages are attractive as they do not allow data races, deadlocks, or similar kinds of concurrency bugs that are caused by unintended (or poorly understood) parallel execution. We present here a simple programming model for deterministic parallel programming that is based on *roles*. The programmer specifies the role that an object plays for a task (e.g., the READONLY role), and compiler and runtime system *together* ensure that only those object accesses are performed that are allowed by this role. An object may play different roles in the course of a program's execution, giving the programmer considerable flexibility in expressing a parallel program.

The model has been implemented in a Java-like language with references and object sharing. Preliminary results indicate that the runtime overhead is moderate (compared to standard Java programs), and that the compiled programs achieve substantial parallel speedups.

1 Introduction

Deterministic parallel programming languages avoid bugs caused by the unintended or poorly understood parallel execution of programs. These languages attempt to make concurrency bugs impossible by design [5,23,24,37,38].

Recently, several projects proposed static effect systems to support deterministic parallel programming (DPP) for imperative and object-oriented languages [6,18,20,25]. In such systems, the programmer declares the side effects of tasks and methods by indicating the *memory regions* that are read or modified. These effect specifications are then used by the compiler or the runtime system to check that tasks with interfering effects are not executed in parallel.

Memory regions as used in effect systems may allow a precise description of which memory locations are read or modified by a program unit. However, object-oriented programs are not structured (or documented) based on memory locations but instead use *objects* as the unit of reasoning. Memory locations provide little abstraction and are at too low a level. Since objects are the foundation of object-oriented programs, our approach to DPP is based on objects. The first idea is to leverage the concept of *roles*, which have a long-standing tradition in sequential object-oriented programming and modeling, where they are used to characterize the different "roles" an object may assume when collaborating with

© Springer Nature Switzerland AG 2019
L. Rauchwerger (Ed.): LCPC 2017, LNCS 11403, pp. 163–181, 2019.
https://doi.org/10.1007/978-3-030-35225-7_12

other objects [15,21,28,30,31]. Our work builds on this foundation and uses roles as the key abstraction to specify and reason about parallelism. Together with the concept of *role transitions*, roles form the basis for a new object-oriented DPP model.

In this model, every object plays a role in each task, and these roles change dynamically when tasks start or finish. Because the role of an object defines the legal interactions with that object, roles provide a concise way to reason about, document, and specify the effects of concurrent tasks. In contrast to effect systems, the model does not focus on pieces of code and their effects on memory regions; instead, it focuses on objects and the roles they play in parallel – hence the name *Parallel Roles*. By employing a specific set of roles and *role transition rules*, the model guarantees that tasks do not interfere. Noninterference is not checked at compile time or before a task is started, like in effect systems; instead, it is enforced *during* the execution of tasks. However, unlike in speculative systems, noninterference is enforced deterministically and without rollback.

This dynamic approach makes it possible to design DPP languages with simple program annotations, without the need for special syntactic constructs for parallel execution, and without any kind of aliasing restriction. To illustrate these points, we give an overview of a roles-based, Java-like language we call *Rolez*. This language enables programmers to parallelize a program by simply marking a method as a "task" and declaring one of three possible roles for its parameters: READWRITE, READONLY, or PURE. When a task is invoked, it is executed in parallel to the invoking code, while the runtime system prevents the two concurrent parts of the program from interfering, based on the declared roles.

Figure 1 illustrates the simplicity of Rolez in a snippet of an encryption program we use in our evaluation. The encryption scheme is block-based, so different parts of the data can be encrypted in parallel. Note that for the sake of clarity, some annotations are left out; Sect. 3.2 explains what additional annotations are required. The `encrypt` task has two main parameters: `src` and `dst`, both of type `Array`. The task declares the READONLY role for the `src` array,

```
def parallelEncrypt(plaintext: Array[byte],
                    tasks: int): Array[byte] {
  val encrypted: Array[Array[byte]] = ...
  for(var i = 0; i < tasks; i++)
    start encrypt(plaintext, encrypted.get(i), i);
  return merge(encrypted);
}

task encrypt(src: readonly Array[byte],
             dst: readwrite Array[byte],
             partition: int): void {
  ...
}
```

Fig. 1. Rolez example. The role declarations are highlighted in green and orange. (Color figure online)

which the task only *reads*, and the READWRITE role for the `dst` array, to which the task *writes* the encrypted data. In addition, the `encrypt` task has a parameter that defines the part of the `src` array that should be encrypted. The `parallelEncrypt` method achieves parallelism by creating multiple destination arrays and starting a separate `encrypt` task for each of them. Noninterference is guaranteed in two ways: First, the `plaintext` array plays the READONLY role in all tasks, which means that it cannot be modified by any of them. Second, every task writes to a separate destination array. In terms of roles, a destination array that plays the READWRITE role in one task plays the PURE role in all other tasks (including the parent task), meaning that it is inaccessible. However, as soon as all tasks have finished, all destination arrays are READWRITE again in the parent task, so they can be merged into a single array. When the `merge` method in the parent task tries to read from the destination arrays, it is automatically blocked until all `encrypt` tasks have finished.

To demonstrate the viability of roles-based languages, we implemented a prototype compiler and runtime system for Rolez and use a suite of parallel programs to assess its effectiveness. These programs contain a range of parallel patterns that are expressible with the three mentioned roles. All programs achieve substantial speedups over a sequential Java version and exhibit a reasonable runtime overhead compared to a manually parallelized Java programs.

To summarize, the key contributions of this paper are the following:

1. an object-oriented parallel programming model, based on three roles: READWRITE, READONLY, and PURE that guarantee determinism (Sect. 2);
2. an overview of the design of Rolez, a roles-based, Java-like DPP language that requires only simple *role declarations* from a programmer (Sect. 3);
3. a preliminary evaluation of the Rolez prototype for 4 parallel programs. Rolez can express many parallel patterns found in these programs and achieves substantial speedups over sequential Java for most of them (Sect. 4).

2   The Parallel Roles Model

This section presents the Parallel Roles programming model. We first present a simple core version for single objects and then extend it to cover object graphs.

2.1   Core Parallel Roles

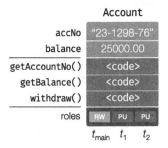

Fig. 2. The components of an object: fields, methods, roles

The main idea behind Parallel Roles is to use the *object*, the key concept of object-oriented programming (OOP) as the basis to reason about concurrent effects and parallelism. In the standard OOP model an object is a collection of fields, which contain the object's state, plus a collection of methods, which define the object's functionality. In the Parallel Roles model, every object has a third component: the *roles* it currently plays for the different *tasks* in the program. This is illustrated in Fig. 2.

The fields and methods of an object define the object's *sequential behavior*. That is, they define how the object behaves when other objects interact with it in a single task. On the other hand, the roles of an object define the object's *concurrent behavior*. Specifically, they define which interactions are legal in which tasks and what happens when an illegal interaction occurs. Like the content of an object's fields, the roles an object plays may change over time. However, in contrast to the fields' contents, which (in general) can be modified arbitrarily, the changing of roles follows strict rules. These *role transition rules* restrict the combinations of roles an object may play in different tasks at the same time. Those restrictions in turn guarantee noninterference and, by extension, determinism. In the following paragraphs, we explain these core concepts, roles, tasks, and role transitions, in more detail.

Roles. The role of an object defines how other objects may interact with that object, i.e., which kinds of field operations they may perform and, by extension, which methods they may invoke. There are three roles: READWRITE,

	PURE	READONLY	READWRITE
final field read	✓	✓	✓
any field read	✗	✓	✓
field write	✗	✗	✓

Fig. 3. Operations permitted by the roles

READONLY, and PURE. READWRITE permits both field read and field write operations, while READONLY permits only read operations. PURE permits neither, except if a field is final (i.e., it cannot be modified, as in Java); then it may be read. Final fields are treated specially because they can never be the source of interference. Figure 3 summarizes these rules.

The set of permitted field operations also defines the set of permitted methods. READWRITE permits calls to any method, while READONLY permits only calls to methods that do not modify the target object. PURE permits only calls to *pure methods*, which are the object-oriented counterpart of a *pure function*: They are side-effect free (i.e., they do not write to any of the target object's fields) and their result is always the same, given the same target object (i.e., they do not read any of the target object's non-final fields). As an example, PURE for some `Account` object would only permit calls to `getAccountNo()` (assuming account numbers are immutable), READONLY would also permit calls to `getBalance()`, and READWRITE would permit calls to all methods, including `withdraw()`.

Tasks and Role Declarations. Tasks are execution contexts, like threads. When the execution of a program begins, all objects interact with each other in the *main task*. A task may start other tasks (called *child tasks*) and thereby create multiple concurrent execution contexts. While tasks are similar to threads, there is a key difference: When defining a task, the programmer needs to declare the role that each object is supposed to play in that task. With these *role declarations*, the programmer controls the role transitions that objects perform, as described next.

Role Transitions. As mentioned earlier, there are rules about when and how the roles of an object change, i.e., when and how an object performs a role transition. Most importantly, role transitions only take place when a task starts or finishes. When a new task starts, every object for which the task declares a role performs a role transition such that its role in that task matches the declared one. Hence, at the beginning of a task, every object plays the declared role in that task. However, a role transition may also change the role an object plays in the parent task (the task that starts the new task). For example, this is the case if the new task declares the READWRITE role for an object. In such a case, the object becomes PURE in the parent task, to prevent interference. Therefore, while an object is guaranteed to play the declared role at the *beginning* of a task, a role declaration does not state that the object plays this role for the whole duration of the task. What a role declaration *does* state is that the object may never play a *more permissive* role than the one declared, in either that task itself or any task that is (transitively) started by it. That is, an object may never play a role that permits an operation the declared role does not permit. For example, if the declared role of an object is READONLY, this object can never play the READWRITE role in that task, since READWRITE is more permissive than READONLY.

1. When an object is created in a task t, it plays the READWRITE role in t and the PURE role in all other tasks.
2. When an object o plays the READWRITE role in a task t, t may share o with a new task t_n that declares the READWRITE role for o. When t_n is started, o becomes READWRITE in t_n and PURE in t.
3. When an object o plays the READWRITE or READONLY role in a task t, t may share o with a new task t_n that declares the READONLY role for o. When t_n is started, o becomes READONLY in t and t_n.
4. Any object o may be shared with a task t that declares the PURE role for it. No transition takes place for o when t is started.

5. When a task t that declared the READWRITE role for an object o is about to finish, t waits until o is READWRITE; then, t finishes and o becomes READWRITE in t's parent task.
6. When a task t that declared the READONLY role for an object o is about to finish, t waits until o is READONLY. After t has finished, if t's parent t_p is the only task left in which o is READONLY, o becomes READWRITE in t_p. Otherwise, o stays READONLY in t_p.
7. When a task that declared an object o as PURE finishes, o performs no role transition.
8. When a task t is about to finish, t waits until every object o created in t (or a child of t) plays the READWRITE role; then, t finishes and o becomes READWRITE in t's parent t_p (if t_p may reach o via some reference).

Fig. 4. The core role transition rules

The rules in Fig. 4 define when and how the roles of an object can change. As we explain shortly, these rules are designed such that they guarantee noninterference for every object. Rule 1 concerns newly created objects, while Rules 2–4 concern the starting of tasks and Rules 5–8 the finishing of tasks.

Figure 5 illustrates these rules by showing a series of role transitions an object can go through. Initially, when the object is created in task t_1, it is READWRITE in t_1 and PURE in the t_{main} task. It is then shared with two tasks: t_2, which declares it as READWRITE, and later t_3, which declares it as READONLY. When t_2 and t_3 start and finish, the object performs a role transition. After t_3 has finished, it is again READWRITE in t_1. Finally, t_1 finishes and the object becomes READWRITE in t_{main}.

Guarding. An object may never play a role that is more permissive than the role declared in a given task. However, the object may temporarily play a *less* permissive role. When this happens, some operations may become illegal, despite being

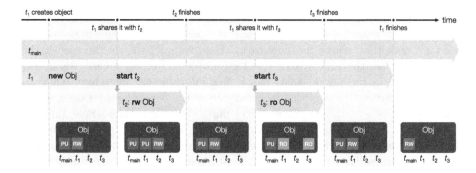

Fig. 5. Illustration of the role transition rules for an object. The gray arrows from the left to the right are tasks, the black boxes represent the same object in different points in time, and the small colored boxes show the roles the object plays in each task. (Color figure online)

legal under the declared role. For example, if an object is declared READWRITE in a task, it might play the READONLY role for some time, because it was shared with another task. This discrepancy between declared and current role is the subject of *guarding*. The idea of guarding is to wait until the current role equals the declared role: When an operation is performed that is legal under the declared but not under the current role of the target object, this operation is not an error but instead is blocked until the object plays its declared role again.

We illustrate guarding with a simplified Rolez snippet (from a program we later use for the evaluation) and a corresponding illustration, in Fig. 6. This program renders animated 3D scenes and encodes the rendered images as frames in a video file. The main loop consists of three steps: First, the scene is rendered for a fixed point in (animation) time, then the resulting image is encoded as a video frame, and finally an animation step is performed to update the scene for the next frame. The encoding and the animation step can be done in parallel, which is why `encode` is declared and invoked as a task. Because `encode` only needs to *read* the image, it declares it as READONLY. When the `encode` task starts, the image performs a role transition and becomes READONLY also in the "main" task. While `animateStep` does not modify the image, the rendering in the next iteration does. In case the `render` method begins execution before the `encode` task has finished, guarding blocks the execution of `render` to prevent it from interfering with the encoding. Once `encode` finishes, the `render` method resumes execution. Note that in the version of the program used for the evaluation, *two* image buffers are used, to enable the `encode` task to also execute in parallel to `render`.

Properties. We now examine the properties of Parallel Roles. First of all, the transition rules ensure the *soundness of role declarations*, i.e., that no object may play a more permissive role than its declared role in both the task that declared it and any task it (transitively) starts. This follows from two observations: First,

```
def animate(scn: Scene): {
    val img = new Image(w, h);
    while(scn.time < scn.length) {
        render(scn, img);
        start encode(img);
        animateStep(scn);
    }
}
task encode(img: readonly Image): {
    ...
}
```

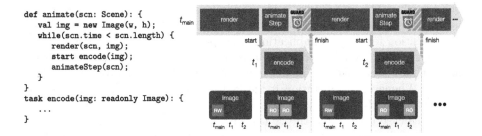

Fig. 6. Guarding example. The left side shows (simplified) Rolez code and the right side illustrates how guarding prevents **encode** from interfering with the **render** method.

no transition rule permits an object with a declared role to play a role it has not played before in a given task. And second, none of the rules permit an object to be shared with a task that declares a more permissive role than the object currently plays. Note that Rule 8 *does* permit objects to play a more permissive role (READWRITE) in the parent task than before (PURE), but since these objects were newly created, they do not have a declared role in the parent task.

Second, the transition rules guarantee that no object ever plays the READWRITE role in one task while it plays the READWRITE or the READONLY role in another task. We call this property *exclusiveness of* READWRITE and we show it using induction: When an object is created, it is READWRITE for the creator task and PURE for all other tasks (Rule 1). This is the base case. For the inductive step, we assume the object is either READWRITE in a single task or READONLY in a number of tasks, but in both cases PURE for all other tasks. After any start transition (Rules 2 or 3), this rule still holds. After any transition at the end of a task (Rules 5, 6, or 8), the condition also still holds. In particular, Rule 6 ensures that an object that is READONLY in any task can only become READWRITE again once there is no task left in which it is READONLY. Therefore, no series of transitions may ever violate the exclusiveness of READWRITE.

Exclusiveness of READWRITE, combined with guarding and the definitions of permitted operations in Fig. 3, implies that if an object can be modified in one task, then the mutable parts of it cannot be accessed by any other task until the modifying task has finished. Thus, the model guarantees *noninterference*. Note that two mechanisms to prevent interference are combined: (i) An operation that is illegal with respect to the *declared* role of an object results in an error. This could be a runtime or a compile-time error, depending on the language. (ii) An operation that is illegal with respect to the *current* role of an object, but not with respect to its declared role, is blocked by guarding until the object plays a role under which the operation is legal.

Note that noninterference is much stricter than data race freedom. Since the exclusiveness of READWRITE holds for all objects in the program, no modification of a task t can be observed by any other task, as long as t is running. Therefore, tasks cannot communicate, except for passing arguments and waiting for each other's results. This restriction is the key to guarantee determinism. However, Parallel Roles could be extended with nondeterministic roles to enable inter-task communication for parallel applications that profit from nondeterminism.

Since noninterference is achieved in part by blocking the execution of operations, it may seem like the model is prone to deadlock. However, this is not the case: Whenever an operation is blocked in a task t_1, it is because the target object currently plays a less permissive role than its declared role. This can only be the case if t_1 shared the object with another task t_2. Since objects can only be shared when a task is started, t_2 must be a child task of t_1. Therefore, tasks can be blocked only by child tasks, and this property precludes cyclic dependences. Thus, Parallel Roles not only guarantees noninterference, but also *deadlock freedom*. Together, these two properties imply that Parallel Roles guarantees determinism.

To summarize, Parallel Roles combines roles, which determine the legal operations for an object, with transition rules, which determine the possible combinations of roles an object may play in parallel. Tasks are prevented from interfering using a combination of runtime or compile-time checking and guarding.

2.2 Object Graphs

A shortcoming of the transition rules presented so far is that they do not consider objects with references to other objects. That is, they do not define what happens to objects that are *reachable* from an object that performs a role transition.

A safe but impractical definition would be that objects are simply unaffected by the role transitions of their referrers. However, with such a definition, an object could easily break when shared with another task, because objects it depends on would play a different role than itself. For example, consider a Bank object, which contains references to all Accounts of that bank. The Bank has a method payInterest, which computes and deposits the yearly interest for each of its accounts. If such a Bank object was shared with a task t that declares it as READWRITE, calling the payInterest method in t would fail, since all of its Account objects would be PURE and their balance could not be accessed in t.

We employ a practical, but simple and safe way to handle object graphs. Expressed as two additional role transition rule, it states:

9. Whenever an object o is about to perform a role transition, all objects that are reachable from o perform the same transition. The transitions only take place once all these objects play one of the roles o is required to play. The implicitly declared role of these objects is the same as for o. In case an object is reachable from multiple objects that perform different role transitions at the start of a task, that object performs the transition that makes it play the most permissive role in the new task.

10. When a task t that declared the READWRITE role for an object o is about to finish, t waits until all objects *that were reachable from o when t started* are READWRITE. Then, t finishes and all these objects become READWRITE in t's parent task.

With Rule 9, when an object is shared with a task, the task will not start until that object *and all objects that are reachable from it* play the required role. For example, when a Bank object is shared with a task that declares it as READWRITE, not only the Bank itself, but also all of its Accounts must play the READWRITE role before the task may start. Once they do, all these objects perform a transition and become READWRITE for the new task. Now, payInterest can be successfully invoked in that task, because all required objects play the READWRITE role.

Finally, Rule 10 concerns object graphs that are shared with a task that unlinks some objects in the graph. Since these objects may still be used in the parent task later, they also revert to their previous roles once the task finishes.

3 Rolez Language Overview

This section gives an informal description of a concrete programming language, *Rolez*, which implements the Parallel Roles model presented in the previous section. It is a Java-like language with a roles-based type system.

```
1   class App {
2       def pure calcInterest(balance: int): int {
3           return (the Consts.intrstRate * balance) as int;
4       }
5       task pure payInterest(acc: readwrite Account): {
6           val intrst = this.calcInterest(acc.getBalance);
7           acc.deposit(intrst);
8       }
9       task pure main: {
10          val acc = new Account;
11          acc.deposit(1000);
12          this start payInterest(acc);
13      }
14  }

15  class Account {
16      var balance: int
17      def readwrite deposit(i: int): {
18          this.balance += i;
19      }
20      def readwrite withdraw(i: int): {
21          this.balance -= i;
22      }
23      def readonly getBalance: int {
24          return this.balance;
25      }
26  }
27  object Consts {
28      val intrstRate: double = 0.015
29  }
```

Fig. 7. Rolez code example for tasks, role declarations, and global singleton objects

3.1 Tasks and Role Declarations

Declaring and Starting Tasks. In Rolez, tasks are declared in the same way as methods. Two different keywords, def and task, are used to distinguish the two. Likewise, starting a task is expressed in the same way as invoking a method, except for the keyword start, which replaces the dot. When an object is supposed to be shared with a task, the programmer simply creates a corresponding parameter for that task and passes the object as an argument when starting it. Figure 7 shows a Rolez example program that illustrates these points. Lines 2 to 8 contain the declarations of a method and a task, while Lines 11 and 12 show how these are called or started, respectively. Note that void return types can be omitted.

Role Declarations. To declare the role of an object in a task, the programmer annotates the corresponding task parameter with that role, as shown on Line 5. This line indicates that the `payInterest` task requires a single object to be shared with it, namely an `Account` object that plays the READWRITE role. The parameter is declared as READWRITE because the `payInterest` modifies the balance of the given account when calling `deposit` on Line 7. So when this task is started on Line 12, the `Account` object that is passed as an argument performs a role transition and becomes READWRITE for the `payInterest` task and PURE for the `main` task.

Incidentally, both the `payInterest` and the `main` task have another parameter: the "`this`". The role for "`this`" is declared right after the `task` keyword and is PURE for both of these tasks. This means that the `App` instance does not perform any role transition (see Rule 4). This instance is created implicitly before the program starts and is the target (the "`this`") of both task start invocations (including the implicit start of the `main` task at the start of the program execution).

Note that, in Rolez, not only task parameters but also method parameters and other constructs have role declarations. Section 3.2 elaborates these aspects.

Global Objects. How can Rolez guarantee that only objects that have been shared with a task are accessed in that task? Simply, a task can only access objects that were passed to it as arguments (including "`this`"), or that are reachable from such. (As per Rule 9, such reachable objects perform the same transitions as their referrers and implicitly have the same declared role.) That is, no objects can be globally accessed in Rolez, in contrast to, e.g., objects in static fields in Java.

However, there is one exception: A programmer may define global singleton objects, using the `object` keyword instead of `class`. To prevent tasks from interfering when they access such global objects, these objects are immutable. In other words, they are (conceptually) initialized at the beginning of the program and then they permanently play the READONLY role for all tasks. An example for the declaration of such a singleton is shown in Fig. 7 on Lines 27 to 29, while Line 3 shows how this singleton is accessed using the keyword "`the`".

3.2 Role Type System

Rolez uses a static type system to report erroneous operations at compile time. Recall that there are two kinds of *illegal* operations with regard to roles, only one of which is considered *erroneous*. The first kind is a *temporarily illegal* operation, which is illegal only with respect to an object's *current* role. Such an operation is not considered an error, but is delayed until it becomes legal, using guarding. The second kind of an illegal operation is illegal with respect to an object's *declared* role. Such an operation can never become legal and must be reported as a *role error*. In Rolez, role errors are reported at compile-time, using a roles-based type system. In this section, we give a brief, informal overview of this type system.

Note that the Rolez type system does not guarantee noninterference on its own, unlike static effect systems. Only in combination with guarding can Rolez guarantee that tasks do not interfere. Thus, the Rolez type system is much less complex than static effect systems or permission-based type systems (see Sect. 5) and does not, e.g., impose any aliasing restrictions.

Role Types. The Rolez type system is an extension of the class-based type system known from Java and other OOP languages. Every variable in such a language has a type that corresponds to a class. A sound type system guarantees that, at runtime, a variable always refers to an object that is an instance of the class that corresponds to the variable's type (or a subclass thereof). Therefore, when accessing a field or calling a method on a variable, the compiler can check whether this member exists in that class, or else report a type error. Likewise, by including an object's declared role in the static type of variables that refer to that object, the Rolez type system enables the compiler to report role errors.

A static type in Rolez, called a *role type*, consists of two parts, the *class part* and the *static role*. The class part corresponds to the class of an object, while the static role corresponds to the declared role of an object in the currently executing task. An example for a role type is `readwrite Account`, where `readwrite` is the static role and `Account` is the class part.

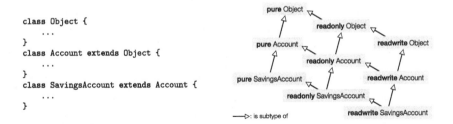

Fig. 8. Rolez type hierarchy example: source code and corresponding type hierarchy

In Java-like languages, a variable may not only refer to instances of the very class that corresponds to the variable's type, but also to instances of subclasses thereof. In Rolez, the same applies to the static role: A variable may refer to objects whose declared role is a *subrole* of the variable's static role. A role is a subrole of another role if it is the same or a more permissive role. Hence, subtyping applies to both the class part and the static role.

Figure 8 illustrates the subtype relation with an example consisting of three classes. In Java, this code would lead to a type hierarchy with a linear structure and three types that correspond to the three classes. On the other hand, in Rolez the code results in a lattice containing nine role types that correspond to all possible combinations of roles and classes.

Type Declarations and Type Checks. In Rolez, like in other languages with a
static type system, all local variables, parameters, fields, and methods need a
type declaration, in general. However, Fig. 7 shows that *type inference* is applied
to local variables to reduce the programmer's annotation burden. If a variable
is assigned right when it is declared, the variable's type is inferred from the
right-hand side of the assignment (Lines 6 and 10). For method parameters,
type inference is not possible under modular compilation, therefore types must
be fully declared. This is true also for the "`this`" parameter of methods (and
tasks), although the class part of the type is implicit, because it corresponds to
the method's class. The role part is still necessary though (Lines 17, 20, and 23).
These type declarations are used by the compiler to perform type checks, with
the ultimate purpose of preventing operations that are not permitted under the
declared role of an object.

Most type checks in Rolez are standard, like "the right-hand side type of
an assignment must be a subtype of the left-hand side type". The roles-specific
checks concern field accesses. A field may only be read if the target's role is
"at least" `readonly` (or if the field is final). Likewise, a field may only be written
to if the target is `readwrite`. Another difference between the field access rules in
Rolez and other OOP languages is that the type of a field read expression depends
on the role of the target expression, and is not simply the declared type of the
field. The reason for this difference is the object graphs extension introduced in
Sect. 2.2. With this extension, the declared role of an object that is reachable
from a task parameter corresponds to the declared role of that parameter. To
reflect this in the type system, the role of a field-read expression must always be
a superrole (the same or a less permissive role) of that of the target expression.

```
1  task pure getOwnerName(a: readonly Account): pure String {   5  class Account {
2      val owner: readonly Client = a.owner;                      6      var owner: readwrite Client
3      return owner.name;                                         7      ...
4  }                                                              8  }
```

Fig. 9. Rolez example to illustrate the field-read type check

The example in Fig. 9 illustrates how this last rule ensures that the static
role of an object that is reachable from a task parameter is always a superrole of
that object's implicitly declared role. The `getOwnerName` task declares an `Account`
parameter with the `readonly` role. When an `Account` object is shared with this
task, it becomes READONLY, like the `Client` object that the `owner` field on Line 6
refers to. When this field is read on Line 2, the role of the `a.owner` expression is
`readonly`, even though the type of the `owner` field is `readwrite Client`. Therefore,
this expression can only be assigned to a variable of type `readonly Client`, making sure that the `Client` object's implicitly declared READONLY role is respected.

4   Evaluation

In this section, we present a preliminary evaluation of the Rolez language that
shows that (i) parallel programs for non-trivial problems can be written in Rolez,

and (ii) parallel Rolez programs realize a speedup over both sequential Rolez and Java programs, despite the runtime overhead of role transitions and guarding.

4.1 Experimental Setup

We implemented a Rolez prototype, i.e., a compiler and a runtime system, on top of the Java platform. The runtime system is implemented as a Java library, while the compiler, implemented with Xtext [1], transforms Rolez source code into Java source code, inserting role transition and guarding operations as method calls to the runtime library where necessary. The generated code is compiled using a standard Java compiler and executed on a standard Java Virtual Machine (JVM).

The following programs were implemented in Rolez: IDEA encryption and Monte Carlo financial simulation, both adapted from the Parallel Java Grande benchmark suite [34]; a k-means clustering algorithm, as in the STAMP Benchmark Suite [10]; and a ray tracer that renders animated scenes (called animator). These programs contain the following parallel patterns, all of which can be expressed in Rolez: data parallelism, task parallelism, read-only data, and task-local data.

We measured the performance of each program on a machine with four Intel Xeon E7-4830 processors with a total of 32 cores and 64 GB of main memory, running Ubuntu Linux. As the Java platform we used OpenJDK 7. To eliminate warm-up effects from the JIT compiler in the JVM, we executed every program 5 to 10 times before measuring. Then we repeated every experiment 30 times inside the same JVM, taking the arithmetic mean.

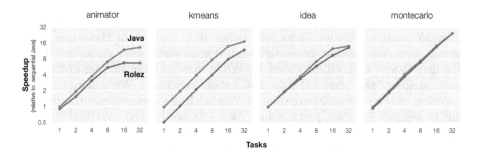

Fig. 10. Speedup of parallel Rolez programs, compared to speedup of parallel Java programs, for different numbers of tasks. All numbers are relative to single-threaded Java. Error bars are omitted since the variation is insignificant for all programs.

4.2 Results

First, we focus on the parallel speedup of the Rolez programs and compare it to that of equivalent Java programs. Note that the Rolez programs reuse some Java classes, such as `System` and `Math`, which contain native code, and also classes like

String and Random, to avoid the porting effort to Rolez. We manually ensured that the use of these classes is deterministic. Figure 10 shows the speedups of the Rolez and Java programs, relative to the single-threaded Java version, for different numbers of tasks. Note the logarithmic scale of both axes.

All Rolez programs achieve substantial speedups. They outperform single-threaded Java already with two tasks, and achieve maximum speedups of 7–20×. The speedup they achieve is practically linear with up to 8 tasks, and for IDEA and Monte Carlo even with 32 tasks. The plots also give a first idea about the Rolez overhead. While for IDEA and Monte Carlo the speedup lines are mostly equal, the overhead is clearly visible for animator and k-means, where the Java versions achieve substantially higher performance.

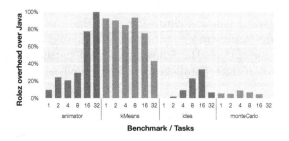

Fig. 11. Relative Rolez overhead when compared to the Java version of the same program and with the same number of tasks. Again, error bars are omitted due to insignificant variation.

Figure 11 shows this overhead in more detail. For IDEA, the overhead stays below 35% and for Monte Carlo even below 10%. In both of these programs, there is a modest amount of sharing and, due to static analysis in the Rolez compiler, almost no need for guarding. While there is more sharing in the animator program, the overhead stays low for up to 8 tasks. With more tasks, a limitation of the current incarnation of Parallel Roles shows: Since there is no built-in support for data partitioning, data sets need to be split and merged explicitly, which may result in a substantial overhead. Finally, k-means contains the most sharing and therefore suffers most from the overhead caused by role transitions.

To summarize, while the runtime concepts of Parallel Roles may inflict a non-negligible performance overhead, our prototype still delivers substantial parallel speedups. We expect that the performance of Rolez could be significantly improved by a more advanced compiler with access to global program information or runtime data (such as a JIT compiler), or by more optimized guarding and role transitions. However, we argue that the current Rolez prototype already provides good performance for many applications, especially on personal devices, where the number of cores has remained relatively small.

5 Related Work

Many approaches have been proposed to make parallel programming in some way safer than with explicit synchronization. Recently, the deterministic-by-default approach for imperative, object-oriented languages has sparked the interest of the research community [5,13,23,24]. In imperative languages, DPP is hard because tasks may have effects on shared mutable state. If not restricted, the non-deterministic interleaving of such effects leads to nondeterministic results [23].

The first imperative DPP language is Jade [22,32], where the programmer specifies the effects of a task using arbitrary code that is executed at runtime. Though extremely flexible, this approach comes with a substantial drawback: The correctness of effect specifications can only be checked at runtime. Such checks impact performance and may lead to unexpected errors. The same applies to Prometheus [2], where the programmer writes code that assigns operations to different *serialization sets*, and to Yada [14], where *sharing types* restrict how tasks may access shared data. Yada's sharing types are similar in spirit to role types, but they were not designed with compile-time checking as a goal.

To avoid these problems, static effect systems enable checking the correctness of effect specifications at compile time. In fact, these systems typically even check *noninterference* statically, avoiding runtime checks altogether. While early systems like FX [26] can only express limited forms of parallelism, recent systems like Liquid Effects [20] or Deterministic Effects [25] can handle many kinds of parallelism, although not necessarily in an object-oriented setting. The effect system used in Deterministic Parallel Java (DPJ) [4,6] and TWEJava [18] brings statically checked effects to Java-like languages. To support a wide range of parallel patterns, it includes many features: region parameters, disjointness constraints, region path lists, indexed-parameterized arrays, subarrays, and invocation effects. This formidable list shows that DPJ and TWEJava require a programmer to understand many and potentially complex concepts. Parallel Roles aims to simplify DPP by using the concepts of roles and role transitions to specify the effects of tasks. In addition, the concept of guarding enables parallelization by simply marking methods as tasks and invoking them like normal methods.

Other effect systems have been proposed to make parallel programming less error-prone, e.g., by enforcing a locking discipline or by preventing data races or deadlocks [7,19]. These systems combine effects with ownership types [11,12] and generally couple the regions and effects of an object with those of its owner. This idea resembles our handling of object graphs, which can be interpreted as coupling the role of an object with that of its "owners", i.e., the objects that have a reference to it. Even though this simple idea of "referrer as owner" has the advantage that no additional notion of ownership is involved, combining roles with a more advanced concept of ownership would be interesting future work.

An alternative to effects are systems based on *permissions* [3,8,9]. Permissions accompany object references and define how an object is shared and how it may be accessed. In ÆMINIUM [37,38] for instance, permissions like *unique*, *immutable*, or *shared* keep track of how may references to an object exist and specify the permitted operations. The system then automatically extracts and exploits concurrency. Similarly, the Rust language [27] features *mutable* or *immutable* references and guarantees that there are either a single mutable or multiple immutable references to an object at any time. Permissions are more object-based than effects and conceptually similar to our roles. However, roles and particularly guarding are dynamic concepts and enable simpler language designs, at the cost of some runtime overhead. For instance, while ÆMINIUM and Rust rigorously restrict aliasing, Rolez is a simpler language that permits arbitrary aliasing.

Another approach for DPP is speculative execution, where the effects of tasks are buffered by a runtime component and rolled back in case they interfere. The two most well-known such approaches, Thread Level Speculation [29,35,36] and Transactional Memory [16,17,33] are not DPP models in a strict sense: The former *automatically* parallelizes sequential programs and the latter usually provides no determinism guarantees. However, there *are* speculative approaches that constitute DPP models: Safe Futures for Java [40] and Implicit Parallelism with Ordered Transactions [39]. In both models, the programmer defines which parts of a sequential program should execute asynchronously. The runtime then executes them as speculative tasks, enforcing their sequential order. In Parallel Roles, speculation is not necessary, because interfering operations are either delayed by guarding or cause an error (in the case of Rolez, at compile time).

6   Conclusion

During the last few years, much research about deterministic parallel programming has focused on static effect or permission systems. In this paper, we presented Parallel Roles to leverage *roles* to express the kinds of access that are permitted for an object. Parallel Roles puts the focus on objects and presents a simple object-oriented way to specify and reason about effects of parallel computations. This paper explores parallel programming with just three simple roles; these are powerful enough to express a wide range of parallel patterns and applications without the burden of complex program annotations. While a certain runtime overhead seems to be the necessary toll for this simplicity, a preliminary evaluation indicates that the overhead is moderate: The implementation of a roles-based language achieves substantial speedups over the corresponding sequential Java version. Furthermore, past programming language innovations such as garbage collection or runtime type checking have shown that a modest runtime overhead is a small price to pay for more safety, simplicity and programmer productivity.

References

1. Xtext. http://www.eclipse.org/Xtext/
2. Allen, M.D., Sridharan, S., Sohi, G.S.: Serialization sets: a dynamic dependence-based parallel execution model. In: Proceedings of the 14th ACM SIGPLAN Symposium on Principles and Practice of Parallel Programming (PPoPP 2009), pp. 85–96. ACM, New York (2009)

3. Bierhoff, K., Aldrich, J.: Modular typestate checking of aliased objects. In: Proceedings of the 22nd Annual ACM SIGPLAN Conference on Object-Oriented Programming Systems and Applications (OOPSLA 2007), pp. 301–320. ACM, New York (2007)
4. Bocchino, R.L., Adve, V.S.: Types, regions, and effects for safe programming with object-oriented parallel frameworks. In: Mezini, M. (ed.) ECOOP 2011. LNCS, vol. 6813, pp. 306–332. Springer, Heidelberg (2011). https://doi.org/10.1007/978-3-642-22655-7_15
5. Bocchino, R.L., Adve, V.S., Adve, S.V., Snir, M.: Parallel programming must be deterministic by default. In: Proceedings of the 1st USENIX Conference on Hot Topics in Parallelism (HotPar 2009). USENIX Association, Berkeley (2009). http://dl.acm.org/citation.cfm?id=1855591.1855595
6. Bocchino, R.L., et al.: A type and effect system for deterministic parallel Java. In: Proceedings of the 24th ACM SIGPLAN Conference on Object Oriented Programming Systems Languages and Applications (OOPSLA 2009), pp. 97–116. ACM, New York (2009)
7. Boyapati, C., Lee, R., Rinard, M.: Ownership types for safe programming: preventing data races and deadlocks. In: Proceedings of the 17th ACM SIGPLAN Conference on Object-Oriented Programming, Systems, Languages, and Applications (OOPSLA 2002), pp. 211–230. ACM, New York (2002)
8. Boyland, J.: Checking interference with fractional permissions. In: Cousot, R. (ed.) SAS 2003. LNCS, vol. 2694, pp. 55–72. Springer, Heidelberg (2003). https://doi.org/10.1007/3-540-44898-5_4
9. Boyland, J.T., Retert, W.: Connecting effects and uniqueness with adoption. In: Proceedings of the 32nd ACM SIGPLAN-SIGACT Symposium on Principles of Programming Languages (POPL 2005), pp. 283–295. ACM, New York (2005)
10. Minh, C.C., Chung, J., Kozyrakis, C., Olukotun, K.: STAMP: stanford transactional applications for multi-processing. In: Proceedings of The IEEE International Symposium on Workload Characterization (IISWC 2008), September 2008
11. Clarke, D.G., Noble, J., Potter, J.M.: Simple ownership types for object containment. In: Knudsen, J.L. (ed.) ECOOP 2001. LNCS, vol. 2072, pp. 53–76. Springer, Heidelberg (2001). https://doi.org/10.1007/3-540-45337-7_4
12. Clarke, D.G., Potter, J.M., Noble, J.: Ownership types for flexible alias protection. In: Proceedings of the 13th ACM SIGPLAN Conference on Object-Oriented Programming, Systems, Languages, and Applications (OOPSLA 1998), pp. 48–64. ACM, New York (1998)
13. Devietti, J., Lucia, B., Ceze, L., Oskin, M.: DMP: deterministic shared memory multiprocessing. In: Proceedings of the 14th International Conference on Architectural Support for Programming Languages and Operating Systems (ASPLOS XIV), pp. 85–96. ACM, New York (2009)
14. Gay, D., Galenson, J., Naik, M., Yelick, K.: Yada: straightforward parallel programming. Parallel Comput. **37**(9), 592–609 (2011)
15. Gottlob, G., Schrefl, M., Röck, B.: Extending object-oriented systems with roles. ACM Trans. Inf. Syst. **14**(3), 268–296 (1996)
16. Harris, T., Fraser, K.: Language support for lightweight transactions. In: Proceedings of the 18th Annual ACM SIGPLAN Conference on Object-Oriented Programming, Systems, Languages, and Applications (OOPSLA 2003), pp. 388–402. ACM, New York (2003)
17. Herlihy, M., Moss, J.E.B.: Transactional memory: architectural support for lock-free data structures. In: Proceedings of the 20th Annual International Symposium on Computer Architecture (ISCA 1993), pp. 289–300. ACM, New York (1993)

18. Heumann, S.T., Adve, V.S., Wang, S.: The tasks with effects model for safe concurrency. In: Proceedings of the 18th ACM SIGPLAN Symposium on Principles and Practice of Parallel Programming (PPoPP 2013), pp. 239–250. ACM, New York (2013)

19. Jacobs, B., Smans, J., Piessens, F., Schulte, W.: A statically verifiable programming model for concurrent object-oriented programs. In: Liu, Z., He, J. (eds.) ICFEM 2006. LNCS, vol. 4260, pp. 420–439. Springer, Heidelberg (2006). https://doi.org/10.1007/11901433_23

20. Kawaguchi, M., Rondon, P., Bakst, A., Jhala, R.: Deterministic parallelism via liquid effects. In: Proceedings of the 33rd ACM SIGPLAN Conference on Programming Language Design and Implementation (PLDI 2012), pp. 45–54. ACM, New York (2012)

21. Kristensen, B.B.: Object-Oriented Modeling with Roles. In: Murphy, J., Stone, B. (eds.) OOIS 1995, pp. 57–71. Springer, London (1996)

22. Lam, M.S., Rinard, M.C.: Coarse-grain parallel programming in Jade. In: Proceedings of the 3rd ACM SIGPLAN Symposium on Principles and Practice of Parallel Programming (PPoPP 1991), pp. 94–105. ACM, New York (1991)

23. Lee, E.A.: The problem with threads. Computer **39**(5), 33–42 (2006)

24. Lu, L., Scott, M.L.: Toward a formal semantic framework for deterministic parallel programming. In: Peleg, D. (ed.) DISC 2011. LNCS, vol. 6950, pp. 460–474. Springer, Heidelberg (2011). https://doi.org/10.1007/978-3-642-24100-0_43

25. Lu, Y., Potter, J., Zhang, C., Xue, J.: A type and effect system for determinism in multithreaded programs. In: Seidl, H. (ed.) ESOP 2012. LNCS, vol. 7211, pp. 518–538. Springer, Heidelberg (2012). https://doi.org/10.1007/978-3-642-28869-2_26

26. Lucassen, J.M., Gifford, D.K.: Polymorphic effect systems. In: Proceedings of the 15th ACM SIGPLAN-SIGACT Symposium on Principles of Programming Languages (POPL 1988), pp. 47–57. ACM, New York (1988)

27. Matsakis, N.D., Klock II, F.S.: The rust language. In: Proceedings of the 2014 ACM SIGAda Annual Conference on High Integrity Language Technology (HILT 2014), pp. 103–104. ACM, New York (2014)

28. Pernici, B.: Objects with roles. In: Proceedings of the ACM SIGOIS and IEEE CS TC-OA Conference on Office Information Systems (COCS 1990), pp. 205–215. ACM, New York (1990)

29. Rauchwerger, L., Padua, D.: The LRPD test: speculative run-time parallelization of loops with privatization and reduction parallelization. In: Proceedings of the ACM SIGPLAN 1995 Conference on Programming Language Design and Implementation (PLDI 1995), pp. 218–232. ACM, New York, June 1995

30. Reenskaug, W., Wold, P., Lehne, O.A.: Working with Objects: OORAM Software Engineering Method. J a Majors, Greenwich, June 1995

31. Riehle, D., Gross, T.: Role model based framework design and integration. In: Proceedings of the 13th ACM SIGPLAN Conference on Object-Oriented Programming, Systems, Languages, and Applications (OOPSLA 1998), pp. 117–133. ACM, New York (1998)

32. Rinard, M.C., Lam, M.S.: The design, implementation, and evaluation of Jade. ACM Trans. Program. Lang. Syst. **20**(3), 483–545 (1998)

33. Shavit, N., Touitou, D.: Software transactional memory. In: Proceedings of the 14th Annual ACM Symposium on Principles of Distributed Computing (PODC 1995), pp. 204–213. ACM, New York (1995)

34. Smith, L.A., Bull, J.M., Obdrzálek, J.: A parallel java grande benchmark suite. In: Proceedings of the 2001 ACM/IEEE Conference on Supercomputing (SC 2001), pp. 8. ACM, New York (2001)

35. Sohi, G.S., Breach, S.E., Vijaykumar, T.N.: Multiscalar processors. In: Proceedings of the 22nd Annual International Symposium on Computer Architecture (ISCA 1995), pp. 414–425. ACM, New York, June 1995

36. Steffan, J., Mowry, T.: The potential for using thread-level data speculation to facilitate automatic parallelization. In: Proceedings of the 4th International Symposium on High-Performance Computer Architecture (HPCA 1998), pp. 2–13. IEEE Computer Society, Washington DC (1998)

37. Stork, S., Marques, P., Aldrich, J.: Concurrency by default: using permissions to express dataflow in stateful programs. In: Proceedings of the 24th ACM SIGPLAN Conference Companion on Object Oriented Programming Systems Languages and Applications (OOPSLA 2009), pp. 933–940. ACM, New York (2009)

38. Stork, S., et al.: Æminium: a permission-based concurrent-by-default programming language approach. ACM Trans. Program. Lang. Syst. 36(1), 2:1–2:42 (2014)

39. von Praun, C., Ceze, L., Caşcaval, C.: Implicit parallelism with ordered transactions. In: Proceedings of the 12th ACM SIGPLAN Symposium on Principles and Practice of Parallel Programming (PPoPP 2007), pp. 79–89. ACM, New York (2007)

40. Welc, A., Jagannathan, S., Hosking, A.: Safe futures for Java. In: Proceedings of the 20th Annual ACM SIGPLAN Conference on Object-Oriented Programming, Systems, Languages, and Applications (OOPSLA 2005), pp. 439–453. ACM, New York (2005)

Mozart: Efficient Composition of Library Functions for Heterogeneous Execution

Rajkishore Barik[✉], Tatiana Shpeisman, Hongbo Rong, Chunling Hu,
Victor W. Lee, Todd A. Anderson, Greg Henry, Hai Liu, Youfeng Wu,
Paul Petersen, and Geoff Lowney

Intel Corporation, Santa Clara, CA, USA
rajbarik@uber.com

Abstract. Current processor trend is to couple a commodity processor with a GPU, a co-processor, or an accelerator. To unleash the full computational power of such heterogeneous systems is a daunting task: programmers often resort to heterogeneous scheduling runtime frameworks that use device specific library routines. However, highly-tuned libraries do not compose very well across heterogeneous architectures. That is, important performance-oriented optimizations such as data locality and reuse "across" library calls is not fully exploited. In this paper, we present a framework, called *Mozart*, to extend existing library frameworks to efficiently compose a sequence of library calls for heterogeneous execution. *Mozart* consists of two components: *library description* (LD) and *library composition runtime*. We advocate library writers to wrap existing libraries using LD in order to provide their performance parameters on heterogeneous cores, no programmer intervention is necessary. Our runtime performs composition of libraries via task-fission, load balances among heterogeneous cores using information from LD, and automatically adapts to runtime behavior of an application. We evaluate *Mozart* on a Xeon + 2 Xeon Phi system using the High Performance Linpack benchmark which is the most popular benchmark to rank supercomputers in TOP500 and show GFLOPS improvement of 31.7% over MKL with Automatic Offload and 6.7% over hand-optimized ninja code.

1 Introduction

The current processor trend is to couple a commodity processor with GPUs, co-processors, or accelerators. Such heterogeneous systems not only offer increased computational power but also deliver high energy efficiency. However, due to the architectural differences between cores of the host processor and device, it is increasingly difficult to extract every-bit of performance out of these platforms, leading to growing "ninja gap" [38] where only a small number of expert programmers are capable of harvesting the full potential of the system.

Although compilers have matured significantly over the years, most of the time, compiler generated code still can not compete with hand-optimized implementation even on a homogeneous architecture. An alternative approach

© Springer Nature Switzerland AG 2019
L. Rauchwerger (Ed.): LCPC 2017, LNCS 11403, pp. 182–202, 2019.
https://doi.org/10.1007/978-3-030-35225-7_13

commonly used in several application domains is to use highly-tuned high-performance libraries to close ninja-gap without placing unnecessary development burden on a programmer. For example, Intel's Math Kernel Library (MKL) and NVIDIA's cuBLAS are two widely used high performance linear algebra libraries for CPUs and GPUs, respectively. These libraries are developed by domain experts who fully exploit the underlying processor architecture.

As heterogeneous systems become ubiquitous, it is challenging to make the existing library frameworks heterogeneity-aware: the libraries have to be specialized for each particular processor or device, the workload has to be properly load-balanced between them, and communication between them must be overlapped with computation as much as possible to gain performance. In order to determine optimal work distribution between devices one must use device specific performance characteristics of libraries (e.g., throughput of a library on each device). More importantly, work distribution and communication generation must look beyond just a single library call to improve data locality and reduce communication overhead. Sometimes the communication latency hiding techniques can be complicated as optimal device offload granularity might depend on the input problem size. Thus, a generic easy-to-use framework is necessary that not only allows automatic learning of device specific performance characteristics of libraries but also efficiently composes multiple library calls without any intervention from the programmer.

Existing research in this area fall into two broad categories:

- *Leverage device specific libraries and use a heterogeneous scheduling runtime for work distribution and communication.* In this approach, the device-specific libraries are treated as black-box and thus, the runtime can not easily take advantage of the expert programmers' domain knowledge related to the properties of a library during scheduling. Moreover, the programmer is responsible for providing wrappers for device-specific library task implementations on her own. There has been a lot of research work in the context of dividing work between CPU-GPU using a scheduling runtime [5,14,23,26,31–33,35,40]. Although, their techniques can be adopted in the context of libraries, they are primarily restricted to the work distribution of a single library call. Important inter-library call optimizations are left unexplored.
- *Library frameworks perform work distribution between heterogeneous cores transparent to the programmer.* Although this approach achieves peak performance for a single library call by having expert programmers' knowledge embedded in it, it can not perform optimizations across library calls. Moreover, the programmer manually instructs the library to execute on a single device or on the heterogeneous system. This approach is recently adopted by MKL by adding a functionality called Automatic Offloading (AO), which can offload part of the library call workload from a Xeon CPU to a Xeon Phi co-processor [3]. However, this advanced feature is currently limited to "sufficiently large problems" exhibiting large computation to data access ratio. Thus, only a hand-full of Level-3 BLAS functions (GEMM, SYMM, TRMM, and TRSM) and three matrix factorization routines (LU, QR, and Cholesky)

have this feature today. Although this approach is best for programmers, our experiments show that it can leave 25% performance on the table when compared to a Hand-tuned version for the High Performance Linpack benchmark on average (details in Sect. 4).

To the best of our knowledge, none of the existing systems exploit inter-library call optimizations such as data locality and reuse. That is, if a series of library tasks are invoked one after another, it is possible to schedule them better by grouping them based on their data access patterns rather than naively executing them one after another. It might also be necessary to decompose a library call to finer granularity in order to improve its scheduling and reduce communication overhead. The goal of this paper is to devise a generic framework that can perform optimizations across library call boundaries in order to efficiently compose them in heterogeneous systems and further reduce the ninja-gap.

In this paper, we propose a framework for library composition, called *Mozart*. *Mozart* consists of two components: *library description* (LD) and *library composition runtime*. *Mozart* transparently composes and decomposes such library calls across heterogeneous processors delivering performance on par with that of expertly tuned hand-written code. LD expresses library routines as tasks and embeds library developer expertise via meta-information about every library routine. The meta-information initially comes from library developers, is subsequently augmented with install-time profiling on the target platform, and is finally used in guiding the scheduling runtime to automatically load balance between heterogeneous processors. The runtime dynamically builds a runtime task graph for an application from the numerous library calls of the application, dynamically decomposes tasks in the graph according to the granularity specified by LD and assigns them for execution to host processor and device as they become available. To facilitate efficient composition of library tasks, our runtime applies a novel optimization, *task-fission*, that pre-processes the task graph as it is being constructed and partitions the tasks into coarse-grain sub-tasks according to data flow between the tasks. We demonstrate that our approach can improve data-locality and reuse, resulting in improved performance compared to existing approaches. To the best of our knowledge, our work is the first attempt to seamlessly perform library call composition for heterogeneous architectures.

Compared to other task based approaches such as [5,9,14,23,26,31,32,35, 40], *Mozart* has the following additional capabilities. First, *Mozart* transparently schedules a decomposable library task between host processor and device cores using library metadata (LD) provided by library writers. Unlike existing systems, programmer is not responsible for writing any wrappers for device specific library implementations. Second, *Mozart* efficiently composes a series of library tasks by performing *task-fission* dynamically on the runtime task graph resulting in improved data locality. Finally, *Mozart* profiles device data transfer overhead and measures host/device throughput at runtime. It then uses this data to adaptively control the number of iterations performed by the device including the offload granularity of device. This results in both improved load-balance and better communication-computation overlap.

The key contributions of this paper include:

- a novel *Library Description* (LD) framework to describe meta-information about libraries. We expect library developers to use this framework to specify their domain knowledge about library routines. The parameters of this framework are either specified by the library developer or determined via install-time profiling of libraries on the target platform.
- a scheduling runtime that performs load balancing among heterogeneous cores using the LD information. The distinguishing features of our runtime include dynamic *task-fission* and adaptation to runtime behavior of an application. Compared to existing scheduling runtimes [6,14,26,31,32,34,40], our runtime enables cross library call scheduling optimizations such as data-locality and communication optimization as well as host and device work distribution.
- an experimental evaluation of *Mozart* in a heterogeneous system consisting of a Xeon CPU and 2 Xeon Phi co-processors using High Performance Linpack benchmark which is the most popular benchmark to rank supercomputers in TOP500. Our results show a GFLOPS improvement of 31.7% over MKL with Automatic Offloading and 6.7% over hand-optimized version of the application. *Please note that, although we perform our experimental evaluation on a Xeon+Xeon Phi system, our technique should be applicable to any host plus device based system including widely used CPU+GPU based systems.*

The rest of the paper is organized as follows. Section 2 describes the library description interfaces. Section 3 describes our heterogeneous scheduling runtime. Evaluations are presented in Sect. 4. We discuss related work in Sect. 5 and conclude in Sect. 6.

2 Library Description Language

In this section, we describe the library description (LD) framework that drives composition of library calls at runtime, so that the calls are effectively executed in a distributed fashion on a heterogeneous system – to take advantage of the rich hardware parallelism in such a system. LD expresses domain knowledge from library developers and uses install-time profiling to build platform-specific performance models. Such expertise, code, and models reflect important aspects of the dynamic behavior of a library function.

Library experts (typically library-writers) build a library description (LD) for each library function during or after library development. This LD is basic in that it might not contain platform-specific information. The expert also builds an extensive set of microbenchmarks to perform install-time profiling in order to fill in the LD parameters of a library. Any relevant performance characteristics of a library function can be put into the LD, but specifically, we propose a set of abstract interfaces as shown in Table 1: `Threads()` and `SubTaskSize()` are described, because the number of threads and the task granularity for offloading

Table 1. Library description APIs

API	Description
In, Out	Returns the inputs and outputs of the library function
Threads(id)	Returns the optimal number of threads to set for this library function for a given device *id*
SubTaskSize(id)	Returns the best sub-task size to set for this library function for a given device *id*
Rate(id)	Returns the computation throughput of the library function on a given device *id* Rate is defined as the ratio of number of iterations processed per unit time
Affinity()	Returns the device affinity of the library function
Task_arch(range)	Returns a task function operating on a sub-range of the original iteration space of the library function for a device, e.g., arch is either CPU or GPU
InsertTask()	Inserts task functions into the runtime's task graph and schedule it for execution when it is ready

are the two most important optimization parameters for most applications. Note that Threads() for memory-bound applications may be much smaller than the maximum available cores on the underlying platform. Similarly, SubTaskSize() determines the offload granularity to a device in order to optimally overlap it's computation with communication. When the library is installed, the microbenchmarks are used to profile the underlying platform and build platform-specific models for the functions in LD, including Threads(), SubTaskSize(), and Rate(). Many different combinations of the inputs of a library function can be used to run the function. With different input combinations and their corresponding execution time of the function, profiling can learn a model for each of Threads(), SubTaskSize(), and Rate(). The learned performance models replace the default Threads(), SubTaskSize(), and Rate() specified by the library-writer.

Figure 1 illustrates the implementation of LD class for a matrix-matrix multiplication library call, dgemm_LD. In this example, Threads() and SubTaskSize() are hard-coded numbers based on library-writer's experiences. Rate() is an auto-generated performance model built from install-time profiling (in particular, we perform a linear approximation of the profiling data after executing the microbenchmarks on each device). Task_arch() and InsertTask() are written manually by expert programmers. Here we have two Task_arch() functions: one for the host, the other for the device. We have used Intel Offload programming model [1] to demonstrate device offloading, but it is not a limitation.

In a specific implementation, the compiler may automatically redirect a library function call in a user program to its corresponding library description,

```
// Library description (LD) for matrix-matrix multiplication using dgemm call on  host and device
class dgemm_LD {
    int Threads(int tid) { return tid == 0 ? 40:240;}
    int SubTaskSize(int tid) { return tid == 0 ? 1500 : 3000; }
    bool Affinity() { return Device0; }
    int Rate(int tid) { // Auto-generated performance model via linear approximation
        if  (1.00000*M -20000.00000 <= 0) {
            dtmp=0.00087*M+0.00087*N +0.00143*K+157.65765;
        } else {
            if  (1.00000*M -25001.00000 <= 0)
                dtmp =0.00220*M + 0.00220*N +0.15566*K;
            else
                dtmp=-0.00008*M-0.00008*N -0.00813*K+360.9299;
        }
        return MAX(dtmp, 1);
    }
    void TaskHost(range r) {
        cblas_dgemm(...); // Host MKL call to matrix-matrix multiply
    }
    void TaskDevice(range r) {
        // Ninja written code
#pragma offload target(DEV0)
        cblas_dgemm(r, ...);  // Device library call to matrix-matrix multiply
    }
    void InsertTask() {
        // set arguments and argument metadata, call to scheduling runtime
        insert_divisible_task(...);
    }
}
```

Fig. 1. LD for matrix-matrix multiplication library, dgemm. The library developer initially writes the dgemm_LD function. During install time of the library, `Threads`, `SubTaskSize`, `Affinity`, and `Rate` are populated via install-time profiling. The `TaskHost` and `TaskDevice` functions operate on sub-ranges in order to let the runtime adaptively decide the work distribution between host and device. The `InsertTask` function calls into runtime (Sect. 3).

which enqueues a divisible task into the runtime system's task graph (described in Sect. 3). For example, for a library function f () with LD as f_LD(), the library wrapper or the compiler performs the following two operations:

$$LD * \quad ld = f\_LD(/ * originalparameters * /);$$
$$ld- > InsertTask();$$

When the user program runs, the above two statements create an LD object, and invoke our runtime through that object's `InsertTask()` function, which inserts the `Task_arch()` function(s) into the runtime system's task graph, and invokes the runtime system. The runtime is described in Sect. 3.

In another implementation, the library writer may hide LD details from the user by wrapping the library functions in new interfaces and expose these interfaces to the programmer. Either way, the newly created runtime task is semantically equivalent to the original library function. The runtime system executes this task in a parallel and perhaps in a distributed fashion on the heterogeneous system.

Figure 2 depicts the high-level flow of LD. At library installation time, a performance model (via linear approximation) is built for how each library function performs on the entire system with such factors as number of threads, sub-task size and the relative performance of each processor in the system. The compiler pattern matches library function call names and replaces a regular function call with a call to the runtime providing access to the model for the given function. The runtime is then responsible for determining how best to execute the function with the current inputs within the system. It will often do so by splitting up the

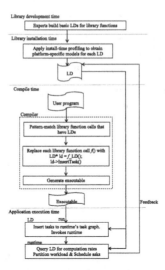

Fig. 2. Detailed work-flow of library description framework.

work into smaller granularity and giving that work to different processors in the heterogeneous system.

One thing to keep in mind is that LD interfaces are developed by library writers, programmer is not involved. Additionally, the LD information for each library routine is written exactly once and thus we believe the complexity is manageable. Augmenting auto-tuning with install-time profiling is a subject for future work.

3   Library Composition Runtime

In this section, we describe our heterogeneous runtime system that performs dynamic task-fission, overlaps communication and computation to hide communication latency of heterogeneous processor, and finally, adapts to runtime behavior of an application. Our runtime system takes advantage of the performance profile information from LD described in Sect. 2. For simplicity of presentation, we treat each task as a library task created from a particular library routine.

Library Task Representation: We introduce the notions of *simple* and *divisible* library tasks in our runtime. A *divisible* task can be further decomposed into sub-tasks. Typical example of a divisible task is a data-parallel library routine which can be decomposed in many different ways including simply varying the number of loop iterations that are grouped into a single task. For example, the classical matrix-matrix multiplication library task is a divisible task since the 2-d iteration range of the output matrix can be blocked into sub-ranges and each sub-range can be processed independently either on host or device.

Runtime Interfaces: Our runtime exposes two key APIs: *insert_{T}_task* where T is either divisible or simple and *task_wait. insert_{T}_task()* communicates all information regarding a task to the runtime. *task_wait()* function waits for the previously issued tasks to complete and their output data become available. Some of the important information passed to an *insert_{T}_task(T,...)* include iteration range and dimensionality (for divisible tasks), function pointers to device task implementations that operate on sub-tasks, arguments and their corresponding metadata information (using array access descriptors as described later in this section), device affinity if known, and performance profile information for the corresponding library function from LD (described in Sect. 2). Each argument to a task is marked as one of the following: IN, OUT, INOUT, VALUE (passed-by-value), ACCUMULATOR (passed-by-reference, typically reduction variables are passed as accumulator variables). Please note that the library developer wraps *insert_T_task* in the LD method InsertTask for a library task and *task_wait* is inferred by our runtime based on input and output dependences.

Array Access Descriptors: Affine array accesses are typical in scientific and HPC applications, therefore are used heavily in library routines. The metadata information for an array argument of a task in our runtime also carries a *descriptor* in order for the runtime to be able to determine the sub-region of the array being accessed by a sub-task, which is crucial to generate the data movements between host and devices. The following array access descriptor captures affine array accesses of the form $a * i + b$, where a and b are compile-time constants and i denotes the loop induction variable:

```
struct array_access_desc_Nd_s {
  unsigned int dim; /* number of array dimensions */
  int64_t *a1, *a2; /* "a" coefficients of ai+b in each dimension */
  int64_t *l_b, *u_b; /* "b" (lower and upper bound) coefficients of ai+b in each dimension */
};
```

The array region accessed by a sub-task can be 1-d linear, 2-d rectangular, or 3-d rectangular prism (our implementation currently does not support beyond 3-d). At runtime, each array region is associated with a location information indicating the device that holds that array region. Runtime uses this information to decide device affinity of a sub-task. Additionally, efficient implementations of standard set operations such as union, intersection, and difference are also provided for array regions in order to reduce the runtime overheads of task graph construction. Note that since we are composing libraries, the array access descriptors are written by expert library developers as part of LD, programmer who uses these libraries is not involved.

Work-Sharing Runtime: The runtime determines task dependencies from the array access descriptor metadata of task arguments, builds a *task dependence graph*, generates necessary data transfers and schedules tasks for execution possibly choosing the device. Once all the predecessors of a task in the task graph have completed execution and all the input data has been transferred to the target device, the task is executed. This might result in the output data transfer to a different device, as well as a trigger for the other task execution (Fig. 3).

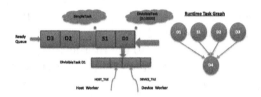

Fig. 3. Work-sharing runtime and runtime task graph

Typically a heterogeneous system node has a few devices leading to fewer contention among devices. Moreover, the optimal task granularity for offload may differ from device to device, e.g., a discrete GPU may choose a sub-task tile that completely hides the data communication latency of an application. With these design choices in mind, we implement a *work-sharing runtime* where an idle device grabs it's own sub-task tile of iterations for a ready divisible task from a common shared queue of the parallel iterations. Note that sub-task tile size for each device is bootstrapped using SubTaskSize() in LD and is adaptively adjusted in the runtime (described later in this section). A proxy host thread (i.e., *worker*) is assigned to each device that offloads work to that device.

When a task becomes ready, i.e., all its predecessors in the task dependence graph finished their execution, it is added to the ready queue. When a worker becomes idle, it tries to retrieve a task from this ready queue and executes it. There could be more than one task available in the ready queue, in which case one of the two following strategies could be used: (1) the idle worker first tries to pick a task that no other worker is working on (that is, *breadth-first* approach); (2) the idle worker picks the first ready task (that is, *depth-first* approach). This is currently implemented via a runtime flag. By default, a simple task has an affinity to the host CPU in our runtime.

Task Fission: Choosing sub-task size is critical to application performance on heterogeneous systems as it affects both scheduling granularity, data locality, and communication latency. It can also artificially limit parallelism and flexibility of scheduling. In general, the sub-task granularity should be large enough to occupy at least a single core of the heterogeneous system, yet small enough to support efficient load balancing and communication/computation overlap. Consider an example program shown in Fig. 4. task1 invoked with parallel iterations [1 . . . 10000] writes 10000 elements of array b, while task2 invoked with parallel iterations [1...500] reads only the first 500 elements of b. Consider the following scheduling constraint on a discrete CPU+GPU heterogeneous system: task2 executes significantly better on CPU than GPU while task1 can be executed on either CPU or GPU. An optimal scheduling solution is to execute first 500 iterations of task1, as well as, all of task2 on CPU and the last 9500 iterations of task1 on the discrete GPU until CPU completes execution, at which point both CPU and GPU can execute the remaining iterations of task1. This enables overlapping of task2 and task1 execution resulting in improved data-locality (that is, task2 might reuse data from the cache prefetches of task1) and reduced communication too (that is, there is no data transfer cost to/from GPU for the first 500 iterations of `task1`. However, if tasks have to be scheduled as indivisible units, a scheduler has to assign all iterations of `task1` to either CPU (leaving GPU unused) or GPU (resulting in data transfer cost) and wait for all of `task1` to complete before starting `task2`. Choosing fine-grain tasks resolves this problem but leads to higher overhead of maintaining task graph and scheduling tasks, potentially defeating benefits from exploiting a higher degree of parallelism.

```
task1(range r, in a, out b) {            task2(range r, in b, out c) {
    for (i = r.start  : r.end)               for (i = r.start : r.end)
        b[i] = f(a[i]) // f is a library call       c[i] = g(b[i]); // g is a library call
}                                        }


main() {                                 main() {
    insert_task([1...10000], task1); // CPU or GPU   insert_task([1...500], task1); // CPU
    insert_task([1...500], task2); // CPU            insert_task([501...10000], task1); // CPU or GPU
    task_wait(); // wait for task completion         insert_task([1...500], task2); // CPU
}                                                    task_wait(); // wait for task completion
                                         }
```

Fig. 4. Optimal task granularity example with dynamic task-fission; `task1` with range $[1 \ldots 10000]$ was split into two tasks with ranges $[1 \ldots 500]$ and $[501 \ldots 10000]$ at runtime based on consumer task `task2`; Now `task2` can start executing immediately after `task1` with range $[1 \ldots 500]$ completes on CPU. This improves locality and reduces communication.

We propose *task-fission* at runtime that automatically adjusts task granularity to discover additional available parallelism while keeping the cost of task graph maintenance and scheduling under control. Tasks are split to achieve exact match between one task output and another task input. Such tasks are further combined into task chains that can be scheduled to a single device to reduce communication cost.

We support two kinds of task-fission. The first one splits an existing task A when a new task B is inserted into task graph whose input is a subset of the output of the task A. In this case, A is split into A1 and A2, such that output of A1 is the same as input of B. This enables execution of B as soon as A1 finishes without waiting for completion of A2. It also allows the runtime to schedule A1 and B to the same device while, in parallel, executing A2 on a different device. The second one splits a new task B when its input is a super-set of the output of an existing task A. In this case, B is split into B1 and B2, such that output of A is the same as input of B1. This enables execution of B2 without waiting of completion of A and allows the runtime to schedule A and B1 to the same device, while scheduling B2 to a different one.

When a task is inserted to our runtime, the argument metadata information (described using array access descriptor) is used to derive task dependencies and to construct the runtime task dependency graph. During this addition of the newly arrived task to the runtime task graph, our runtime checks if it is feasible to perform task-fission with the immediate predecessor task or with the immediate successor task (as described in the previous paragraph). If the immediate predecessor task is not already executing and offers opportunities for task-fission, we perform task fission and update the runtime task graph. We enqueue the newly created tasks from task-fission to our runtime when they are ready. In most cases, we expect that the cost of task-fission be mitigated by the benefits we get from task-fission. Our runtime augments online profiling to decide whether to perform task-fission or not.

Task-fission results in the following benefits: (1) increased task parallelism, due to precise matching between task dependencies and task granularity; (2) reduced communication cost, as sub-tasks with the same input/outputs can be scheduled to the same device without affecting scheduling of the whole task; (3) improved data locality and reuse, as sub-tasks with the same input/output can reuse data from caches.

Overlap Communication and Computation: Accelerators including GPUs and Xeon Phi are typically connected to the host processor via PCIe interconnect. Thus, communication overhead is one of the dominant factors in obtaining performance of these systems. There are many existing approaches for hiding communication latency [2]. We use the *double buffering* technique transparently in our runtime to overlap communication to device with computation on host CPU. This transparency is feasible in *Mozart*, since tasks can be divided into sub-tasks and the argument array regions accesses by sub-regions can be computed from the array access descriptors. Our runtime creates two temporary buffers for every argument array region corresponding to sub-tasks and while the current buffer holds the array region for computation on the device of sub-task A, the next buffer holds the array region that is used for transferring data from the device to the host (for output transfer) for sub-task B. Sub-tasks A and B originate from the same divisible task. Similarly, we can also overlap input data transfer of one sub-task with computation of another sub-task. The granularity of the sub-tasks are chosen such that the two temporary buffers fit on the device memory and more importantly, the ratio of communication to computation time of the sub-tasks must be close to 1. This results in optimal performance as it hides the communication latency completely. Our runtime initially uses LD information to choose this sub-task granularity (via `SubTaskSize()`), but later on adjusts adaptively at runtime.

Strided Data Access: Several scientific and HPC applications access strided data. Strided data can be tricky to transfer to devices using pragma based compilers such as Intel Offload compiler [1] as they are limited by their expressibility resulting in unnecessary data transfer. Consider the shaded regions to the left of Fig. 5. In order to transfer only the shaded regions to Xeon Phi using current Intel Offload compiler, entire rows and columns corresponding to the shared regions need to be transferred. This incurs runtime overhead and can be significant if the matrix is large and the shaded region is very small. We mitigate this by transparently copying data in runtime to contiguous memory locations and then remapping the index space of this data in the library kernels for both Xeon and Xeon Phi. The code snippet to the right of Fig. 5 depicts the argument offset data structure used in our runtime and its use in a matrix multiplication Xeon Phi library kernel. This data structure stores dimensionality information (dim), row/column size (depending on row-major or column-major) using max_size, and the original indices using index_offset for each dimension. Each library kernel now takes an additional argument for this offset data structure offset and replaces each access to $A[i]$ by $A[i -$ offset$- >$ index_offset$[0]]$. The offset data structure is transparently populated by runtime and passed to the library kernel before executing it on the device. This approach avoids unnecessary data transfer and is likely to improve performance for strided data access applications. Based on the above design, the library developer needs to write Task_arch(range) functions for libraries dealing with non-contiguous data.

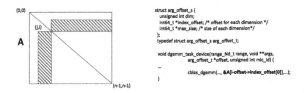

Fig. 5. Strided and non-contiguous data transfer

Runtime Adaptation: Even though LD provides platform-specific performance sketch of libraries to runtime, it is also possible to adaptively learn and improve these library parameters such as Affinity, Threads, Rate, and SubTaskSize. For instance, if an application repeatedly invokes the same library task (perhaps with a different range), we can estimate its optimal tile size for overlapping computation and communication from invocation to invocation even before executing it. We can also predict if task-fission is beneficial across library tasks (due to the overhead involved in splitting a task). Our runtime maintains an *online profiling database* in order to track performance profile of library tasks as they execute on devices. Following data structure depicts our online profiling database:

```
typedef struct task_profile_s {
    unsigned int task_type; // 0 for simple_task, 1 for divisible_task
    /* host execution profile */
    int64_t host_num_iters; /* Number of iterations executed by host */
    double host_time; /* Time taken by host */

    /*device execution profile */
    int64_t device_num_iters; /* Number of iterations executed by devices */
    int64_t num_bytes_xfered; /* Bytes of output transferred from devices */
    double xfer_time; /* Time taken for output data transfer */
    double compute_time; /*Device computation time*/

    /* task fission*/
    double task_split_time;
} task_profile_t;

/* Map from phase signature (id) to task name (string) to profiling database*/
map< int64_t, map<string, task_profile_t> > profile_db;
```

We divide a program execution into phases. Each phase consists of all the tasks being executed in between two consecutive wait_task(). We profile each phase and accumulate their information in profiling data-base. Each worker locally gathers profiling information for each task executing in a profiling phase. After the phase completes, wait_task() accumulates the per-worker profiles into the data structure above. Typical information we collect include data transfer time, computation time on host and device, and number of parallel iterations performed by host and device. These information can be used to improve LD's `Affinity()` and `Rate()` information. Additionally, during runtime task graph construction, we use the profiling database to estimate execution time of each new invocation of a task and determine if it is beneficial to perform task-fission in the current phase or not. That is, the total estimated time with and without task-fission is computed using the throughput and data transfer overhead of each device (computed from prior iterations). Since we estimate execution time and data transfer time on device for each task, we also adjust the tile size (i.e., `SubTaskSize()`) in order to reduce the communication to computation gap.

4 Evaluation

In this section, we investigate the performance of *Mozart* in High Performance Linpack (HPL) benchmark. This program is typically written using several library calls and hence, offering opportunities to our runtime to efficiently compose them. We compare *Mozart* with `MKL Offload` and hand-tuned optimized implementations of the same computation. The details of the hand-tuned HPL implementation is described in [19]. With better load balancing, efficient library composition, and adaptation to runtime behavior, *Mozart* is able to comprehensively outperform `MKL Offload` and is also able to beat the hand-tuned ninja version.

Implementation: Figure 6 depicts our implementation framework. We have implemented *Mozart* on top of the Julia compiler infrastructure [8]. The standard Julia compiler converts a Julia program into the Julia AST, then transforms it into LLVM IR, and finally generates native assembly code. We intercept the Julia compiler at the Julia AST level, recognize the library calls via AST pattern matching and rewrote them to create the corresponding LD object and invoke the *InsertTask()* function on it (as described in Sect. 2). Finally, we generate C++ code from Julia AST. Please note that the techniques described in this paper are not tied to our choice of implementation language and can be applied to other languages as well.

Platform: We use a host server with two Intel® Xeon® E5-2690v2 processors and 128 GB RAM. The processors are code-named Ivy Bridge and manufactured using 22 nm technology. Each processor has 10 cores (20 cores total) with base frequency of 3.00 GHz. The cache sizes are 32 KB for L1I, 32 KB for L1D, 256 KB for L2, and 25 MB for the L3 cache. It runs CentOS v6.6 distribution of Linux. This host server is connected via PCIe (with bandwidth 6 GB/s) to two massively parallel Xeon Phi co-processor with 61 in-order Pentium cores with each core being 4-way hyper-threaded. Applications can use up to 240 threads simultaneously (one core is reserved for the Linux OS running on it). Each core of Xeon Phi is embedded with a 512-bit vector unit for increased SIMD parallelism. Furthermore, each core has 32 KB L1 data cache, 32 KB L1 instruction cache and

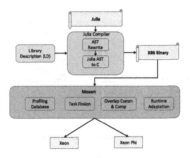

Fig. 6. Overall implementation framework of *Mozart*

512 KB partition of globally coherent L2 cache. Each Xeon phi co-processor has 8 GB of GDDR memory.

We use the Intel®C++ Compiler (ICC) v15.0.2 with "-O3" flag for compilation of the *Mozart* runtime and the C++ code generated from the Julia AST. We report execution times using the average of five runs.

High Performance Linpack (HPL) Performance. HPL is the most popular benchmark to rank supercomputers in TOP500, and it spends majority of time in numeric libraries. The key routine in HPL is LU factorization. LU factorization decomposes a matrix A into a lower-triangular matrix L and an upper triangular matrix U. We use a blocked LU factorization version that demonstrates the benefits of library composition using *Mozart*. The high-level blocked LU formulation code is shown in Fig. 7.[1] This algorithm proceeds from left to right of matrix A in blocks of nb until entire A is factorized. In each iteration of the loop, nb column panels are first factorized using dgetrf library call, nb block of matrix rows are swapped based on the pivot vector ipiv from panel factorization using two dlaswp library calls (denoted as dlaswpL and dlaswpR), and a portion of row panel is updated using dtrsm forward solver library call. The trailing submatrix of A is then updated using dgemm library call.

```
for( j = 0; j < n; j += nb ) {
    dgetrf(A[j:n-1][j:j+nb-1], ipiv[j:j+nb-1]);
    dlaswpL(A[j:j+nb-1][0:j], ipiv[j:j+nb-1]);
    dlaswpR(A[j:j+nb-1][j+nb:n-1], ipiv[j:j+nb-1]);
    dtrsm(A[j:j+nb-1][j:j+nb-1], A[j:j+nb-1][j+nb:n-1]);
    dgemm(A[j+nb:n-1][j:j+nb-1], A[j:j+nb][j+nb:n-1], A[j+nb:n-1][j+nb:n-1]);
}
```

Fig. 7. HPL blocked version demonstrating library composition.

We wrote the LD specifications for the library tasks from Fig. 7. The performance models for `Threads()`, `SubTaskSize()` and `Rate()` were built using

---

[1] Note that we specifically choose the blocked version of HPL to highlight the contribution of this paper, which is library composition. We do not directly use the LU factorization algorithm provided by MKL.

Fig. 8. HPL: task-fission performed via *Mozart*

simple curve-fitting from an extensive set of micro-benchmarking executions on our platform. The library tasks were then inserted inserted into our runtime using `InsertTask()` LD interfaces. Our runtime automatically identifies the task dependencies between them based on their input-output dependencies on matrix A and builds the task graph. The runtime task graph for two consecutive iterations $j-nb$ and j is shown to the left of Fig. 8. Our runtime identifies an opportunity to detect partial loop-carried dependency between dgemm($j-nb$) task and dgetrf(j) task, i.e., dependency between previous iteration $j-nb$ dgemm call and next iteration j dgetrf call. It then splits dgemm($j-nb$) into dgemm_1($j-nb$) and dgemm_2($j-nb$) tasks using task fission (as shown in the middle of Fig. 8). This allows dgemm_1($j-nb$) task to execute concurrently with both dgemm_2($j-nb$) and dgetrf(j) tasks (as shown to the right of Fig. 8). Both dgemm_2($j-nb$) and dgetrf(j) are executed on Xeon based on the affinity of dgetrf(j) task specified in LD. On the other hand, dgemm_1($j-nb$) starts by executing on Xeon Phi but is subsequently executed on both Xeon and Xeon Phi when dgemm_2($j-nb$) and dgetrf(j) tasks are completed.

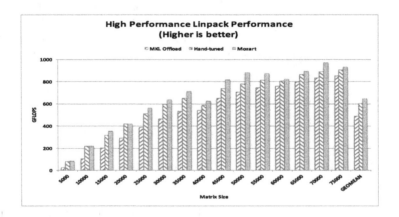

Fig. 9. Performance of High Performance Linpack running on a Xeon + 2 Phi Ivy Bridge system (higher is better). On average, `MKL Offload` approach achieves 489 GFLOPS, `Hand-tuned` achieves 604 GFLOPS, and *Mozart* achieves 644 GFLOPS for matrix sizes 5K–75K.

Figure 9 presents our experimental evaluation comparing *Mozart* with MKL Offload and Hand-tuned ninja version [19]. We vary the matrix size from 5K until 75K in steps of 5K. We observe an average GFLOPS improvement of 31.7% for *Mozart* vs. MKL Offload, primarily due to the fact that MKL Offload does not perform any cross library optimization for the blocked version of HPL, although it is able to execute the dgemm and dtrsm library functions across both Xeon and Xeon Phi and achieves peak performance for them individually. When compared to hand-tuned ninja version, *Mozart* yields an average GFLOPS improvement of 6.7%. Although hand-tuned ninja version performs library composition using a manual implementation of task fission, it does not perform the following tasks effectively: (1) the ninja version is unable to load balance effectively – it does not use a performance model like ours (via LD) to divide work between Xeon and Xeon Phi instead uses a platform-specific hand-tuned step function to determine the number of dgemm_1$(j - nb)$ iterations to be performed on Xeon[2]; (2) the ninja version does not perform runtime adaptation like ours as described in Sect. 3.

Performance Breakdown: The GFLOPS improvement of 31.7% for *Mozart* vs. MKL Offload can be explained as follows: we observe 10–15% benefit for small size matrices (5K–25K) and close to 20% benefit for larger matrices (>=30K) from our task-fission optimization, which MKL-Offload can not perform in the blocked version of HPL. Remaining benefits of close to 10–15% is obtained from runtime adaptation via sub-task granularity determination (i.e., SubTaskSize()) and cost-benefit analysis of task-fission (that is whether to perform task fission or not) as described in Sect. 3.

Discussion: The HPL application has the following properties that *Mozart* exploits:

- *dgemm* matrix-matrix multiplication task is computationally expensive and can be decomposed into smaller granularity which can distributed to host and device cores;
- *dgemm* can be split via task-fission into two sub-tasks where one of them can execute in parallel with *dgetrf* of the next iteration in order to reduce the critical path length.

One of the key ideas of the paper is to dynamically perform task-fission optimization across library calls. Task-fission opportunities are prevalent in many data parallel application domains including emerging AI and machine-learning that compose many data parallel libraries, e.g., Intel's DAAL and CUDA-DNN within a network model. Existing HPC applications such as LU, Cholesky and QR factorization already exhibit task-fission patterns. Thus, we believe efficient library composition via task fission will play an important role in optimizing future applications. Although it is possible to implement task-fission statically, it may not be straightforward in the presence of complicated control-flow such as the one present in HPL. In summary, the techniques described in *Mozart*

---

[2] Hand-tuned implementations are rarely performance portable.

including library description and library composition runtime are general and can be applied to other heterogeneous architectures and applications.

5 Related Work

Heterogeneous Execution: There have been several efforts [5, 7, 10–12, 14, 18, 20, 22, 25, 26, 29, 31, 32, 32, 34–36, 39, 40, 44] to make heterogeneous execution of applications more efficient. [4] is most closely related to our work as it analyzes a series of GPU library calls in order to minimize the CPU-GPU communication overheads by caching the reused data. Our work is different from the above body of works in two key aspects: *Mozart* performs task-fission at runtime and dynamically adapts device tile sizes. It augments library description metadata framework to decompose libraries for efficient heterogeneous execution.

Dynamic Task Graph: Dynamic task graph is widely used in parallel systems. StarPU [5], OMPSs [9, 13, 33], and BDDT [43] build dynamic task graphs, but they do not dynamically split tasks into subtasks. There is previous work [15] on dividing/consolidating tasks to make better use of resource or to achieve better load balance, but it considers only independent tasks. [17, 19] manually splits tasks in application level to enable dynamic load-balancing on a Xeon Phi system. To the best of our knowledge, no known work splits tasks in a dynamic task graph based on the dependencies between tasks.

Overlapped Communication and Computation: [5, 9, 28] present runtimes that overlap communication with computation. [37] describes a hybrid threading approach where one thread handles all MPI-related operations and all other threads handle computation. [24] provides an OpenCL communication library and programming interface to optimize communication between host and accelerators. [40] uses static inter-node data and task distribution in large-scale GPU-based clusters, and dynamic task scheduling within a node to overlap communication with computation. [41] uses source-to-source compiler optimization to enable streaming for offloaded computations for Xeon Phi. In our work, we use performance models from LD and dynamically adjust tile size to completely overlap communication and computation for heterogeneous systems.

Telescopic Languages: The idea of annotating libraries in order to generate fast specialized code at the translation of scripting languages has been explored in [21]. Our library description metadata is inspired by this work, but extends it to enable cross-library heterogeneous execution via task-fission. Library annotation has also been explored in [16].

Skeleton Composition: Efficient composition of algorithmic skeletons such as map, reduce, and zip for shared-memory systems and clusters has been explored in the STAPL Skeleton Framework [42, 45, 46].

6 Conclusion

In this paper, we show that library composition plays a crucial role in achieving peak performance in heterogeneous architectures. We propose a framework, *Mozart*, consisting of two components: a *library description* (LD) interface for library writers and a generic *library composition runtime*. The runtime performs task-fission on-the-fly in order to improve data locality and data reuse across library calls using the performance parameters from LD. *Mozart* transparently composes library calls across heterogeneous cores and delivers close-to expertly tuned performance. Our experimental evaluation on a heterogeneous system consisting of a Xeon CPU and 2 Xeon Phi co-processors executing High Performance Linpack benchmarks shows that *Mozart* achieves an average GFLOPS improvement of 31.7% over MKL+AO and 6.7% over hand-optimized code. In future, we would like to augment auto-tuning within our framework to further improve our performance results. We would also like to extend *Mozart* to handle non-affine array accesses. A tool that can automatically generate LD specifications for library routines is also a subject for future work.

References

1. Effective Use of the Intel Compiler's Offload Features. https://software.intel.com/en-us/articles/effective-use-of-the-intel-compilers-offload-features
2. How to Overlap Data Transfers in CUDA C/C++. https://devblogs.nvidia.com/parallelforall/how-overlap-data-transfers-cuda-cc/
3. Intel Math Kernel Library Automatic Offload for Intel Xeon Phi Coprocessor. https://software.intel.com/en-us/articles/math-kernel-library-automatic-offload-for-intel-xeon-phi-coprocessor
4. AlSaber, N., Kulkarni, M.: Semcache: semantics-aware caching for efficient GPU offloading. In: Proceedings of the 27th International ACM Conference on International Conference on Supercomputing, ICS 2013, pp. 421–432. ACM, New York (2013)
5. Augonnet, C., Thibault, S., Namyst, R., Wacrenier, P.-A.: StarPU: a unified platform for task scheduling on heterogeneous multicore architectures. Concurr. Comput.: Pract. Exp. **23**(2), 187–198 (2011)
6. Barik, R., et al.: Efficient mapping of irregular C++ applications to integrated GPUs. In: IEEE/ACM International Symposium on Code Generation and Optimization (CGO) (2014)
7. Belviranli, M.E., Bhuyan, L.N., Gupta, R.: A dynamic self-scheduling scheme for heterogeneous multiprocessor architectures. ACM Trans. Archit. Code Optim. **9**(4), 57:1–57:20 (2013)
8. Bezanson, J., Karpinski, S., Shah, V.B., Edelman, A.: Julia: a fast dynamic language for technical computing. CoRR, abs/1209.5145 (2012)
9. Bueno, J., Martorell, X., Badia, R.M., Ayguadé, E., Labarta, J.: Implementing OmpSs support for regions of data in architectures with multiple address spaces. In: Proceedings of the 27th International ACM Conference on International Conference on Supercomputing, ICS 2013, pp. 359–368. ACM, New York (2013)
10. Cederman, D., Tsigas, P.: On dynamic load balancing on graphics processors. In: Proceedings of the 23rd ACM SIGGRAPH/EUROGRAPHICS Symposium on Graphics Hardware, GH 2008, Aire-la-Ville, Switzerland, pp. 57–64 (2008)

11. Chatterjee, S., Grossman, M., Sbîrlea, A., Sarkar, V.: Dynamic task parallelism with a GPU work-stealing runtime system. In: Rajopadhye, S., Mills Strout, M. (eds.) LCPC 2011. LNCS, vol. 7146, pp. 203–217. Springer, Heidelberg (2013). https://doi.org/10.1007/978-3-642-36036-7_14

12. Chen, L., Villa, O., Krishnamoorthy, S., Gao, G.R.: Dynamic load balancing on single- and multi-GPU systems. In: IEEE International Symposium on Parallel and Distributed Processing (IPDPS), pp. 1–12 (2010)

13. Chronaki, K., Rico, A., Badia, R.M., Ayguadé, E., Labarta, J., Valero, M.: Criticality-aware dynamic task scheduling for heterogeneous architectures. In: Proceedings of the 29th ACM on International Conference on Supercomputing, ICS 2015, New York, NY, USA, pp. 329–338 (2015)

14. Grewe, D., Wang, Z., O'Boyle, M.F.P.: OpenCL task partitioning in the presence of GPU contention. In: Caşcaval, C., Montesinos, P. (eds.) LCPC 2013. LNCS, vol. 8664, pp. 87–101. Springer, Cham (2014). https://doi.org/10.1007/978-3-319-09967-5_5

15. Guo, Z., Pierce, M., Fox, G., Zhou, M.: Automatic task re-organization in MapReduce. In: 2011 IEEE International Conference on Cluster Computing (CLUSTER), pp. 335–343 (2011)

16. Guyer, S.Z., Lin, C.: Broadway: a software architecture for scientific computing. In: IFIPS Working Group 2.5: Software Architecture for Scientific Computing (2000)

17. Haidar, A., Tomov, S., Arturov, K., Guney, M., Story, S., Dongarra, J.: LU, QR, and Cholesky factorizations: programming model, performance analysis and optimization techniques for the Intel Knights Landing Xeon Phi. In: 2016 IEEE High Performance Extreme Computing Conference (HPEC), pp. 1–7, September 2016

18. Harris, T., Maas, M., Marathe, V.J.: Callisto: co-scheduling parallel runtime systems. In: Proceedings of the Ninth European Conference on Computer Systems, EuroSys 2014, pp. 24:1–24:14. ACM, New York (2014)

19. Heinecke, A., et al.: Design and implementation of the Linpack benchmark for single and multi-node systems based on Intel Xeon Phi coprocessor. In: 2013 IEEE 27th International Symposium on Parallel and Distributed Processing (IPDPS), Washington, DC, USA, pp. 126–137 (2013)

20. Hugo, A.-E., Guermouche, A., Wacrenier, P.-A., Namyst, R.: Composing multiple StarPU applications over heterogeneous machines: a supervised approach. IJHPCA 28(3), 285–300 (2014)

21. Kennedy, K., et al.: Telescoping languages: a strategy for automatic generation of scientific problem-solving systems from annotated libraries. J. Parallel Distrib. Comput. 61(12), 1803–1826 (2001)

22. Kim, J., Kim, H., Lee, J.H., Lee, J.: Achieving a single compute device image in OpenCL for multiple GPUs. In: Proceedings of the 16th ACM Symposium on Principles and Practice of Parallel Programming, PPoPP 2011, NY, USA, pp. 277–288 (2011)

23. Kim, J., Seo, S., Lee, J., Nah, J., Jo, G., Lee, J.: SnuCL: an OpenCL framework for heterogeneous CPU/GPU clusters. In: Proceedings of the 26th ACM International Conference on Supercomputing, ICS 2012, pp. 341–352 (2012)

24. Komoda, T., Miwa, S., Nakamura, H.: Communication library to overlap computation and communication for OpenCL application. In: Proceedings of the 2012 IEEE 26th International Parallel and Distributed Processing Symposium Workshops and Ph.D. Forum, IPDPSW 2012, Washington, DC, USA, pp. 567–573 (2012)

25. Lee, J., Samadi, M., Park, Y., Mahlke, S.: Transparent CPU-GPU collaboration for data-parallel kernels on heterogeneous systems. In: Proceedings of the 22nd International Conference on Parallel Architectures and Compilation Techniques, PACT (2013)
26. Luk, C.-K., Hong, S., Kim, H.: Qilin: exploiting parallelism on heterogeneous multiprocessors with adaptive mapping. In: Proceedings of the 42nd Annual IEEE/ACM International Symposium on Microarchitecture, MICRO, NY, USA, pp. 45–55 (2009)
27. Majo, Z., Gross, T.R.: A library for portable and composable data locality optimizations for NUMA systems. ACM Trans. Parallel Comput. **3**(4), 20:1–20:32 (2017)
28. Marjanović, V., Labarta, J., Ayguadé, E., Valero, M.: Overlapping communication and computation by using a hybrid MPI/SMPSs approach. In: Proceedings of the 24th ACM International Conference on Supercomputing, ICS 2010, New York, NY, USA, pp. 5–16 (2010)
29. Ogata, Y., Endo, T., Maruyama, N., Matsuoka, S.: An efficient, model-based CPU-GPU heterogeneous FFT library. In: IEEE International Symposium on Parallel and Distributed Processing, IPDPS, pp. 1–10 (2008)
30. Pan, H., Hindman, B., Asanović, K.: Lithe: enabling efficient composition of parallel libraries. In: Proceedings of the First USENIX Conference on Hot Topics in Parallelism, HotPar 2009, p. 11. USENIX Association, Berkeley (2009)
31. Pandit, P., Govindarajan, R.: Fluidic kernels: cooperative execution of OpenCL programs on multiple heterogeneous devices. In: Proceedings of Annual IEEE/ACM International Symposium on Code Generation and Optimization, CGO 2014, NY, USA, pp. 273:273–273:283 (2014)
32. Phothilimthana, P.M., Ansel, J., Ragan-Kelley, J., Amarasinghe, S.: Portable performance on heterogeneous architectures. In: Proceedings of the Eighteenth International Conference on Architectural Support for Programming Languages and Operating Systems, ASPLOS 2013, NY, USA, pp. 431–444 (2013)
33. Planas, J., Badia, R.M., Ayguadé, E., Labarta, J.: SSMART: smart scheduling of multi-architecture tasks on heterogeneous systems. In: Proceedings of the Second Workshop on Accelerator Programming Using Directives, WACCPD 2015, pp. 1:1–1:11 (2015)
34. Ravi, V.T., Ma, W., Chiu, D., Agrawal, G.: Compiler and runtime support for enabling generalized reduction computations on heterogeneous parallel configurations. In: Proceedings of the 24th ACM International Conference on Supercomputing, ICS 2010, NY, USA, pp. 137–146 (2010)
35. Ravi, V.T., Agrawal, G.: A dynamic scheduling framework for emerging heterogeneous systems. In: 2011 18th International Conference on High Performance Computing (HiPC), pp. 1–10, December 2011
36. Rey, A., Igual, F.D., Prieto-Matías, M.: HeSP: a simulation framework for solving the task scheduling-partitioning problem on heterogeneous architectures. In: Dutot, P.-F., Trystram, D. (eds.) Euro-Par 2016. LNCS, vol. 9833, pp. 183–195. Springer, Cham (2016). https://doi.org/10.1007/978-3-319-43659-3_14
37. Satish, N., Kim, C., Chhugani, J., Dubey, P.: Large-scale energy-efficient graph traversal: a path to efficient data-intensive supercomputing. In: Proceedings of the International Conference on High Performance Computing, Networking, Storage and Analysis, SC 2012, Los Alamitos, CA, USA, pp. 14:1–14:11 (2012)

38. Satish, N.: Can traditional programming bridge the ninja performance gap for parallel computing applications? In: Proceedings of the 39th Annual International Symposium on Computer Architecture, ISCA 2012, Washington, DC, USA, pp. 440–451 (2012)
39. Schaa, D., Kaeli, D.: Exploring the multiple-GPU design space. In: IEEE International Symposium on Parallel Distributed Processing, IPDPS, pp. 1–12 (2009)
40. Song, F., Dongarra, J.: A scalable framework for heterogeneous GPU-based clusters. In: Proceedings of the 24th ACM Symposium on Parallelism in Algorithms and Architectures, SPAA 2012, NY, USA, pp. 91–100 (2012)
41. Song, L., Feng, M., Ravi, N., Yang, Y., Chakradhar, S.: COMP: compiler optimizations for manycore processors. In: Proceedings of the 47th Annual IEEE/ACM International Symposium on Microarchitecture, MICRO-47, Washington, DC, USA, pp. 659–671 (2014)
42. Thomas, N., Tanase, G., Tkachyshyn, O., Perdue, J., Amato, N.M., Rauchwerger, L.: A framework for adaptive algorithm selection in STAPL. In: Proceedings of the Tenth ACM SIGPLAN Symposium on Principles and Practice of Parallel Programming, PPoPP 2005, pp. 277–288. ACM, New York (2005)
43. Tzenakis, G., Papatriantafyllou, A., Vandierendonck, H., Pratikakis, P., Nikolopoulos, D.S.: BDDT: block-level dynamic dependence analysis for task-based parallelism. In: Wu, C., Cohen, A. (eds.) APPT 2013. LNCS, vol. 8299, pp. 17–31. Springer, Heidelberg (2013). https://doi.org/10.1007/978-3-642-45293-2_2
44. Wu, W., Bouteiller, A., Bosilca, G., Faverge, M., Dongarra, J.: Hierarchical DAG scheduling for hybrid distributed systems. In: 29th IEEE International Parallel and Distributed Processing Symposium (IPDPS), Hyderabad, India, May 2015
45. Yu, H., Rauchwerger, L.: An adaptive algorithm selection framework for reduction parallelization. IEEE Trans. Parallel Distrib. Syst. **17**(10), 1084–1096 (2006)
46. Zandifar, M., Jabbar, M.A., Majidi, A., Keyes, D., Amato, N.M., Rauchwerger, L.: Composing algorithmic skeletons to express high-performance scientific applications. In: Proceedings of the 29th ACM on International Conference on Supercomputing, ICS 2015, pp. 415–424. ACM, New York (2015)

Lock-Free Transactional Adjacency List

Zachary Painter$^{(\boxtimes)}$, Christina Peterson, and Damian Dechev

University Of Central Florida, Orlando, FL 32816, USA
zacharypainter@knights.ucf.edu

Abstract. Adjacency lists are frequently used in graphing or map based applications. Although efficient concurrent linked-list algorithms are well known, it can be difficult to adapt these approaches to build a high-performance adjacency list. Furthermore, it can often be desirable to execute operations in these data structures transactionally, or perform a sequence of operations in one atomic step. In this paper, we present a lock-free transactional adjacency list based on a multi-dimensional list (MDList). We are able to combine known linked list strategies with the capability of the MDList in order to efficiently organize graph vertexes and their edges. We design our underlying data structure to be node-based and linearizable, then use the Lock-Free Transactional Transformation (LFTT) methodology to efficiently enable transactional execution. In our performance evaluation, our lock-free transactional adjacency list achieves an average of 50% speedup over a transactional boosting implementation.

1 Introduction

Lock-free data structures aim to fully utilize the computing resources of multi-core processors without the drawbacks of lock-based counterparts such as deadlock or priority inversion. However, lock-free data structures are difficult to design due to the consideration of all possible thread interleavings when reasoning about safety or liveness properties. Even more so are lock-free transactional data structures because in addition to the safety and liveness properties of traditional lock-free data structures, isolation must be preserved such that a series of operations appear to occur in one atomic step.

An adjacency list data structure maps graph nodes, or "vertexes," to other nodes by their connections, or "edges." Generally, if a vertex i is adjacent to another vertex j, then vertex j is contained in the sublist of vertex i. In order to implement such a data structure concurrently, one would need to overcome the challenges of traversing in multiple dimensions, organizing vertex and edge nodes, and properly disposing of all children of a vertex before deleting the vertex.

This research was supported by the National Science Foundation under NSF OAC 1440530, NSF CCF 1717515, and NSF OAC 1740095.

© Springer Nature Switzerland AG 2019
L. Rauchwerger (Ed.): LCPC 2017, LNCS 11403, pp. 203–219, 2019.
https://doi.org/10.1007/978-3-030-35225-7_14

Previous work on lock-free linked list data structures are designed for sets and queues. Since elements of these abstract data types do not account for relationships between elements, they are unsuitable to be directly used for an adjacency list data structure. An adjacency list data structure needs to support operations that can insert and remove vertexes and edges, as well as check whether a vertex or edge is contained in the list. Additional synchronization is required to ensure that an operation that deletes a vertex i does not modify or remove nodes that are currently part of i's sublist of adjacent nodes. Further synchronization is required to ensure that two operations are able to simultaneously modify the sublist of a vertex despite those operations appearing to take place at the same vertex.

A lock-free adjacency list provides atomicity at the granularity of an individual operation. However, in some cases one may want to perform a sequence of operations such that the entire sequence appears to take place in one atomic step. One such case is during the deletion of a vertex, in which case it must first be guaranteed that all edges from that vertex have already been deleted. In such a case, a sequence of operations such as the following would be useful.

1: **if** ISEMPTY(*vertex.List*) **then**
2:     DELETE(*vertex*);

This code should be able to verify that a given node's sublist is empty before deleting that node. Unfortunately, this operation fails to complete its goal. Since the composition of the methods is not atomic, another thread a could insert an edge between the time that thread b reads that the list of edge nodes is empty, and thread b deleting the vertex, thus invalidating the operation.

In order to perform a series of operations such as those previously mentioned, all involved operations need to appear to take place in a single atomic step. Additionally, if any operation fails, it must appear as though none of the operations took place. Some implementations, such as Transactional Boosting [9], use fine-grained locking in order to create a transactional data structure from an underlying concurrent data structure. This, however, reduces the performance of the data structure, and negates any lock-free progress guarantee the underlying data structure might have had. Software Transactional Memory (STM) can also be used to create transactional data structures from existing ones. Unfortunately, this approach also creates significant performance loss. In an STM data structure, transactions maintain a list of read and write locations. If a transaction's read and write set overlaps with another transaction's write set, those transactions conflict. In the case of a conflict, one of the transactions must abort. This results in a significant amount of unnecessary aborts, as conflicts detected in this way do not necessarily correspond to high-level semantic conflicts. These excessive aborts can severely limit the degree of concurrency when executing transactions on a data structure.

In this paper, we present a high performance lock-free transactional adjacency list. The primary goal of the data structure presented in this work is to (1) implement a lock-free adjacency list base data structure, and (2) enable transactional execution of operations in this data structure.

In order to achieve the first goal, we implement lock-free adjacency list using a lock-free linked list of vertexes, where each vertex contains a pointer to a Multi-Dimensional List (MDList) [24] to allow fast lookup of edges. We depict the adjacency list structure in Fig. 1. An MDList guarantees a worst-cast search time complexity of $O(\log N)$, an improvement over a worst-cast search time complexity of $O(N)$ provided by design alternatives such as a linked list or skiplist. A skiplist provides an average search time complexity of $O(\log N)$, but has a worst-cast search time complexity of $O(N)$ if shortcuts to the node of interest do not exist. We place all vertexes in the primary linked list, and all adjacent edges to that vertex as a node in its associated MDList. This allows us to take maximum advantage of the multi-dimensional property of the MDList, while also easily organizing the relative locations of each vertex and their corresponding edges. Background details on the MDList are provided in Sect. 2.

We refer to elements in the primary linked list as vertexes, and elements in the sublist of a vertex as nodes. A node a contained in vertex b's associated MDList indicates that vertex a is adjacent to vertex b. When inserting or deleting a vertex, we traverse along the main list of vertexes, checking each key, until we find the location to insert or delete our vertex. While allocating the vertex we also allocate a new MDList for that vertex to point to.

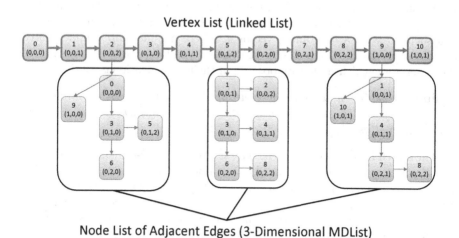

Fig. 1. Adjacency list structure

In order to achieve the second goal, we adopt Lock-Free Transaction Transformation (LFTT) [25] by storing descriptor objects within each node in both the main list and each MDList. LFTT uses high-level semantic conflict detection to avoid low-level read/write conflicts, and a logical rollback to avoid the performance penalties of a physical rollback. Background details on LFTT are provided in Sect. 2.

The contribution made by this paper is as follows:

- To the best of our knowledge, this paper presents the only lock-free transactional adjacency list.
- This data structure experiences an average speedup greater than 50% when compared to similar approaches based on transactional boosting and STM.

2   Background

An MDList partitions a linked list into shorter lists organized in multi-dimensional space to improve search time. A node in a D-dimensional MDList comprises a key-value pair, a coordinate vector of integers $k[D]$, and an array of child pointers where the dth pointer links to a child node of dimension d. A list of arbitrary dimension D is formally defined as follows.

Definition 1. *A D-dimensional list is a rooted tree in which each node is implicitly assigned a dimension of $d \in [0, D)$. The root node's dimension is 0. A node of dimension d has no more than $D - d$ children, and each child is assigned a unique dimension of $d' \in [d, D)$* [24].

Given a key range of $[0, N)$ in a D-dimensional space, the maximum number of keys in each dimension is $b = \lceil \sqrt[D]{N} \rceil$. The mapping of an integer key to its D-dimension vector coordinates is performed by converting the key to a b-based number and using each digit as an entry in the vector coordinates. Each node is associated with a coordinate vector k, where a dimension d node shares a coordinate prefix of length d with its parent. The following definition provides the criteria for which nodes are ordered in their D-dimensional list.

Definition 2. *Given a non-root node of dimension d with coordinate $k = (k_0, ..., k_{D-1})$ and its parent with coordinate $k' = (k'_0, ..., k'_{D-1})$ in an ordered D-dimensional list: $k_i = k'_i, \forall i \in [0, d) \land k_d > k'_d$* [24].

The search for a node is performed by starting at the 0-dimension and traversing all nodes at this dimension until either a node with the same 0th coordinate as the key of interest is reached, or the current node being traversed has a greater 0th coordinate than the key of interest. If a node with a 0th coordinate identical to the key of interest exists, then the search advances to the next dimension d. The search will continue advancing dimensions given that a node with the same dth coordinate as the key of interest is found. The search terminates when either a node with the same coordinates as the key of interest is found, or no node exists with the same dth coordinate as the key of interest.

The worst-case time complexity of a search in an MDList is $O(D \cdot b)$, where b is the maximum number of nodes in a dimension. Replacing b in the worst-cast time complexity, we have $O(D \cdot b) = O(D \cdot \sqrt[D]{N})$. If we choose $D \propto \log N$, then $O(D \cdot \sqrt[D]{N}) = O(\log N \cdot \sqrt[\log N]{N}) = O(\log N \cdot 2) = O(\log N)$.

Insertion into an MDList is performed by splicing and child adoption. Splicing consists of updating the new node's child pointer to point to the predecessor's child, and updating the predecessor's child pointer to point to the new node. Child adoption is necessary when the dimension of an old child has changed due to the insertion of a new node, where the old child will be adopted as a higher dimension child of the new node. Deletion of a node in an MDList is performed by updating the predecessor's child point to point to the child of the node to be deleted. In the case of a deletion, the child of the node to be deleted is adopted as a lower dimension child of the predecessor.

Lock Free Transactional Transformation (LFTT) is a methodology for creating transactional data structures from lock-free node-based data structures. LFTT handles conflicts between operations by utilizing descriptor objects referenced by each node. These transaction descriptors contain all information necessary for an arbitrary thread to perform any given operation or sequence of operations belonging to a transaction. For a thread to perform an operation at a node as part of a transaction, it is must first create a reference to its transaction descriptor in the node. If there already exists a transaction descriptor at that node, a conflict between two transactions accessing the same node has been detected. LFTT resolves these conflicts by having the thread that finds an existing transaction descriptor at a node help complete the conflicting transaction by executing all remaining operations that are part of that transaction, thus eventually causing the conflicting transaction to either succeed or fail. Once the transaction referenced by the transaction descriptor at a node is complete, a thread may place a reference to its own transaction descriptor in the node and proceed with its operation.

LFTT additionally handles the recovery of failed transactions through its transaction descriptors. A transaction descriptor may be marked as *committed*, indicating that all operations that are part of the transaction have been successfully completed. Alternatively, a transaction descriptor may be marked *aborted*, indicating that none of the operations in the transaction should occur. LFTT is able to avoid the need to physically undo already completed operations that are part of an aborted transaction by interpreting the logical status of a node based on its transaction descriptors status. A nodes status in the list is interpreted inversely if it is part of an aborted transaction. This results in the *appearance* that all completed operations that are part of an aborted transaction have been undone.

3   Lock-Free Transactional Adjacency List

The primary challenge in creating a lock-free transactional adjacency list is its multi-dimensional structure, which poses a major challenge to performing transactional synchronization for non-commutative operations. INSERTEDGE and DELETEEDGE create a relation between two vertexes by adding or removing a node from the sublist of an existing vertex. Any INSERTEDGE or DELETEEDGE operation occurring at vertex j would have their outcome affected by a transaction that modifies vertex j. As a result, two edge operations occurring at the same vertex are able to commute, while an edge operation and an operation that modifies the vertex itself are not. The DELETEVERTEX method requires special consideration. The case in which a transaction deletes a vertex at which one or multiple threads are performing an edge operation must be prevented. A DELETEVERTEX operation on a vertex should help complete all pending edge operations currently accessing the MDList contained at that vertex. Simultaneously, any subsequent operations attempting to access that MDList will first help complete the pending DELETEVERTEX.

The constants provided by LFTT are detailed in Algorithm 1. We introduce a *currentOpid* field to each descriptor to track the current progress of each transaction. The IsNODEPRESENT, IsKEYPRESENT, EXECUTEOPS, MARKDELETE, LOCATEPRED, and pointer marking operations are provided in Lock-Free Transactional Transformation [25].

Algorithm 1. LFTT Definitions

```
 1: enum TxStatus              14: struct Desc
 2:     Active                 15:     int size
 3:     Committed              16:     TxStatus status
 4:     Aborted                17:     int currentOpid
 5: enum OpType                18:     Operation ops[]
 6:     InsertVertex           19: struct NodeDesc
 7:     DeleteVertex           20:     Desc* desc
 8:     InsertEdge             21:     int opid
 9:     DeleteEdge             22: struct Node
10:     Find                   23:     NodeDesc* info
11: struct Operation           24:     int key
12:     OpType type            25:     MDList* list
13:     int key                26:     ...
```

Algorithm 2. Update Info Pointer

```
 1: function UPDATEINFO(Node* n, NodeDesc* info, bool wantkey)
 2:     NodeInfo *oldinfo ← n.info
 3:     if IsMARKED(oldinfo) then
 4:         Do_DELETE(n)
 5:         return retry;
 6:     if oldinfo.desc ≠ info.desc then
 7:         if oldinfo.desc.ops[oldinfo.opid] == DeleteVertex & oldinfo.desc.currentOpid == old-
            info.opid then
 8:             EXECUTEOPS(oldinfo.desc, oldinfo.opid)
 9:         else
10:             EXECUTEOPS(oldinfo.desc, oldinfo.opid+1)
11:     else if oldinfo.opid >= info.opid then
12:         return success
13:     haskey ← IsKEYPRESENT(oldinfo)
14:     if (!haskey & wantkey) || (haskey & !wantkey) then
15:         return fail
16:     if info.desc.status ≠ Active then
17:         return fail
18:     if CAS(&n.info, oldinfo, info) then
19:         return success
20:     else
21:         return retry
```

Algorithm 2 contains the UPDATEINFO operation provided by Lock-Free Transactional Transformation [25], which has been modified in the following way to allow for a special case regarding DELETEVERTEX. At line 2.6 we check the info pointer at node n. If a different operation is currently taking place at node n, that operation must be completed before the desired operation can begin. At line 2.7 we check if the operation that occurred at node n was a DELETEVERTEX operation. If so, we check whether the DELETEVERTEX operation is pending. The *currentOpid* variable stores what step the transaction is currently on. If this value is equal to the value of the operation that occurred at node n, then the DELETEVERTEX operation is not complete and the current thread should use the descriptor object to attempt to delete the vertex. For all other operations, the presence of an info pointer at node n indicates that the operation described by *n.info* is already complete. Thus, EXECUTEOPS is called on the next operation in the transaction.

Algorithm 3. Transformed Delete Vertex

```
1:  function DELETEVERTEX(int vertex, NodeDesc* nDesc)
2:      Node *curr ← head
3:      Node *pred ← NULL
4:      while true do
5:          LOCATEPRED(pred, curr, vertex)
6:          if ISNODEPRESENT(curr, vertex) then
7:              ret ← (UPDATEINFO(curr, nDesc, true) == success)
8:              if ret then
9:                  MDList *list ← curr.list
10:                 ret ← list.FINISHDELETE(list.head, 0, nDesc)
11:         else
12:             ret ← false
13:         if ret then
14:             return true
15:         else
16:             return false
```

Algorithm 4. Finish Pending DELETEVERTEX Operation

```
1:  function FINISHDELETE(MDList::Node* n, int dc, NodeDesc* nDesc)
2:      while true do
3:          if UPDATEINFO(n, nDesc, true) == success then
4:              Break
5:          else
6:              return false
7:      for i ∈ [dc,DIMENSION) do
8:          MDList::Node *child ← n.child[i]
9:          CAS(&n.child[i], child, SET_MARK(child))
10:         if child! = NULL then
11:             ret ← FINISHDELETE(child, i, nDesc)
12:             if ret == false then
13:                 return false
14:         else
15:             return true
```

3.1   Adjacency List Operations

This adjacency list supports 5 operations: INSERTVERTEX, DELETEVERTEX, INSERTEDGE, DELETEEDGE, and FIND. The INSERTVERTEX operation adds a vertex to a primary linked list of vertexes. The INSERTEDGE operation adds a node to a specific vertex's sublist, thus establishing that node as adjacent to the specified vertex. The DELETEVERTEX and DELETEEDGE operations are the inverses of their counterparts. The FIND operation searches for a node within the sublist of vertex j, returning whether or not that node shares an edge with vertex j.

Algorithm 5. Find Vertex Operation

```
1: function FINDVERTEX(int vertex, NodeDesc* nDesc, int opid)
2:     Node *curr ← head
3:     Node *pred ← NULL
4:     while true do
5:         LOCATEPRED(pred, curr, vertex)
6:         if ISNODEPRESENT(curr, vertex) then
7:             NodeDesc *cDesc ← curr.info
8:             if cDesc != nDesc then
9:                 EXECUTEOPS(cDesc.desc, cDesc.opid+1)
10:            if ISKEYPRESENT(cDesc) then
11:                if nDesc.desc.status != ACTIVE then
12:                    return NULL
13:                else
14:                    return curr
15:        else
16:            return NULL
```

Algorithm 3 details the DELETEVERTEX operation. DELETEVERTEX traverses the main list of vertexes by calling LOCATEPRED on line 3.5. If the node with the target key already exists, then LOCATEPRED will return when *curr* points to the node with that key, otherwise, *curr* will point to the logical successor of the node to be deleted. We check for the case that the node with the desired key already exists on line 3.6. We then call UPDATEINFO to attempt to redirect the *info* pointer. If this succeeds, we must then call FINISHDELETE on the vertex's *list* object. FINISHDELETE traverses *list* calling UPDATEINFO on all the nodes it contains. Additionally, we must mark the next pointer of all nodes as they are traversed, which will interrupt competing INSERTEDGE operations that have already begun inserting their node on line 6.15, causing them to re-traverse. The goal of this operation is to logically delete all edges adjacent to the vertex to be deleted. This process allows all pending transactions occurring within the sublist to commit due to the call to UPDATEINFO at line 4.3. Once it can be guaranteed that all nodes within the vertex's list are deleted, the operation is complete. Physical deletion is later done by using Compare-And-Swap to change *pred.next* to point to *curr.next*, thus removing the vertex from the main list.

The INSERTVERTEX algorithm is similar to DELETEVERTEX. INSERTVERTEX traverses the list using LOCATEPRED, but can only succeed if its value is not already in the list (!IsNodePresent($curr, vertex$)). In this case, it allocates a new vertex and inserts it into the list using Compare-And-Swap to change *pred.next* to *curr*.

Algorithm 5 details the main method used to help the insertion of edge nodes. To begin, it searches the list until it finds the correct vertex node and verifies that it is logically in the list, and that no other transaction currently holds the *info* pointer. If another thread does hold the *info* pointer, the thread will help complete that transaction at line 5.9. Otherwise, the function returns a pointer to the node.

Algorithm 6. Insert key:edge at target vertex

```
1: function INSERTEDGE(int vertex, int edge, NodeDesc* nDesc, int opid)
2:     while true do
3:         Node  *currVertex ←
4:         FINDVERTEX(vertex, nDesc, opid))
5:         if currVertex == NULL then
6:             return false
7:         Node *pred ← NULL
8:         Node *currEdge ← currVertex.list.head
9:         while true do
10:            currVertex.list.LOCATEPRED(pred, currEdge)
11:            if IsNODEPRESENT(currEdge, edge) then
12:                return (UPDATEINFO(currEdge, nDesc, false) == success)
13:            else
14:                MDList::Node *n ← new MDList::Node
15:                n.info ← nDesc
16:                return currVertex.list.DO_INSERT(n)
```

Algorithm 7. Delete key:edge at target vertex

```
1: function DELETEEDGE(int vertex, int edge, NodeDesc* nDesc, int opid)
2:     while true do
3:         Node  *currVertex ←
4:         FINDVERTEX(vertex, nDesc, opid))
5:         if currVertex == NULL then
6:             return false
7:         Node *pred ← NULL
8:         Node *currEdge ← currVertex.list.head
9:         while true do
10:            currVertex.list.LOCATEPRED(pred, currEdge)
11:            if IsNODEPRESENT(currEdge, edge) then
12:                return (UPDATEINFO(currEdge, nDesc, true) == success)
13:            else
14:                return false
```

Algorithm 6 details the insertion of a node into an MDList in order to create an edge with a vertex. INSERTEDGE begins by calling FINDVERTEX to get the proper vertex node for insertion. If the node exists, then we traverse the MDList pointed to by the vertex to find the proper location to insert the new edge node. Once the traversal is complete, insertion is done the same way as in INSERTVERTEX.

Algorithm 7 details the deletion of a node in an MDList in order to remove an edge with a vertex. DELETEEDGE traverses to the target vertex using the same logic as INSERTEDGE. Once it has acquired a valid vertex, it traverses the MDList looking for the target edge node to delete. If the target node is found in the MDList, deletion is done by updating the $info$ pointer of the target node.

4   Correctness

The lock-free transactional adjacency list is designed for the correctness property strict serializability. According to conclusion by Herlihy et al. [9], a committed transaction is strictly serializable given that a data structure contains linearizable operations and obeys commutativity isolation.

4.1   Definitions

According to Herlihy et al. [9], a *history* is a sequence of instantaneous events. Events occur during the transition of a transactions status between pending, committed, and aborted.

Definition 3. *A history h is strictly serializable if the committed series of transactions is equivalent to a legal history in which all transactions executed sequentially in the order they commit.*

Definition 4. *Two method calls I,R and I',R' commute if: for all histories h, if $h \cdot I \cdot R$ and $h \cdot I' \cdot R'$ are both legal, then $h \cdot I \cdot R \cdot I' \cdot R'$ and $h \cdot I' \cdot R' \cdot I \cdot R$ are both legal and define the same abstract state.*

Operations are said to commute if executing them in any order yields the same abstract state. The commutativity of adjacency list operations are as follows, assuming vertexes x,y and nodes i,j:

INSERTVERTEX(x) $\leftrightarrow$ INSERTVERTEX(y), x ≠ y

DELETEVERTEX(x) $\leftrightarrow$ DELETEVERTEX(y), x ≠ y

INSERTVERTEX(x) $\leftrightarrow$ DELETEVERTEX(y), x ≠ y

INSERTEDGE(x, i) $\leftrightarrow$ INSERTEDGE(x, j), i ≠ j

INSERTEDGE(x, i) $\leftrightarrow$ INSERTEDGE(y, i), x ≠ y

DELETEEDGE(x, i) $\leftrightarrow$ DELETEEDGE(x, j), i ≠ j

DELETEEDGE(x, i) $\leftrightarrow$ DELETEEDGE(y, i), x ≠ y

INSERTEDGE(x, i) $\leftrightarrow$ DELETEEDGE(x, j), i ≠ j

INSERTEDGE(x, i) $\leftrightarrow$ DELETEEDGE(y, i), x ≠ y

FINDVERTEX(x) $\leftrightarrow$ INSERTVERTEX(x)/*false* $\leftrightarrow$ DELETEVERTEX(x)/*false*

FINDEDGE(x, i) $\leftrightarrow$ INSERTEDGE(x, i)/*false* $\leftrightarrow$ DELETEEDGE(x, i)/*false*

Rule 1. *Linearizability: For any history h, two concurrent invocations I and I' must be equivalent to either the history $h \cdot I \cdot R \cdot I' \cdot R'$ or the history $h \cdot I' \cdot R' \cdot I \cdot R$*

Rule 2. *Commutativity Isolation: For any non-commutative method calls* $I_{1,1} \in T_1$ *and* $I_2, R_2 \in T_2$, *either* T_1 *commits or aborts before any additional method calls in* T_2 *are invoked, or vice-versa.*

To meet the specifications of the correctness condition linearizability, we identify an operation's linearization points. Furthermore, we will identify an operation's decision points and state-read points. The decision point of an operation occurs the moment the outcome of the operation is decided atomically. A state-read point occurs when the deciding state of the data structure is read.

Lemma 1. *The adjacency list operations* INSERTVERTEX, DELETEVERTEX, INSERTEDGE, DELETEEDGE, *and* FIND *are linearizable.*

Proof. In the DELETEVERTEX operation, execution can branch at multiple points. Beginning at 3.6, if the vertex to be deleted is not found, the operation returns a *fail* status. The state-read point of this execution occurs during traversal, when the thread reads *pred.next* and does not find a node with the desired key. If the vertex is successfully found, but the operation returns *fail* at line 2.15 or 2.17, then the state-read point occurs when *oldinfo.desc.status* and *info.desc.status* are read, respectively. Following a successful logical status update, the decision point is when the CAS operation at line 2.18 succeeds.

The code path for FINISHDELETE, in which all nodes in the vertex's sublist are acquired by the transaction, is identical to the code path followed by DELETEVERTEX because of the call to UPDATEINFO at line 4.3. Thus, the state-read and decision points for FINISHDELETE are the same as the respective cases in DELETEVERTEX. The code path for the physical deletion of the vertex is linearizable because DO_DELETE, which is provided by the base data structure, is linearizable.

The same reasoning applies to the INSERTVERTEX, INSERTEDGE, DELETEEDGE and FIND operations because they share the same UPDATEINFO procedure for updating the logical status of a node.

Lemma 2. *The adjacency list operations* INSERTVERTEX, DELETEVERTEX, INSERTEDGE, DELETEEDGE, *and* FIND *satisfy the commutativity isolation rule.*

Proof. As previously shown, commuting operations are those that access different vertexes, or those that access different nodes within the same vertex so long as no operation is operating on that vertex. This means that commuting operations must either operate on different vertexes or operate on different nodes rooted at the same vertex without operating on the vertex itself. Let T_1 denote a transaction that currently accesses vertex *n1*. If another transaction T_2 were to access *n1*, it must first perform EXECUTEOPS for T_1 which will either commit or abort T_1 before it is finished executing. Alternatively, let T_1 denote a transaction that currently accesses node *m1* stored in the sublist of vertex *n1*. If a transaction T_2 were to try to access vertex *n1* it would first perform EXECUTEOPS for T_1 when it traverses to node *m1* during the call to FINISHDELETE at 2.10, which will either commit or abort T_1.

Theorem 1. *The transformed lock-free adjacency list is strictly serializable*

Proof. Following Lemmas 1 and 2, we can claim that the lock-free adjacency list is strictly serializable due to the conclusions by Herlihy and Koskinen [9].

5   Experimental Evaluation

We compare the scalability and performance of our lock-free transactional adjacency list to related approaches based on transactional boosting [9] and NOrec Rochester Software Transactional Memory [13]. We create a related approach using transactional boosting by converting the lock-free transactional adjacency list's base data structure operations transaction boosting methodology. Additionally, an undo log is maintained per-thread for rollbacks in the boosted implementation.

We evaluate the performance of these implementations using varying compositions of adjacency list operations. The compositions of operations are selected to highlight "vertex" operations and "edge" operations separately, as well as measuring the effects of non-commutative or expensive operations like DELETEVERTEX. Each test consists of a series of fixed-size transactions made up of INSERTVERTEX, DELETEVERTEX, INSERTEDGE, DELETEEDGE and FIND operations on random keys. The tests are performed on two systems; a 64-core NUMA system containing 4 AMD opteron 6272 16 core CPUs @2.1 GHz, and a 12-core system containing an Intel(R) Xeon(R) CPU E5-2697 v2 @ 2.7 ghz.

Figure 2 shows the performance results of the 64-core NUMA system. Figure 3 shows the results for the 12-core system. Throughput is measured in terms of operations per second. Only operations that are part of a committed transactions are counting in the calculation of throughput in order to measure the performance impact of various conflict detection and rollback schemes. The x-axis represents the number of threads running the test. In each figure, graph (a) shows a work-load dominated by operations occurring at vertexes, whereas graph (b) represents a work-load made up of relatively more operations occurring at edges. This test measures the performance impact of non-commutative operations such as DELETEVERTEX and INSERTEDGE as well as the performance impact of rollbacks on lengthy operations such as DELETEVERTEX. Each thread executed 20,000 transactions with a key range of 500.

In Fig. 2, the difference between the lock-free transactional adjacency list, denoted 'LFTT,' the transactional boosting implementation, denoted 'Boost,' and the Software Transactional Memory implementation, denoted 'STM' is shown. In the boosting implementation, threads must acquire locks on nodes for each operation. In the case of DELETEVERTEX, threads may need to acquire a number of locks equal to the size of the vertex's sublist. In this case, the lock-free algorithm has the advantage of only needing to allocate a single descriptor object for the entire transaction. Additionally with regards to Boost, the cost of rolling back aborted operations is very high in operations like DELETEVERTEX. Not only must the vertex be restored after an aborted transaction, but all

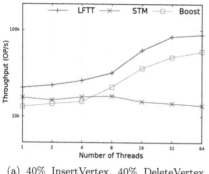 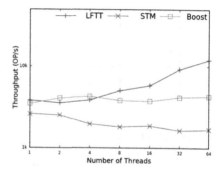

(a) 40% InsertVertex, 40% DeleteVertex, 10% InsertEdge, 10% DeleteEdge

(b) 20% InsertVertex, 20% DeleteVertex, 25% InsertEdge, 25% DeleteEdge, 10% Find

Fig. 2. Performance Results

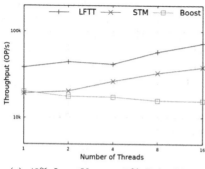 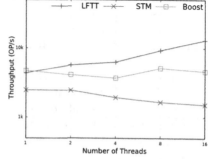

(a) 40% InsertVertex, 40% DeleteVertex, 10% InsertEdge, 10% DeleteEdge

(b) 20% InsertVertex, 20% DeleteVertex, 25% InsertEdge, 25% DeleteEdge, 10% Find

Fig. 3. Performance Results

nodes from the vertex's sublist must be re-added using INSERTEDGE. This creates a very low performance for aborted transactions in transactional boosting. Because of LFTT's logical status update, the lock-free transactional adjacency list is able to rollback these operations in a single atomic step. Similarly, STM experiences a heavy performance loss due to its high number of spurious aborts. STM is very likely to detect a conflict between operations like DELETEVERTEX, which modify a great number of nodes, despite there being no semantic conflict between transactions. These results are highly similar to the ones gathered from the 12-core system displayed in Fig. 3.

In general, the lock-free transactional adjacency list outperforms transactional boosting implementation by an average of 50%, and frequently outperforms RSTM by as much as 150%.

6   Related Work

Transactions can be enabled in similar data structures using related approaches such as STM or Transactional Boosting. We focus our discussion on transactional Lists and Skiplists, which provide similar node-based store and search time complexities.

6.1   Transactional Memory

Transactional memory is a programming paradigm initially proposed by Herlihy et al. [11] intended to simplify concurrent programming by allowing user-specified blocks of code to be executed in hardware, exhibiting both atomicity and isolation. Software transactional memory, proposed by Shavit et al. [18], was developed to facilitate transactional programming without hardware transactional memory support. Herlihy et al. [10] present DSTM, an application programming interface for obstruction-free STM designed to support dynamic-sized data structures. Dalessandro et al. [2] present NOrec, a low-overhead STM that utilizes a single global sequence lock shared with the transactional mutex lock system, an indexed write set, and value-based conflict detection to provide features such as livelock freedom, full compatibility with existing data structure layouts, and starvation avoidance mechanisms. Dice et al. [4] present Transactional Locking II (TL2), an STM algorithm that uses a novel version-clock validation to guarantee that user code operates only on consistent memory states. Other STM designs include [6,13,16]. STM implementations rely on low-level conflict detection to enable transactions. These implementations generally suffer from high spurious abort counts, making them less desirable for concurrent data structures.

Initial performance experiments were performed with Hardware Transactional Memory (HTM) by Dice et al. [3]. Intel introduced Transactional Synchronization Extensions (TSX) to the x86 instruction set architecture of the Intel 4th Generation Core^{TM}Processors [23]. IBM introduced HTM in the Power ISA [1]. Both implementations offer a best-effort HTM, which means that there is no guarantee provided that a hardware transaction will commit to memory. The disadvantage of a best-effort strategy is that HTM may experience frequent aborts due to data access conflicts, hardware interrupts, limited transactional resources, or false sharing due to unrelated variables mapping to the same cache line [12].

Herlihy et al. [9] present transactional boosting, a methodology for transforming highly-concurrent linearizable objects into highly-concurrent transactional objects. Transactional boosting uses a high-level semantic conflict detection to allow commutative operations in separate transactions to proceed concurrently using the thread-level synchronization of the base linearizable data structure; non-commutative operations require transaction-level synchronization through the acquisition of an abstract lock. If a transaction aborts, it recovers the correct abstract state by invoking the inverse operations recorded in the undo log.

6.2   Linked Lists

Valois [22], Harris [7], Michael [14], and Fomitchev et al. [5] present individual algorithms for a lock-free linearizable linked list based on the Compare-And-Swap operation. Valois' algorithm addresses the problem of (1) a concurrent deletion and insertion on an adjacent cell, and (2) a concurrent deletion and deletion on an adjacent cell, by requiring that every normal node in the list have an auxiliary node with only a next field as both its predecessor and successor. The auxiliary nodes prevent the undesirable circumstance of performing an insertion or deletion on a node adjacent to a node to be deleted. Harris' algorithm uses the bit-stealing technique to logically mark a node for deletion. A lazy approach is taken for the physical deletion in which a delete operation attempts to physically delete a node once using Compare-And-Swap. If Compare-And-Swap fails, then the physical deletion is left for other threads to perform if they traverse the logically deleted node. Michael's algorithm is compatible with efficient lock-free memory management methods, including IBM freelists [21] and the safe memory reclamation method [15]. Fomitchev et al.'s algorithm uses backlinks that are set when a node is deleted to allow a node to backtrack to a predecessor that is not undergoing a deletion. An MDList provides a worst-case search time complexity of $O(\log N)$ an improvement over the $O(N)$ worst-cast search time complexity provided by a linked list.

Transactional linked list implementations based on transactional boosting use coarse-grained locking to ensure that non-commutative method calls are never allowed to execute simultaneously. The underlying linked list algorithm's linearizability is preserved during this process to handle thread level synchronization. Rollbacks are performed by calling a method's inverse operation, which causes a performance loss for aborted transactions. Zhang and Dechev [24] present a lock-free transactional linked list alongside LFTT which takes advantage of a node based conflict detection scheme to preserve the underlying algorithm's lock-freedom. This approach additionally reduces the performance hit of rollbacks by introducing a logical status update scheme capable of aborting a transaction in a single atomic step. LFTT provides transformation templates for the set abstract data type, which does not account for operations in which elements are related to each other.

6.3   Skiplists and Queues

Sundell et al. [20] present a lock-free priority queue based on a lock-free skiplist adapted from Lotan et al. [17]. Fomitchev et al. [5] use their lock-free linked list design [5] to implement a lock-free skiplist. Each node is augmented with a pointer to the next lower level and a pointer to the base level. Herlihy et al. [8] present a lock-free skiplist based on an algorithm developed by Faser [6]. Skiplists eliminate global rebalancing and provide a logarithmic sequential search time on average, but the worst-case search time is linear with respect to the input size. An MDList improves upon the skiplist by providing a worst-case logarithmic sequential search time.

Spiegelman et al. [19] presented a transactional skiplist that uses STM-like techniques combined with node locking in an attempt to reduce overhead and false aborts. Spiegelman et al. additionally present a transactional queue using a pessimistic lock-based approach. In this queue, the execution of ENQUEUE operations are deferred to the final phase of the transaction, the commit phase, in order to avoid keeping track of the current head of the queue. Meanwhile, DEQUEUE operations acquire a lock on the queue until their transaction is complete. Zhang and Dechev [24] preserved lock-freedom in their algorithm by transforming a skiplist using LFTT which, again, offers a performance improvement on transaction rollbacks.

7 Conclusion

In this paper we introduced an efficient lock-free adjacency list algorithm based on MDList, then enabled transactions using the LFTT methodology. We allowed for multiple threads to concurrently modify nodes rooted at the same vertex thus increasing the amount of operations that commute. When compared to similar implementations based on related approaches, our algorithm experiences performance gains across several compositions of methods.

References

1. Cain, H.W., Michael, M.M., Frey, B., May, C., Williams, D., Le, H.: Robust architectural support for transactional memory in the power architecture. In: ACM SIGARCH Computer Architecture News, vol. 41, pp. 225–236. ACM (2013)
2. Dalessandro, L., Spear, M.F., Scott, M.L.: NOrec: streamlining STM by abolishing ownership records. In: ACM Sigplan Notices, vol. 45, pp. 67–78. ACM (2010)
3. Dice, D., Lev, Y., Moir, M., Nussbaum, D., Olszewski, M.: Early experience with a commercial hardware transactional memory implementation. Sun Microsystems Technical report (2009)
4. Dice, D., Shalev, O., Shavit, N.: Transactional locking II. In: Dolev, S. (ed.) DISC 2006. LNCS, vol. 4167, pp. 194–208. Springer, Heidelberg (2006). https://doi.org/10.1007/11864219_14
5. Fomitchev, M., Ruppert, E.: Lock-free linked lists and skip lists. In: Proceedings of the Twenty-Third Annual ACM Symposium on Principles of Distributed Computing, pp. 50–59. ACM (2004)
6. Fraser, K.: Practical lock-freedom. Technical report, University of Cambridge, Computer Laboratory (2004)
7. Harris, T.L.: A pragmatic implementation of non-blocking linked-lists. In: Welch, J. (ed.) DISC 2001. LNCS, vol. 2180, pp. 300–314. Springer, Heidelberg (2001). https://doi.org/10.1007/3-540-45414-4_21
8. Herlihy, M., Lev, Y., Shavit, N.: A lock-free concurrent skiplist with wait-free search. Unpublished Manuscript, Sun Microsystems Laboratories, Burlington, Massachusetts (2007)
9. Herlihy, M., Koskinen, E.: Transactional boosting: a methodology for highly-concurrent transactional objects. In: Proceedings of the 13th ACM SIGPLAN Symposium on Principles and Practice of Parallel Programming, pp. 207–216. ACM (2008)

10. Herlihy, M., Luchangco, V., Moir, M., Scherer III, W.N.: Software transactional memory for dynamic-sized data structures. In: Proceedings of the Twenty-Second Annual Symposium on Principles of Distributed Computing, pp. 92–101. ACM (2003)
11. Herlihy, M., Moss, J.E.B.: Transactional memory: architectural support for lock-free data structures, vol. 21. ACM (1993)
12. Intel. Intel 64 and IA-32 architectures optimization reference manual (2016)
13. Marathe, V.J., et al.: Lowering the overhead of nonblocking software transactional memory. In: Workshop on Languages, Compilers, and Hardware Support for Transactional Computing (TRANSACT) (2006)
14. Michael, M.M.: High performance dynamic lock-free hash tables and list-based sets. In: Proceedings of the Fourteenth Annual ACM Symposium on Parallel Algorithms and Architectures, pp. 73–82. ACM (2002)
15. Michael, M.M.: Safe memory reclamation for dynamic lock-free objects using atomic reads and writes. In: Proceedings of the Twenty-First Annual Symposium on Principles of Distributed Computing, pp. 21–30. ACM (2002)
16. Saha, B., Adl-Tabatabai, A.-R., Hudson, R.L., Minh, C.C., Hertzberg, B.: McRT-STM: a high performance software transactional memory system for a multi-core runtime. In: Proceedings of the Eleventh ACM SIGPLAN Symposium on Principles and Practice of Parallel Programming, pp. 187–197. ACM (2006)
17. Shavit, N., Lotan, I.: Skiplist-based concurrent priority queues. In: 2000 Proceedings of the 14th International Parallel and Distributed Processing Symposium, IPDPS 2000, pp. 263–268. IEEE (2000)
18. Shavit, N., Touitou, D.: Software transactional memory. Distrib. Comput. **10**(2), 99–116 (1997)
19. Spiegelman, A., Golan-Gueta, G., Keidar, I.: Transactional data structure libraries. In: Proceedings of the 37th ACM SIGPLAN Conference on Programming Language Design and Implementation (PLDI 2016), vol. 51, pp. 682–696. ACM (2016)
20. Sundell, H., Tsigas, P.: Fast and lock-free concurrent priority queues for multi-thread systems. In: 2003 Proceedings of the International Parallel and Distributed Processing Symposium, pp. 11–pp. IEEE (2003)
21. Treiber, R.K.: Systems programming: coping with parallelism. International Business Machines Incorporated, Thomas J. Watson Research Center (1986)
22. Valois, J.D.: Lock-free linked lists using compare-and-swap. In: Proceedings of the Fourteenth Annual ACM Symposium on Principles of Distributed Computing, pp. 214–222. ACM (1995)
23. Yoo, R.M., Hughes, C.J., Lai, K., Rajwar, R.: Performance evaluation of intel® transactional synchronization extensions for high-performance computing. In: 2013 International Conference for High Performance Computing, Networking, Storage and Analysis (SC), pp. 1–11. IEEE (2013)
24. Zhang, D., Dechev, D.: An efficient lock-free logarithmic search data structure based on multi-dimensional list. In: 2016 IEEE 36th International Conference on Distributed Computing Systems (ICDCS), pp. 281–292. IEEE (2016)
25. Zhang D., Dechev, D.: Lock-free transactions without rollbacks for linked data structures. In: Proceedings of the 28th ACM Symposium on Parallelism in Algorithms and Architectures, pp. 325–336. ACM (2016)

GPU Applications

Efficient Inspected Critical Sections in Data-Parallel GPU Codes

Thorsten Blaß$^{(\boxtimes)}$, Michael Philippsen, and Ronald Veldema

Programming Systems Group, Friedrich-Alexander University, Erlangen, Germany
{Thorsten.Blass,Michael.Philippsen,Ronald.Veldema}@fau.de

Abstract. Optimistic concurrency control and STMs rely on the assumption of sparse conflicts. For data-parallel GPU codes with many or with dynamic data dependences, a pessimistic and lock-based approach may be faster, if only GPUs would offer hardware support for GPU-wide fine-grained synchronization. Instead, current GPUs inflict dead- and livelocks on attempts to implement such synchronization in software.

The paper demonstrates how to build GPU-wide non-hanging critical sections that are as easy to use as STMs but also get close to the performance of traditional fine-grained locks. Instead of sequentializing all threads that enter a critical section, the novel programmer-guided Inspected Critical Sections (ICS) keep the degree of parallelism up. As in optimistic approaches threads that are known not to interfere, may execute the body of the inspected critical section concurrently.

Keywords: GPGPU · CUDA · SIMT · Critical section · Mutual exclusion

1 Introduction

Optimistic concurrency control – as it is implemented in Software Transactional Memory (STM) – comes with some overhead for logging and rollback [5]. This overhead grows with the number of threads that collide in their memory accesses. On asynchronous multicores often only a few of the running threads are in an atomic region at any time, whereas on a GPU with its data-parallel/lock-step execution model, all threads must enter this critical section at exactly the same time. Hence, optimistic approaches may cause significant overhead on GPUs.

Assume you want to study this hypothesis. You pick benchmarks from the GPU-STM community, you take (or re-implement) an STM prototype for GPUs [6, 12,16,20], and to gauge the overhead, you re-work the atomic regions of the benchmark codes into pessimistic concurrency control,

```
1  while(atomicCAS(&lock, −1, TID) != −1); //spin
2  // critical section code here
3  atomicExch(lock, −1);
```

```
1  bool leaveLoop = false; //thread local
2  while(!leaveLoop){
3    if(atomicCAS(&lock, −1, TID) == TID){
4      // critical section code here
5      leaveLoop = true;
6      atomicExch(lock, −1);
7    }
8    // point of convergence
9  }
```

Fig. 1. Spin lock implementations, with and w/o a SIMT-deadlock. TID is the global thread Id.

© Springer Nature Switzerland AG 2019
L. Rauchwerger (Ed.): LCPC 2017, LNCS 11403, pp. 223–239, 2019.
https://doi.org/10.1007/978-3-030-35225-7_15

Table 1. Fraction of the runs affected by dead- or livelocks; see Appendix.

	Hash table		Bank	Graph		Labyrinth	Genome	Kmeans	Vacation
Problem size	1,572,864	786,432	25,165,824	25%	75%	(512,512,7)	Configuration see Appendix		
# threads	1,572,864		25,165,824	10,280		512	811,008	3,014,656	4,194,304
FGL	43%	42%	45%	29%	42%	33%	49%	37%	53%
STM	39%	45%	49%	35%	43%	37%	50%	41%	55%

i.e., your threads simply acquire a fine-grained lock for each of the data items that they may access concurrently at runtime. If threads need to acquire multiple locks, you use a global order to avoid deadlocks. Since you know that the Single Instruction Multiple Thread (SIMT) execution model is prone to deadlocks[1] [9,11] you re-work your code as shown in Fig. 1, i.e., you pull the loop out of the if-statement that holds the CAS. With the resulting convergence point after the if-statement, regardless of the SIMT-scheduling, both sets of threads make progress; the lock is eventually released.

At this point you will understand the first motivation of our work. In our experiments and with a particular STM framework [20], our otherwise correct benchmark code (see Appendix) often hangs in dead- or livelocks that are beyond our control, see Table 1. Your mileage will vary. It depends on the size, configuration, version and vendor of your GPU, the number of threads that your code spawns, the unknown scheduling strategies that run on your GPU, ..., and the compiler version that you are using.[2] Hence, either it works by coincidence or you need to carefully fine-tune your setup to avoid similar dead- or livelocks – both for the STM codes and for the codes with the fine-grained locks (FGL). While the FGL-codes are straightforward to construct, unfortunately in general they are incorrect. The STM codes hang on the GPU because the STM framework internally uses such error prone synchronization.

In Sect. 2 we discuss that there are fundamental architectural reasons for those dead- and livelocks on current GPUs. We also show how to construct a non-hanging GPU-wide critical section.

This brings us to our second motivation: In all the successful, non-hanging runs (and only those), the FGL-code has less overhead and clearly outperforms

---

[1] Recall that the upper code in Fig. 1 can deadlock on a GPU. Generally speaking, the while-condition splits the threads (of a warp/wavefront) into two sets. One set has the thread that has acquired the lock, the other set holds all the other threads. The SIMT instruction scheduler then runs the sets in turn, one after the other, and up to a convergence point where the sets are combined again. The problem is that there is no yield and that the instruction scheduler does not switch between sets. If the scheduler chooses to issue instructions to the set of the spinning threads first, the set with the winning thread never receives a single instruction, it does not make any progress, and thus it never releases the lock.

[2] For Table 1 we compiled with -O0. If we use -O3 all the runs hang. In our benchmark environment the compiler seems to undo the manual anti-SIMT-deadlock transformation shown in Fig. 1.

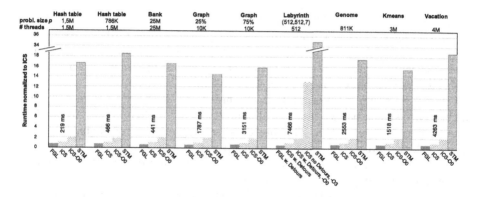

Fig. 2. Runtimes, normalized to ICS codes (-03).

the optimistic concurrency control on the GPU, see the first and last bar of each bundle in Fig. 2. With more collisions (smaller hash table and $p = 75\%$ for the Graph benchmark) the STM versions get even slower.

Sections 3 and 4 then extend our GPU-wide critical section to so-called Inspected Critical Sections (ICS) that get close to the FGL-performance (without the hanging) and that also make the reasoning for the programmer as straightforward as for the FGL-codes. See the ICS-columns in Fig. 2 that we have used to normalize the other runtimes.[3]

2   Non-hanging GPU-wide Critical Sections

To explain where the dead- and livelocks come from, we sketch a GPU's execution model and its vendor-provided schedulers. When a GPU programmer creates a grid of threads s/he also organizes them into b **groups** of t threads each (NVIDIA: block, AMD: workgroup). We call t the **group-size**. The GPU breaks up a group into **warps** of typically 32 threads (AMD: wavefront). To keep the discussion simple, assume that the grid size is exactly $b \cdot t$ and that

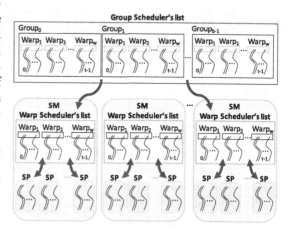

Fig. 3. GPU architecture and schedulers.

---

[3] Since we can only show -00 numbers for STM and FGL due to the compiler issue, we show those numbers for ICS as well, even though the compiler issue did not prevent -03 for our approach.

t is a multiple of 32. Figure 3 shows a grid of threads in the work list of the GPU's *group scheduler*. It picks a group and assigns it to one of the GPU's Streaming Multiprocessors (SM). Groups are never preempted before they have completed execution. Since in general, there are unassigned groups (even if some SMs can process more than a group), there cannot be a GPU-wide barrier for all threads of the grid. Assume that all threads of all the SM-assigned groups had reached such a barrier. As they all still have work to do beyond that barrier, these groups are unfinished. This prevents pending groups from being assigned to an SM; the SM-assigned threads wait forever.

When a group is assigned to an SM, its *warp scheduler* dispatches the threads of the group's warps to the SM's many Stream Processors (SP). Multiple SPs then execute all the threads of the warp in SIMT-mode. To achieve this, the *instruction scheduler* spawns the same instruction to all threads at the same time in a lock-step fashion.

GPU vendors do not disclose the strategies that their schedulers use and could change them at will between hardware releases and compiler versions. As it is unspecified for which of the branches of a condition the instruction dispatcher spawns the instructions first, the upper spin lock of Fig. 1 was incorrect and prone to SIMT-deadlocks. As there are no fairness guarantees for the warp scheduler on when to replace unfinished warps with pending ones, the code in the lower part of Fig. 1 is also incorrect. It can cause a livelock because in contrast to the group scheduler, the warp scheduler *can* take back unfinished warps from the SPs at any time. Assume that more warps are dispatched to an SM than it has SPs. Some of these warps can be part of the same group, or they can belong to other groups assigned to the same SM. Immediately after a winning thread has entered the critical section (line 4), the warp scheduler can choose to replace the winner's warp by another warp. Afterwards all the SPs run warps whose threads all wait for the critical section to become available again. From the viewpoint of the warp scheduler all the scheduled warps perform useful work because they all process the `while` loop. So there is no need to (ever) schedule back in the winner; the other warps may hence spin forever. The code hangs in a livelock.[4]

Figure 4 shows our new non-hanging GPU-wide critical section. It hoists the lock-acquisition and the lock-release out of the individual threads of a group. Instead of having *each* of the t threads of a group compete for the global lock, the lock is acquired only once per group.

```
1   if (GID == 0) // 1 thread has Group-level ID 0
2       global.lock();  // exclude other groups
3   <thread-group-barrier> //CUDA: __syncthreads()

4   // Run threads in the group one after the other
5   for (i=0 .. GROUP_SIZE-1) {
6       if (i == GID)
7           // critical section code here
8       <thread-group-barrier>
9   }

10  if (GID == 0) // 1 thread of the set (= group)
11      global.unlock(); // allow other groups
```

Fig. 4. Non-hanging GPU-wide critical section.

---

[4] To circumvent this problem, many codes use the incorrect spin lock with a grid size that stays below (warp size · # of SPs). With such an underutilization of the GPU the warp scheduler does not have to re-schedule because there is no more than one warp per SP.

All the threads of an SP-assigned warp execute the code in Fig. 4 concurrently in a lock-step fashion. In each of the SM-assigned groups the one thread with the group-level ID 0 within that group acquires the GPU-wide lock `global` (of the critical section) in line 2. (Release is in line 11.)

In Fig. 5 time flows from top to bottom. The thread with GID = 0 (red) of a group acquires and releases the lock. Let us ignore the global locking (and unlocking) for now – it only matters that the locking is followed by a `<thread-group -barrier>` in line 3 of the code (or the dotted line in Fig. 5, resp.). This is the SM-wide barrier that interacts with the warp scheduler. The GID-condition in line 1 splits a warp into two sets. The set with the single thread acquires the lock and runs into the barrier. The threads in the other

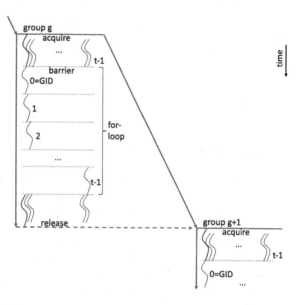

Fig. 5. Schematic execution of Fig. 4. (Color figure online)

set also run into the barrier. Which set of threads receive their SIMT-instructions first is irrelevant as the convergence point for all threads is before the barrier. Note that the warp scheduler replaces such warps (whose threads all are inactive) with other (pending) warps that still have active threads. As more and more warps find all their threads inactive in the barrier, eventually all warps of a group will be assigned to SPs and will reach the barrier. Thus, regardless of the scheduler's internal strategy, the hanging-problem is gone.

Note that it is irrelevant whether and when other groups that are scheduled to other SMs reach their barriers. It only matters that all the threads of the warp with the winning thread eventually finish their work. Then other warps finish because of the same reasoning. Then eventually an SM finishes and another (pending) group can be assigned to this SM.

There are two issues left to explain. First, the global lock (lines 2 and 11) can be implemented with any CPU-style lock, e.g., with the upper spin lock from Fig. 1. As the group scheduler never takes back the group that acquired the lock before completion, this group is still active when it eventually releases the lock.

The second question is, how the group's threads actually perform the body of the critical section sequentially. In line 3 there is an SM-wide barrier. After that barrier *all* threads of the group are active again (not just the thread that acquired the lock). However, the critical work needs to be performed sequentially by one thread at a time. This is what the code in lines 4–9 achieves. In SIMT-mode *all* threads execute the for loop. But in each iteration only one of them finds the loop counter to be equal to its own GID. This thread executes the body of the critical section, the others pause, before all threads meet again in the SM-wide barrier in line 8 which is the point of convergence for all threads. This barrier is needed to prevent other threads from prematurely starting with their critical section work. After the barrier the next thread executes the body of the critical section, as shown in the for-loop area of Fig. 5. When all threads are done, the thread with GID = 0 releases the lock to let the next group proceed.

We will later reuse this idea for each of the architectural levels of a GPU (and for more levels) to efficiently implement inspected critical sections.

3   Inspected Critical Sections

Now that we have non-hanging GPU-wide critical sections we can let the threads execute the code sequentially. However, this is obviously overly restrictive as threads that work on disjoint data should be able to do their work in parallel.

Thus, we introduce ics(list of items) { block }, an **I**nspected **C**ritical **S**ection wherein the programmer declares all the items (data elements, memory addresses, fields, . . .) up front that each of the data-parallel threads needs isolated access to (in the block). As for the FGL-codes, the programmer must know what is thread-local data and what is shared between threads and thus needs to be mentioned in the list of items. For the hash table with chaining, the list holds the number of the bucket that a put uses. This number represents the shared data that potentially causes a conflicting access. It is more straightforward than the memory address of the bucket.

The semantics of the inspected critical sections is inspired by the classic inspector-executor paradigm [3]. Upon entry to the critical section, it is checked whether the lists of items intersect between threads. If so, the code will run sequentially, otherwise the threads run the body in parallel, as they would do for an atomic region. For the inspection, the threads atomically register their items in a bitmap. If a bit is already set when they try to set it, a conflict is detected.

There are three differences to the traditional inspector-executor. First, we start from parallel code and the inspector downgrades to a sequential execution, whereas originally the inspector is used to parallelize a loop if possible. Second, we rely on the programmer to identify where conflicts may be. As there is no automatic detection of all the accessed memory addresses, the programmer can leave out irrelevant addresses. There is also no longer the problem that computed memory addresses may fool the automatic detection (think of a[foo()] where foo is impure). In general, there is not even the need to consider all memory addresses. Instead, smaller data structures suffice. For the hash table a bitmap with one bit per bucket is large enough. A traditional inspector works with the full memory addresses of the buckets.

Therefore, in addition to the ics-statement, the developer *has to* specify an __upperBound() of the size of the shared data structure and hence the size of the bitmap. The developer *can* also overwrite the mapping function __idx() with an application-specific one that maps a potentially conflicting item (data element, memorylocation, ...) to an index of the bitmap.[5] For the hash table, the number of available buckets is the upper bound; as the bucket number used by the put is a good index, there is no need to use the memory address.

The third difference to the traditional inspector-executor is that we do better than all-or-nothing. Instead of sequentializing as soon as there is a conflict, Sect. 4 introduces a gradual retrenchment of parallelism that keeps up the degree of parallelism for those threads that do not interfere.

Some algorithms (like the Labyrinth benchmark) can find a detour if an initially available resource can no longer be used because another thread has taken it. Instead of sequentializing to deal with this conflict, there may be an application-specific way around. For such situations the developer *can* provide a method __alternative(item) that exploits knowledge about which item causes the conflict, finds a detour, and retries the conflict check with a new list of items.

The pseudo code in Fig. 6 shows how the initial inspection checks whether there are conflicts between the concurrent threads. (For a better understanding, ignore the level-indices for now and assume single values instead – Sect. 4 will fill in the details.) All threads run the code in parallel. For each potentially critical item the threads use a CAS operation to set the

```
1   void check4confl(level, items[]) {
2       // precondition: hasConflict = false;
3       resetBits(bitmap);
4       barrier[level]();
5       iter = 0;
6       retries = 0;
7       do {
8           item = items[iter];
9           if (atomicCAS(&bitmap[__idx(item)],
10                  0, 1) == 1) {
11              if(__alternative != NULL) {  // Detour?
12                  resetMyBits(bitmap, items);
13                  items = __alternative(item);
14                  iter = 0;
15                  retries++;
16                  continue;
17              }
18              hasConflict = true;
19          }
20          iter++;
21      } while (items.size()>iter && retries!=3);
22  }
```

Fig. 6. Check for conflicts, with "Detour" option.

corresponding bit (line 9) in the bitmap. The index of the bit is determined by means of __idx(). If there is a conflict and if there is a valid function pointer to an application-specific __alternative() callback function in line 11, then the application gets the chance to modify the local results and to retry with a different set of potentially conflicting items (lines 11–17). There is an upper bound on the number of retries. If the application cannot find a patch/an alternative that avoids the conflicting item, the global conflict flag is set. We optimize this if there is only a single item to inspect.

---

[5] Note that if needed, the developer can trade time for space: Ideally __idx() is an injective projection of an item to [0...__upperBound()-1]. With a smaller co-domain of __idx(), the bitmap can be smaller, but the conflict detection may announce false positives that then cause sequential execution and hence longer runtimes.

4   Gradual Retrenchment of Parallelism

Sequentializing all threads once a conflict is found is too slow to be practical. To make inspected critical sections efficient, we use a divide-and-conquer approach that instead of instantly switching to a fully sequential execution, splits the threads into smaller sets [7]. We process these sets in order, set after set. Within such a set, the threads *could* still modify the data without a conflict. Hence, before the threads of a set perform their work sequentially, they again check for conflicts, but this time only among themselves. If there is no conflict, this set of threads can run in parallel. Otherwise we apply this idea recursively. Since all the sets of the same level are always processed one after the other, the threads that caused the initial conflict can never run at the same time.

The GPU architecture from Fig. 3 guides the hierarchical splitting into sets of threads. If the conflict is on the first level of the recursion, between the threads that run on all the SMs, then we split them into their groups. The SMs those groups are assigned to process them sequentially. One level down it may be possible that all the threads in a group can run without a conflict.

If there is still a conflict among all the threads on that SM, then the SM needs to process its warps (i.e., the next level of sets) sequentially. One level down, potentially all the threads in a warp can run without a conflict.

The next level down are pairs of threads. To keep it simple, we have left this out in Fig. 4. Pairs are executed in order, but within a pair the two threads can run concurrently unless they interfere.

The base level is a full sequentialization of the threads as shown in the figure.

The recursive pseudo code is shown in Fig. 7. This code is a generalization of the code shown in Fig. 4. As discussed above, there cannot be GPU-wide barriers. Thus the recursion does not start from the full grid but from the SM level. To implement the user's ics-statement, all active threads execute **retrench** (which calls the **body** of the **ics**). As in Sect. 2 only one of them

```
1   static bool hasConflict;
2   void retrench(level, items[]) {
3       lock[level].acquire();//includes ?ID==0 test
4       hasConflict = false;
5       barrier[level]();
6       if (level < 4) {
7           check4confl(level, items[]);
8           barrier[level]();
9       }
10      if (!hasConflict) {
11          //critical section code here; body of ics
12      } else {
13          retrench(level+1, items[]);
14      }
15      barrier[level]();
16      lock[level].release(); //include ?ID==0 test
17  }
```

Fig. 7. Hierarchical retrenchment of parallelism.

acquires the lock of the current level (line 3). The **acquire** method comprises the ?ID==0 test known from before (? stands for the level, e.g., G for group level). The other sets of that hierarchy level wait; the lock acquisition serializes them. All threads of the winning set leave the barrier in line 5. There are different barrier implementations for each level: a (home-grown spin-based) barrier across the SMs, the hardware-supported SM-wide <thread-group-barrier>, a (home-grown) warp-wide barrier, and conceptually even a barrier for a pair of threads in a warp. The recursion **level** is used to pick the appropriate type of barrier. In line 7 all those threads inspect the items that they intend to work with for conflicts. If there is none, they can execute the critical section code concurrently (line 11). Otherwise, we recursively split the set of threads into smaller sets. Notice that on the lowest level 4, there is no checking for conflicts as there is only one active thread. Thus the recursion always ends in line 11 as soon as it reaches the level of a single thread. On the way out of the recursion, one thread releases the level's lock (line 16). This releases another set of threads that is waiting for the lock.

Figure 8 shows what happens at the group level. Initially the thread with GID = 0 (red, on the left) acquires the lock. Then all the group's threads check whether there are conflicts (c4c for check4confl). If there is none, the threads concurrently execute the critical section code (bottom left of the figure) and the thread with GID = 0 releases the lock so that another SM can proceed with its group (not shown). Otherwise the recursive invocation of retrench splits the t threads into warps. Each of the warps has a thread with WID = 0 that

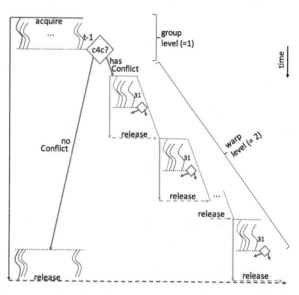

Fig. 8. From group to warp level. (Color figure online)

tries to acquire the (orange) lock (line 3 of the code; conflict side of Fig. 8). The warps are processed in sequence, one after the other. For each of the warps there is again the concurrent checking for conflicts. A warp can either run in parallel or – if there is a conflict among the warp's threads – the recursion proceeds to pair level. This decision can vary from warp to warp.

The above recursive pseudo code is simplified to get the idea across. The actual implementation not only unrolls the recursion, but it also cuts off the recursive descent as soon as it reaches warp level (=2). Here the for-loop known from the non-hanging GPU lock, see Fig. 4, suffices due to the SIMT-execution. Moreover, for pairs of threads that execute in a lock-step fashion anyway, check4confl can be optimized as no longer bitmaps with atomic operations are needed. Due to space restrictions, we cannot get into details, but eventually the lower two levels of the retrenchment are fused into a single efficient for-loop that also saves on the number of synchronization barriers.

5   Evaluation

Recall that the quantitative results are the motivation of this work, see Sect. 1: The STM versions (with mostly given atomic regions) and the FGL versions (written by us) of the benchmark codes (see Appendix) frequently hang in dead- or livelocks, see Table 1. The ICS versions never hang, they use straightforward __idx functions to indicate where the threads may be in conflict at runtime,[6] and they are much faster than the STM codes and often get close to the FGL-versions (provided the latter do not hang), see Fig. 2.

Table 2. Level on which ICS executes the critical code.

	Hash table		Bank	Graph		Labyrinth	Genome	Kmeans	Vacation
Problem size	1,572,864	786,432	25,165,824	25%	75%	(512,512,7)	Configuration see Appendix		
# threads	1,572,864		25,165,824	10,280		512	811,008	3,014,656	4,194,304
8-SM	215,040	23,040	5,360,640	0	0	0	122,880	872,448	906,240
group	1,282,560	416,128	11,438,336	3456	128	0	318,080	1,482,240	2,129,536
warp	72,608	799,648	8,233,856	6176	3392	160	351,904	639,936	1,085,856
pair	2642	333,980	132,844	648	6698	312	18,102	19,988	72,634
single	14	68	148	0	62	40	42	44	38

Let us now look into three more aspects of these general results. First, as the key idea of our approach is to retrench parallelism gradually so that threads that work on non-conflicting parts of the shared data can run concurrently instead of being sequentialized, Table 2 shows on which level of the retrenchment cascade the threads actually execute the critical code (average over 100 runs).

For the large hash table 215,040 (14%) of the threads execute the critical section code in parallel on the first level of the retrenchment cascade. Since the recursive decent stops on the first level only a few barriers cause overhead. The majority of the threads (82%) can retain group-level parallelism, where 128 threads run in parallel. Only 14 threads need to run in isolation. For the smaller hash table with more collisions the numbers shift towards the lower end of the scale; still retaining a high degree of parallelism. Bank is similar. The other four benchmarks have more collisions, but they also achieve a bell-shaped distribution of levels.[7]

---

[6] For Hash we use the number of the bucket, for Bank it is the account numbers. Labyrinth uses the coordinates of the points in the mesh as __idx. Genome uses a common subsequence (string) to identify a hash bucket that holds common DNA-segments. Kmeans uses the Id of a cluster. Vacation uses Ids of hotel rooms, flighs, and cars. We never use memory addresses as items.

[7] If we force ICS to always assume a conflict and to go down to the *single* thread level, runtimes are much slower than the STM version (Hash table: 14x and 11x, Bank: 13x, Graph: 6x and 2x, Labyrinth: 2x, Genome: 12x, Kmeans: 10x, Vacation: 15x).

Second, let us study the overhead. STM research separates the run-time spent in the atomic region from the

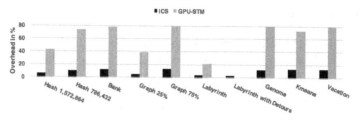

Fig. 9. Fraction of overhead of ICS and STM.

time spent for logging, commit processing, and rollback. We mimic this and also isolate the time spent in the retrenchment cascade and the barriers from the critical section bodies. Figure 9 shows that the GPU-STMs overhead is 24%–84% (similar results can be found in [20]), while the ICS codes only have an overhead of 2.7%–13%.

To understand where this small overhead comes from, Fig. 10 compares an ICS with both an empty `block` and with no items to check for conflicts, to the non-hanging GPU-wide critical section from Fig. 4 with its full sequentialization. The first bar of each group depicts this base line (total runtime of all threads; the overhead per thread is given in the table on the side of Fig. 10).[8]

The bars that follow show the runtimes of the recursive retrenchment cascade. For a certain retrenchment level (60 · $SM, group, \ldots, single$), we let `check4confl` on the surrounding levels (if any) always signal a conflict. On the measured level there is no conflict so that the parallel threads perform their (empty) critical section in parallel. Hence, on the 60 · SM level, on each of the 60 SMs of our GPU all the 128 threads of the assigned group run in parallel (i.e., there is a total number of 60 · 128 = 7,680 parallel

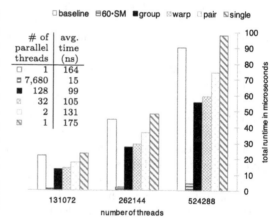

	# of parallel threads	avg. time (ns)
☐	1	164
☐	7,680	15
■	128	99
☒	32	105
☐	2	131
⊠	1	175

Fig. 10. Overhead of the `retrench` cascade.

threads). On the *group* level, the SMs process their assigned groups sequentially, while within a group all 128 threads run in parallel. The last bar shows that the worst case overhead of the level-wise retrenchment adds about 7% to the base line.

There are additional aspects to note. (a) The overhead per thread is better with fewer retrenchment, see side table, since higher levels have fewer barriers along the cascade. Hence, the fewer dynamic dependences an application has, the smaller is the runtime fee that it pays. (b) The warp-level optimizations and the pairing of threads pay off. (c) Doubling the number of threads approximately

---

[8] All measurements with -O3; the compiler did not remove the empty `block`.

doubles the total runtime and leaves the overhead per thread fixed. (d) If the body had not been empty, the inner four bars of each bundle would shrink in relation to the fully sequential execution of both the first and the last bar.

Third, if there is a conflict in the Labyrinth benchmark, the STM has to completely undo the transaction. The results in Fig. 2 show that due to the enhanced expressiveness, the FGL-code and the ICS-code with the optional __alternative() can do much better. It also lowers the overhead in Fig. 9.

6 Limits

Inspected critical sections trade STM-comfort for runtime performance. When using the inspected critical section, a programmer may miss items that can be in conflict between threads. Failure to declare such items is likely to cause races. Because of the lock-step execution it may be a bit easier to avoid such bugs than in general MIMD codes. For collision detection, ICS expects that all accessed memory addresses are known a-priori. If there are unforeseeable addresses, i.e., conflicting accesses to computed memory addresses it is much more difficult to keep the degree of parallelism up.

The programmer can trick the inspected critical sections into a buggy behavior with wrong auxiliary functions. Examples are a too narrow __upperBound() that does not match the co-domain of the mapping function __idx(), or an __idx() that is stateful and yields different answers when invoked for a single item (data element, memoryaddress, ...) twice and/or by different threads.

The pseudo code that this paper uses to explain how an inspected critical section is implemented, assumes that (like in all the benchmark codes) all data-parallel threads of the GPU kernel do enter the critical section, i.e., there cannot be a surrounding condition that lets some threads avoid the critical section. (The reasons are: (a) current GPUs require that *all* threads must reach a thread-group-barrier, and (b) for correctness our pseudo code requires that the thread with ?ID=0 has entered the critical section.) So far, we circumvent this problem by (manually) hoisting the critical section out of the condition. In general, there is a performance penalty for this as the critical sections get larger.

7 Related Work

Several authors study how to correctly and efficiently implement synchronization, locking, and barriers on the GPU and on its architectural levels. A general difference to our work is that most of the related work comes from MIMD-parallelism and deals with threads that perform individual tasks. Our base line is different because we assume that all threads follow the same instructions in data-parallel code, but there are some code fragments that need synchronization. So whenever a locking is needed, conceptually all threads are involved.

ElTantawy and Aamodt [9] work on the SIMT-induced deadlocks and build their solution into a compiler transformation. Another published workaround moves the convergence point to a statement that all threads can reach – no matter if they have the lock [15]. At the lowest level of our recursive approach, we use similar ideas, but we also guarantee progress.

Xiao et al. [17,18] also work on inter-group barriers for GPUs. Whereas our threads also proceed after the ICS in parallel, there is also the `block` of code that conceptually they execute in isolation – running in parallel if there are no data dependences. Another difference is that on every level, our recursive retrenchment of parallelism uses smaller barriers that wait for fewer threads. The fewer and the more local the threads are that wait in a barrier, the more efficient the barrier code gets. On some levels of the GPU architecture there is even hardware support for barriers. Their group-level locking cannot use a similar optimization. Xu et al. [19] build livelock-free lock stealing and lock virtualization for GPUs. Their techniques only work on warp level, whereas our mechanisms not only work across all levels of the GPU architecture, but we also present optimizations on sub-warp level, e.g., for pairs of threads. Another difference is that their lock stealing makes it necessary that the developer provides undo-methods that reinstate functional correctness in case of a stolen lock. We do not need to supply such code.

With respect to low-level locks and barriers there is orthogonal work that we may be able to incorporate and benefit from. Whenever our system-level implementation needed a barrier or lock, we used a basic CPU-style spin lock (except where discussed in detail in the paper). Operating systems research has targeted the efficiency of locking techniques. Some authors improve the time delay, the memory traffic, and storages costs compared to locks based on atomics [21]. Others optimize for situations in which many locks are acquired and released often [13]. SmartLocks [8] is a library for spin lock implementations. Its goal is that the scheduler always picks from the spinning threads the one that probably contributes most to a certain goal, e.g., the overall runtime, the energy consumption, etc. It is orthogonal research to port such ideas to the GPU and to use the best types in our system-level implementation, especially as some ideas require hardware support that is not (or not yet?) available on GPUs.

There are several Transactional Memory implementations in software (STM) for GPUs [6,12,16,20]. Their common principle is to log all read and write operations that happen in a critical section. Multiple threads execute the critical section concurrently. If they detect a conflicting access in the logs at commit time, then they undo the work. All of this causes storage costs and memory traffic. In our approach we also execute critical sections concurrently, but only if we can check beforehand that there will be no conflicts. We assume that the developer knows the application well enough to be able to indicate those data elements/memory locations that at runtime threads may access in a conflicting way. This is less costly because there is no need to rollback. Moreover, instead of logging all memory accesses, we use application-specific knowledge and only check those memory accesses that the developer knows to be potentially critical. This lowers the checking overhead even further. STMs are general-purpose. They hence need to be conservative and check and log every single memory access to achieve correctness.

Systems that rely on a static code analysis to find spots where concurrent threads can have conflicting access to data usually face a similar type of drawback. Due to their conservative approach, these systems, like race detection tools, in general produce many false positives. If these tools cannot prove the absence of a dependence, then they must assume that there is one. They do not benefit from application-specific knowledge. In contrast, we let the programmer specify the potentially critical data elements – and in a converse reasoning – it is known that other data does not cause any correctness problems. Synchronize via Scheduling (SvS) by Best et al. [4] is such a static analysis that checks whether certain tasks can run in parallel because they access disjoint variables. Because of the many false positives, SvS instruments the tasks with runtime checks that compare the working sets of the tasks. In a way, this is similar to our check4confl. However, we only have to consider a few programmer-indicated data elements while SvS – due to its general-purpose approach – has to process the whole state of a thread, if not the reachable graph of objects on the heap. SvS also does not optimize for GPUs whereas we carefully map the checking to the GPU architecture so that we retain as much parallelism as possible, even for the checking itself.

CUDA 9 is announced to offer so-called Cooperative Groups [1] that can bundle threads for collective operations. On current NVIDIA GPUs these bundles stick to the GPU hardware hierarchy and are unlikely to impede the results of this paper. On the announced Volta architecture [2] there will be a thread scheduling that is independent of the GPU hardware hierarchy. Although that will potentially make some dead- and livelocks go away, the programmer still has to make sure by hand that all threads are active that need to synchronize. We expect this to be as complicated as the mechanisms presented here. These issues and performance comparisons are future work.

8   Conclusion

On current GPUs, thread synchronization often suffers from dead- and livelocks (because of the SIMT execution and the schedulers). This makes porting of parallel applications to GPUs error-prone, especially when efficient fine-grain synchronization is needed. *Inspected Critical Sections* that make use of application-specific knowledge on which data items may cause dynamic data-dependences among data-parallel threads, outperform optimistic STM approaches on GPUs and get close to (unreliable) implementations with fine-grain locking. The key to the efficiency of ICS is a divide-and-conquer approach that exploits the architectural levels of GPUs and that employs a dead- and livelock free GPU-wide barrier with guaranteed progress.

Appendix

Benchmark Infrastructure

For all measurements we use a 1,5 GHz Desktop NVIDIA TITAN Xp GPU with 12 GBytes of global memory and 3.840 cores in 60 SMs (with 64 SPs each) that runs CUDA (Version 8.0) code.

The group-size in all measurements is 128 threads. The reason is that on our GPU the kernels can use up to 32.000 registers per group, i.e., 250 registers per thread. Both the retrenchment cascade and the STM framework need 70 of those registers. This leaves 180 registers for the local variables of the applications. Since the benchmarks need that many, we could not use larger group-sizes. While smaller group-sizes are possible, we only present measurements for a group-size of 128 threads because our experiments did not show qualitatively different results for smaller group-sizes.

We repeated all measurements 100 times; all given numbers are averages. For the code versions with fine-grained locks and the STM-based implementations we only measured those runs that did not face a dead- or livelock.

Benchmark Set

We use seven benchmarks, some of which are taken from the STAMP benchmark suite [14] with given atomic regions. We always use the largest possible shared data structure and/or the maximal number of threads that fit onto our GPU.

Hash Table. We use $1.5M$ threads and a hash table with the same number of buckets, each of which holds the linked lists of colliding entries. The threads randomly put a single entry into the shared hash table. ICS uses the bucket number as item to check for conflicts. The bucket operation is the atomic region in the STM code. The fine-grained lock code (FGL) uses one lock per bucket. To study the effect of the number of collisions, we also use half the buckets.

Bank. There are $24M$ accounts. $24M$ parallel threads withdraw an amount of money from one randomly picked account and deposit it to another. The two accounts are the items for conflict checking. There is a conflict if two threads use an account in common. STM: the transfer happens in the atomic region. FGL: there is one lock per account.

Graph. The $G(n, p)$-instance of the Erdős-Rényi Graph Model (ERGM) [10] starts from an edgeless graph with $n = 10K$ nodes. A thread per node adds an undirected edge to any other node ($=$ICS item for conflict checking) with probability p. To illustrate the effect of the number of collisions we study the two probabilities $p = 25\%$ and $p = 75\%$. STM: the atomic region is the insertion of an edge. FGL: the code locks the adjacency lists of both the nodes that the new edge connects.

Labyrinth. The largest 3D-mesh from the STAMP input files that fits into our memory has size $(512, 512, 7)$. Thus 512 threads plan non-intersecting routes in parallel. All nodes of the route are the items for conflict checking. STM: a full routing step is the atomic region. FGL: there is a lock per mesh point. FGL and ICS: if a route hits a spot that is already part of another route, the thread tries (three times) to find a detour around it. This avoids recalculating the full route.

Genome. $8M$ threads try to reconstruct a genome from DNA segments that reside in a shared pool, that is a hash table. There may not be duplicates and only one thread may check whether and where a segment from the pool matches the given genome. ICS checks conflicts on the bucket number. We consider a genome size of $65,536$, DNA segments have a size of 192, and there are $1,677,726$ such segments. STM and FGL: see Hash table.

Kmeans. $3M$ threads partition the same number of data items from a 32-dimensional space into $1,536$ subsets (clusters). Until a fix point is reached, all threads check the distance to the centers of all of the clusters and migrate a data item to the closest cluster (= item for conflict checking). STM: the migration is the atomic region. FGL: there is one lock per cluster; the code locks the two clusters that are affected by a migration.

Vacation. The travel reservation system uses hash tables to store customers and their reservations for a hotel, a flight, and a rental car, i.e., on three potentially conflicting items. $4M$ parallel threads perform $4M$ (random) reservations, cancellations, and updates for full trips. There may be conflicts. There are configuration parameters for the likelihood of such conflicts and the mix of operations (for the STAMP expert: we use $r = 629148$, $u = 93$, $q = 90$). STM: one operation on all three components of a trip is in the atomic region. FGL: there is a lock per hotel, flight, and car.

References

1. CUDA 9 Features Revealed: Volta, Cooperative Groups and More (2017). https://devblogs.nvidia.com/parallelforall/cuda-9-features-revealed/. Accessed 03 July 2017
2. Inside Volta: The World's Most Advanced Data Center GPU (2017). https://devblogs.nvidia.com/parallelforall/cuda-9-features-revealed/. Accessed 03 July 2017
3. Baxter, D., Mirchandaney, R., Saltz, J.H.: Run-time parallelization and scheduling of loops. In: (SPAA 1989): Symposium on Parallel Algorithms and Architecture, Santa Fe, NM, pp. 603–612, June 1989
4. Best, M.J., Mottishaw, S., Mustard, C., Roth, M., Fedorova, A., Brownsword, A.: Synchronization via scheduling: techniques for efficiently managing shared state. In: (PLDI 2011): International Conference on Programming Language Design and Implementation, San Jose, CA, pp. 640–652, June 2011
5. Cascaval, C., et al.: Software transactional memory: why is it only a research toy? Queue **6**(5), 40:46–40:58 (2008)
6. Cederman, D., Tsigas, P., Chaudhry, M.T.: Towards a software transactional memory for graphics processors. In: (EG PGV 2010): Eurographics Conference on Parallel Graphics and Visualization, Norrköping, Sweden, pp. 121–129, May 2010

7. Dang, F.H., Rauchwerger, L.: Speculative parallelization of partially parallel loops. In: (LCR 2000): International Workshop Languages, Compilers, and Run-Time Systems for Scalable Computers, Rochester, NY, pp. 285–299, May 2000

8. Eastep, J., Wingate, D., Santambrogio, M.D., Agarwal, A.: Smartlocks: lock acquisition scheduling for self-aware synchronization. In: (ICAC 2010): International Conference on Autonomic Computing, Washington, DC, pp. 215–224, June 2010

9. ElTantawy, A., Aamodt, T.M.: MIMD synchronization on SIMT architectures. In: (MICRO 2016): International Symposium on Microarchitecture, Taipei, Taiwan, pp. 1–14, October 2016

10. Erdős, P., Rényi, A.: On random graphs I. Publ. Math. (Debrecen) **6**, 290–297 (1959)

11. Habermaier, A., Knapp, A.: On the correctness of the SIMT execution model of GPUs. In: (ESOP 2012): European Symposium on Programming, Tallinn, Estonia, pp. 316–335, March 2012

12. Holey, A., Zhai, A.: Lightweight software transactions on GPUs. In: (ICPP 2014): International Conference on Parallel Processing, Minneapolis, MN, pp. 461–470, September 2014

13. Li, A., van den Braak, G.J., Corporaal, H., Kumar, A.: Fine-grained synchronizations and dataflow programming on GPUs. In: (ICS 2015): International Conference on Supercomputing, Newport Beach, CA, pp. 109–118, June 2015

14. Minh, C.C., Chung, J., Kozyrakis, C., Olukotun, K.: STAMP: Stanford transactional applications for multi-processing. In: (IISWC 2008): International Symposium on Workload Characterization, Seattle, WA, pp. 35–46, September 2008

15. Ramamurthy, A.: Towards scalar synchronization in SIMT architectures. Master's thesis, University of British Columbia, September 2011

16. Shen, Q., Sharp, C., Blewitt, W., Ushaw, G., Morgan, G.: PR-STM: priority rule based software transactions for the GPU. In: (Euro-Par 2015): International Conference on Parallel and Distributed Systems, Vienna, Austria, pp. 361–372, August 2015

17. Xiao, S., Aji, A.M., Feng, W.C.: On the robust mapping of dynamic programming onto a graphics processing unit. In: (ICPADS 2009): International Conference on Parallel and Distributed Systems, Shenzhen, China, pp. 26–33, December 2009

18. Xiao, S., Feng, W.: Inter-Block GPU communication via fast barrier synchronization. In: (IPDPS 2010): International Symposium on Parallel and Distributed Processing, Atlanta, GA, pp. 1–12, April 2010

19. Xu, Y., Gao, L., Wang, R., Luan, Z., Wu, W., Qian, D.: Lock-based Synchronization for GPU architectures. In: (CF 2016): International Conference on Computing Frontiers, Como, Italy, pp. 205–213, May 2016

20. Xu, Y., Wang, R., Goswami, N., Li, T., Gao, L., Qian, D.: Software transactional memory for GPU architectures. In: (CGO 2014): International Symposium on Code Generation and Optimization, Orlando, FL, pp. 1:1–1:10, February 2014

21. Yilmazer, A., Kaeli, D.R.: HQL: a scalable synchronization mechanism for GPUs. In: (IPDPS 2013): International Symposium on Parallel and Distributed Processing, Cambridge, MA, pp. 475–486, May 2013

Scalable Top-K Query Processing Using Graphics Processing Unit

Yulin Zhang$^{(\boxtimes)}$, Hui Fang, and Xiaoming Li

University of Delaware, Newark, DE 19716, USA
{yzhan,hfang,xli}@udel.edu

Abstract. Top-K query processing is one of the fundamental and the most performance-deciding components in Web search engines. A number of techniques such as dynamic pruning have been proposed to reduce the query processing time on CPU. However, it has become increasingly difficult to further improve Top-K query processing's efficiency without hurting its effectiveness. On the other hand, Graphic Processing Unit (GPU), a powerful computing accelerator on almost every computer today, is barely tapped in Web search engines. The biggest challenge to accelerate top-K query processing on GPU is that the parallel nature of execution model of GPU prevents many CPU top-K query processing optimizations from being directly ported to GPU. GPU with hundreds of cores is ideal for applications with massive parallelism, which is not readily available in existing CPU-oriented top-K query implementations.

This paper exploits the GPU computation power for top-K query processing. In particular, we propose a new domain-specific parallelization framework to utilize GPU to parallelize it. The proposed framework is general enough for both disjunctive and conjunctive query processing modes. Experiments on TREC collections show that our proposed GPU top-K query processing framework is able to improve the query processing time by a factor of 7 when compared with state-of-the-art dynamic pruning methods for the disjunctive mode and by a factor of 6 when compared with the conjunctive mode. Our results show that our GPU top-K query processing framework is faster than previously known GPU baseline method. In particular, our framework is shown to be more scalable and efficient than the CPU and GPU baselines when K is large.

Keywords: Query processing · GPU · Scalable

1 Introduction

Large-scale Information Retrieval (IR) systems, such as Web search engines, rely on fast response and high throughput to deal with rapid growing number of queries and web pages. The efficiency of a search engine can directly affect its revenue as well as users' search experience [17]. Given a query, an IR system needs to compute the relevance score for each document based on a underlying retrieval function, and then returns top K documents with the highest relevant scores.

© Springer Nature Switzerland AG 2019
L. Rauchwerger (Ed.): LCPC 2017, LNCS 11403, pp. 240–261, 2019.
https://doi.org/10.1007/978-3-030-35225-7_16

This process is known as top-K query processing. Although most Web search engines adopt a multi-stage distributed architecture to process queries [3,23], top-K query processing on a single node is still the first step to quickly identify a set of promising documents that need to be re-ranked with more complicated ranking mechanisms. Clearly, reducing top-K query processing time is a crucial step to improve search efficiency.

The most basic query processing strategy is exhaustive query processing using *disjunctive* (OR) mode, which evaluates all documents containing at least one query term and then ranks them based on their relevance scores. Although this strategy is simple, the computational cost would be quite high, in particular when an IR system has to deal with hundreds of millions of documents. An alternative is to process queries using *conjunctive* (AND) mode, which means that relevance scores are computed only for documents that contain all the query terms. This significantly decreases the number of evaluated documents and thus reduce the query processing time. However, it hurts the retrieval effectiveness significantly since many relevant documents do not contain all query terms [15,25]. Various dynamic pruning methods [5,9,22] have been proposed to reduce the query processing time for the disjunctive mode without hurting the retrieval effectiveness. The main idea is to avoid evaluating documents which are unlikely to make to the top-K search results. Although these methods can improve the search efficiency when the number of returned documents (i.e., K) is small, they are not scalable for larger $K's$ [25]. This is probably because the overhead of the dynamic pruning methods (such as pre-computing necessary statistics and storing them on the disk) increases as K gets larger. In fact, it becomes increasingly difficult to further improve the efficiency of top-K query processing without any degradation of effectiveness in the search results. Recently, researchers have started to look into how to sacrifice effectiveness for the sake of further reducing the query processing time [21,25].

Almost all of today's top-K query processing implementations were developed on and tuned for CPU. A significant source for computation power in today's computers is unused. Most of today's computers have not only CPU but also GPU, i.e., Graphics Processing Unit. GPU is a powerful platform that has been successfully used to accelerate various computer-intensive applications. Despite its great potential, GPU has not been fully utilized to improve the search efficiency. This is largely because porting top-K query processing to GPU is hard. The first challenge is how to effectively utilize GPU's massive parallelism in top-K query processing. The number of computing cores on a GPU is large, e.g., thousands cores in most powerful GPU models, which makes it possible for massive parallelism. However, top-K query processing is not a task that can be easily massively parallelized. One naive way is to set the number of threads the same as the number of query terms. However, the degree of parallelism here, i.e., the number of query terms, is much smaller than what the GPUs can do, leading to under-utilization of the GPUs. The second challenge is how to structure the computations and the data transfers involved in the top-K query processing so that we can effectively leverage the programming model offered by the

GPU. In particular, GPU runs most efficiently when threads execute the same workload at the same time, which is called SIMT (Single-Instruction-Multiple-Thread). SIMT requires very different way to express computation workload than on CPU. It means that the computations in CPU-oriented top-K query processing need to be structured in a way that all threads that are executed at the same time better to perform the same task. This is not trivial because many steps in the top-K query processing are adaptive and it requires careful designs when we need to massive parallelize each step. Ding et al. [8] tried to leverage the GPU for query processing, but they focused on query processing for a small value of K (i.e., $K = 10$). It remains unclear whether there is a general strategy for GPU-based top-K query processing and how well it can scale with K.

In this paper, we propose a novel framework of exploiting the parallelism of top-K query processing on GPUs. Our framework presents the same interface as existing top-K query processing implementations, that is, queries are submitted to a CPU. However, for each query, the CPU transfers the compressed inverted indexes related to the query to a GPU, and the GPU then evaluates documents and returns top-K results back to the CPU. The processing time of a query consists of the query processing time spent on the GPU as well as the data transfer time. The main innovation of our framework is that we leverage the data-parallel programming model provided by the GPU to speed up the process of document evaluation. Generally speaking, the document evaluation process consists of three steps: *index decompression, score calculation* and *top-K selection*. Since these three steps require different types of computations, we have designed different strategies, such as blocked scan, double-level binary search, bucket selection, to parallelize each step. Unlike the previous study [8], our framework is general enough to process queries in both disjunctive and conjunctive modes.

Experiments are conducted over multiple TREC Web collections. Results show that the proposed GPU top-K query processing framework can significantly improve the efficiency compared with the CPU baseline method in both disjunctive and conjunctive mode over all collections. When compared with the exhaustive query processing on CPU, the average speedup is around 33 for the disjunctive mode and 6 for the conjunctive mode. The GPU-based methods are more efficient than the state of the art dynamic pruning methods. It can also outperform the previously proposed GPU-based method [8], in particular, when K is larger. Moreover, empirical results consistently show that the GPU-based methods are scalable with respect to K, i.e., the speedup remains the same as K gets larger. Finally, it is interesting to note that, with the proposed GPU optimization methods, the processing time of the disjunctive mode is comparable to that of the conjunctive mode, which means that we can significantly improve the efficiency without any sacrifice in terms of the effectiveness.

2   Related Work and Background

Improving search efficiency has been an active research topic since the beginning of the IR field. Commonly used strategies include index compression [26], caching

[7], dynamic pruning [5,9,22], distributed computing [4], query processing on multicore architecture [20] etc.

Although GPU is a powerful platform used to accelerate computing-intensive applications, not many studies focus on top-K query processing on GPUs. There are a few studies that used GPUs to improve the efficiency for applications related to the top-K query processing, such as list intersection [2,24] and relational operations [11]. However, they only solve one step involved in the top-K query processing, and none of them provided a complete solution to top-K query processing.

Ding et al. [8] was the first and probably the only study done on using GPUs for top-K query processing so far. They mainly focused on conjunctive query processing mode and the results are evaluated only when K is set to 10. On the contrary, we propose a general framework that can process queries in both disjunctive and conjunctive modes with scalability. We evaluated the proposed methods on multiple values of K, and found that the proposed framework is scalable and can still keep large speedup even when K is large. Finally, another key difference is that we do not assume that inverted lists are available in GPU global memory when processing queries on the GPUs, which is an assumption made in the previous study [8]. The assumption might give unrealistic advantage to GPU-based implementations. Instead, when measuring the performance, the query processing time includes the time spent on transferring data between CPU and GPU memories. This transfer is often considered to be one of the bottlenecks when applying GPU to accelerate applications, but, as shown in this paper, even with this overhead the proposed GPU framework can still achieve significant speedup.

The contribution of this paper can be summarized as follows. First, we propose a novel framework that can fully exploit the massive parallelism power of GPU to speedup the top-K query processing time. The framework is general enough for both disjunctive and conjunctive modes. Second, experiment results show that the proposed GPU framework is more efficient and scalable than the state-of-the-art CPU and GPU top-K query processing methods. Finally, with the GPU optimization, for the first time, the query processing time for the disjunctive mode is comparable to that for the conjunctive mode, making it possible to improve the efficiency significantly without hurting the search effectiveness.

2.1 Top-K Query Processing Background

Web search engines use inverted indexes to facilitate the search process. For each term in the collection, an inverted index was built to store the information about the occurrences of the term in the documents. An inverted list consists of a list of postings, where each posting contains a document ID and the occurrences of the term in the corresponding document. Indexes are often stored in a highly compressed format. The compression not only reduces the total size of index, but also improves efficiency by decreasing the number of disk reads. Since the indexes are compressed, the first step of the top-K query processing is often to decompress the indexes to get the term statistics.

With the decompressed statistics, search engines need to traverse inverted indexes to compute relevance scores for all documents based on a underlying retrieval function. There are two commonly used index traversal methods: Term-At-A-Time (TAAT) [6] and Document-AT-A-Time (DAAT) [5]. TAAT sequentially processes one query term at a time. It goes through the inverted list of a term and accumulates the partial document scores contributed by the term. The partial scores are stored in an accumulator, and will later be accumulated to compute the final document scores. On the contrary, DAAT processes one document at a time. It goes through the inverted lists of all query terms in parallel. A document needs to be fully evaluated before moving on to the next one. Since DAAT requires the synchronization among posting lists, it is not suitable for the highly parallel architecture of the GPUs due to data dependency. Therefore, in the proposed GPU implementation, we use the TAAT query processing strategy.

Given a query, it can be processed either using *disjunctive* (OR) mode or *conjunctive* (AND) mode. In the disjunctive mode, we compute the scores for all documents with at least one query term. In the conjunctive mode, we compute the scores only for documents with all query terms. The conjunctive mode is often considered more efficient and less effective, since it evaluates fewer documents and some relevant documents may not contain all query terms [25]. In this paper, we develop a general framework that can process queries in both modes.

3   GPU-Based Top-K Query Processing

Our GPU-based top-K query processing framework works as follows. Given a query, CPU sends the query as well as the inverted indexes of all the query terms to GPU. The GPU then evaluates documents based on the query and the inverted indexes, and returns top-K ranked documents to the CPU. Note that the query processing time here includes the time spent on transferring the indexes, the time spent on document evaluation, and the time spent on returning the search results.

Unlike the previous study where the entire inverted indexes are assumed to be kept in the GPU memory, our framework keeps only simple global statistics such as document lengths and IDF values in the GPU memory. The main reason of our design is that GPU memory has limited size and it may not be able to hold the entire inverted indexes for large data collections. Therefore, all the inverted indexes are kept on the CPU side, and only those related to the query will be transferred to the GPU. As we will show in the experiments, even with the overhead of the data transfer, the proposed GPU framework is still able to improve the search efficiency significantly.

The transfer of data between GPU and CPU is pretty straightforward. The main challenge, also the main technical contribution of our framework, is the parallel implementation of document evaluation for the GPU-based top-K query processing. During the document evaluation, the system first needs to read the compressed indexes and decompress them to get the posting information. After that, we need to traverse the indexes and compute the relevance scores. As discussed earlier, we use the TAAT method for index traversal. In particular, a large array is allocated to record the relevance score for each document with respect to a query term, where the size of the array is the total number of documents for the query term. When processing a query with TAAT, the GPU would first go through each posting list and compute the partial relevance score of a document with respect to the corresponding query term. After that, we can compute the relevance scores of all documents by combining the partial scores in all the posting lists of a query. To do this, list operations (either intersection or union) need to be performed. Finally, we need to select top-K ranked documents from the list based on their scores.

Clearly, when implementing the query processing with GPUs, we can divide document evaluation into the following three steps: (1) *index decompression,* which decompresses the indexes related to the query terms; (2) *score calculation,* which calculates the partial relevance scores of documents for the posting list of each query term and then combines scores from multiple posting lists through different list operations (i.e., list intersection for conjunctive query processing mode and list union for disjunctive query processing mode); and (3) *top-K selection,* which goes through the final list and selects documents with top-K highest scores. We describe how to parallelize each component for GPUs in the following subsections.

3.1   Parallel Index Decompression

As mentioned in the previous section, given a query, the CPU transfers the inverted indexes of the query terms to the GPU. Since the indexes are compressed, the first step is to decompress the indexes.

One possible solution to parallelize index decompression is to decompress the inverted index for all the terms in parallel. Since the number of terms in a query is not big, such parallelism would under-utilize the GPU. Recall that each term has an inverted index with a list of postings, and the posting list of a common term could contain billions of postings. Thus, a more sensible solution could be to parallelize the decompression of the posting list of a common term. We now provide more details on how we tackle this challenge.

PForDelta is a commonly used index compression method for IR systems [27]. Like all the other index compression methods, PForDelta does not directly store the document IDs in each posting list because the document IDs can be fairly large numbers. Instead, it stores the differences between the sorted document IDs in each posting list, and these gaps are then compressed. PForDelta first splits the data into blocks and decompresses one block at a time. The size of a block needs to be a multiple of 32, and we set it to 64 in this paper. For each block, PForDelta chooses an integer b so that a certain percentage (e.g., 90%) of the gaps in a list can fit into a fixed length field with b bit. The remaining gaps, i.e., those are larger than 2^b, are referred to as exceptions. PForDelta can be tuned by choosing different thresholds for the number of exceptions allowed. Because exceptions and non-exceptions are compressed using different numbers of bits, it is difficult to decompress both of them simultaneously on the GPU in one CUDA kernel invocation. In order to exploit more parallelism, we set the number of exceptions allowed to zero. In other words, for each block, we choose the value of b such that all the gaps in the block are smaller than 2^b. As a result, all the information in the indexes are compressed using the same strategy. It is expected that the compressed index size would increase because of this new increased value of b. Our result shows the compressed size of Gov2 collection increases from 8.2 GB to 11 GB. However, the major benefit of using this variant is to eliminate the kernel invocation overhead of exceptions decompression as well as provide a uniformly parallel decompression scheme for the whole block. It is worth pointing out the decompression technique CPU query processing used in this work is PForDelta since it is more efficient than our parallel decompression method.

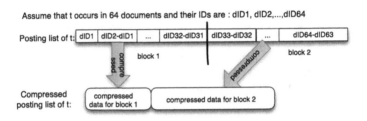

Fig. 1. An example of index compression

Figure 1 illustrates the basic idea of index compression method with a simplified example. We assume that the term t occurs in multiple documents whose IDs are $dID_1, dID_2, \ldots, dID_{64}$. Instead of storing these IDs directly in the posting list, we store the gaps, i.e., the differences between the sorted document IDs such as $dID_2 - dID_1$. Note that other information (such as term frequency and term position) also needs to be stored together with document ID gaps. We want to keep the example simple, so did not show those information here. The posting list can be divided into blocks (32 postings per block in this example), and each block can then be decompressed using different values of b to make sure that all of the gaps in the block are smaller than 2^b. Since the sizes of the compressed data blocks could be different, when storing the compressed postings for each block, we also need to store the value of b and the length of the compressed block.

When decompressing the indexes, we need to recover the posting lists including the document ID and term frequency for each document and term pair. Since an inverted list needs to be split into blocks when using PForDelta for compression, we can first look at the main computations involved in each block and then discuss how to process the entire list. The main computations involved in each block include:

– *block address calculation*, to compute the starting address of each compressed data block;

- *block decompression*, to read and decode a block based on the block address;
- *document ID recovery*, to read the document ID gaps from the decompressed blocks for the document ID gaps, and recover the original document IDs based on the ID gaps.

Fig. 2. The layout of compressed data for each block in compressed postinglist

Block Address Calculation. The first step of the decompression is to read each compressed block. Since the length of each block is not fixed, we need to use the lengths of compressed blocks to recover the address for each block. Figure 2 zooms in the compressed data for block in Fig. 1, and it shows the internal layout for each compressed data block in the compressed postinglist. The respective values of b and the length of each compressed block are denoted as B and Len in Fig. 2. If we want to read the compressed blocks in parallel, we have to figure out how to compute the starting addresses of all the blocks in parallel.

Take Fig. 1 as an example, the address of the second compressed block can be computed by summing up the address of the first block and the length of the first block. Similarly, the address of the third compressed block, if there is any, can be computed by adding the address of the second block with the length of the second block. In fact, this process is essentially to compute the prefix sum for all the lengths of compressed blocks, and can be parallelized using parallel scan. Parallel scan is a widely used parallel operation on GPU and can be used in applications such as sorting, stream compaction, building histogram, etc. [10,18]. When computing the starting address of a block, we do not use the length of the current block, so this kind of prefix sum is exclusive. In this paper, we apply an exclusive parallel scan to compute the starting address of each compressed block of data. Regarding the GPU configuration, we set the thread block size to 1,024, and each thread is assigned to process an integer, which contains the information about two postings.

Block Decompression. After reading all the compressed blocks, the next step is to decompress these blocks in parallel. This step is pretty straightforward. Since an inverted list is split into blocks and each block contains the information about 64 postings, we launch a block of 64 threads to decompress each compressed data block and the total number of threads is equal to the number of document in the posting list, and thus, the compressed posting can be decompressed simultaneously.

Document ID Recovery. After decompressing the data blocks, we can get the document ID gaps for each posting list. The next step is to recover the original document IDs. For example, as shown in Fig. 1, dID_1 and $dID_2 - dID_1$

are stored in the posting list and we can get the original document ID of the second document, i.e., dID_2, by adding the gaps up. How do we parallelize this process to recover a large number of document IDs in the same time? This can still be solved using parallel scan since the computation is inclusive prefix sum. However, since the posting lists could be very long, it may require multiple levels of recursions to finish the scan, adding extra scan kernel invocations. To improve the efficiency, we propose a segment-based parallel scan. The main idea is to split each posting list into segments and apply an inclusive parallel scan on each segment. For each inverted list, we build an array called *FirstID* to store the original ID for the first document in each segment, and the array elements are then later used together with the segment-based parallel scan results to recover the original ID for all the documents. We also tune the thread block size and set it to 128 based on our preliminary results, and each thread processes 8 postings to better cover the global memory latency for each thread [14]. So, the size of a segment is set to 1,024, meaning each segment contains 1024 postings. Our preliminary results show that the proposed segment-based parallel scan is more efficient than the original parallel scan, achieving a speed up of 1.4 for an array with 2^{24} elements.

3.2 Parallel Score Calculation

After decompressed the indexes, the system can then traverse the indexes to compute the relevance scores for all the documents. The relevance scores of a document with respect to a query is often computed by summing up the partial relevance score of a document with respect to a term for all the query terms [16]. Thus, two main computations involved in this step include:

- *partial score calculation*, which computes partial relevance scores of a document for matching each of the query term based on a underlying retrieval function;
- *score accumulation*, which accumulates all the partial scores of a document with respect to each query term and computes the final relevance score for the document;
- *unique document filtering*, which filters out duplicate documents between posting lists, and leave unique documents with final score for top-K selection.

In the *partial score calculation* step, for each query term, we need to go through its posting list, calculate the partial scores of each document on the list and record them in large score arrays. They are allocated in GPU global memory with size of the total number of documents for each term, as we already mentioned in the introduction of our general framework. Auxiliary information such as total number of documents for each term is saved as part of the indexes. Since we need to compute the partial score for each term and its associated document, we can parallelize this step by allocating one GPU thread for each document in the term utilizing BM25 [16] function. Specifically, it is a combination of inverse document frequency, term frequency in the document, the length of the document and average document length in the collection.

Here, we have completed partial score calculation for each document with respect to the query, our next step is to accumulate partial score and compute the final score. When computing the final score of a document, we need to find all the posting lists that contain the document and sum up the partial scores. Specifically, given a document (i.e., posting) in an inverted list, we need to locate the document in the other inverted lists so that the partial scores of this document could be accumulated. The main computation here is to look up the document in the posting lists. To speed up the process, we propose to leverage the *FirstID* arrays discussed in Sect. 3.1. Recall that we split an inverted index into segments, and FirstID stores the original ID of the first document in each segment. The FirstID array are preprocessed offline, as a part of auxiliary data structure to the indexes. Its space overhead is acceptable, e.g., FirstID array in GOV2 is 345 MB comparing with 11.5 GB for the compressed posting lists. The ratio between them is 3%. Thus, given a document, we employ a two-level binary search to locate its location in the posting lists. We first use FirstID arrays to narrow down the search space, and then use the document IDs to identify the exact location. To parallelize the above process, we allocate a thread for each document, and then conduct two-level parallel binary searches to locate the positions of the posting in all the inverted lists and compute the final score. In this step, we utilize a predicate array to save boolean variables, if a duplicate document is found during two-level search, the corresponding location of predicate array is marked as TRUE. Before the parallelization process, we sort the decompressed posting lists by their lengths in an ascending order, which minimizes the number of allocated thread blocks and further reduces the overhead on GPU.

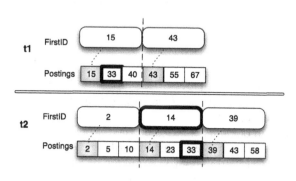

Fig. 3. An example of two-level search

Figure 3 illustrates an example. Assume that a query has two terms t_1 and t_2 and each segment contains 3 postings in this example. t_1 has a shorter posting list than t_2, so we would first go through the postings of t_1 to calculate the final document scores for each of them. When computing the final score for document 33, instead of search a match on the posting list of t_2, we first search over the *FirstID* array for t_2 to identify the corresponding segment on the posting list of t_2 and then search the elements in the segments.

There might be duplicate documents between posting lists. Suppose a query contains term A and B, both posting lists of A and B have duplicate document I (called I_A and I_B). In the previous score accumulation step, the score array of I_B contains the total score for the query while I_A contains partial score. Thus, it requires to filter out duplicate document with partial score. Otherwise, duplicate documents might be selected into tok-K results. In this unique document filtering step, we adopt the implementation in [1]. Its key idea is to use shared memory atomics to filter out duplicate documents by the Predicate array mentioned above.

Note that the above parallel method can be applied to both disjunctive and conjunctive query modes. For disjunctive mode, we need to allocate threads for documents that occur in the inverted lists of the query terms, i.e., those containing at least one query term. For conjunctive mode, we need to allocate threads to only documents that occur in the shortest posting list. To establish a connection among these three steps, we present the following pseudocode for conjunctive mode. The disjunctive mode can be established similarly. In Algorithm 1, N is the number of query terms. PRED represents the predicate array mentioned in two-level search. It is also used in document filtering step. $DocID_i$ represents the corresponding decompressed posting lists for each term. They are sorted by their length in ascending order.

Algorithm 1. Parallel Score Calculation

Function{ScoreCalculation}{$DocID, Score, FirstID, PRED, N$}

PartialScoreCalulation{$DocID, Score$}

for $i \in \{2, \ldots, N\}$ **do**

ScoreAccumulation{$DocID_1, DocID_i, Score, FirstID, PRED$}

end for

DocumentFiltering{$DocID, Score, PRED$}

EndFunction

3.3   Parallel Top-K Selection

We have discussed how to leverage GPU to parallel decompress indexes and compute the final relevance scores for documents. This section focuses on how to select top-K ranked documents using GPU.

The simplest strategy is to sort all documents based on their scores and pick the top-K ranked documents. However, this might unnecessarily waste a lots of computational power because we do not care about the ranking of a document if it does not make it into the top-K and K is often much smaller than the total number of documents in the collection. To speed up this process, we propose a method based on bucket sorting. The main idea is to first distribute documents into a number of buckets based on their relevance scores, select a minimum number of buckets that can cover the top-K ranked documents, and identify top-K ranked documents from the selected promising buckets.

The first step is to divide documents into buckets based on the scores and then select a minimum number of buckets that can cover top-K documents. Assuming there are a number of buckets, each of them corresponds to a range of relevance scores, and the documents in a bucket should be within the corresponding score range of the bucket. Therefore, the relevance score of a document decides which bucket it would be put in.

When deciding on the score range for each bucket, we first use the collection statistics to compute the maximal and minimal values for the relevance score and then divide the score range evenly based on the number of buckets, e.g., Based on the statistics about the GOV2 collection and BM25 function, we choose max value to be 74, and min value is 0. Thus, let B denotes the number of buckets, max and min denote that maximum and minimum of the relevance scores, and $score[i]$ denotes the relevance score of document i. We can determine the bucket number for the document (i.e., $bucket[i]$) as: $bucket[i] = B - \lfloor \frac{B}{max-min} \cdot (score[i] - min) \rfloor$.

During the process of documents distribution, we also maintain an array in GPU global memory to save the bucket number for each document. After assigning a document to its corresponding bucket based on the above equation, we need to count the number of documents in each bucket. We now explain how to parallelize this step. Each bucket maintains a counter to record the number of documents in the bucket. We allocate one thread for each document. So when we assign a document to a bucket, the corresponding thread needs to *atomically* increase the counter of the corresponding bucket by 1. When multiple threads need to add the value to the same bucket, we may encounter the problem of collision and need to make sure the operation to be atomic. It is well known that atomic operations on global memory in GPU is computationally expensive, especially in the case of large collision volume, and atomic operations in the shared memory is faster than in the global memory. Therefore, we have adopted a method from the previous study [19] to simulate atomic add in the shared memory. Our preliminary results show that this method can reduce the collision rate of atomic operations and achieve a speed up of 2. After counting the number of documents for each bucket, we can perform a serial accumulative sum and figure out how many buckets include the top-K documents.

With the identified buckets, we can then sort all the candidate documents with any existing sorting algorithms. We used radix sorting algorithms [13] in this paper, since it is considered as one of the fastest sorting algorithm on GPU, and Thrust library [12] in CUDA includes its implementation. Radix sorting is a non-comparison based sorting algorithm, which considers one bit from each key, and partitions the unsorted array elements so that all elements with a 0 in that bit precede those with 1 in that bit. When GPU finishes selecting top-K documents, it returns the retrieval results back to CPU.

4   Experiments

To evaluate the efficiency of the proposed GPU-based top-K query processing framework, first, we compare the proposed parallel GPU top-K query processing methods with the CPU top-K query processing methods for the *exhaustive* evaluation, where all the candidate documents are evaluated and ranked. The methods are compared in both disjunctive and conjunctive modes. Second, we compare the proposed GPU methods with several state of the art top-K query processing methods, which includes dynamic pruning methods maxScore [22] and Block-Max WAND [9] as well as the previously proposed GPU top-K query processing method for both conjunctive and disjunctive modes [8]. Additionally, we conduct more analysis to further understand the proposed GPU methods.

The proposed GPU framework is implemented on Nvidia Tesla C2075 with 448 CUDA cores. All CPU query processing methods are evaluated on a single core of Intel Core i7 CPU. All the methods use the same indexes, which are kept in the CPU memory. Relevance scores are computed based on Okapi BM25 [16] in our experiments, but the proposed GPU framework can work with any retrieval functions. The number of buckets (i.e., B in Sect. 3.3) is set to 32 because the size of a warp in GPU is 32 and it is easier to implement the atomic operation in shared memory when setting B to the same value as the number of threads in a warp. The code of our proposed methods will be made available at GitHub for other researchers to use and study in the future.

Experiments are conducted over multiple TREC collections. The first three were used in the TREC 2004–2006 Terabyte tracks, and their document collection (i.e., GOV2) consists of 25 millions of webpages. The data sets are denoted as *TB04*, *TB05* and *TB06*. The other four data sets were used at the TREC 2009–2012 Web track, and their document collection (i.e., ClueWeb09 category B) contains 50 million web pages. These data sets are denoted as *Web09*, *Web10*, *Web11*, and *Web12*.

When measuring the performance, we report the average query processing time for each data set. As discussed earlier, the query processing time of the GPU-based implementations includes the time spent on identifying top-K documents on GPU as well as the data transfer time between CPU and GPU.

4.1   Performance Comparison

Comparison with Exhaustive Evaluation (CPU-Based). The most basic query processing method is to *exhaustively* evaluate all candidate documents, i.e., all documents with at least one query term for the disjunctive processing mode, and all documents with all query terms for the conjunctive processing mode. Our proposed GPU framework essentially computes the relevance scores of all the candidate documents, and can be considered as an exhaustive query processing method. Therefore, it would be interesting to compare its performance with its counterparts on CPU. The proposed GPU-based query processing methods are denoted as *GPU-OR* and *GPU-AND*. The exhaustive CPU-based top-K query processing methods are denoted as *CPU-OR* and *CPU-AND*.

Table 1a shows the performance comparison for the disjunctive query processing methods when K is set to 1000. It is clear that GPU-OR consistently outperforms CPU-OR methods. It indicates that processing queries in the disjunctive mode on the CPU is significantly slower than in the conjunctive mode no matter what the value of K is. However, the performance differences between

Table 1. Performance comparison on exhaustive evaluation (ms)

(a) Disjunctive (OR) mode (K=1,000)

	TB04	TB05	TB06	Web09	Web10	Web11	Web12
CPU-OR	683.99	577.70	545.55	1038.70	752.26	1557.03	1054.51
GPU-OR	21.09	17.94	16.40	31.08	21.82	43.45	31.15
(Speedup)	(32.4)	(32.2)	(33.3)	(33.4)	(34.5)	(35.8)	(33.9)

(b) Conjunctive (AND) mode (K=100)

	TB04	TB05	TB06	Web09	Web10	Web11	Web12
CPU-AND	73.53	43.16	43.81	172.78	106.72	103.55	172.76
GPU-AND	12.90	11.12	10.40	22.80	15.80	25.50	20.67
(Speedup)	(5.7)	(3.9)	(4.2)	(7.6)	(6.8)	(4.1)	(8.4)

the two GPU methods are very small. The latencies are almost comparable for all the values of K. This is a very encouraging finding. It has been very difficult to further improve the query processing efficiency, so researchers have started looking into how to sacrifice effectiveness, such as using conjunctive mode or document prioritization [25], to reduce the query latency. Previous study on using GPU for top-K query processing [8] proposed to optimize the efficiency by executing the conjunctive mode first and then disjunctive if there are not enough results, which indicates that there is still a performance gap between these two modes when using their GPU-based method. Interestingly, our results show that, using our proposed GPU optimization methods, we can finally bridge the efficiency gap between the disjunctive and conjunctive processing modes without making any sacrifice on the retrieval effectiveness.

Comparison with Dynamic Pruning Methods (CPU-Based). Since there have been many efforts on developing more efficient query processing methods on CPU, we further compare our efforts with a few stronger baseline methods. We compare our methods with two state of the art dynamic pruning methods: maxScore [22] and Block-Max WAND (BMW) [9]. Results are summarized in Table 2. Clearly, the GPU-based method is much more efficient than the two baseline methods over all the data sets.

Table 2. Performance comparison for disjunctive processing (ms): GPU vs. dynamic pruning (K = 1,000)

	TB04	TB05	TB06	Web09	Web10	Web11	Web12
BMW	199.61	125.12	106.52	171.96	113.66	258.47	169.48
Maxscore	130.52	108.72	74.30	329.33	190.60	234.94	223.31
GPU-OR	**21.09**	**17.94**	**16.40**	**31.08**	**21.82**	**43.45**	**31.15**

Furthermore, we conduct experiments to examine how the query processing time would be affected by K. Figure 4 shows the average query processing time of the GPU-OR and the two baseline methods for different values of K on the *TB05* data set. The plots on other data sets show similar trends. It is very interesting to see that the execution time of GPU-OR remains nearly the same as K gets larger, while the speed of dynamic pruning methods increases. This observation demonstrates the scalability of the proposed GPU-based framework. It is mainly due to the final radix sorting of the framework, where the number of documents (K) to be sorted is several orders of magnitude smaller than the original document lists, accounting for only 5% of the total execution time. As K increases in Fig. 4, the GPU approach stays nearly constant. A deeper analysis on the break-down of performance is presented below. On the other hand, the dynamic pruning methods evaluate more documents as K increases. Consequently, the performance difference between our GPU method and dynamic pruning ones becomes larger. The speedup scalability is a desirable property because previous studies [15, 25] suggested that a large value of K can lead to more satisfying search results.

Table 3. Performance comparison with the GPU baseline in disjunctive mode (ms) (K = 2,000)

	TB04	*TB05*	*TB06*	*Web09*	*Web10*	*Web11*	*Web12*
BL-GPU-OR	95.14	94.97	96.51	95.12	93.33	100.82	95.35
GPU-OR	**21.61**	**17.47**	**16.90**	**32.14**	**22.08**	**44.19**	**32.01**
(Speedup)	**(4.5)**	**(5.3)**	**(6.0)**	**(3.1)**	**(4.3)**	**(2.3)**	**(3.1)**

Comparison with Previous GPU-Based Method. We now compare the proposed GPU methods with the baseline methods proposed in the previous

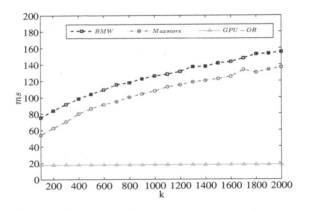

Fig. 4. GPU-OR vs dynamic pruning (TB05)

Table 4. Performance comparison with the GPU baseline in conjunctive mode (ms) (K = 1,000)

	TB04	*TB05*	*TB06*	*Web09*	*Web10*	*Web11*	*Web12*
BL-GPU-AND	29.17	26.64	27.21	29.80	24.82	34.77	32.06
GPU-AND	**12.79**	**11.08**	**11.42**	**23.93**	**16.2**	**25.73**	**21.73**
(Speedup)	**(2.3)**	**(2.4)**	**(2.4)**	**(1.3)**	**(1.5)**	**(1.4)**	**(1.5)**

study [8], since this study was the first and probably the only complete solution for GPU-based top-K query processing. The authors of the previous study have kindly shared the code with us, so we directly used their codes to generate the results to ensure the correctness. Note the baseline methods assume the inverted list are stored in GPU memory and do not consider the data transfer time in the query processing time. On the contrary, our methods do not make such an assumption and the query processing time includes the data transfer time between CPU and GPU.

Table 3 summarizes the performance comparison for the disjunctive mode when K is set to 2000. We want to point out that, due to the different assumption made in the methods, the reported query processing time for the baseline methods (i.e., BL-GPU-OR and BL-GPU-AND) does not include the data transfer time while the reported time for our proposed method (i.e., GPU-OR and GPU-AND) includes it. As shown in the results, even when we include the data transfer time, our proposed method can still achieve an average speedup of 4 over all the collections. The results for the conjunctive mode are reported in Table 4. The proposed method can still outperform the baseline method.

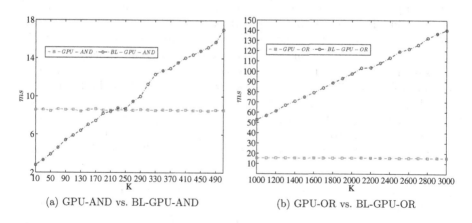

(a) GPU-AND vs. BL-GPU-AND   (b) GPU-OR vs. BL-GPU-OR

Fig. 5. Speed comparison of GPU and BL-GPU as K increases (TB05)

Next, we examine how the performance comparison changes with different values of K. Figure 5b shows the trend for the disjunctive mode. It is clear that

GPU-OR method is scalable and the query processing time does not change much when we increase the value of K, while the BL-GPU-OR method does not have such a nice property. Thus, as K increases, the speedup of the GPU-OR over the BL-GPU-OR would be larger. Figure 5a shows the trend for the conjunctive mode. Here, we use a smaller value of K because the number of documents that contain all the query terms is not large. One interesting observation is that when K is small, GPU-AND performs worse than the baseline method. But as the value of K increases, GPU-AND becomes more efficient since the processing time of the baseline method increases linearly but the processing time of the GPU-AND does not change much.

Finally, we decompose the computations involved in the query processing time to better understand the impact of K on our methods as well as the baseline methods. In particular, we report the time spent on the three main steps: i.e., *index decompression*, *score calculation* and *top-K selection*.

Figure 6a shows the results for the conjunctive mode. We can see that, for the BL-GPU-AND method, the time spent on *top-K selection* increases linearly because it used maximum reduction to select top-K documents, and the overhead of looping through the maximum reduction grows almost linearly with K. On the contrary, for the GPU-AND method, the time spent on top-K selection stays nearly constant. Furthermore, BL-GPU-AND only decompressed and computed score for the intersected posting lists while GPU-AND decompressed and computed score for all the posting lists of query terms. As a result, decompression and scoring in BL-GPU-AND are more efficient than in GPU-AND. However, for the BL-GPU-AND methods, as K increases, the performance gain in the decompression and scoring steps can not compensate for its performance degradation in the top-K selection step. Therefore, the GPU-AND starts to outperform GPU-AND-BL when K increases as shown in Fig. 5a.

Similarly, Fig. 6b shows the decomposed query processing time for the disjunctive mode. It is clear that the performance gap between GPU-OR and BL-GPU-OR mainly comes from the top-K selection step. BL-GPU-OR spent significant amount of time on this step, because the maximum reduction overhead increases with the value of K. Moreover, we can see that the time spent on the decompression and scoring is about the same for GPU-OR and BL-GPU-OR. This is because when we processing queries in the disjunctive mode, the subset of the documents that the baseline method needs to consider becomes much larger.

In summary, our proposed methods demonstrate their advantages in terms of the efficiency and scalability when compared with both CPU and GPU baselines.

Time Analysis. We break down the performance to understand where the speedup comes from. Particularly the data transfer time to-and-from GPU is included in our results. Figure 7a and b show the respective percentage of the query processing time spent on each task for CPU and GPU. Note that the last step is named differently, which is document synchronization and top-K selection, respectively. CPU uses document pointers to synchronize among the posting lists to evaluate document in a DAAT fashion. The GPU method does not introduce

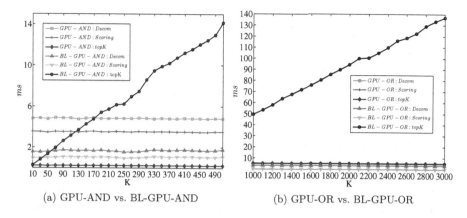

(a) GPU-AND vs. BL-GPU-AND   (b) GPU-OR vs. BL-GPU-OR

Fig. 6. Speed comparison of GPU and BL-GPU as K increases (TB05)

such a document synchronization. Instead it deploys top-K selection to evaluate the candidate documents. For the purpose of a fair performance comparison, they should be put into the same category. We use Nvidia profiler to measure kernel running time. It is clear that each of the three steps (i.e., decompression, scoring and top-K selection) takes a big chunk of time (31%, 29%, and 27%, respectively). Beside them, the data transfer from CPU to GPU (CtoG transfer) takes the most time (12%). For each query to be executed on GPU, CPU transfers it corresponding compressed inverted index and FirstID to GPU. When GPU finishes top-K query processing, it transfers back the top-K results to the CPU. Only less than 1% is spent on GPU to CPU transfer since the size of top-K results is relatively small.

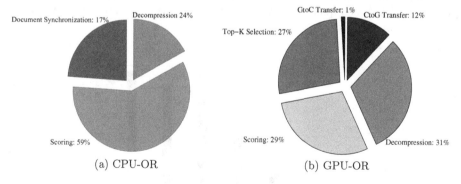

(a) CPU-OR   (b) GPU-OR

Fig. 7. Query processing time decomposition for CPU-OR when K = 1000 (TB05)

When comparing the time spent on each step by GPU and CPU, we find that the speedup of our GPU-based framework mainly comes from the score computation and the index decompression and Top-k selection gains the least speedup. The massive parallelism used in the score computation makes it possible to decrease the time spent on computing the scores significantly. More specifically, with the CPU-based implementation, around 59% of the processing time were spent on calculating the scores. But with the GPU-based implementation, only 29% were about score calculation. In situation where massive parallelism exists, such as BM25 function in scoring step, GPU outperforms CPU significantly. Moreover, the block-based posting list is a highly regular structure with relatively high number of warp divergence and uncoalesced memory access, they lead to a loss of efficiency on GPU for decompression step. Apart from these two inefficiencies, top-K selection also suffers from atomics operation, which incurs additional performance penalty on GPU.

Moreover, the break-down analysis also reveals the scalability of the GPU-based methods. As shown in Figs. 4 and 5a, the performance of the GPU methods does not change much with the value of K. This is because the value of K only affects the *radix sorting* and *GPU to CPU transfer (GtoC)* steps. Which only consists of less than 5% of query processing time. As a result, the efficiency of GPU-OR query processing methods nearly stay constant.

Speedup for Different Query Lengths. One great advantage of the GPU-based implementation is the ability to process the posting lists of multiple terms in parallel, so it would be interesting to see how the speedup changes for different query lengths. Figure 8 shows how the speedup of GPU-OR over CPU-OR changes for queries with different lengths. It is quite encouraging to see that the speedup increases when the query length gets longer. This is a desirable property because the query processing time is closely related to the number of terms in the query. Long queries often have a long query processing time, which can cause load unbalancing and search user dissatisfaction. It is very hard to improve the efficiency of these queries without hurting the effectiveness [21]. However, our proposed GPU-based query processing framework has been shown to have great advantages in this aspect.

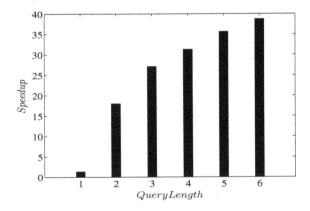

Fig. 8. Speedup over different query lengths (*TB05*) (K = 1000)

5   Conclusions

It is critical to improve the efficiency of Web search engines. Many CPU-based optimization strategies have been proposed for top-K query processing. Unfortunately, GPU, another powerful computational resource that is available on today's computers, has been largely under-utilized in IR systems. Our paper is one of a few studies that try to bridge the gap through studying how to leverage GPU to accelerate top-K query processing.

In this work, we proposed and implemented a one-of-the-first GPU-based top-K query processing framework for both disjunctive and conjunctive modes. We identified three important components in the framework, and discussed how to design and implement each of them by exploiting the parallel functionality provided by GPU. Empirical results over multiple TREC collections showed that the proposed GPU-based query processing methods are very efficient and highly scalable compared with both CPU and GPU baselines, in particular when the number of returned results (i.e., K) is large. Additionally, the proposed GPU-based framework can be used to achieve high efficiency and effectiveness in search system. The implemented system and its code will be made publicly available so that others could utilize them for their own work.

This paper shows that GPUs can be harnessed to accelerate top-K query processing in particular when K is large in Web search engines. There are several interesting future directions. First, there is the study of the GPU top-K execution time model to be able to predict the incoming query to GPU. Second, it would be interesting to study how to design a hybrid CPU-GPU system to co-process incoming queries based on the time model. Third, there is the possibility of exploiting the use of GPU to accelerate other components (e.g., query expansion and feedback) in a Web search engine that can potentially further improve the search efficiency. Finally, it would be interesting to study how to automatically set the parameter values in our proposed methods.

References

1. Adinetz, A.: CUDA pro tip: optimized filtering with warp-aggregated atomics. Parallel Forall. Np (2014)
2. Ao, N., et al.: Efficient parallel lists intersection and index compression algorithms using graphics processing units. Proc. VLDB Endow. **4**(8), 470–481 (2011)
3. Asadi, N., Lin, J.: Effectiveness/efficiency tradeoffs for candidate generation in multi-stage retrieval architectures. In: Proceedings of the 36th International ACM SIGIR Conference on Research and Development in Information Retrieval, pp. 997–1000. ACM (2013)
4. Barroso, L.A., Dean, J., Holzle, U.: Web search for a planet: the Google cluster architecture. IEEE Micro **23**(2), 22–28 (2003)
5. Broder, A.Z., Carmel, D., Herscovici, M., Soffer, A., Zien, J.: Efficient query evaluation using a two-level retrieval process. In: Proceedings of the twelfth International Conference on Information and Knowledge Management, pp. 426–434. ACM (2003)

6. Buckley, C., Lewit, A.F.: Optimization of inverted vector searches. In: Proceedings of the 8th Annual International ACM SIGIR Conference on Research and Development in Information Retrieval, pp. 97–110. ACM (1985)
7. Büttcher, S., Clarke, C.L.: Index compression is good, especially for random access. In: Proceedings of the Sixteenth ACM Conference on Information and Knowledge Management, pp. 761–770. ACM (2007)
8. Ding, S., He, J., Yan, H., Suel, T.: Using graphics processors for high performance IR query processing. In: Proceedings of the 18th International Conference on World Wide Web, pp. 421–430. ACM (2009)
9. Ding, S., Suel, T.: Faster top-k document retrieval using block-max indexes. In: Proceedings of the 34th International ACM SIGIR Conference on Research and Development in Information Retrieval, pp. 993–1002. ACM (2011)
10. Harris, M., Sengupta, S., Owens, J.D.: Parallel prefix sum (scan) with CUDA. GPU Gems **3**(39), 851–876 (2007)
11. He, B., et al.: Relational query coprocessing on graphics processors. ACM Trans. Database Syst. (TODS) **34**(4), 21 (2009)
12. Hoberock, J., Bell, N.: Thrust: a parallel template library (2010)
13. Lee, S.J., Jeon, M., Kim, D., Sohn, A.: Partitioned parallel radix sort. J. Parallel Distrib. Comput. **62**(4), 656–668 (2002)
14. Lichterman, D.: Course project for UIUC ECE 498 AL: programming massively parallel processors. Wen-Mei Hwu and David Kirk, instructors (2007)
15. Macdonald, C., Santos, R.L., Ounis, I.: The whens and hows of learning to rank for web search. Inf. Retrieval **16**(5), 584–628 (2013)
16. Robertson, S.E., Walker, S., Jones, S., Hancock-Beaulieu, M.M., Gatford, M., et al.: Okapi at TREC-3. NIST Special Publication SP, p. 109 (1995)
17. Schurman, E., Brutlag, J.: Performance related changes and their user impact. In: Velocity Web Performance and Operations Conference (2009)
18. Sengupta, S., Harris, M., Garland, M., Owens, J.D.: Efficient parallel scan algorithms for many-core GPUs. In: Scientific Computing with Multicore and Accelerators, pp. 413–442 (2011)
19. Shams, R., Kennedy, R., et al.: Efficient histogram algorithms for NVIDIA CUDA compatible devices. In: Proceedings of the International Conference on Signal Processing and Communications Systems (ICSPCS), pp. 418–422. Citeseer (2007)
20. Tatikonda, S., Cambazoglu, B.B., Junqueira, F.P.: Posting list intersection on multicore architectures. In: Proceedings of the 34th International ACM SIGIR Conference on Research and Development in Information Retrieval, pp. 963–972. ACM (2011)
21. Tonellotto, N., Macdonald, C., Ounis, I.: Efficient and effective retrieval using selective pruning. In: Proceedings of the Sixth ACM International Conference on Web Search and Data Mining, pp. 63–72. ACM (2013)
22. Turtle, H., Flood, J.: Query evaluation: strategies and optimizations. Inf. Process. Manag. **31**(6), 831–850 (1995)
23. Wang, L., Lin, J., Metzler, D.: A cascade ranking model for efficient ranked retrieval. In: Proceedings of the 34th International ACM SIGIR Conference on Research and Development in Information Retrieval, pp. 105–114. ACM (2011)
24. Wu, D., Zhang, F., Ao, N., Wang, G., Liu, J., Liu, J.: Efficient lists intersection by CPU-GPU cooperative computing. In: 2010 IEEE International Symposium on Parallel & Distributed Processing, Workshops and Ph.D. Forum (IPDPSW), pp. 1–8. IEEE (2010)

25. Wu, H., Fang, H.: Document prioritization for scalable query processing. In: Proceedings of the 23rd ACM International Conference on Conference on Information and Knowledge Management, pp. 1609–1618. ACM (2014)
26. Zhang, J., Long, X., Suel, T.: Performance of compressed inverted list caching in search engines. In: Proceedings of the 17th International Conference on World Wide Web, pp. 387–396. ACM (2008)
27. Zukowski, M., Heman, S., Nes, N., Boncz, P.: Super-scalar RAM-CPU cache compression. In: Proceedings of the 22nd International Conference on Data Engineering, ICDE 2006, p. 59. IEEE (2006)

Fast Dynamic Graph Algorithms

Gaurav Malhotra, Hitish Chappidi, and Rupesh Nasre[✉]

IIT Madras, Chennai, India
{gaurav,hitish,rupesh}@cse.iitm.ac.in

Abstract. We show that dynamic graph algorithms are amenable to parallelism on graphics processing units (GPUs). Evolving graphs such as social networks undergo structural updates, and analyzing such graphs with the existing static graph algorithms is inefficient. To deal with such dynamic graphs, we present techniques to (i) represent evolving graphs, (ii) amortize the processing cost over multiple updates, and (iii) optimize graph analytic algorithms for GPUs. We illustrate the effectiveness of our proposed mechanisms with three dynamic graph algorithms: dynamic breadth-first search, dynamic shortest paths computation and dynamic minimum spanning tree maintenance. In particular, we show that the dynamic processing is beneficial up to a certain percentage of updates beyond which a static algorithm is more efficient.

1 Introduction

Graphs are fundamental data structures to represent varied real-life phenomena such as interaction among molecules, friendships across persons, and city roads. Applications from various disciplines operate on these graphs to extract useful information such as placement of molecules, communities in social networks, and shortest path from one place to another. As data sizes grow, fast graph analytics rely on parallel graph processing. Former research has shown evidence that static graph algorithms contain enough parallelism to keep GPU cores busy [1–4]. However, several real-world graphs continue evolving. For instance, molecules change positions based on interaction and forces; new friendships get formed in social networks leading to new communities; while roads get blocked due to traffic management. A naïve way to deal with such dynamic updates is to rerun the static graph algorithm on each update to keep the information up-to-date. However, this is often time-consuming. Hard time-constraints in several applications (such as those dealing with streaming data or large-scale simulations) demand faster processing of dynamic updates, and quicker solutions.

In this work we deal with GPU-based dynamic graph algorithms. Following technical challenges get surfaced in such a setup, which fuel our work.

- **Graph representation:** Existing popular formats such as compressed sparse-row (CSR) storage for representing graphs are ill-suited for dynamic updates. A small change in the graph structure leads to a considerable data-movement in the CSR format. We devise a dynamic CSR storage format

© Springer Nature Switzerland AG 2019
L. Rauchwerger (Ed.): LCPC 2017, LNCS 11403, pp. 262–277, 2019.
https://doi.org/10.1007/978-3-030-35225-7_17

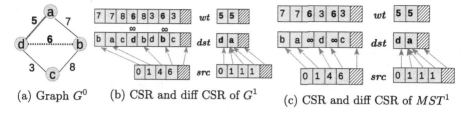

(a) Graph G^0 (b) CSR and diff CSR of G^1 (c) CSR and diff CSR of MST^1

Fig. 1. Dynamic graph representation. Edge $b - d$ is deleted from G^0 and edge $a - d$ is added to get G^1. *src* stores index in the *dst* array.

which continues its benefits for static graphs while allowing dynamic updates (Sect. 2).

- **Data-driven versus topology-driven processing:** It has been shown that a topology-driven processing *can* be beneficial for static graph algorithms [5]. However, a limitation of the existing topology-driven methods (wherein all graph elements are processed in each iteration) is their work-inefficiency. Especially in the context of dynamic updates, a topology-driven processing leads to wasted resources. We propose a data-driven approach to deal with dynamic updates. Unlike traditional static data-driven graph algorithms which use a single worklist, our dynamic graph algorithms necessitate use of multiple worklists for efficient data-driven processing (Sect. 3).

- **Synchronization:** Synchronization is a major challenge in graph algorithms in case of highly concurrent setting such as GPUs. This issue is exacerbated in the dynamic setting when the underlying graph structure is arbitrarily changed by threads. We propose a combination of lock-free updates and barrier-based processing to tame the synchronization cost (Sect. 4).

- **Interplay of incremental and decremental updates:** Fully dynamic graph algorithms may insert and remove graph elements that may affect their concurrent processing. For instance, in maintaining the minimum spanning tree, a higher-weight spanning tree edge may be deleted while a lower-weight new edge may be added. Taking advantage of such scenarios is critical for efficient dynamic processing of graphs.

We address the above challenges with effective mechanisms and illustrate that it is indeed beneficial to process dynamic graphs on GPUs. We apply the proposed techniques to three graph theoretic algorithms: dynamic breadth-first search (BFS), dynamic single-source shortest paths (SSSP) computation and dynamic maintenance of the minimum spanning tree (MST). Using several graphs from SNAP [6], we show that our GPU-based dynamic graph algorithms are faster than their static counterparts up to 15–20% of updates.

2   Graph Representation

An evolving graph is denoted using its version number as a sequence $G^0, G^1, \ldots$. Node addition and deletion can be simulated by edge addition and deletion.

Similarly, edge updates can be simulated using deletion (of the edge) followed by addition. Therefore, we focus on edge addition and deletion in our setup.

CSR: A traditionally popular representation for GPU-based graph processing is compressed sparse-row (CSR) storage format [4]. It essentially concatenates the adjacency lists of nodes and uses offsets to mark the beginnings of adjacency lists. A sample graph and its CSR representation is depicted in Fig. 1.

Unfortunately, traditional CSR has limitations when applied to dynamic graph algorithms as in our case. First, for adding a new edge $u \to v$, we need to append v to u's adjacency list (two updates are required for an undirected edge). However, this necessitates moving the adjacency lists of all the nodes after u. Additionally, this changes the offsets of all the nodes after u, requiring updates to src, dst as well as wt array if applicable (see Fig. 1). Second, adding multiple edges in parallel by multiple threads requires heavy synchronization to move elements in the CSR arrays. Third, CSR does not allow us to take advantage of interacting edge additions and removals.

diff-CSR: We address these issues (and retain benefits of CSR) by augmenting CSR representation with a diff-CSR. Thus, the initial graph G_0 is represented using CSR format. The next graph version G_1 is formed by following the transformations to the original CSR array by processing deleted edges followed by the newly inserted edges. The deleted edges are marked by overwriting with a sentinel ∞ in dst array. For inserting an edge $u - v$, our method checks if any deleted edge exists for each source node (u and v), and if it does, it is replaced with the new destination in the original CSR array. If such a deleted entry is not found, then the new edge is pushed into an additional diff-CSR array which contains only the additional insertions which could not be fitted into the original CSR array. These two arrays together represent the graph G_1.

For the subsequent versions G_i we reuse the original CSR array of G_{i-1} and allocate a new diff array if required. Such a representation can form a chain of diffs over the original array. In our setup, we merge the two diffs to create a single consolidated diff array. This allows us to remove the sequential bottleneck of chain-traversal while processing a graph update. For deletion of edges in the graph, the original and the diff arrays of G_{i-1} are checked for the corresponding node, and it is marked as deleted. Insertions are tried to be fitted into one of these arrays. Additional insertions are copied into a bigger diff array by copying all the edges already present in the previous array to the new diff array. As the diff arrays are small, such a copying does not incur any noticeable overhead.

MST Representation: In the case of dynamic MST computation, the MST itself needs to be maintained. We take advantage of our diff-CSR to store the MST. For instance, the MST of G^0 in Fig. 1a consists of edges $\{a-b, b-d, d-c\}$ with the MST cost of 16 (note that edge $a-d$ is not present in G^0). After edge $a-d$ is added and edge $b-d$ is deleted to get version G^1 (Fig. 1b), the modified MST denoted as MST^1 consists of edges $\{a-b, a-d, d-c\}$ with cost 15. MST^1 can be stored in diff-CSR format as shown in Fig. 1c.

3   Data-Driven Processing

GPUs are ideal for regular dense matrix computations. A topology-driven processing is useful in such scenarios as most of the elements are almost always *active*; that is, work is required to be done at these elements. On the other hand, in a data-driven approach, only the active graph elements are processed, making better use of the available resources. The down-side of a data-driven approach is that the active graph elements need to be stored explicitly and maintained during the parallel processing. This demands maintenance of a concurrent worklist in the presence of thousands of threads on the GPU. Thus, there is a tension between work-efficiency and synchronization cost in topology-driven versus data-driven graph processing. In the context of dynamic graph algorithms, we advocate the use of a data-driven approach. This stems from the fact that typically the updates are sparse; that is, there are only a few updates.

3.1   Incremental Graph Processing

In an incremental setting, edges are only added to the graph and no edge-deletion is performed. Given a graph G^0 and a statically computed information I^0, the goal here is to incrementally compute the modified information I^1 for the superset graph G^1. For BFS, I^1 is the updated level information; for SSSP, it is the updated shortest path from a designated source; while for MST, it is the modified minimum spanning tree. An efficient implementation of such incremental algorithms would exploit the following properties:

- BFS: In I^1, no vertex has a level larger than its level in I_0. In other words, level numbers can only reduce across incremental updates.
- SSSP: In I^1, no vertex has a distance longer than its distance in I_0.
- MST: The MST cost cannot increase due to incremental updates.

BFS: In incremental BFS, when a new edge $u \rightarrow v$ is added, the levels of only those nodes that are reachable via edge $u \rightarrow v$ *may* reduce. Such a processing can be readily modeled by mapping incremental work in the context of static graph processing. Thus, vertex u can be added to the worklist and concurrent level-synchronous BFS can proceed, exactly as in the static version. If v's level reduces, the processing may continue to the next level; otherwise, no other vertices need to be processed further. Figure 2 shows the processing steps when edge $a - d$ is added and a is the source in the graph of Fig. 1a.

SSSP: Similar to incremental BFS, in incremental SSSP also, when an edge $u \rightarrow v$ is added, the distances of only those vertices that are reachable via edge $u \rightarrow v$ may reduce. Therefore, the processing can also piggyback on the static processing by inserting vertex u into the worklist of active vertices. An important difference with respect to BFS is that SSSP computation is asynchronous, enforcing a different synchronization requirement (discussed in Sect. 4).

Iteration	Vertex levels				Active vertices
	a	b	c	d	
0	0	7	15	13	{a}
1	0	7	15	5	{d}
2	0	7	8	5	{c}
2	0	7	8	5	{}

Fig. 2. Incremental BFS on the graph from Fig. 1a

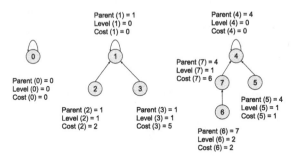

Fig. 3. Level-order traversal of the minimum spanning forest

MST: Unlike BFS and SSSP, incremental MST requires special consideration, which we discuss next. In MST, addition of an edge creates a cycle. Our implementation allows such a cycle to be created, and later traverses the cycle to remove the maximum weight edge (which could as well be the newly added edge). However, a naïve traversal to find the cycle is expensive. Therefore, we resort to preprocessing of the MST (in general, minimum spanning forest MSF) which reduces the traversal and improves incremental MST computation. The preprocessing ensures that there is a dedicated directed path (note that the MST is undirected) to traverse to find that cycle. In this step, we find out the representative vertices for each disjoint component of the MSF and start a level-order traversal from each vertex in parallel. During the traversal, we maintain three attributes with each vertex: *Parent, Level* and *Cost*. Whenever an unvisited vertex v is reached from the current vertex u, Parent$(v) = u$, Level$(v) =$ Level(u) $+ 1$, Cost$(v) =$ Wt$(u - v)$. This data-driven worklist-based process continues until all the vertices are visited as shown in Fig. 3.

We perform incremental updates as below. We first add the incremental edges that connect two different MSTs in the MSF. This is because such cut-edges would always be part of the new MSF and are guaranteed not to create cycle. After all such inter-component edges are processed, any new edge would be intra-component and would necessarily create a cycle. This necessitates finding the maximum-weight cycle edge. To do this, we start from the two ends of the incremental edge; say, $first\_end$ and $other\_end$. Without loss of generality, assume that Level$(first\_end) \geq$ Level$(other\_end)$. So, we start from the $first\_end$ and then following the vertices from the parent array, we update the

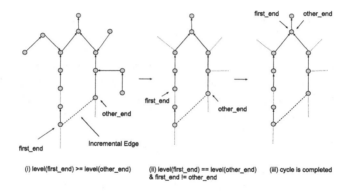

Fig. 4. Path traversal to find maximum weight edge in a cycle

parent of the $first\_end$ to be the new $first\_end$. We continue with this until we get to a point where Level($first\_end$) == Level($other\_end$). At this point, also if $first\_end$ == $other\_end$, then we have found the cycle and we return with the maximum weight edge found on the path traversed. This is depicted in Fig. 4.

When we add multiple incremental edges in parallel, there exists a chance that two incremental edges pick up the *same* maximum weight edge during its cycle traversal. In such cases, we must consider only one of the two incremental edges in that iteration and process the other edge later. Otherwise, there is a danger of forming a cycle in the maintained spanning tree.

3.2 Decremental Graph Processing

In a decremental setting, edges are only removed from the graph and no edge-insertion is performed. Given a graph G^0 and a statically computed information I^0, the goal here is to decrementally compute the modified information I^1 for the subset graph G^1. For BFS, I^1 is the updated level information; for SSSP, it is the updated shortest path from a designated source; while for MST, it is the modified minimum spanning tree. An efficient implementation of such decremental algorithms would exploit the following properties:

- BFS: In I^1, no vertex has a level smaller than its level in I_0. In other words, level numbers can only increase across decremental updates.
- SSSP: In I^1, no vertex has a distance shorter than its distance in I_0.
- MST: The MST cost cannot reduce due to decremental updates.

BFS: Unlike in incremental BFS, the decremental version poses a challenge that the next shortest path (new parent) is not known. To address this issue, we use a multi-worklist approach, which we explain below. The static BFS processes G^0 in level-synchronous worklist-based manner and computes the level values in I^0. Next, to compute I^1, the dynamic version processes all the deleted edges $a \rightarrow b$ to check if a is a parent of b in the BFS tree (BFST). If it is, then we check all the incoming nodes of b (to check for the new shortest path) and update b's level. If its level *increases* then it is added to a special worklist. Processing threads remove nodes from this worklist and check if any of their outgoing vertices is a child in BFST to the currently removed node. If a vertex is indeed a child, it is pushed to the special worklist. For each vertex in the special worklist, we update its level based on its incoming nodes, whereas the regular worklist is used to propagate distances to the outgoing neighbors. If a vertex's level increases, we mark it special. The change is propagated to the special nodes' children by checking their parents in the BFST as discussed.

SSSP: Similar to decremental BFS, decremental SSSP also uses a multi-worklist approach. A key difference from BFS is that SSSP computation is asynchronous, enforcing a different synchronization requirement (discussed in Sect. 4).

MST: Similar to BFS and SSSP, decremental MST also uses a data-driven worklist-based approach, but its operators are quite different [7]. We first mark and delete all the decremental edges in the previous version of the MST. This is done by a level-order traversal of the MST where we start from representative vertices of the MSTs in the MSF and vertices from which edges are being deleted. After deleting the decremental edges, we will have different MST components.

For every such MST segment, we will have one representative vertex. We need to connect MSTs (if possible) by using other non-tree edges from the original graph. Similar to the processing in the incremental setting, we first add the cut edges across different representative vertices from the non-tree edges of the graph. Threads operate on representative vertices and start finding the minimum weight edge representative vertex adjacent to them. Since each representative vertex chooses at most one representative vertex, cycles may be introduced while adding edges between them. We borrow the technique of choosing the lower of the vertex identifiers for same-weight edges from Vineet et al. [8]. This ensures that only 2-length cycles are possible as illustrated in Fig. 5. Threads can quickly check for 2-length cycles by finding if a reverse-edge is chosen by the end-point of the chosen-edge. After this step, minimum weight edges from the remaining vertices are added to the MST. Finally, all the vertices connected by minimum weight edges form one super-vertex component and all these disjoint components form new vertices for the next iteration. This process continues until no more edges can be added between any two components.

3.3   Fully Dynamic Graph Processing

BFS: Fully-dynamic BFS can be built upon the concepts of incremental and decremental BFS. For each deleted edge $u \rightarrow v$ in parallel, we push v to the special worklist, while for each inserted edge $u \rightarrow v$, we push u to the regular worklist. Threads then extract vertices from the special worklist, and process their incoming edges. A vertex is marked as special if there is an increase in its level compared to the previous version. Then, similar to the decremental algorithm, the special node is pushed into the regular worklist for propagating the

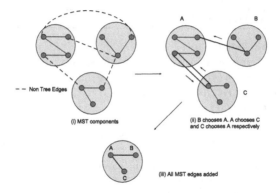

Fig. 5. Adding non-tree edges to get final MST

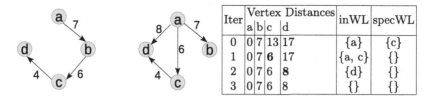

Fig. 6. Dynamic SSSP on graph versions G^0 and G^1

level information to its children. Threads extract vertices from the worklist and check if any of them is special. For each special vertex, similar to the decremental algorithm, we check if it has any child in the BFST in its outgoing edges. If there is, the child is pushed into the special worklist. For the remaining children, we propagate the (special) parent's change along its outgoing edges. If an outgoing neighbor's level reduces, it is pushed to the regular worklist. This repeats until both the worklists are empty.

SSSP: The incremental and the decremental algorithms can be combined and this can be used when both insertions and deletions are happening simultaneously. The algorithm is listed in Algorithm 1 which uses the results of iteration $i-1$ in iteration i. For each deleted edge (u, v) where u is the SPT parent of v, we push v to the special worklist. We also check if the vertex has a new outgoing edge (due to incremental updates). If it does, we push it into the (regular) worklist. We then process vertices from the special worklist, we relax all the incoming edges of each node and update the node's distance. We then check if the node's distance increased. If so, then the node is marked as special and pushed into the worklist. We loop through the worklist for special vertices. For special vertices, similar to the case of the decremental algorithm, we check if it is a parent to any node in the SPT in its outgoing edges. If so, then the child is pushed to the special worklist. For the others, we propagate the change along the outgoing edges. The two worklists are processed until they get empty.

Algorithm 1. Fully Dynamic SSSP

```
1   function SSSP-static(G⁰)
2       for each iteration Gⁱ other than G⁰
3           readGraph(Gⁱ)
4           copyResult(distᵢ₋₁, distᵢ)
5           preprocess(Gᵢ)
6           while(! both worklists are empty)
7               for each vertex a in specWL
8                   specFunc(a)
9               for each node a in inWL
10                  regularFunc(a)
11              swap(inWL, outWL)
12
13  function preprocess(Gⁱ)
14      for each vertex a in Gⁱ
15          if newoutgoing[a] = true
16              push a to inWL
17      for each deleted edge a → b
18          if a is the parent of b in SPT
19              push b to specWL
20
21  function regularFunc(a)
22      if(a is special)
23          for each outgoing neighbor b of a
24              if a is the parent of b in SPT
25                  push b to specWL
26      else
27          for each outgoing neighbor b of a
28              if dist[a] + wt(a,b) < dist[b]
29                  dist[b] := wt(a,b) + dist[a]
30                  push b to outWL
31
32  function specFunc(a)
33      prevdist := dist[a]
34      dist[a] := ∞
35      for each parent b of a
36          update dist[a] via b
37          if dist[a] > prevdist
38              push a to outWL
39              mark a as special
40          else if dist[a] < prevdist
41              push a to outWL
```

Consider the example shown in Fig. 6. Edge $b \to c$ is deleted and edges $a \to d$ and $a \to c$ are added. Vertex c is a child of vertex b in SPT and we push c to the special worklist. Then vertex a is pushed into the regular worklist because it has new outgoing edges. We extract vertex c from the special worklist, process its incoming vertices, and update its distance to 6. Then we push c to the worklist because of reduced distance. Then we process all the nodes in the worklist. This reduces d's distance to 8 and it is pushed to the worklist. This finally leads to the fixed-point.

MST: In contrast to BFS and SSSP, for dynamic MST, we first follow the steps of the incremental algorithm. However, instead of picking only the maximum weighted edges from either of the ends, if we get a decremental edge having weight greater than the incremental edge during the cycle traversal, then we replace the incremental edge with the decremental edge. This mechanism is valid because we are replacing a valid incremental edge whose weight is less than the decremental edge, if found. However, if we do not find any decremental edges or any decremental edges whose weight is less than the incremental edges, then we continue with our above proposed incremental algorithm. After processing all the incremental edges in this fashion, we process the remaining decremental edges which have to be deleted.

4   Synchronization Considerations

Irregular procedures such as graph algorithms necessitate thread-synchronization for safe concurrent processing. The synchronization requirement is heavy when the graph undergoes structural updates, as in our case. Thus, for instance, while a thread is updating an MST to include a new edge, some other thread may be deleting the same edge. The synchronization issue gets exacerbated on GPUs as logical locks are prohibitively expensive.

BFS: Level-by-level static BFS can be implemented without using atomic instructions as the data-races are benign. However, synchronization may still be necessary while maintaining the frontier, depending upon its implementation. Thus, if the frontier is implemented as a bit-vector (one bit per vertex), then no explicit atomics are necessary (as single word writing is atomic in CUDA and most other hardware). However, if the frontier is implemented as a compact worklist containing vertex identifiers, then synchronization in terms of either atomics or prefix-sum barriers is necessary to insert vertices. Removal of elements need not require synchronization as all the elements can be read in parallel and the worklist can be emptied by setting its size variable to 0. However, a barrier is necessary between reading and resetting the worklist. All these synchronization requirements are applicable in case of the dynamic setting also. In addition, efficient processing of special and regular worklists demands careful synchronization. In particular, we need to insert two barriers between the iterative processing of special and regular worklists (after for loops at lines 7 and 9 in BFS code similar to Algorithm 1).

SSSP: Synchronization considerations of dynamic SSSP are similar to those of BFS. However, since SSSP is implemented in an asynchronous manner, it demands usage of atomicMin instruction while updating distances.

MST: Dynamic MST poses more synchronization challenges. First, all primitive data type updates rely on atomic instructions. Performing level-order traversal to find maximum weight edge in a cycle needs BFS-like synchronization. The underlying data structure to keep track of MSTs also necessitates careful synchronization. For instance, various components of the minimum spanning forest (MSF) are efficiently stored in a concurrent union-find data structure. Updating parent pointers of vertices (union) and identifying if two vertices belong to the same component (find) need to be separated either by a barrier or protected using atomics. Note that find is not a read-only operation when path-compression is enabled. Further, if the incremental and the decremental phases are separated by a barrier, it helps reduce intra-phase synchronization. Note, however, that the fully-dynamic version takes advantage of the decremental edges while inserting new edges for efficiency (as discussed in Sect. 3.3).

5   Experimental Results

We implemented dynamic BFS, SSSP and MST in CUDA. The experiments are run on an Intel Xeon X5675 with Tesla M2070 GPU with 6 GB RAM and 14 SMs containing 448 cores. We compare our dynamic BFS and SSSP with the static versions from LonestarGPU 2.0 [9], and dynamic MST with our implementation of the static version by Vineet et al. [8]. We call the static versions as *Base*. Our code is publicly available[1] which contains optimized incremental, decremental as well as fully-dynamic versions.

In the evaluation below, the base implementation creates the graph with all the dynamic updates and then runs the static version on it. We present results directly for fully-dynamic version. We select an edge for addition or removal by selecting two random vertex identifiers, and checking if the edge already exists. We add edge-weight as a random number between 1 and 100. Figure 7 shows the characteristics of various graphs from SNAP [6].

Graph	$|V| \times 10^6$	$|E| \times 10^6$	Graph	$|V| \times 10^6$	$|E| \times 10^6$
Livejournal	3.9	70.0	R4-2e20	1.0	8.3
R4-2e23	8.3	67.0	Amazon2008	0.7	7.0
Soc-Pokec	1.6	61.0	Wiki	2.4	5.0
Patent	6.0	33.0	Amazon0505	0.4	4.8
Flickr	0.4	17.0	Road-CA	2.0	3.0
Rmat20	1.0	16.5	Youtube	1.2	3.0
Skitter	1.6	11.0	Road-TX	1.4	2.0

Fig. 7. Input graphs

---

[1] http://www.cse.iitm.ac.in/~rupesh/?mode=Research.

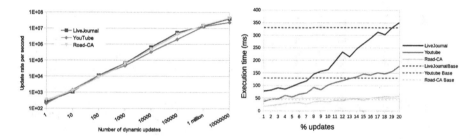

Fig. 8. diff-CSR throughput and performance of fully-dynamic BFS (Color figure online)

5.1 Performance

diff-CSR: To evaluate our diff-CSR representation, we added and removed randomly selected edges to various graphs. Figure 8 shows throughput (number of updates performed per second) for various number of updates. We find that (i) the throughput improves almost linearly, (ii) the throughput reaches a plateau after 10 million updates, and (iii) is largely the same independent of the graph.

BFS: Figure 8 shows the performance of fully-dynamic BFS. It plots the execution time with varying number of dynamic updates (as a percentage of $|E|$ from 1..20) for a subset of graphs (to avoid clutter, but others have similar behavior). The plot also indicates the execution time of the static version by the dotted lines (with the same color). We observe that the dynamic version takes much lesser time compared to its static counterpart for a few updates. As the number of dynamic updates increases, the amount of processing and, in turn, the execution time of the dynamic version increases almost linearly. In practice, we believe the number of dynamic updates would be small and our dynamic version would prove useful.

SSSP: Figure 9 shows the performance of fully dynamic SSSP with varying insertion and deletion percentage for a few graphs. Similar to BFS, dynamic SSSP performs better than its static counterpart until a graph-dependent threshold.

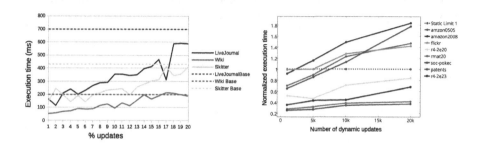

Fig. 9. Performance of fully dynamic SSSP and MST

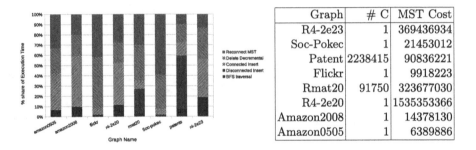

Fig. 10. Dynamic MST performance, and computed statistics

MST: Figure 9 shows the performance of the fully dynamic MST with varying insertions and deletions. The plot differs from the earlier ones (BFS and SSSP) in two aspects. One, dynamic MST is a complicated algorithm, its benefits get reduced due to higher synchronization costs. Therefore, it works better only up to a few thousand dynamic updates (which may be good for several applications). Hence, we plot directly the number of updates (1..20K) rather than a percentage (which would be very small). Second, we plot the performance over several graphs. Hence, instead of showing two lines per graph, we plot normalized execution times. We observe a trend similar to that of BFS and SSSP, with dynamic MST performing better than the static version for a few thousand updates.

In Fig. 10 we show the execution time split-up for dynamic MST across five stages of the algorithm: (i) level order BFS traversal to initialize *Parent*, *Level* and *Cost* arrays, (ii) connecting incremental edges across the disjoint MST components, (iii) inserting incremental edges within the MST component, (iv) marking and deleting decremental edges in the MST to form disjoint MST components, and (v) reconnecting the MST components to get the MST or MSF. We observe that fully dynamic MST is dominated in execution time by the decremental part which involves complicated processing in deleting the decremental edges and then reconnecting the MST components. Secondly, for graphs like rmat20 and patents, where there are multiple components, time consumed in adding incremental edges *across* the MST components is more than the time consumed for adding incremental edges *within* the MST tree component. This is because in these graphs most of the incremental edges have been added across the MST components rather than within an MST component. Figure 10 also shows the statistics obtained by our MST computation. #C indicates the number of connected components, and Cost indicates the total MST (MSF) cost. It shows that Patent and Rmat20 are disconnected.

Overall, we illustrate that our dynamic versions of graph algorithms provide benefits over recomputing the graph analytic information from scratch. In particular, when the number of updates is relatively small – which happens in social networks, dynamic molecular simulations and control-flow graphs across code versions, our dynamic methods offer promising results.

6   Related Work

There exists a body of work on speeding up processing of evolving graphs [10–12]. While Chronos [10] introduces a novel memory layout to improve cache locality during serial or parallel graph processing, much of the other work restricts type of queries or are designed for a specific algorithm (e.g., Ren et al. [11] and Kan et al. [12] consider queries that depend upon the graph structure alone).

There are many implementations of parallel static graph algorithms on a variety of architectures, including distributed-memory supercomputers [13], shared-memory supercomputers [14], and multicore machines [15]. Harish and Narayanan [16] pioneered CUDA implementations of graph algorithms such as BFS and single-source shortest paths computation. BFS has received significant attention [4,17,18]. Hong et al. [3] propose a warp-centric approach for implementing BFS. In Pregel-like graph processing systems [19] some of the underlying algorithms like Page Rank, SSSP and DMST have been proposed for distributed processing. Vineet et al. [8] and Nobari et al. [20] propose computing the minimum spanning tree and forest, respectively, on GPUs. MST computation on temporal graphs [21] has also been proposed in the sequential setting.

Ashari et al. [22] propose an adaptive CSR layout for sparse matrix-vector multiplication. Their method reduces thread-divergence on GPUs by sorting vertices based on their degrees and binning the vertices with similar degrees. Adaptive CSR also uses dynamic parallelism supported in the latest GPUs to improve work-efficiency. King et al. [23] propose a dynamic CSR layout for graphs with changing structures. The difference between dynamic CSR and our diff-CSR (Sect. 2) is that dynamic CSR keeps track of additional segments to accommodate new edges. This leads to fragmentation when the segments are not full, and the authors propose a defragmentation step to compact the segment. In contrast, diff-CSR maintains a diff in the same CSR format, but the diff is separately maintained from the original CSR. diff-CSR may also incur fragmentation due to deletions, but since it never allocates more memory than required in a step, it does not incur fragmentation on insertion. cuSTINGER [24] proposes to store dynamic graphs on GPUs. It also uses arrays to store adjacency lists; however, diff-CSR uses two arrays (original and diff). Further, unlike diff-CSR, cuSTINGER separates insertions and deletions, and needs a host-device copying of adjacency lists when the current storage space is insufficient for the dynamic updates. cuSTINGER also compacts the storage at the end of a batch deletion; diff-CSR does not perform compaction, but retains the deleted markings.

Closest to our work is the work on morph algorithms on GPUs [25] wherein structurally changing graphs are analyzed on the GPUs. While similar in spirit, our work proposes a new dynamic graph representation and highlight new synchronization challenges. Automatic code generation for morph algorithms has been proposed by Cheramangalath et al. [26].

7   Conclusion

We illustrated the promise in processing dynamic graph algorithms on GPUs. To address challenges posed by the structural updates, we proposed a backwards-compatible dynamic CSR representation, advocated data-driven processing, carefully chose the synchronization primitives, and took advantage of the interplay of incremental and decremental updates. By implementing and optimizing three popular graph algorithms in CUDA, we illustrated the promise in our proposed techniques. Using a collection of real-world and synthetic graphs, we showed that the proposed techniques work effectively and provide performance benefits over static graph algorithms up to a certain percentage of structural updates. We believe our techniques can be applied to other propagation-based algorithms such as Page Rank, Betweenness Centrality, and Coloring.

Acknowledgments. We thank the reviewers and our shepherd Nancy Amato for their comments which considerably improved our work. This work is partially supported by IIT Madras Exploratory Research Grant CSE/16-17/837/RFER/RUPS.

References

1. Wang, Y., Davidson, A., Pan, Y., Wu, Y., Riffel, A., Owens, J.D.: Gunrock: a high-performance graph processing library on the GPU. In: PPoPP (2015)
2. Gharaibeh, A., Costa, L.B., Santos-Neto, E., Ripeanu, M.: A yoke of oxen and a thousand chickens for heavy lifting graph processing. In: PACT (2012)
3. Hong, S., Kim, S.K., Oguntebi, T., Olukotun, K.: Accelerating CUDA graph algorithms at maximum warp. In: PPoPP, pp. 267–276 (2011)
4. Merrill, D.G., Garland, M., Grimshaw, A.S.: Scalable GPU graph traversal. In: PPoPP (2012)
5. Nasre, R., Burtscher, M., Pingali, K.: Data-driven versus topology-driven irregular computations on GPUs. In: IPDPS, pp. 463–474 (2013)
6. Leskovec, J., Sosič, R.: SNAP: a general purpose network analysis and graph mining library in C++, June 2014. http://snap.stanford.edu/snap
7. Pingali, K., et al.: The tao of parallelism in algorithms. In: PLDI, pp. 12–25 (2011)
8. Vineet, V., Harish, P., Patidar, S., Narayanan, P.J.: Fast minimum spanning tree for large graphs on the GPU. In: HPG, pp. 167–171 (2009)
9. Burtscher, M., Nasre, R., Pingali, K.: A quantitative study of irregular programs on GPUs. In: IISWC, pp. 141–151 (2012)
10. Hant, W., et al.: Chronos: a graph engine for temporal graph analysis. In: ECCS, p. 1 (2014)
11. Ren, C., Lo, E., Kao, B., Zhu, X., Cheng, R.: On querying historical evolving graph sequences. Proc. VLDB Endow. 4(11), 726–737 (2011)
12. Kan, A., Chan, J., Bailey, J., Leckie, C.: A query based approach for mining evolving graphs. In: Proceedings of the Eighth Australasian Data Mining Conference, vol. 101, pp. 139–150. Australian Computer Society Inc. (2009)
13. Yoo, A., Chow, E., Henderson, K., McLendon, W., Hendrickson, B., Catalyurek, U.: A scalable distributed parallel breadth-first search algorithm on BlueGene/L. In: SC, p. 25 (2005)

14. Bader, D.A., Madduri, K.: Designing multithreaded algorithms for breadth-first search and st-connectivity on the Cray MTA-2. In: ICPP, pp. 523–530 (2006)
15. Kulkarni, M., Pingali, K., Walter, B., Ramanarayanan, G., Bala, K., Chew, L.P.: Optimistic parallelism requires abstractions. SIGPLAN Not. (PLDI) **42**(6), 211–222 (2007)
16. Harish, P., Narayanan, P.J.: Accelerating large graph algorithms on the GPU using CUDA. In: Aluru, S., Parashar, M., Badrinath, R., Prasanna, V.K. (eds.) HiPC 2007. LNCS, vol. 4873, pp. 197–208. Springer, Heidelberg (2007). https://doi.org/10.1007/978-3-540-77220-0_21
17. Luo, L., Wong, M., Hwu, W.-M.: An effective GPU implementation of breadth-first search. In: DAC, pp. 52–55 (2010)
18. Hong, S., Oguntebi, T., Olukotun, K.: Efficient parallel graph exploration on multi-core CPU and GPU. In: PACT. PACT 2011 (2011)
19. Han, M., Daudjee, K.: Giraph unchained: barrierless asynchronous parallel execution in pregel-like graph processing systems. Proc. VLDB Endow. **8**(9), 950–961 (2015)
20. Nobari, S., Cao, T.-T., Karras, P., Bressan, S.: Scalable parallel minimum spanning forest computation. In: Proceedings of the 17th ACM SIGPLAN Symposium on Principles and Practice of Parallel Programming. PPoPP 2012, pp. 205–214. ACM, New York (2012). http://doi.acm.org/10.1145/2145816.2145842
21. Huang, S., Fu, A.W.-C., Liu, R.: Minimum spanning trees in temporal graphs. In: Proceedings of the 2015 ACM SIGMOD International Conference on Management of Data. SIGMOD 2015, pp. 419–430. ACM, New York (2015). http://doi.acm.org/10.1145/2723372.2723717
22. Ashari, A., Sedaghati, N., Eisenlohr, J., Parthasarathy, S., Sadayappan, P.: Fast sparse matrix-vector multiplication on GPUs for graph applications. In: SC, pp. 781–792 (2014)
23. King, J., Gilray, T., Kirby, R.M., Might, M.: Dynamic sparse-matrix allocation on GPUs. In: Kunkel, J.M., Balaji, P., Dongarra, J. (eds.) ISC High Performance 2016. LNCS, vol. 9697, pp. 61–80. Springer, Cham (2016). https://doi.org/10.1007/978-3-319-41321-1_4
24. Green, O., Bader, D.A.: cuSTINGER: supporting dynamic graph algorithms for GPUs. In: 2016 IEEE High Performance Extreme Computing Conference (HPEC), pp. 1–6, September 2016
25. Nasre, R., Burtscher, M., Pingali, K.: Morph algorithms on GPUs. In: PPoPP, pp. 147–156 (2013)
26. Cheramangalath, U., Nasre, R., Srikant, Y.N.: Falcon: a graph manipulation language for heterogeneous systems. ACM Trans. Archit. Code Optim. **12**(4), 54:1–54:27 (2015). http://doi.acm.org/10.1145/2842618

Posters

Towards Fine-Grained Dataflow Parallelism in Big Data Systems

Sebastian Ertel$^{(\boxtimes)}$, Justus Adam, and Jeronimo Castrillon

Technische Universität Dresden, Dresden, Germany
{Sebastian.Ertel,Justus.Adam,Jeronimo.Castrillon}@tu-dresden.de

1 Introduction

Over the last decade big data analytics became the major source of new insights in science and industry. Applications include the identification of mutations in cancer genome and the tracking of other vehicles around an autonomously driving car. The big data systems (BDSs) that enable such analyses have to be able to process massive amounts of data as fast as possible. To do so, current BDSs apply coarse-grained data parallelism, i.e., they execute the same code on each core of the nodes in a cluster on a different chunk of the data. Such an application is said to scale with the number of cores in the cluster. However, not every aspect of a big data application exposes data parallelism. For these aspects, current BDSs fail to scale.

2 Scalability Issues of Big Data Systems

A typical big data analysis program assembles a set of predefined operations and applies them to the data in multiple phases. For example, the famous MapReduce programming model defines exactly two phases: a map and a reduce phase [1]. The map phase is data parallel by definition but the data parallelism of the reduce phase depends on the application. For example, in data analytics queries, the join operation for two tables can not be performed in a data parallel way (when the input data is not partitioned). In such a case, a single node receives all results from the map phase and becomes the throughput bottleneck.

BDSs have been traditionally designed to execute applications in a massive coarse-grained data parallel fashion across a cluster of machines. The underlying assumption was that applications would process large amounts of simply structured data, such as text. The effort to serialize and deserialize such data structures, i.e., transforming them to bytes (and its dual operation on the receiver side), is negligible. This setup led to the common belief that network I/O, instead of computation, is the performance bottleneck in these systems.

Only recently, researchers have shown that I/O is not always the limiting factor for performance [3]. Authors in [4] benchmarked the current state-of-the-art BDSs Apache Spark and Apache Flink in a high bandwidth cluster setup. They show that reduce operations do not profit from modern multi-core architectures

© Springer Nature Switzerland AG 2019
L. Rauchwerger (Ed.): LCPC 2017, LNCS 11403, pp. 281–282, 2019.
https://doi.org/10.1007/978-3-030-35225-7

since their cores do not take advantage of fine-grained parallelism. As a result, the data throughput does not increase for faster network devices, i.e., it does not scale with the network.

To better exploit new hardware, the design of BDSs must be revisited [4]. Redesign is non trivial due to the complexity of the code bases of state-of-the-art BDSs, e.g., with over 1.4 million lines of code in Hadoop MapReduce (HMR). Approaching this task with common parallel programming means, like threads, tasks or actors and their respective synchronization via locks, futures or mailboxes, inevitably increases code complexity. As a result, these systems become harder to reason about, maintain and extend. We believe that this redesign can be better achieved with new programming abstractions together with associated compilers and runtimes to help automatically optimize the code depending on the application characteristics. This paper represents first steps in this direction.

3   Implicit Dataflow Programming

In our work, we investigate rewrites for the processing cores of current big data systems to increase data throughput, effectively improving scalability with new hardware. Our rewrites use the implicit parallel programming language, Ohua [2], to provide concise code that is easy to maintain. The corresponding compiler transforms the program into a dataflow graph that the runtime system executes in a pipeline and task parallel fashion across the cores of a single machine. To verify the claim that all BDSs face the

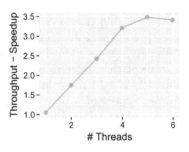

Fig. 1. Map task execution of a black list filter on TPC-H data.

above scalability issues, we analyzed the code base of HMR, Spark and Flink. We found that all three systems use the same design patterns to build their data processing pipelines and use them as an indicator for code that can execute in parallel. The rewrite of the data processing cores of HMR with Ohua resulted in concise code that is free of concurrency abstractions and reuses existing code to a large extend. Figure 1 presents first performance results with speed-ups of up to 3.5× for compute-intensive configurations.

References

1. Dean, J., Ghemawat, S.: Mapreduce: simplified data processing on large clusters. In: OSDI 2004. USENIX Association (2004)
2. Ertel, S., Fetzer, C., Felber, P.: Ohua: implicit dataflow programming for concurrent systems. In: PPPJ 2015. ACM (2015)
3. Ousterhout, K., Rasti, R., Ratnasamy, S., Shenker, S., Chun, B.G.: Making sense of performance in data analytics frameworks. In: NSDI 2015. USENIX Association (2015)
4. Trivedi, A., et al.: On the [ir]relevance of network performance for data processing. In: HotCloud 2016. USENIX Association (2016)

JIT for Intelligent Manufacturing

Lei Zhang$^{(\boxtimes)}$, L. N. C. Annadorai, Atin Angrish, Xipeng Shen, Binil Starly,
Yuan-Shin Lee, and Paul Cohen

North Carolina State University, Raleigh, NC 27695, USA
{lzhang45, lcoimba, aangris, xshen5, bstarly, yslee, pcohen}@ncsu.edu

Modern manufacturing machines center on computer numerical control (CNC). Despite years' of progresses, today's manufacturing still runs upon an old paradigm as shown in Fig. 1. Through CAD/CAM software, engineers produce a computer file containing some high-level instructions on how to manufacture a product on a CNC machine (with some drilling, milling tools). The file is then translated into a low-level format called G-code [1] through vendor-provided non-disclosed postprocessors. The generated machine-specific G-code is sent as input to a CNC, which drives the motors and tools in the machine to make the product.

G-code is a standard programming language for CNC machines, created in 1950s. Vendors have added many extra features into G-code that are specific to some CNC machines, resulting in thousands of variations of G-code. Consequently, code for part fabrication is often customized to a physical CNC machine on a shop floor, not portable across CNC machines.

In current manufacturing, there are usually some humans called *CNC operators* who need to closely monitor the operations of CNC machines throughout the manufacturing process. Because the tool wearing conditions and initial positions of a particular CNC machine may differ from what the product designers had assumed when they create the high-level designs of the manufacturing code, these operators often need to manually modify the G-code of the product at manufacturing time to meet the quality requirement. Given the many variations of G-code, the operators usually have to learn the G-code of a particular CNC machine to be able to do the work. In other instances, there is often variability in the raw material dimension and physical properties that results in the operator having to edit the G-code to add additional steps that the manufacturing process engineer may not have accounted for in the initial G-code.

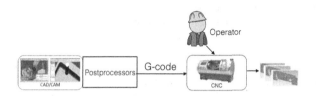

Fig. 1. Conventional manufacturing process.

This paper advocates that the key to removing the main barrier lies in programming systems, esp. Just-In-Time (JIT) compilation techniques. We use

L. Rauchwerger (Ed.): LCPC 2017, LNCS 11403, pp. 283–284, 2019.
https://doi.org/10.1007/978-3-030-35225-7

Fig. 2 to outline the role that JIT can play in enabling intelligent manufacturing. The CNC machine is equipped with a JIT-based runtime, which transforms the IM code (a replacement of G-code) at manufacturing time to adapt the machine operations to dynamic conditions. The automatic feedback-driven paradigm may improve the productivity and quality of future manufacturing dramatically. There are two-fold opportunities and challenges.

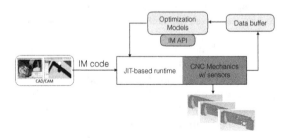

Fig. 2. JIT-based intelligent manufacturing framework. "IM" stands for intelligent manufacturing, Optimization model is a model for optimizing the manufacturing, written by domain experts with IM API.

The first fold of challenges are on how to derive optimization decisions from the feedback data reported by the sensors. A runtime system may need to monitor the dispatch and executions of instructions and map the data to the currently running instructions and manufacturing steps. Meanwhile, a set of programming interface or descriptive programming language shall be designed to facilitate the interactions between domain experts and the runtime software.

The second fold of challenges are on how to materialize the desired optimizations. A portable programming language shall be introduced to replace G-code such that the code can carry the high-level features of the product. The representation shall be generic across CNC machines. Vendor-specific machine instructions shall be part of the backend of the code generator that generates native instructions from the new language. The development of the new language could be based upon some existing high-level languages proposed in manufacturing. The code transformation challenge could be addressed through a JIT compiler, which runs on CNC machines, and compiles the product code in the portable programming language into the native code at manufacturing time. There are some research challenges in the JIT development, including the compilation speed for high responsiveness, safety constraints in manufacturing, and more complex optimization criteria in manufacturing.

Acknowledgments. This material is based upon work supported by NSF Grant #1547105. Any opinions, findings, and conclusions or recommendations expressed in this material are those of the authors and do not necessarily reflect the views of NSF.

Reference

1. Jones, F.D., Ryffel, H.H., Amiss, J.M.: Machinery's Handbook. Industrial Press (1996)

Static Reuse Time Analysis Using Dependence Distance

Dong Chen[1]([⊠]), Fangzhou Liu[1], Chen Ding[1], and Chucheow Lim[2]

[1] Department of Computer Science, University of Rochester, Rochester, NY, USA
{dchen39, fliu14, cding}@cs.rochester.edu
[2] Qualcomm, Santa Clara, CA, USA
chucheow@qti.qualcomm.com

Introduction: Locality analysis is an important problem in program optimization. Compile time locality analysis can provide detailed feedback related to code structure. Compared to trace based analysis, compiler analysis does not require the program input and does not execute a program.

We present a new technique that is based on the recent Higher-Order Theory of Locality (HOTL). HOTL shows when and how reuse time can be used to derive the cache performance, both for cache misses by Xiang et al. [4] and writebacks by Chen et al. [3] Here *reuse time* is the number of memory accesses between use and its next reuse. The new technique differs from past techniques in targeting the reuse time instead of the reuse distance, as in [2], or the miss ratio, which we can now compute from the reuse time using HOTL.

In this paper, we show how to derive the reuse time distribution using dependence analysis, in particular the dependence distance described in Sect. 2.2 of [1]. Furthermore, we extend the analysis to reuses at the cache line granularity.

Reuse Time Analysis: Reuse Time Analysis (RTA) assumes a loop nest whose dependence distances for all pairs of memory references to each array are all vectors of constants. Among all the dependences from a single source *src*, the shortest distance $v(src)$ is contributed by its reuse, calculated in Eq. 1.

$$v(src) = min(\{v(src, snk) \mid snk \in ref \}) \tag{1}$$

By iterating $v(src)$ for all the loop ranges containing the source, the reuse time histogram can be constructed. However, not all dependence distances give valid reuses in all iterations. Some sink iterations may be outside the loop bound. For each dependence distance, precise RTA must consider the iteration range for which the sink is valid.

Using Eq. 1, we can derive the reuse time of each reference from the dependence distances originated from the reference. This analysis assumes that the granularity of data access is a single data element.

Cache Line Granularity: A cache line contains $b > 1$ data elements, which is calculated by the ratio of the cache line size (CLS) to the data element size (DS), $b = \frac{CLS}{DS}$. A cache line reuse can happen between accesses to different data elements. For cache line RTA, we extend the basic RTA with additional information: the data position p inside the cache line. For 32B cache line size and 8B data element size, b is 4 and p ranges from 0 to 3.

© Springer Nature Switzerland AG 2019
L. Rauchwerger (Ed.): LCPC 2017, LNCS 11403, pp. 285–286, 2019.
https://doi.org/10.1007/978-3-030-35225-7

Adding the position information, we expand the dependence distance to find the reuses between the source cache line accessed at data position p_{src} and the sink cache line accessed at data position p_{snk}. The block granularity dependence distance v_b is given by Eq. 2:

$$v_b(src, p_{src}, snk, p_{snk}) = v(src, snk) + (0, 0, ..., 0, p_{snk} - p_{src}) \qquad (2)$$

Equation 2 relaxes the requirement of reuse. That is, instead of requiring that the source and the sink access the same data element, it requires that they access the same cache lines. The dependence distance $v_b(src, p_{src}, snk, p_{snk})$ can be derived by adding the position difference between source and its sink to the innermost dimension of the original distance $v(src, snk)$. Note this calculation of distance assumes: (1) The innermost loop accesses the array contiguously. Otherwise it will need more sophisticated calculation, and the result may be the same as that of element granularity. (2) Some iterations of the last dimension of $v_b(src, p_{src}, snk, p_{snk})$ may be outside the loop bound.

The cache line reuse time for source src at position p_{src} is given by $v_b(src, p_{src})$, which is the shortest dependence distance $v_b(src, p_{src}, snk, p_{snk})$ for all its sinks that access the same cache line, shown by Eq. 3:

$$v_b(src, p_{src}) = min(\{v_b(src, p_{src}, snk, p_{snk}) \mid snk \in ref, p_{snk} \in 0 \ldots b-1\}) \qquad (3)$$

In addition to making sure the sink happens within the iteration space, we also need to make sure the iteration space we are analyzing does not contain a cache line with data across different iterations in higher dimensions (except the innermost dimension). By iterating $v_b(src, p_{src})$ for all the loop ranges containing the source, we obtain the cache line granularity reuse time distribution.

Acknowledgements. We thank Chunling Hu, Kath Knobe, Zoran Budimlic for discussion of the ideas. The research is partially supported by the National Science Foundation (Contract No. CCF-1717877, CCF-1629376) and IBM CAS Faculty Fellowship.

References

1. Allen, R., Kennedy, K.: Optimizing Compilers for Modern Architectures: A Dependence-Based Approach. Morgan Kaufmann Publishers, October 2001
2. Beyls, K., D'Hollander, E.H.: Generating cache hints for improved program efficiency. J. Syst. Archit. **51**(4), 223–250 (2005)
3. Chen, D., Ye, C., Ding, C.: Write locality and optimization for persistent memory. In: Proceedings of the Second International Symposium on Memory Systems, pp. 77–87. ACM (2016)
4. Xiang, X., Ding, C., Luo, H., Bao, B.: HOTL: a higher order theory of locality, 343–356 (2013)

Analyzing Auto-Vectorization Rates and Quality in C/C++ Compilers

Angela Pohl[✉], Biagio Cosenza, and Ben Juurlink

Technische Universität Berlin, Berlin, Germany
{angela.pohl, cosenza, b.juurlink}@tu-berlin.de

Data Level Parallelism (DLP) is one of three types of parallelism in applications. A typical source for DLP are loops, where multiple iterations of the same instruction can be executed in parallel. In recent years, straight-line code vectorization, called Superword Level Parallelism (SLP) or Basic Block (BB) vectorization, has been exploited as well. Here, algorithms work on BBs, i.e. straight-line code sequences with only one entry and exit point, instead of loops. SLP tries to group instructions into vectors by analyzing all data dependence graphs within and across BBs. Using both, Loop Level Vectorization (LLV) and SLP, it is possible to achieve speedups up to the Vectorization Factor (VF), i.e. the number of elements processed in parallel, and beyond; such super-linear speedups can be obtained by applying pattern substitutions, for example. Nonetheless, there are codes where a vectorization is not possible, would require alterations to the sources, or is not beneficial. Herein lie the challenges of vectorization: determining the most suitable code transformation and assessing its prospective benefit.

In this work, we assessed the vectorization capabilities of today's most popular C/C++ compilers: GCC, ICC, and LLVM. Based on a study from 2011 [1], we used the same TSVC benchmark [3] to determine the progress that has been made in the past six years. In addition, we studied the LCALS [2] benchmark to cover C++ codes as well.

We ran both benchmarks without further code enhancements or annotations to obtain pure auto-vectorization results; they are shown in Fig. 1. Out of the 151 TSVC loop patterns, GCC is able to vectorize 83 loops (55%) on the Intel i5 and 89 loops (59%) on the Intel E5, while ICC vectorizes 107 (71%) on either platform, as does LLVM with 75 loops (50%). All numbers are taken from the compilers' vectorization reports. Based on these results, it can be seen that all of the compilers fail to efficiently vectorize a certain amount of codes. Some of these patterns exhibit only a minor speedup after vectorization, i.e. up to 15%, while others show the exact scalar performance, or even a slowdown.

We identified one of the patterns exhibiting a slowdown in LLVM to be loops with non-constant but loop invariant anti dependences. Here, vectorized code is produced, but not executed due to runtime checks for overlapping memory regions. When enhancing the run-time check to determine the value of the dependence distance, we were able to safely execute the vectorized code for positive distances, yielding a $2\times$ speedup for our patterns.

© Springer Nature Switzerland AG 2019
L. Rauchwerger (Ed.): LCPC 2017, LNCS 11403, pp. 287–288, 2019.
https://doi.org/10.1007/978-3-030-35225-7

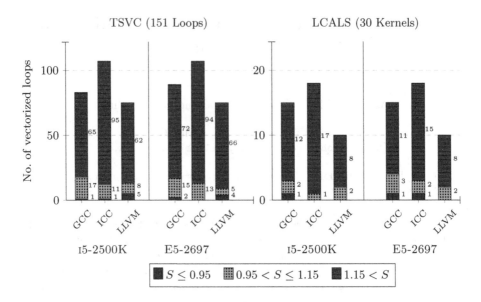

Fig. 1. Vectorization rates of the TSVC and LCALS benchmarks, classified by speedup factor.

Another observation was that SLP barely contributed to the overall vectorization rate, i.e. the number of vectorized patterns. Since the benchmark consists of short body loops, the SLP vectorizer did not find enough statements to group together. When applying loop unrolling before the vectorization pass, the SLP vectorization rate increased significantly by 33%.

In this work, we furthermore compared the results that were achieved by either vectorization pass, LLV or SLP. With unrolling, the SLP vectorizer is able to optimize 69 loops, only three less than the LLV pass; this vectorization rate is constant when the unrolling factor is greater or equal than the vectorization factor. Surprisingly, only 40 loops are optimized by both compiler passes, i.e. each vectorizer is able to improve ∼30 loops exclusively. As a second metric, we analyzed the speedups obtained by each pass for a qualitative analysis. As only 40 loops are vectorized by both, we limited our investigation to these test patterns. Our measurements indicate that speedups are similar, with LLV typically having a slight advantage. Nonetheless, there are codes where SLP with unrolling outperforms LLV; here, LLV would benefit from a higher unrolling factor of its vectorized loop.

References

1. Maleki, S., Gao, Y., Garzarán, M., Wong, T., Padua, D.: An Evaluation of vectorizing compilers. In: PACT 2011, Galveston Island, USA (2011)
2. Hornung, R.: Livermore Compiler Analysis Loop Suite. https://codesign.llnl.gov/LCALS.php
3. Extended Test Suite for Vectorizing Compilers. http://polaris.cs.uiuc.edu/~maleki/TSVC.tar.gz

Author Index

Printed in the United States
By Bookmasters